# Time Out Book of

Book of

# New York Walks

Edited by Andrew White

**Edited and designed by**
Time Out Guides Limited
Universal House
251 Tottenham Court Road
London W1P 0AB
Tel + 44 (0)20 7813 3000
Fax+ 44 (0)20 7813 6001
guides@timeout.com
www.timeout.com

**Editorial**
**Editor** Andrew White
**Editorial Director** Peter Fiennes
**President/Editor-in-Chief New York** Cyndi Stivers
**Managing Editor** Nicholas Royle
**Consultant Editor New York** Shawn Dahl
**Researchers** Lu Chekowsky, Christopher Bollen, Louise Gore
**Editorial Assistant** Jenny Noden
**Proofreader** Tamsin Shelton
**Indexer** Selena Cox

**Design**
**Art Director** John Oakey
**Art Editor** Mandy Martin
**Senior Designer** Scott Moore
**Designers** Benjamin de Lotz, Lucy Grant
**Scanning/Imaging** Dan Conway
**Picture Editor** Kerri Miles
**Assistant Picture Editor** Olivia Duncan-Jones
**Picture Admin** Kit Burnett

**Administration**
**Publisher** Tony Elliott
**Managing Director** Mike Hardwick
**Financial Director** Kevin Ellis
**General Manager** Nichola Coulthard
**Marketing Director** Christine Cort
**Marketing Manager** Mandy Martinez
**Accountant** Sarah Bostock
**Production Manager** Mark Lamond

**The Editor would like to thank the following:**
Stephanie Adler, Lanning Aldrich, Joe Angio, Victor Bockris, Sophie Blacksell, Gavin Brown, Jonathan Cox, Alan Christea, Lily Dunn, Paul Fairclough, Lesa Griffith, Sarah Guy, Hazel Hagger, Wally Hammond, Mike Hardwick, Danny Hoch, Ruth Jarvis, Alkarim Jivani, Arabella Keatley, Michelle Lavery, Sunny Lee, Mandy Martinez, Lesley McCave, Jenny Noden, Nana Ocran, Cath Phillips, Alex Poots, Allen Robertson, Greg Sanders, François Sergent, Gene Skolnikoff, the staff and editors of *Time Out New York*, Janet Steen, Cyndi Stivers, Amy Struck, Aimee Szparaga, Caro Taverne, Horatia Thomas, Jill Tulip, Kelvin White, Susan White.

**Maps by** JS Graphics, 17 Beadles Lane, Old Oxted, Surrey RH8 9JG

**Photography by Adam Eastland** except for: p104,175 Archive Photos; p138, 139 Victor Bockris; p237 Andrew White; p266 Jerome Albertini; page 172, 275 (bottom) Andrew Hill/Corbis-Bettmann.

Published by the Penguin Group
Penguin Books Ltd., 27 Wrights Lane, London, W8 5TZ, England
Penguin Putnam Inc., 375 Hudson Street, New York, New York 10014, USA
Penguin Books Australia Ltd., 487 Maroondah Highway (PO Box 257), Ringwood, VIC 3134, Australia
Penguin Books Canada Ltd., 10 Alcorn Avenue, Toronto, Ontario, Canada M4V 3B2
Penguin Books (NZ) Ltd., Private Bag 102902, NSMC, Auckland, New Zealand

Penguin Books Ltd., Registered offices: Harmondsworth, Middlesex, England

First published 2000
10 9 8 7 6 5 4 3 2 1

Colour reprographics by Westside Digital Media, 9 Bridle Lane, London W1.
Printed by Cayfosa-Quebecor, Ctra. de Caldes, Km 3 08 130 Sta, Perpètua de Mogoda, Barcelona, Spain.

# Using this book

We recommend that you read the entire text of any walk before setting out. Not only should this whet your appetite for the journey ahead, it will also help you to plan stopping-off points according to opening times provided in the listings. Indeed, for the longer walks, it'll give you a chance to plan at which point you want to abandon the walk and stagger to the nearest café/bar.

In the interests of not interfering with the flow of the prose, we have avoided endless directions in the text. The text and the maps should be used alongside each other, so if one seems unclear, consult the other. That said, every one of the routes has been walked and scrupulously checked, so we hope you'll find it very hard to get lost…

## Maps

The route is marked in red, including short diversions. The dotted lines mark a *possible* diversion, or the route between different sections of a walk, when a subway or bus ride is, in truth, recommended. Some, but not all, of the sites highlighted in the walk are marked on the maps. We have always indicated the subway stations, and the trains that stop there, on the maps – apologies to bus travellers. Free bus maps are available from all subway stations. Fifth Avenue serves as the backbone of Manhattan's grid system – street numbers start here, and rise East or West across the island.

## Distance

The distances given are to the nearest half-mile or half-kilometre.

## Time

The timing of the walks obviously depends on the speed of the walker, and the length and frequency of any stops. The times given are therefore approximate, and assume that there are no lengthy stops en route (though of course these are highly recommended), and that a healthy, though not frenetic, pace is maintained.

## Notes

The notes at the start of each text are largely self explanatory and merely aim to help walkers plan the timing of the walk, and forewarn them of any peculiar features. Links with other walks in the collection are also mentioned.

## Listings

We have listed virtually every café, bar, restaurant, shop, museum, gallery, church, park and relevant organisation mentioned in the text of the walk that is open to the public. They are arranged by category and alphabetically, not following the chronology of the walk. They were all accurate at the time of writing.

For the eating and drinking sections at the end of each walk, we have listed the opening hours of the establishment, and where we can, included a brief summary of the venue. Those included that are not mentioned in the walks are taken from the annual *Time Out New York Eating & Drinking Guide 2000*. For those venues appearing in the *Eating & Drinking Guide* we have added a short description of the fare. A *'TONY* 100' venue indicates that it has earned special praise from the guide.

All the remaining listings are taken from the text, and are divided, sometimes somewhat crudely, into categories. The final 'Others' category, where it occurs, may list organisations that readers might wish to contact should the walk inspire further investigation.

## Walks' accessibility

Under New York city law, all facilities constructed after 1987 must provide complete access to the disabled – restrooms and entrances/exits included. In 1990, the Americans with Disabilities Act made the same requirements federal law. Due to widespread compliance with the law, we have not noted the availability of disabled facilities in our listings. However, it's a good idea to call ahead and check.

A guide to accessibility for the disabled to the city's cultural institutions, *Access for All* ($5), is available from **Hospital Audiences, Inc** (212 431 8710/212 575

5790). **The Society for the Advancement of Travel for the Handicapped (SATH)** is based on Fifth Avenue and **The Mayor's Office for People with Disabilities** also organises services for the disabled. In addition, the organisation **Big Apple Greeter** will help any person with disabilities enjoy New York City. All buses are equipped with wheelchair lifts – contact the **MTA** (718 330 1234).

### SATH
*347 Fifth Avenue, suite 610, between 33rd & 34th (212 447 7284/fax 212 725 8253).* **Open** 10am-5pm Mon-Fri.

### Lighthouse Incorporated
*111 East 59th Street, between Park & Lexington Avenues (212 821 9200/800 334 5497).* A store and advice line for the sight-impaired and blind.

### Mayor's Office for People with Disabilities
*52 Chambers Street, at Broadway, room 206 (212 788 2830).* **Open** 9am-5pm Mon-Fri.

### New York Society for the Deaf
*817 Broadway, at 12th Street (212 777 3900).* **Open** 9am-5pm Mon-Thur; 9am-4pm Fri.

### Big Apple Greeter
*1 Centre Street, at Chambers Street, 20th floor (212 669 2896/fax 212 669 3685).* **Open** 9.30am-5pm Mon-Fri.

## General tips

Sales tax (8.25 per cent) is added to the price of most purchases and there is a lot of tipping to do: waitstaff get 15 to 20 per cent, bartenders $1 a drink and cabbies 15 per cent (many New Yorkers round up to an even dollar amount on small fares). Most museums are closed on Mondays and in some cases Tuesdays, and public holidays – check the listings. Unless otherwise stated, the public parks are generally open from 6am-1am, daily.

## Tourist information

**New York City's Official Visitor Information Center**
*810 Seventh Avenue, at 53rd Street (212 484 1222).* **Open** 8.30am-6pm Mon-Fri; 9am-5pm Sat, Sun.

# Contents

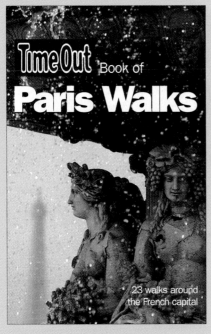

# Introduction

People have been coming to New York for centuries. Ever since the Dutch first colonised the island through a dubious 'purchase' in 1624, wave upon wave of people have settled here, each for their own reasons. Refugees escaping religious intolerance, radicals fleeing ideological dogma, minorites driven here by racial prejudice; economic refugees seeking to better themselves, aspiring youngsters hungry for success, loners seeking the anonymity of a city. The welcome they have received has varied according to contemporary sentiment, but the guiding principle has been Darwinian – survive and prosper, or sink and suffer.

To accommodate this growing population, New York has had to expand. Much of Manhattan has been levelled, the surplus rocks and stones serving as landfill in the steady broadening of the island. In 1898 the outlying areas – Brooklyn, the Bronx, Queens and Staten Island, each differently flavoured – were aborbed into New York City, although somehow the focus always seems drawn back to Manhattan.

North from 14th Street the grid system dominates the island, and is only marginally upset by the old Indian trail, Broadway, snaking its way up the spine of the island. Neighbourhoods have evolved, from the largely unresidential Financial District, to gay Greenwich Village, the grand Upper East Side and the neglected Spanish Harlem – all have their own vitality, their own ways of being New York.

These walks attempt to provide some reflection of the city from those who know its charms and understand its foibles. Resident New Yorkers and expat admirers have lent their views of the streets, buildings and people here – telling us not only about the city around us, but also the way in which New Yorkers see their home turf, their 'Babylon on the Hudson'.

Some contributors retrace a route through their favoured neighbourhoods. Linda Yablonsky revisits the ever-changing Lower East Side, Phillip Lopate sings the virtues of his native Brooklyn, and Maitland McDonagh bounces us through Riverside Park.

Other walks follow a theme – the who, where, when and why of a city's history. Edwin G Burrows lifts the lid on Lower Manhattan's past, from fur trading to share trading; Barry Miles pinpoints Beat writers' hangouts in Greenwich Village; while the lives of notable New Yorkers Dorothy Parker and Damon Runyon are explored through Midtown by Marion Meade and Minda Novek respectively.

Some walks provide a still more obscure angle on the city. Lee Stringer retraces the route he often trudged when he was homeless; Lady Bunny takes us on a tour of gay Manhattan, encouraging us to dress up en route; and Cristina Verán hip hops between graffiti sites in the Bronx.

And so on. In all there are 23 walks, covering Manhattan, the Bronx, Queens and Brooklyn. It's a huge trek, marching up avenues and across streets, in and out of museums, through parks and over bridges. But anything feels possible here, even walking for miles across the granite island, with horns honking in your wake and traders hollering across the street in one of any number of languages. And as you wander the diverse neighbourhoods, you'll begin to understand why the city has earned so many names – the Big Apple, Gotham, Fun City, Metropolis. Perhaps you'll find one of your own. At least until you set off on the next walk.

Have a nice day.

*Andrew White*

# Up Madison, down Lexington

William Boyd

Moments of Hopper-like stillness and calm amid the hustle and bustle of the Upper East Side.

---

**Start:** The Lowell Hotel, 28 East 63rd Street
**Finish:** The Lowell Hotel, 28 East 63rd Street
**Time:** 1-2 hours
**Distance:** 2 miles/3km
**Getting there:** subway trains B or Q to Lexington Avenue station at 63rd Street
**Getting back:** subway trains B or Q from Lexington Avenue station at 63rd Street
**Note:** most of the fashion stores on Madison Avenue are open late on Thursdays.

---

Since 1996 I've spent between 40 and 50 days a year in New York and, if I can't claim to be a local, I do feel I've come to know the place better than your average tourist: I have my habits, I have my little routines and short cuts, I am a regular in certain bars and restaurants. I may not be at home but I feel I occupy a kind of residential limbo – in prolonged and agreeable transit. I am, as they would say in France, *un familier*.

One measure of this familiarity is that there is a walk I do most Mondays to Fridays that has become as much a part of my life as similar walks are in London. It starts where I live when I'm in New York, a small hotel on 63rd Street between Park and Madison, and it forms a rough oblong shape that covers a fair bit of the Upper East Side. The Upper East Side suffers a

little from its reputation as a place where only the truly wealthy New Yorkers live, hidden away in immaculate, doorman-guarded apartment blocks. Like all stereotypes this one possesses a fair degree of truth. But the denizens of this bit of Manhattan do make for a fascinating passing parade, and the one place you'll see them out of their apartments and town cars is on the streets around here. People-watching doesn't come much better than on Madison Avenue.

Yet the Upper East Side is a far more heterogeneous place than its snootily upscale reputation might suggest and the first and most intriguing aspect of this walk is that, over its couple of miles or so, you will encounter as many facets of Manhattan life as you would almost anywhere else.

I leave the hotel and turn left towards Madison Avenue and, a few paces later, reaching Madison, turn north, heading uptown. In the four years I've been coming regularly to New York, Madison has turned itself into one of the most remarkable shopping streets in the world, a mile-long hymn of praise to labels and logos, high prices and haute couture. This is fine if you're interested in shopping but, even if you're not, these immaculate temples of consumerism are still diverting to the eye. The Madison run actually starts a few blocks south of 63rd with Nicole Farhi, Donna Karan and Calvin Klein, but as I turn northward pretty soon I'm flanked by Armani and Valentino and

# Up Madison, down Lexington

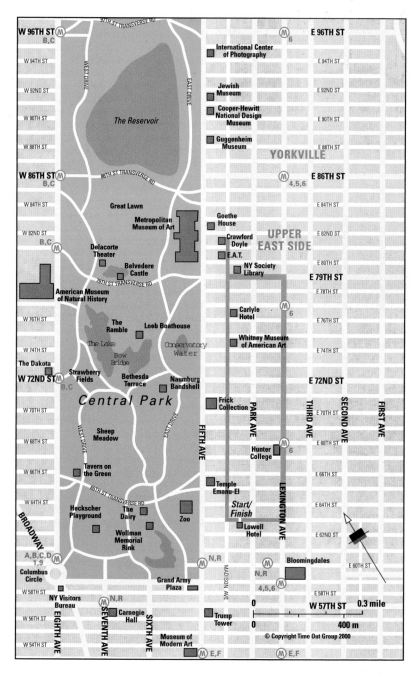

Reflected glory – **Ralph Lauren**'s mansion.

walk provides. This is the Madison Avenue Bookshop, small and well stocked, famous for the contemptuous aloofness of its erudite staff.

We've been walking slightly uphill thus far, on the east side of the Avenue. At the crest of this gentle hill stands what was once the Westbury Hotel, now converted into condominiums, and looking left down the cross-streets you can see narrow, tree-crowded vistas of Central Park.

Strolling easily downhill you pass on your right the impossible fantasy that is Ralph Lauren's shop/mansion on 72nd, a two-way cross-street. It's worth visiting this shop if only to see the quintessence of the Ralph Lauren vision of the good life: the dream made flesh. Across 72nd is the Madison Avenue Presbyterian Church. None of New York's churches is particularly distinguished, architecturally, but they are to be valued for their Victorian Gothic contribution to the 20th-century skyscape. Gargoyles, teetering finials and flying buttresses make the perfect decorative counterpoint to the concrete and plate glass angularities of the skyscrapers and office blocks. Diverted as you might be by the life at street level it is always worth looking up in New York every 50 yards or so. It never palls, this prospect of lofty buildings, and, particularly at night, it can be astonishingly beautiful, these soaring masses of stacked lights and the wavy ripple of mirror glass.

Up ahead, on 74th Street, is the inverted grey ziggurat that is the Whitney Museum of American Art. The Whitney is a great museum, not so much for what it periodically contains (though its permanent collection is superb) but for the building itself. Solidity, moneyed heft, integrity are the quiet messages its stone, brass and mahogany seem emphatically to convey. The lifts are gigantic, the finish flawless (no expense has been spared), its scale is impressive and it is astoundingly easy to use. I don't know what it is about the Whitney that draws me so. I prefer it

up ahead loom Krizia, Ungaro and Bulgari and so on. Also in this stretch of the Avenue are found small see-and-be-seen restaurants, such as Nello, Café Nosidam and La Goulue, serving international food to an international clientele, but my first break usually occurs, mundanely, at an ATM in Citibank and then, on 67th, I am occasionally obliged to stop for breakfast at the Gardenia Café. The Gardenia is a classic diner, although, fittingly for the neighbourhood, it seems slightly more genteel than most. A long, thin, dark room, serving American reliables – eggs, bacon, potatoes – with astonishing speed and fussless taciturnity. I drink my coffee and, if it's a Wednesday, read my *New York Observer*, a weekly, and, just possibly, the most interesting and best written newspaper in the world.

On up Madison the march of brand names continues – Dolce & Gabbana, Yves St Laurent, Sonia Rykiel. More intriguingly we encounter (on 70th) the first of five independent bookshops this

The **Whitney Museum** – a window on the world of American art.

*A Woman in the Sun*, and (opposite) *Second Story Sunlight* – just a couple of **Edward Hopper** delights at the Whitney.

to the Guggenheim and MoMA (not so far away, either). I think it must be something to do with the proportion and massiveness of its construction. As I pass it every day I can go in when it's just opened. I often find myself wandering around with only the museum guards for company. In any given week I may flit in for half an hour two or three times. It's famous for its Biennial exhibition of contemporary American art but it is the permanent collection that draws me back again and again. The Whitney has some superb Edward Hoppers, half a dozen or so. Seeing them, up close, side by side, you understand why Hopper is the great American artist of the 20th century – uniquely and hauntingly so.

On up Madison past the discreetly sumptuous wonders of the Carlyle Hotel. For such a large hotel, the Carlyle seems always calm, its marble lobby strangely free of bustle. In the café and the Bemelmans Bar you have consistently the best and most sophisticated cabaret New York can offer: Bobby Short, Barbara

Cook, Eartha Kitt, Barbara Carroll. And on Monday nights Woody Allen, on clarinet, sits in with his band.

We are now approaching my destination on 79th Street. This is the New York Society Library – where I work. This is an ancient institution by American standards, dating back to the 18th century. The library has moved many times in its history before ending up here in a capacious townhouse on 79th, between Madison and Park. The library is private – it costs $135 or so a year to join – but it provides personal access to a huge collection of books and journals (you can browse in the stacks) and, more importantly for someone like me, at its summit, rooms with desks where a transitory writer can plug in his computer and, in theory at least, work. It remains a defiantly unmodernised place, with filing cards as well as computerised catalogues, marble sculptures on the wide stairways and a politely formal way of dealing with its members. Its reading room could come out of a gentlemen's club in London – tall,

elegant windows, leather armchairs, periodicals displayed on circular tables, people speaking rarely and then in the quietest of whispers.

And this is where I spend my day, venturing out at lunchtime a little further up Madison to E.A.T (80th Street) – the closest thing to a New York brasserie (as opposed to a pseudo-French one) that the city provides. It welcomes many solo diners, which seems an almost forgotten pleasure these days. Eating a proper lunch alone (rather than a bite of something on the run) is an agreeable pastime but it mustn't be rushed and needs to be accompanied by some sort of reading matter – book, newspaper or magazine. They don't chase you out, either, when you've finished. You can easily spend an hour in E.A.T reading and eating and covertly watching the people around you at the same time.

And afterwards, if you require more diversion, just a block away on Fifth Avenue is the sprawling bulk of the Metropolitan Museum, an incomparable

treasure trove and again the sort of museum, in my opinion, that favours the periodic half-hour visit over the day-long, enervating culture-trawl. And, if the Met doesn't beguile, a couple of blocks north of E.A.T. is my favourite bookstore in the city – Crawford Doyle, another independent bookshop, which not only sells (with great charm and friendliness) everything in print you might want to read, but has a thriving antiquarian business to tempt you as well.

The library shuts at the end of the working day and the second leg of my walk commences. I prefer not to walk back down Madison – it's more of a morning thing, Madison Avenue – so I stroll along 79th, heading eastwards towards Lexington Avenue. This involves crossing Park Avenue and here you are afforded one of the great American vistas: the view south down Park Avenue towards the Met-Life building at its foot. It's probably best at dusk, with some blue still left in the sky, but with enough gathering gloom to set the refulgent windows of the towering, lit buildings glowing like banked coals.

On to Lexington and a right turn southwards. Lexington is smaller (in that its buildings are lower), narrower and shabbier than its two adjacent avenues to the west and it provides a welcome contrast. From gleaming, pricey, exclusive New York, you enter a neighbourhood, a place where people actually live and shop for themselves. Gone are the designer stores, to be replaced by supermarkets, delis, Chinese laundries. Lexington has its own special bonus, however: as you walk south you are aiming for the Chrysler Building, the world's most beautiful skyscraper, its silver, art deco, hypodermic needle gleaming gold – if you're lucky – in the orange evening sun.

You start to walk uphill again, fairly soon, up the steeper rise of Lennox Hill, heading towards Hunter College (part of New York University) with its two aerial pedestrian-ways crossing the avenue. Here there is an intriguing congregation of antique shops and, within the space of a few blocks, three more independent bookstores: Lennox Hill Bookstore (on 73rd), Bookberries (on 71st) and Shakespeare & Co on 69th. All have their own distinct character and all are worth stopping in to browse. The hegemony of Borders and Barnes & Noble does not seem to have affected independent bookselling in this part of the city, and a visit to any of the five on this walk will remind you of the advantages of plucky independence versus the chain store.

My pit stop on the walk back is on 73rd, called the Café Word of Mouth. Downstairs is a takeaway, upstairs is almost a tearoom: Rennie Mackintosh meets art deco, all cherrywood and taupe. The last time I did this walk I inverted it – came up Lex, went down Mad. It had snowed in the night and there were foot-high banks of frozen snow on the sidewalks. It was bitter cold, with a wind that seemed to take the skin off your face. I stopped in Café

Word of Mouth for sustenance. A big caffe latte, scrambled eggs and crispy bacon. I read the newspaper and thawed out, then plodded off up Lexington to the library, full and warm.

If you want alcohol on this walk, you have to go into hotels (the Mark or the Carlyle on Madison) or go further afield to the bars of Third Avenue where you're spoilt for choice. Though it's worth remembering that you can go into any New York restaurant and just have a drink at the bar without any problems. There used to be a bar on Madison called the Madison Pub – a dark semi-basement – but it closed recently. Things come and go with astonishing swiftness in New York, and the Upper East Side is no exception: in the last two years I've seen

Light reading – **New York Society Library**.

an entire skyscraper rise up from Park Avenue to dominate the view from my hotel room. A favourite café closed (where reputedly you could get the best espresso in Manhattan); a famous landmark bookstore – Books & Co – went, almost overnight. But this walk up Madison and down Lexington seems to me to contain, for all its regular and sudden transformations, something that remains a representative mixture of the whole city. Fashion, commerce, philanthropic art, the quaint, the banal, the unique, the down-and-dirty, high culture and nail parlours.

It's all downhill from Hunter College's crossroads. Students mill about smoking, sprawled on the steps. They seem all to be foreign, reminding you of this city's polyglot heritage, the welcome it gives (or gave) to immigrants. And indeed many of the shops on this last stretch down to 63rd and the hotel reflect that ethnic mix: pizza joints, kebab houses, Korean nail parlours, Chinese takeaways. And just at the end at the last block is A&B Stationers, home, it seems, to every foreign newspaper and magazine you could ask for. The British papers arrive 24 hours later and it seems bizarre, at six o'clock on a New York evening, to see the racks outside filled with the *Guardian, Independent* and the *Telegraph*. Bizarre but therefore somehow normal in this place, if the paradox doesn't seem too forced. Nothing, in New York, is really surprising, when you come to think about it – once you've got over your surprise.

## Eating & drinking

### Café Nosidam

*768 Madison Avenue, between 65th & 66th Streets (212 717 5633).* **Open** 11.30am-11.30pm Mon-Sat; 11.30am-10.30pm Sun. Light Italian-American dishes.

### Café Word of Mouth

*1012 Lexington Avenue, between 72nd & 73rd Streets (212 734 9483).* **Open** 8am-7pm Mon-Fri; 9am-6pm Sat; 10am-5pm Sun. Popular quality American food in upstairs eat-in café and tearoom.

### E.A.T

*1064 Madison Avenue, between 80th & 81st Streets (212 772 0022).* **Open** 7am-10pm daily. Famous for its breads and salads to eat in or take out.

### Gardenia Café

*797 Madison Avenue, between 67th & 68th Streets (212 628 8763).* **Open** 7am-10pm daily. Unpretentious setting for salads and sandwiches.

### La Goulue

*746 Madison Avenue, between 64th & 65th Streets (212 988 8169).* **Open** noon-11.30pm Mon-Sat; noon-10.30pm Sun. Simple, indulgent French bistro fare.

### Nello

*696 Madison Avenue, between 62nd & 63rd Streets (212 980 9099).* **Open** 11.30am-midnight daily. Designer Italian dishes in plush surroundings.

## Accommodation

### Carlyle Hotel

*35 East 76th Street, between Park & Madison Avenues (212 744 1600/800 227 5737).*

### The Lowell Hotel

*28 East 63rd Street, between Park & Madison Avenues (212 838 1400).*

### The Mark

*25 East 77th Street, between Fifth & Madison Avenues (212 744 4300/800 843 6275).*

## Bookshops

### Bookberries

*983 Lexington Avenue, at 71st Street (212 794 9400).* **Open** 10am-6.30pm Mon-Sat; 10.30am-5.30pm Sun.

### Crawford Doyle Booksellers

*1082 Madison Avenue, between 81st & 82nd Streets (212 288 6300).* **Open** 10am-6pm Mon-Sat; noon-5pm Sun.

### Lennox Hill Bookstore

*1018 Lexington Avenue, between 72nd & 73rd Streets (212 472 7170).* **Open** 10am-7pm Mon, Fri; 10am-8pm Tue-Thur; 11am-6pm Sat, Sun.

### Madison Avenue Bookshop

*833 Madison Avenue, between 69th & 70th Streets (212 535 6130).* **Open** 10am-6pm Mon-Sat.

### Shakespeare & Co Booksellers

*939 Lexington Avenue, between 68th & 69th Streets (212 570 0201).* **Open** 9am-8pm Mon-Fri; 10am-8pm Sat; 10am-5pm Sun.

## Shopping

### Bulgari

*730 Fifth Avenue, at 57th Street (212 315 9000).* **Open** 10am-5.30pm Mon-Sat.

### Calvin Klein

*654 Madison Avenue, at 60th Street (212 292 9000).* **Open** 10am-6pm Mon-Wed, Fri, Sat; 10am-8pm Thur; noon-6pm Sun.

### DKNY

*655 Madison Avenue, at 60th Street (212 223 3569).* **Open** 10am-7pm Mon-Wed, Fri, Sat; 10am-9pm Thur; noon-6pm Sun.

### Dolce & Gabbana

*825 Madison Avenue, between 68th & 69th Streets (212 249 4100).* **Open** 10am-6pm Mon-Wed, Fri, Sat; 10am-7pm Thur.

### emanuel ungaro

*792 Madison Avenue, at 67th Street (212 249 4090).* **Open** 10am-6pm Mon-Sat.

### Emporio Armani

*601 Madison Avenue, between 57th & 58th Streets (212 317 0800).* **Open** 10am-8pm Mon-Fri; 10am-7pm Sat; noon-6pm Sun.

### Krizia

*769 Madison Avenue, at 66th Street (212 879 1211).* **Open** 10am-6.30pm Mon-Wed, Fri; 10am-7.30pm Thur; 10am-6pm Sat.

### Nicole Farhi

*10 East 60th Street, between Fifth & Madison Avenues (212 223 8811).* **Open** 10am-7pm Mon-Fri; 11am-6pm Sat.

### Polo Ralph Lauren

*867 Madison Avenue, at 72nd Street (212 606 2100).* **Open** 10am-6pm Mon-Wed, Fri, Sat; 10am-8pm Thur.

### Sonia Rykiel

*849 Madison Avenue, between 70th & 71st Streets (212 396 3060).* **Open** 10am-6pm Mon-Sat.

### Valentino

*747 Madison Avenue, at 65th Street (212 772 6969).* **Open** 10am-6pm Mon-Sat.

### Yves St Laurent

*855-859 Madison Avenue, between 70th & 71st Streets (212 988 3821).* **Open** 10am-6pm Mon-Sat.

## Galleries

### Metropolitan Museum of Art

*1000 Fifth Avenue, at 82nd Street (212 535 7710).* **Open** 9.30am-5.15pm Tue-Thur, Sun; 9.30am-8.45pm Fri, Sat. **Suggested donation** $10; $5 concessions; free under-12s. No pushchairs on Sundays.

### Museum of Modern Art

*11 West 53rd Street, between Fifth & Sixth Avenues (212 708 9400).* **Open** 10.30am-5.45pm Mon, Tue, Thur, Sat; 10.30am-8.15pm Fri. **Admission** $10; $6.50 concessions; free under-16s; voluntary donation 4.30-8.15pm Fri.

### Solomon R Guggenheim Museum

*1071 Fifth Avenue, at 89th Street (212 423 3500).* **Open** 9am-6pm Mon-Wed, Sun; 9am-8pm Fri, Sat. **Admission** $12; $7 concessions; free under-12s; voluntary donation 6-8pm Fri.

### Whitney Museum of American Art

*945 Madison Avenue, at 75th Street (212 570 3600/recorded information 212 570 3676).* **Open** 11am-6pm Wed, Fri-Sun; 1-8pm Thur. **Admission** $12.50; $10.50 concessions; free under-12s. Free to all 6-8pm Thur.

## Others

### A&B Stationers

*38 Lexington Avenue, between 63rd & 64th Streets (212 888 1064).* **Open** 6am-10pm daily.

### Hunter College

*695 Park Avenue, between East 68th Street & Lexington Avenue (212 772 4000).*

### Madison Avenue Presbyterian Church

*921 Madison Avenue, between 72nd & 73rd Streets (212 288 8920).* **Open** *office* 9am-5pm Mon-Fri. **Services** *Summer* 10.30am Sun; *fall* 9am, 11.15am Sun.

### New York Society Library

*53 East 79th Street, between Park & Madison Avenues (212 288 6900).* **Open** 9am-5pm Mon, Wed, Fri-Sat; 9am-7pm Tue, Thur.

The chrome needle of the **Chrysler Building** punctures the skyline as Lexington Avenue heads towards Midtown.

# The upside of the real low-down

Linda Yablonsky

The melting pot is the same as it ever was. Only different.

---

**Start:** corner of Spring Street and the Bowery
**Finish:** Chaos club on East Houston Street
**Time:** 2-3 hours
**Distance:** 4 miles/6.5km
**Getting there:** subway train 6 to Spring Street station, or trains J or M to Bowery station
**Getting back:** short walk to F train at Second Avenue station
**Note:** the best days for this walk are Wednesday to Sunday; if you are set on seeing the magnificent Eldridge Street Synagogue, note that opening times are limited (see listings).

---

I never used to think of the Lower East Side as a pleasant place to walk, but that's beside the point. The neighbourhood that gave New York its identity as a cultural melting pot offers anyone peeking under its colourful skirts a dizzying variety of experience; for the amateur anthropologist, it's a goldmine – perhaps for the resident as well, I don't know. It may well be a better place just to visit.

My parents, who both grew up on the Lower East Side during the Depression, and had few kind words for the neighbourhood when I was a child. That didn't stop me from heading there as soon as I left our suburban home. Best known for its pushcart peddlers, gangsters, derelicts, floozies and junkies, it represented humanity's poor, dark side –

who could resist exploring it? (Indeed, for a time in the early 1980s I was one of the junkies.) But as the first stop for thousands of German and East European immigrants (including members of my own family) who poured through Ellis Island at the turn of the 19th century, it also represented my roots.

With its oppressive tenements and plethora of very cheap goods, the Lower East Side was where you had to go when you didn't have anywhere else; today, you could do a whole lot worse. If no gracious mansions line its streets, those streets still channel into expansive boulevards. If its most distinctive skyscrapers are what first appear to be ungodly public housing projects, well… God, as they say, is in the details, and details – historical, ethnographical, architectural, entrepreneurial – are what reveal themselves to the walker, beautiful in their scruffy, low-rent sort of way. This is a tour of another world. Actually, many.

The Bowery is the area's western border. Owing to its decades-long rule by the sheiks of scam, it remains, in some quarters, a metaphor for disgrace. You can see vestiges of its one-time flophouses, saloons, sweatshops and shooting galleries behind the artists' lofts and restaurant supply shops there now, but bar stools and bakery ovens are scattered on the sidewalk instead of tottering bums. Still, the Bowery Mission, between Stanton and Rivington, hasn't lasted to this day for nothing. Like the rest of the Lower East Side, this broad

# The upside of the real low-down

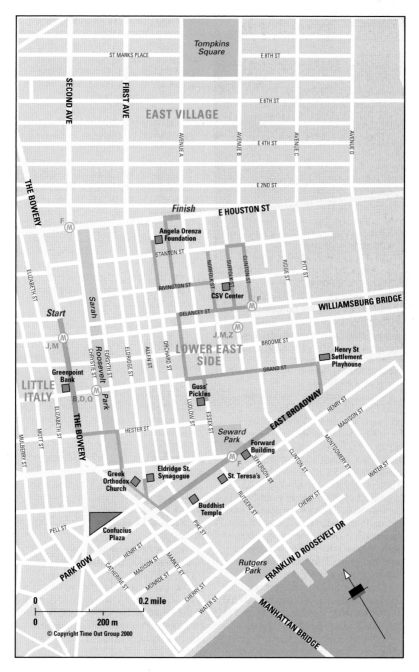

ST MARKS PLACE

*Tompkins Square*

E 8TH ST

SECOND AVE

FIRST AVE

E 6TH ST

**EAST VILLAGE**

AVENUE A

AVENUE B

AVENUE C

AVENUE D

E 4TH ST

E 2ND ST

THE BOWERY

*Finish*

**E HOUSTON ST**

**Angela Orenza Foundation**

STANTON ST

*Sarah*

ELIZABETH ST

RIVINGTON ST

NORFOLK ST

SUFFOLK ST

CLINTON ST

RIDGE ST

PITT ST

**CSV Center**

**WILLIAMSBURG BRIDGE**

DELANCEY ST

*Start*

*Roosevelt Park*

J,M

CHRYSTIE ST

FORSYTH ST

ELDRIDGE ST

ALLEN ST

ORCHARD ST

**J,M,Z**

BROOME ST

**LOWER EAST SIDE**

GRAND ST

**Henry St Settlement Playhouse**

**Greenpoint Bank**

ELIZABETH ST

B,D,Q

HESTER ST

**Guss' Pickles**

LUDLOW ST

ESSEX ST

**LITTLE ITALY**

THE BOWERY

MULBERRY ST

MOTT ST

*Seward Park*

**EAST BROADWAY**

HENRY ST

MADISON ST

MONTGOMERY ST

WATER ST

**Forward Building**

JEFFERSON ST

CLINTON ST

CHERRY ST

**Greek Orthodox Church**

**Eldridge St. Synagogue**

**St. Teresa's**

RUTGERS ST

**Buddhist Temple**

PELL ST

**Confucius Plaza**

HENRY ST

MADISON ST

PIKE ST

*Rutgers Park*

**FRANKLIN D ROOSEVELT DR**

CHERRY ST

WATER ST

PARK ROW

CATHERINE ST

MARKET ST

MONROE ST

CHERRY ST

0            0.2 mile

0            200 m

© Copyright Time Out Group 2000

**MANHATTAN BRIDGE**

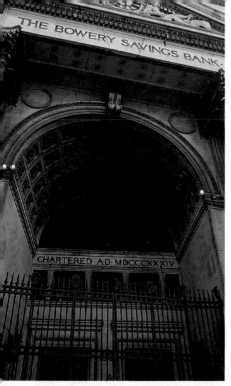

Savour the ceiling of the **Greenpoint Bank**.

thoroughfare is in many ways the same as it ever was. Only different.

I start at Spring Street and Bowery this warm Sunday afternoon, because I'm curious about the mysterious stone fortress standing rather grimly on the corner, its façade nearly blackened by almost a century's worth of grime. A friend who wants to walk with me (New Yorkers are born perambulators), and lives nearby, tells me that it was built as the Germania Bank, whose doors closed during World War II and never opened again. It still looks abandoned; whenever I pass, its windows are always dark, its marble-columned doorway always gated. But my friend says it's actually a private residence, the home and studio of a commercial fashion photographer. What must it be like to live in such a hugely forbidding place? Fabulous, probably.

Moving south across Delancey, the honking conduit to the Williamsburg

Bridge and Brooklyn, we amble towards Chinatown through what is, for all intents and purposes, New York's centre for lighting fixtures. At 155 Bowery, near Broome, we stop by O'Lampia, whose proprietor does only handcrafted custom work and has decorated his shop not just with samples but objects from his personal collection of antiques. Resisting the temptation to browse, we continue on to Grand Street and the Pioneer Hotel, an unmarked relic of the past. (From the mid to late 19th century, it was the home of Tammany Hall, the New York Democratic Party's scandalous political machine.) There are a number of these old hotel buildings along here – some are even still hotels – but what are those fascinating gabled houses at Nos.133-136? Something left from the time New York was New Amsterdam, I think, and thank Heaven this part of Manhattan has so far been immune to gentrification. I like relics.

Caught in the undertow of Chinatown's eternally thick pedestrian traffic we nearly have to claw our way to the spectacle of the Bowery Savings Bank (now the Greenpoint) at Grand Street. It was built on the High Renaissance model and, if one is lucky enough to happen by during business hours, its gilded ceilings and immense proportions are definitely worth a look.

Nearly crazed by the bustling crowds, the smells emanating from endless food shops and restaurants, the goods spilling on to the chaotic sidewalk from novelty shops and produce stands, we pass up a chance to visit the Well-Timed Wedding on Grand and veer left, on Hester, because it's calmer.

Crossing the tree-lined Sarah Roosevelt Park between Chrystie and Forsyth, we round the cylindrical outer walls of a modern public school at the bottom of the park, off Frank D'Amico Plaza (a reminder of the neighbourhood's sometime Italian presence); we pause at 27 Forsyth, just south of Canal, to admire an impressive Greek Orthodox church that was once a synagogue and could care less that it's now surrounded by delis, hardware stores and lumber yards flying Buddhist flags and bearing Chinese signage – as good a symbol of the incongruity of this neighbourhood as any. For a moment, we feel silly speaking English.

Rounding the corner to the left, we start up a slight hill on what might easily be a street in Hong Kong to reach the imposing Gothic eminence at Nos.12-16 – the Eldridge Street Synagogue, a notable building and proud landmark. Completed in 1887, it was the centre of religious life for thousands of immigrant Eastern European Jews. By the 1950s, however, it had fallen on hard times. Now it's been saved from ruin by a conscientious local restoration association and you don't have to be Jewish to love its faded Moorish glory. The sanctuary is missing a few stained glass windows above its rickety balcony, but there's nothing shabby about the intricate wood

carvings, glowing brass fixtures or what remains of the constellation of gold stars painted on the peeling, midnight-blue wall above the Holy Ark. In such surroundings, it's hard to believe we're still in New York. It's hard to feel that our feet are on the ground at all.

But when we hit the street again, turning left and heading down alongside the Manhattan Bridge, past the enclosed, 1960-something Chinese shopping mall at Market Street, we run smack into a modern Shishedo cosmetics outlet at 97 East Broadway. A lone Japanese store surrounded by countless Vietnamese and Chinese restaurants? Of course! We have no common language with the sales girls except that of vanity (and cash), and after a halting purchase of lipstick and face cream we continue east. Crossing the Pike Street Mall, we note a Greek Revival Buddhist temple in what may have been a synagogue… or a church… or possibly a large public bath house, for all we know.

The faded Moorish glory of the **Eldridge Street Synagogue** has an uplifting effect.

China comes to town on **East Broadway**...

Bath houses were once numerous in these environs, as were public toilets – necessities brought on by the cold-water flats of cramped, surrounding tenements; except for the occasional ritual Jewish baths for women, they seem to be gone. Yet, by the time we reach Straus Square, where East Broadway meets Canal and Essex near the southern end of Seward Park (one of the city's more bucolic), the Asian influence has begun a slow dissolve into what remains of the Jewish community that formed here a hundred years ago.

There are many small, 19th-century synagogues scattered along this route, which parallels the park along the East River. Shops are few, there's less traffic and more trees. At 147 East Broadway we come upon a Yeshiva, or school, but there's no hiding the fact that St Teresa's, a graceful Roman Catholic church built in 1841, sits a few steps away at the junction of Henry and Rutgers. It's always been this way down here, I guess, one culture bumping up against another. But it's so peaceful here, so small-town quiet that we begin to feel we've not only stepped back in time but out of it.

At Straus Square, we stop for a reality check by taking a backward glance. The view from here is rather extraordinary: the Woolworth Building, City Hall, and the World Trade Center in the west soar over the steely Manhattan Bridge roadway, where a subway is crossing to Brooklyn; the Chrysler and Citicorp buildings catch the sun in the north. It's New York in a nutshell is what it is – a teeming, gleaming cat's cradle of geometric patterns set in motion against a clear blue sky. Helluva town.

Standing at the granite war memorial at the centre of the square, we take a gander at the terracotta façade of the old, ten-storey Forward Building – a veritable skyscraper in these parts – once the offices of New York's main Yiddish newspaper and soon to be apartments. Who says the Lower East Side has no distinguished architecture? A half-block

away, the red-brick palazzo that is the Seward Park branch of the New York Public Library faces the David Sarnoff building, a Romanesque Revival settlement house refurbished with a gaping arch at the entrance. Around the corner on Jefferson Street, a group of middle-aged white theatre-goers are lining up for the afternoon performance of the Yiddish Mazer Theater, though the kids playing on the side street appear to be Latino. This is their neighbourhood too. A little way down East Broadway, a new Spanish church sits beside a very old, rather nondescript synagogue, hardly distinguishable from the three- and four-storey Federal row houses that fill out the rest of the block. A retired rabbi taking in the sun before one of them tells us it's a Torah study centre and had 'always' been there. He certainly has, God bless him.

A moment later we're at Clinton Street and the Bialystoker Home for the Aged, which looks like nothing else in the neighbourhood. In fact, it resembles an

# The upside of the real low-down

Art Deco hotel in Miami Beach. Those aren't housing projects standing behind it: they're among the earliest co-op cities in New York – by today's standards, the biggest bargain in apartment houses in town and the reason this neighbourhood still has a Jewish population. Who would give up such a good deal?

We turn north at Samuel Dickstein Square, on to Pitt Street, which will take us back to Grand, much wider here than it is in Chinatown and nearly devoid of traffic. If the decibel level has dropped, the centuries still clash as we near No.438 and the Georgian-style Henry Street Settlement Playhouse opposite, whose new red-brick addition is completely out of synch with the Ottoman spires of the Church of St Mary (the oldest Catholic church in town) now dominating the skyline. We stop here a moment, for our eyes to adjust.

But we've worked up an appetite now, and lucky for us we're nearing the Doughnut Plant at 379 Grand. It stays open, as a sign in the window reads, 'until we are sold out', which is generally around noon and we're too late. Fortunately, a few doors away, Kossar's bakery still has a few of its fresh onion and garlic rolls left on its cooling racks. Scrumptious. But we also turn left a bit at Essex, just to get a whiff of the Guss' Pickles stand, a holdover from the pushcart days that still draws fans to its streetside wooden barrels of pickles and sauerkraut throughout the day (except Saturdays – the Jewish Sabbath). It gives us a second wind. We're going to need it.

Returning to and left on Grand, we pass through what must once have been the centre of the hosiery trade, none too stylish now. Too bad; I could use some new underthings. We keep going, turning right on to Ludlow, where we reckon with the shell of Seward Park High School, which takes up the whole block. The roof has been removed, the interior gutted. I feel a spell of nostalgia coming on: this is my parents' *alma mater*. The last time I passed by, years

ago, it was completely dishevelled. Now it's getting a whole new suit. But so is the rest of the neighbourhood.

If the streets south of Delancey Street are keeping the old world alive, those between Delancey and Houston (pronounced 'how-stun'), Allen and Pitt – Nowheresville just a few years ago – have become the revenge of the young and hip. Even the Formica heaven of Ratner's – an ageless, 24-hour dairy restaurant at 138 Delancey (between Norfolk and Suffolk) whose bakery still turns out the best breakfast rolls in town – is being turned into a nightclub to be known as Lansky's Lounge. As we snake up and down Clinton, Norfolk, Suffolk, Ludlow and Orchard Streets, we fairly trip over chic new bars, restaurants, clubs and small shops purveying everything from handbags to furniture to sex toys. And though there are plenty of longtime black and Latino residents of all ages, all

... while the **Financial District** looks on.

Too weird to pass by, too red to miss – the **Angel Orensanz Foundation** shines forth.

around, we don't see any white people over thirty, and that's stretching it.

Clinton Street, on the north side of the Williamsburg Bridge entry ramp, seems the least changed, but that's an illusion. With its mixed population, steep tenement stoops and family-owned appliance shops and bodegas, it's about as close as the Lower East Side gets to Main Street, USA. Except that it also has, at No.71, one of the more upscale restaurants in New York, so chi-chi we're almost afraid to go in. No matter. It's so popular with people from other parts of town, we can't get a table anyway. But disappointment turns to delight at No.57, which is New York's one and only Freakatorium. Run by Johnny Fox, a personable fellow who happens to be a genuine sword-swallower (we get a free demonstration), it displays a collection of freak-show memorabilia that ranges from Tom Thumb's vest to photos of a two-headed boy to the right hand of an 'unrepentant murderer'. Needless to say, it's a fun place to visit.

Turning left on to Stanton, we soon reach a New Age candle shop that's far too precious for these precincts, while the custom décor at a coffee shop down the street is strictly New Age medieval. Turning left down Suffolk, however, we see that the Streit's matzoh factory at Rivington is still open for business, totally unencumbered by any décor at all. Yet, across the street, an ornate, neo-Gothic structure that was once a public school has become the Centrol Cultural Clemente Soto Velez, hosting theatre groups of all nationalities. Down at 107 Suffolk, a hole-in-the-wall storefront selling cute, handmade pocketbooks calls itself, appropriately, Duh.

Turning right on Delancey and right again up Norfolk, we get to No.107 and my favorite underground cabaret. This is Tonic, a comfortable, even laid-back, venue for experimental jazz and electronic music that offers a Klezmer brunch on Sundays and also has a bookstore that stays open late and sells books from small,

# The upside of the real low-down

independent presses only. It's unique in every way. But we keep going – it's too early for this one. Up Norfolk, on the pretty (yes, pretty!) block north of Stanton, stands the Angel Orensanz Foundation, the new name for another cathedral-like former synagogue in the Gothic/Romantic, Eldridge Street Synagogue mould, except it's even older. And newer. Built in 1849 for the German Jews who later settled the East 80s, it's open pretty much around the clock and now rents itself out for weddings, bar mitzvahs and fashion shoots – nothing if not eclectic. The façade is bright red – you can't miss it. And you shouldn't. It's too weird.

And ahead, atop a bland square appartment block, stands a bronze statue of Lenin, saluting the city from on high. Our heads suitably spun around, we're not sure where to turn. So we backtrack to Rivington and make a right. More shops. Lots of them, mostly clothes – some vintage, some hot off the loom. All these shops – this is New York as it was before the big chain stores hit. This may be the only area in town that doesn't have them.

Crossing Essex again, we reach Orchard, the original pushcart plaza. On Sundays, it's closed to vehicular traffic and the street swarms with shoppers. But the cheap stores are quickly outnumbered by the new couturiers who have established themselves among the luggage and shoe salesmen. And there are new bars here too. We're welcomed into Baby Jupiter, an Island-themed restaurant at the corner of Stanton with eye-bugging low prices. There's a Jamaican band performing in the back room; admission is free and the music is fantastic. We can't get over it – or how the old Beckenstein fabric building, near Delancey, has turned into a luxury condo. Down here! In Low Rent City! We turn back to Rivington to get our bearings but there, between Orchard and Ludlow, we find Lucky Wang, which sells all manner of objects covered in bright acrylic Astro-turflike fuzz, and Toys, a lesbian sex shop, right across the street from a Bangladeshi deli and yet another old synagogue. Where else on the planet does this sort of conjunction happen? Hold on – we still have to do Ludlow.

**Katz's Delicatessen** – a childhood memory for some, kosher delight for others.

Ludlow Street is the Times Square of the neighbourhood. No.157 was a brothel up to about 1980 but now the street has it all: the kitschy Max Fish bar (which pioneered the new scene); the Pink Pony Café (great smoothies); the Nada storefront theatre; Iggy's Irish bar; a couple of cool, stainless lounges; a fancy Mexican place across the street from El Sombrero (more down-home Mexican fare); one of the best leather shops in town; a retro furniture shop; a French bistro; and on the corner at Houston, Katz's Delicatessen – the carnivore's answer to Ratner's. My parents used to bring me to this smoked-meat emporium for kosher hot dogs or pastrami sandwiches when I was a kid. Salamis still hang in the window. It doesn't seem so attractive now, but as in every other establishment here, business is booming.

It's night now, and as we turn right on to Houston, we see they're lining up at the Mercury Lounge for rock music. At the corner of Essex, another crowd queues up at a booming, velvet-roped disco known as Chaos. It was a bank, once upon a time. I also remember when it was the studio for the artist Jasper Johns; he moved out after someone broke in and stole some paintings. But well, you know – that's history now.

# Eating & drinking

### 71 Clinton Fresh Food
*71 Clinton Street, between Rivington & Stanton Streets (212 614 6960).* **Open** 6-10pm Mon-Thur; 6-11pm Fri, Sat.

### Baby Jupiter
*170 Orchard Street, at Stanton Street (212 982 2229).* **Open** 11am-1am Mon-Thur, Sun; 11am-3am Fri, Sat. Asian-Cajun fare for a hip crowd.

### Doughnut Plant
*379 Grand Street, between Clinton & Essex Streets (212 505 1493).* **Open** 7am-till they are sold out Tue-Sun.

### El Sombrero
*108 Stanton Street, at Ludlow Street (212 254 4188).* **Open** 9am-4am daily. Popular for the Mexican dishes, but this place also serves the undisputed champion of Manhattan margaritas.

### Guss' Pickles
*35 Essex Street, between Grand & Hester Streets (212 254 4477).* Open 9am-6pm Mon-Thur, Sun; 9am-3.30pm Fri. The undisputed Pickle King sells them sour, half-sour and in all sizes.

### Iggy's
*132 Ludlow Street, between Rivington & Stanton Streets (212 529 2731).* **Open** 2pm-4am daily.

### Katz's Delicatessen
*205 East Houston Street, at Ludlow Street (212 254 2246).* **Open** 8am-10pm Mon, Tue, Sun; 8am-11pm Wed, Thur; 8am-3am Fri, Sat. Grab a meal ticket at the door, and sample pastrami piled high or the city's best hot dog in this venerable New York institution.

### Kossar's Bialystoker Kuchen Bakery
*367 Grand Street, between Clinton & Essex Streets (212 473 4810).* **Open** 24 hours daily except closed 3pm Fri-10pm Sat. Buy warm bialy fresh from the oven and take it to their café round the corner on Essex Street.

### Max Fish
*178 Ludlow Street, between Stanton & Houston Streets (212 529 3959).* **Open** 5.30pm-4am daily.

### Pink Pony Café
*176 Ludlow Street, between Stanton & Houston Streets (212 253 1922).* **Open** 1pm-3am Mon-Thur, Sun; 1pm-4am Fri, Sat.

### Streit's
*150 Rivington, at Suffolk Street (212 475 7000).* Open 9am-4.30 Mon-Thur, Sun.

# Arts centres & theatres

### Angel Orensanz Foundation
*172 Norfolk Street, between Stanton & Houston Streets (212 780 0175).* **Open** 9am-5pm daily.

### Clemente Soto Velez Cultural and Educational Center
*107 Suffolk Street, at Rivington Street (212 260 4080).* **Open** 10am-6pm daily.

### Freakatorium
*57 Clinton Street, at Rivington Street (212 375 0475).* **Open** noon-6pm Wed-Sun. Phone to confirm.

### Henry Street Settlement Playhouse
*466 Grand Street, at Pitt Street (212 598 0400).* **Open** 10am-10pm daily.

## Nada
*167 Ludlow Street, between Stanton & Houston Streets (212 420 1466).* **Open** phone for details.

## David Sarnoff Building of the Educational Alliance
*197 East Broadway, at Jefferson Street (212 780 2300).* **Open** 6am-10pm Mon-Fri.

# Clubs

## Chaos
*225 East Houston Street, between Essex & Ludlow Streets (212 475 3200).* **Open** *office* 11am-5pm Wed-Sat; *club* 10pm-4am Wed-Sat.

## Mercury Lounge
*217 East Houston Street, between Essex & Ludlow Streets (212 26 4700).* **Open** *office* noon-7pm Mon-Fri.

## Tonic
*107 Norfolk Street, between Delancey & Rivington Streets (212 358 7503).* **Open** 8-11pm daily. **Admission** $8-$12. **No credit cards**.

# Public services

## Bialystoker Home for the Aged
*228 East Broadway, between Clinton & Pitt Streets (212 475 7755).*

## Bowery Mission
*227 Bowery, between Stanton & Rivington Streets (212 674 3456).*

## Greenpoint Bank
*130 Bowery, at Grand Street (212 334 6955).* **Open** 8.30am-3pm Mon-Thur; 8.30am-6pm Fri; 9am-noon Sat.

## Pioneer Hotel
*341 Broome, between Bowery & Elizabeth Street (212 226 1482).*

## Seward Park Public Library
*192 East Broadway, between Jefferson & Clinton Streets (212 477 6770).* **Open** noon-8pm Mon; 10am-6pm Tue,Wed, Fri; noon-6pm Thur; 10am-5pm Sat.

# Religion

## Eldridge Street Synagogue
*12 Eldridge Street, between Canal & Division Streets (212 219 0888).* **Open** 11am-4pm Sun. *Tours* 11.30am, 2.30pm Tue, Thur.

## St Barbara Greek Orthodox Church
*27 Forsyth Street, between Canal & Division Streets (212 226 0499).* **Open** 9am-4pm Mon-Fri; 9am-3pm Sat; 9am-1pm Sun.

## St Mary's Church
*440 Grand Street, between Pitt & Clinton Streets (212 260 0018).* **Open** 8am-6pm daily.

## St Teresa's
*141 Henry Street, at Rutgers Street (212 233 0233).* **Open** 8.15am-9am Mon-Thur; 7.15am-8am Fri; 11am-7pm Sat; 7.30am-1pm Sun.

## Sung Tak Buddhist Association of New York City
*15 Pike Street, between East Broadway & Henry Street (212 587 5936).* **Open** 9am-7pm daily.

# Shops

## Ageless
*156B Stanton Street, between Clinton & Suffolk Streets (212 533 7707).* **Open** 1.30-7pm Tue-Sun.

## Duh
*102 Suffolk Street, between Rivington and Delancey Streets (212 253 1158).* **Open** 1-7pm Wed-Sun.

## Lucky Wang
*100 Stanton Street, between Orchard and Ludlow Streets (212 353 2850).* **Open** noon-7pm Wed-Fri; 1-7pm Sat; noon-6pm Sun.

## O'Lampia
*155 Bowery Street, between Broome & Delancey Streets (212 925 1660).* **Open** 10am-6pm Tue-Sun. Mon by appointment only.

## Shishedo
*97 East Broadway, between Market & Pike Streets (212 577 6133).* **Open** 10am-7pm daily.

## Toys
*94 Rivington Street, between Orchard & Ludlow Streets (212 375 1701).* **Open** noon-10pm Mon-Sat; noon-8pm Sun.

## Well-Timed Wedding
*126 Bowery, at Grand Street (212 219 8338).* **Open** 9am-7pm daily.

# Other

## William H Seward Park
*Canal to Hester Streets, Essex to Jefferson Streets.*

# Eyeball kicks

Barry Miles

On the road in the wake of the Beat Generation.

---

**Start:** Chelsea Hotel, West 23rd
Street
**Finish:** Caffe Reggio, 121
MacDougal Street
**Time:** 2-3 hours
**Distance:** 2 miles/3km
**Getting there:** subway trains C, E,
1 or 9 to 23rd Street station
**Getting back:** subway trains A, B,
C, E, F or Q from West 4th Street-
Washington Square station
**Note:** check the opening times
for the General Theological
Seminary's garden. It is also
worth noting that Maitland
McDonagh's walk *You Gotta
Have Park*, and Greg Sanders'
walk, *Men of Letters*, both refer
to Beat locations.

---

New York in the 1940s and '50s was the
artistic capital of the world. In virtually
every area, from modern dance to bebop,
from rock 'n' roll to avant-garde theatre,
from abstract expressionist painting to the
independent cinema, a series of remarkable
artistic developments occurred that
continues to shape the arts to this day.

On the literary front, New York was the
hometown of the Beat Generation. The
principal members – Allen Ginsberg, Jack
Kerouac and William Burroughs – all met
back in 1943-4 in the areas surrounding
the Columbia University campus, where
for about a year they all shared an
apartment on 115th Street. Gregory Corso,
the youngest member, came on the scene
in 1952. Even if we restrict ourselves to
these four individuals, there are hundreds
of sites which could legitimately claim a

Beat connection: in half a century of life
they visited virtually every street and
public building in the city. I am restricting
myself to sites of Beat activity up until the
late 1960s, when the hippies took over as
the dominant form of bohemianism.

The Beat Generation was a term coined
by Jack Kerouac and John Clellon Holmes
in the fall of 1949; in typically Beat
confusion, their accounts of its origin
differ. Jack Kerouac: 'We were talking
about the Lost Generation, and what this
generation would be called, and we
thought of various names and I said, "Ah,
this is really a Beat Generation!" – and he
leaped up and said, "You've got it!" – see,
just like that.' Holmes said: 'Jack and I
never talked about the Lost Generation
particularly. You see, when Jack used that
phrase, we certainly didn't say, "That's it!
That's it!" and make a big issue out of it.'
Holmes, however, was the first to use it,
three years later, in his book *Go*: 'You
know, everyone I know is kind of furtive,
kind of beat … a sort of revolution of the
soul, I guess you'd call it.' The *New York
Times* noticed the catchy phrase and
commissioned Holmes to write a piece on
it. 'This Is the Beat Generation' appeared
November 16 1952 and the movement was
born. As far as the public was concerned,
Kerouac's definition, from *On the Road*,
pretty much summed it up: 'The only
people for me are the mad ones, the ones
who are mad to live, mad to talk, mad to be
saved, desirous of everything at the same
time, the ones who never yawn or say a
commonplace thing but burn, burn, burn,
burn like fabulous yellow roman candles
exploding like spiders across the stars and
in the middle you see the blue centerlight
pop and everybody goes "Awww!".'

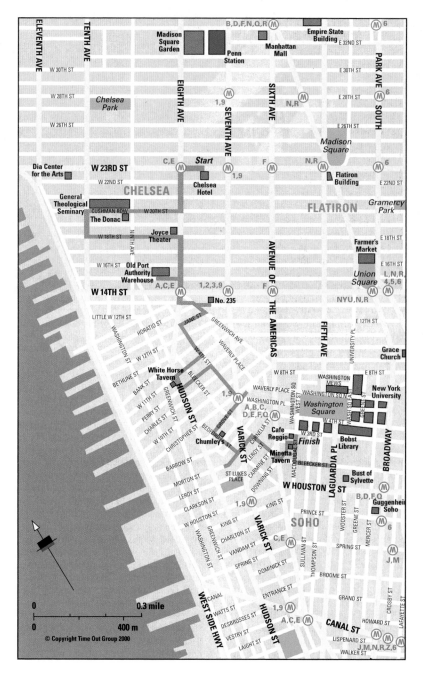

The staircase at the **Chelsea Hotel** has witnessed the rise and fall of many literary figures.

We start at the headquarters of New York bohemia, the Chelsea Hotel at 222 West 23rd. This old building, built as a luxury apartment block in 1884 with artists' studios on the top floor, is the only structure in New York protected both as an historical monument and an architectural one. Look around the lobby, filled with art collected by owner Stanley Bard in lieu of rent. Christo, Larry Rivers, Jackson Pollock, de Kooning, Alice Neal all lived here – the exhibition changes. Jimi Hendrix lived here and Dylan wrote 'Sad Eyed Lady of the Lowlands' here for Sarah. Sid Vicious, of course, murdered Nancy Spungen in room 100 in 1978, and Warhol shot *Chelsea Girls*. Valerie Solanas, author of the SCUM manifesto (Society for Cutting Up Men), was living at the Chelsea when she tried to murder Warhol. When the Beats were around, the hotel was known for its earlier batch of residents: Mark Twain, Nelson Algren, Thomas Wolfe, Sarah Bernhardt. Dylan Thomas was living at the Chelsea when he drank himself to death – he collapsed here – and Brendan Behan, another great

drinker, also lived here during his time in New York. It was home to Mary McCarthy, and composer Virgil Thompson lived here for more than 40 years. George Kleinsinger, composer of the children's hour favourite *Tubby the Tuba,* lived in a room converted to a private menagerie – the bellman would walk the alligators down the corridor. Arthur Miller fled here after breaking up with Marilyn Monroe, Arthur C Clarke had a telescope in his room during the 1960s. The Beat connection began when Jack Kerouac and Gore Vidal took a front balcony room for the night together in 1953, described coyly by Kerouac in *Subterraneans*, and in extreme graphic detail in Vidal's *Palimpsest*. William Burroughs lived here in 1964, during which time he filmed part of Antony Balch's *The Cut-Ups* from a room in back overlooking 22nd Street. Brion Gysin spent many months here that year, painting and trying to sell his Dreamachine to American museums. Gregory Corso first lived here in the mid-'60s and stayed months, even years at a time, after that. When bedbugs overran

Allen Ginsberg's Lower East Side apartment in 1970, it was the Chelsea he moved to.

Make a right at the desk and take the flight of stairs to see the ornate Victorian iron balustrades rising ten floors up the open stairway. Back down and continue out of the hotel, and turn left, passing the El Quixote, where Janis Joplin often closed the bar at 4am. Miller Lite was the favoured beer in the '60s, or a Pina Colada if you could afford it. Other regulars then were Leonard Cohen, the Jefferson Airplane, Grateful Dead and Johnny Winter. Continue west to Eighth Avenue, turn left and walk south. Now the main street of gay Chelsea, this used to be a Hispanic area, filled with Cuban Chinese restaurants, much loved by Ginsberg and company. Turn right at 20th Street and across Ninth Avenue to 402 West 20th – the Donac building – where playwright LeRoi Jones – later known as Amiri Baraka – and Hettie Cohen lived from 1958 until 1960. Here they published *Yugen* magazine – the first of the little magazines of Beat poetry. Frequent visitors included Jack Kerouac, Allen Ginsberg, Gregory Corso, Herbert Selby Jr (author of *Last Exit to Brooklyn*) and dozens of other lesser known Beats – the parties were legendary and many of the Beats first met each other here. The story is told in *The Autobiography: LeRoi Jones/Amiri Baraka*, and in *How I Became Hettie Jones*. The Donac was built in 1897 by CPH Gilbert and makes a nice transition from the avenue to the set back of the Greek Revival row on West 20th. 'Donac' is taken from Don Alonzo Cushman, who built many of the townhouse rows in Chelsea.

Continue down the street. No.404 is the oldest Greek Revival building in Chelsea, built 1830. The row makes up the south side of Chelsea Square, the remainder being the General Theological Seminary on the other side of the street. Though it's private, you can go in (entrance on Ninth Avenue); this was a favourite spot for

Chelsea Hotel residents to picnic in the summer. Ginsberg liked to walk there with Kerouac, who lived a little further along West 20th at No.454. It was here Kerouac wrote *On the Road*.

Kerouac had married 20-year-old Joan Haverty in November 1950, just two weeks after they met. The marriage was doomed: Jack was a mother's boy and he insisted they live with her out in Queens. Mother and son both treated Haverty more or less as a slave, and she quickly moved out, telling Kerouac he could move in with her, or not, as he liked. She took the apartment at 454 West 20th and when she went to see how the removal men were doing during her lunch break, she found Kerouac sitting on top of his desk in the road outside. While Joan worked as a waitress, Jack typed *On the Road* on a 120-foot roll of paper, made from taped-together 20-foot teletype rolls. Fuelled by Benzedrine, soaked in sweat, typing day and night with short exhausted naps, he completed the book in about three weeks during April 1951. It remains a classic of the genre.

Follow the map down to 319 West 18th, where Allen Ginsberg's mother, Naomi, lived in 1943 after breaking up with Allen's father. Allen used her apartment as a mail address and sometimes stayed with her there. Her residency is recorded in detail in *Kaddish*, the story of her developing insanity and eventual death in the madhouse. It is often regarded as his greatest work. It was here she saw God: 'He looked tired. He's a bachelor so long, and he liked lentil soup.'

Turn right on Eighth Avenue and continue down to West 15th Street. The whole city block on the north side is taken up by what used to be a giant Port Authority warehouse, so big it had elevators inside capable of carrying a ten-wheel truck (it's now a cancer outpatients centre and apartment block). For about a year from December 1951, Allen Ginsberg lived in an attic room at No.346 across the street, the period described by Kerouac in *The Subterraneans*. He wrote many poems

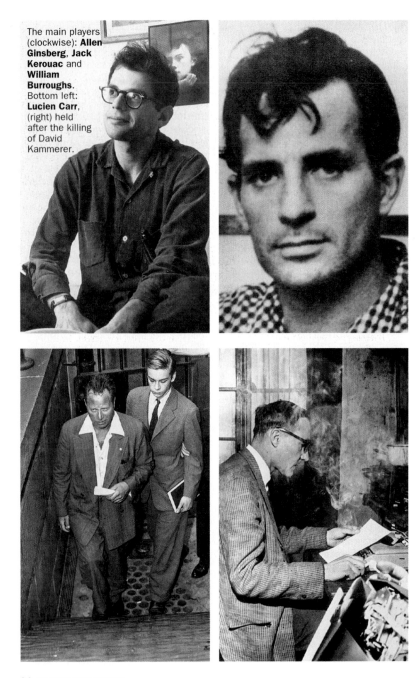

The main players (clockwise): **Allen Ginsberg**, **Jack Kerouac** and **William Burroughs**. Bottom left: **Lucien Carr**, (right) held after the killing of David Kammerer.

Ginsberg and Kerouac used to wander together in the **Theological Seminary Gardens**.

there including *Walking Home at Night*:
> *… reaching my own block*
> *I saw the Port Authority*
> *Building hovering over*
> *the old ghetto side*
> *of the street…*

From here a path he must have taken hundreds of times would take him down Eighth Avenue, then curving along Bleecker Street to the San Remo bar at MacDougal Street.

Return to Eighth Avenue. Cross 14th Street and to the left, just off the corner of Greenwich Avenue at 235 West 13th Street, is the wisteria-clad redbrick building where Lawrence Ferlinghetti lived in 1946 while doing graduate work at Columbia University on the GI Bill (whereby GIs got free education at the government's expense). However, it was not until 1954 in San Francisco that he met Ginsberg and the other Beats. In 1955 he published Ginsberg's *Howl*.

A block down Greenwich make a right at Jane and walk back towards Eighth Avenue. Turn sharp left on to West 4th Street, which – confusingly – crosses West 12th Street one block down. On this corner, at 323 West 4th Street, lived Lucien Carr. Carr was a member of the original Beat group at Columbia in the 1940s and was responsible for introducing Ginsberg and Kerouac to Burroughs. He transferred to Columbia from the University of Chicago to escape from David Kammerer, a homosexual almost twice Carr's age, who had become obsessed with Carr while teaching him at his junior school play group. He pursued Carr relentlessly, even though Carr was not gay, following him everywhere. Carr left St Louis, and attended Bowdoin College in Maine and various other schools, but Kammerer would always arrive to pester him and demand his friendship. In August 1944, while Carr and Kammerer were sitting in Riverside Park on the banks of the Hudson, after the West End Bar had closed, matters came to a head. Kammerer threatened to harm Carr's girlfriend, Celine, and made a lunge for him. Carr defended himself with a boy scout knife and stabbed Kammerer twice through the heart, killing him. It was described by the newspapers as 'an honour killing'. Carr spent two years in jail before becoming a journalist. He was a lifetime friend of Allen Ginsberg, who lived at this address in March 1953, while Lucien was away in Mexico.

Continue down West 4th to West 11th Street and make a right. Two blocks down is the White Horse Tavern, at 567 Hudson Street. The bar only occupied the corner building in the 1950s and '60s but has since expanded along the avenue. This was a major hangout for William Styron and Norman Mailer as well as the Beats. Jack Kerouac was thrown out of here many times, but they always let him back in. It is also where Dylan Thomas drank the evening that he collapsed and died back at the Chelsea Hotel. In a small courtyard on the other side of 11th Street is No.307 where Jack Kerouac lived with Helen Weaver. Early one morning in late November 1956, Kerouac, Allen Ginsberg, Allen's boyfriend Peter Orlovsky and his brother Lafcadio Orlovsky, were dropped off here after a share-drive car trip all the way from Mexico City. They needed to get out of the cold and find a place to stay, so Ginsberg called up to Helen Elliot's apartment, on the third floor. Helen was an ex-girlfriend of Lucien Carr, and shared her apartment with Helen Weaver, so when Allen yelled her name up from the street, the two Helens poked their heads from third floor windows to see who was calling. Jack and Helen Weaver took an immediate liking to each other, so while Allen, Peter and Lafcadio slept in a row on the floor in their sleeping bags, Jack cuddled up in Helen Weaver's warm bed. Kerouac calls them the 'two Ruths' in *Desolation Angels*.

Return to Hudson and walk south one block to Perry, make a left and walk over Bleecker Street to West 4th. Turn right and walk two blocks to the Riviera Café at 225 West 4th at Seventh Avenue South. This was a favourite hangout for Kerouac in the early '50s, who used it as a meeting place as he had no pad of his own. His old friend Henri Cru – called Remi Boncoeur in

'Eighty-six it' through **Chumley's** grille door.

*On the Road* – worked there as a bouncer.

Across the avenue is Sheridan Square. It's not a square, neither is Times Square, but like Times Square it gives its name to all the surrounding blocks. On the corner with West 4th was Jack Delaney's Steak House at 72 Grove Street (now a Starbuck's coffeeshop). Kerouac records in *Vanity of Duluoz* how he and his father ate there on Armistice Day, 1939, to celebrate a victory for his high school football team: 'So we go down to Jack Delaney's steak restaurant on Sheridan Square, myself little knowing how much time I was destined to spend around that square, in Greenwich Village, in darker years, but tenderer years to come.'

In the late '50s Kerouac often stayed at Lucien Carr's apartment at 92 Grove Street, one block along. He described it in *Desolation Angels*: '… a small balcony overlooking all the neons and trees of Sheridan Square, and a kitchen refrigerator full of ice cubes and coke to go with ye old Partners Choice Whiskey-boo.'

One evening, he and Lucien slipped down the fire escape to a bar while Helen Weaver and Carr's wife Cessa talked. Jack fell ten feet from the counterweighted ladder to the sidewalk and cut his head.

Retrace your steps back down Grove, cross Seventh Avenue and continue two blocks to Bedford Street. Make a left, and a few doors down is No.86, the unmarked, rather forbidding doorway to Chumley's. Chumley's opened as a speakeasy in 1928, at the height of Prohibition, and has always been a writers' bar: a list of one-time regulars includes John Steinbeck, Ernest Hemingway, Eugene O'Neill, Sinclair Lewis, Arthur Miller, William Faulkner, Norman Mailer, Anaïs Nin, ee cummings, Dylan Thomas, Margaret Mead and JD Salinger. In 1944 William Burroughs lived around the corner and ate there at least once a week, usually with David Kammerer, Lucien Carr or Chandler Brossard, author of *Who Walk in Darkness*, generally regarded as the first Beat Generation novel. Ginsberg often came down from Columbia to meet him there and it was one of the places where Burroughs and Kerouac drank while working on *And the Hippos Were Boiled in Their Tanks*, their fictional version of the death of David Kammerer. The hamburgers are pretty good, so's the beer. There is another secret, arched, entrance around the corner in Pamela Court, at 58 Barrow Street. Legend has it that the Bedford Street entrance was only used when Prohibition agents showed up at the Pamela Court entrance. While the bartender stalled them, the customers 'eighty-sixed it' through the door at 86 Bedford – thus coining the term for a rapid departure.

Continue down Bedford. In 1943 William Burroughs arrived from Chicago and took an apartment at No.69 on the first floor: 'It wasn't big but it was adequate. A smallish living room with a couch, a little walk-in kitchen with a fridge, a range, a bathroom and a bedroom and that was it, facing on to the

street. And it was comfortable. David Kammerer lived right around the corner.'

The chronology and details of this part of Burroughs' life are accurately portrayed in *Junky*. It was in this apartment, just before Christmas 1943, that Lucien Carr first introduced Allen Ginsberg to Burroughs. Ginsberg was 17 and Burroughs an old man of 29. And it was to here that the panic-striken Lucien Carr fled after pushing Kammerer's body into the Hudson River. Burroughs advised him to get a good lawyer and turn himself in.

Continue down Bedford and make a right on Morton Street; Kammerer had a room at No.48. Chandler Brossard, then a reporter for the *New Yorker*'s 'Talk of the Town' column, lived in the same building, as did a lesbian friend of both Burroughs and Kammerer called Ruth McMann, described by Burroughs as 'straightforward, manly and reliable'. She is called Agnes in *And the Hippos Were Boiled in Their Tanks*. Burroughs: 'I knew Dave Kammerer from Saint Louis, he went to my school. He was my age, a little older. He was a friend. He became obsessed with Lucien, I told him, "This is silly, this is awful," I said, "It's also completely selfish, you're not really interested in him, you're interested in some idea of him that you have. And what you're trying to do is not at all to his advantage." Which it sure wasn't. He just couldn't see it. But otherwise he was very witty, very charming. Dave Kammerer, he was a charmer.'

Burroughs saw Kammerer almost every night. They would go out to dinner at Chumley's or to Little Italy or Chinatown. Burroughs would often meet for dinner with Ginsberg, Kerouac and his girlfriend Edie Parker, and Carr with his girlfriend Celine Young. Chandler Brossard sometimes joined them. Kerouac wrote in *Vanity of Duluoz*: 'Burroughs bought us fine dinners, in Romey Marie's, in San Remo's, in Minetta's, and inevitably Kammerer would always find us and join in.' The Minetta Tavern still exists and we head toward there next.

Double back and walk east on Morton, crossing Seventh Avenue, to Bleecker Street where you make a right. Cross Sixth Avenue – now also called Avenue of the Americas, except by New Yorkers – and make an immediate left into Minetta Street. At the end make a right into Minetta Lane.

On the next corner is the Minetta Tavern at 113 MacDougal Street. Another former speakeasy, once frequented by Hemingway and John Dos Passos, it was the favoured Village drinking place for the teenage Allen Ginsberg and Lucien Carr in the early '40s. Joe Gould was a regular; he would flap his arms and imitate a seagull for a drink – he claimed to have mastered seagull language. He spent decades writing *An Oral History of Our Time*, and though many people doubted its existence, a substantial amount of the manuscript surfaced after his death. The walls are filled with photographs and memorabilia of celebrated customers, including a portrait of Joe Gould in the place of honour.

In the early '50s Gregory Corso became a Minetta regular and it was here that he fought a rival for the attentions of the sculptor Marisol Escobar. Gregory smashed a glass into the other man's face, cutting his own hand. (She left with the other man.) This area was once home to an Italian community, and the Minetta still serves reasonably priced Italian food.

This section was the centre of Beat Generation activity in the '40s and '50s. Across the street, in the basement of No.116, is the site of the Gaslight Café, where owner John Mitchell organised the first coffeeshop poetry readings: Ginsberg, Corso and the whole line-up read here at some time in the late '50s. Kerouac's school friend, Henri Cru, lived on the top floor. Next door, at No.114, is the site of the Kettle of Fish, a popular Beat hangout throughout the '50s and '60s. In addition to Ginsberg, Kerouac and

Corso, it was also one of Andy Warhol's haunts before the back room at Max's Kansas City opened.

Continue south a half-block to Bleecker Street. On the north-west corner, at 93 MacDougal, stood the San Remo. A neighbourhood bar since 1925, it got taken over by artists and intellectuals in the early '40s. It is the Mask in Kerouac's *The Subterraneans*, and appears in John Clellon Holmes's *Go* and Chandler Brossard's *Who Walk in Darkness*. William Burroughs, Gregory Corso and Allen Ginsberg all drank here and Kerouac was often thrown out for his rowdy behaviour. Jay Landesman, the first person to publish Ginsberg – in his magazine *Neurotica* – was a regular. The idea of the Living Theater was born here to Julian Beck and Judith Malina. John Cage and Merce Cunningham drank here, as did Miles Davis, Jackson Pollock, Tennessee Williams, Larry Rivers, Frank O'Hara, Gore Vidal and James Agee. Ginsberg met Dylan Thomas in there one night, who complained that he had just been offered money for sex. The San Remo's clientele were the who's-who of American avant-garde and it appears in many memoirs.

The corner of Bleecker and MacDougal was the cultural centre of Village life in the post-war period. Gregory Corso gets the highest street credibility by actually being born here, above a funeral parlour on the south-west corner at 190 Bleecker (well, he was actually born at St Vincent's, but was brought here immediately afterward).

The Figaro Café on the south-east corner is not the original one, which was at 195 Bleecker. Walk east down Bleecker to No.160, the Atrium. In the early '50s this was the Mills Hotel – 'Mills House' can still be seen on the pediment – where Allen Ginsberg lived in 1951. Then it was a $2-a-night flophouse with 1,500 rooms. Kerouac also used to stay there, usually in Allen's room and claimed to have been traumatised by some sexual activity he had observed, voyeuristically, from his window there.

Turn back to one of the many bars and cafés in the neighbourhood, perhaps visiting Caffe Reggio, at 121 MacDougal, the first European-style coffeehouse in the village, which opened in 1927 and which all subsequent coffeehouses used as their model. The Beats read their poetry here in the '50s and, in 1960, it was the site of John Kennedy's first presidential campaign speech. With its pressed tin ceiling, huge paintings and hissing espresso machine, it is one of the few survivors from the long-gone days of the Beat Generation.

## Eating & drinking

### Chumley's
*86 Bedford Street, at Barrow Street (212 675 4449).* **Open** 5.30pm-midnight Mon-Thur; 5.30pm-2am Fri; 2pm-2am Sat; 2pm-midnight Sun. Dark and still reminiscent of a speakeasy, a bar with a literary past.

### Le Figaro Café
*184 Bleecker Street, at MacDougal Street (212 677 1100).* **Open** 10am-2am Mon-Thur, Sun; 10am-4am Fri, Sat.

### Minetta Tavern
*113 MacDougal Street, at Minetta Lane (212 475 3850).* **Open** noon-1am daily. Closed Mon June-Aug.

### El Quijote
*226 West 23rd Street, between Seventh & Eighth Avenues (212 929 1855).* **Open** noon-midnight daily. Straight-faced old-school Spanish cuisine.

### Caffe Reggio
*119 MacDougal Street, between West 3rd & Bleecker Streets (212 475 9557).* **Open** 10am-2am Mon-Thur, Sun; 10am-4am Fri, Sat. Great spot for people-watching and coffee-drinking.

### Riviera Café
*225 West 4th Street, at Seventh Avenue South (212 929 3250).* **Open** 11am-1.30am Mon-Thur, Sun; 11am-2.30am Fri, Sat. TVs, beers, and outdoor seating.

### The West End
*2911 Broadway, between 113th & 114th Streets (212 662 8830).* **Open** 11am-3am (varies) daily. The wide draught selection still draws students from Columbia.

### White Horse Tavern
*567 Hudson Street, at 11th Street (212 989 3956).* **Open** 11am-2am Mon-Thur, Sun; 11am-4am Fri, Sat. As the name suggests, reminiscent of an English pub, now popular with young tourists.

## Films & music
**Chelsea Girls** (Andy Warhol, 1967, US)
**The Cut-Ups** (Antony Balch, 1967, US)
**Sad Eyed Lady of the Lowlands** Bob Dylan from *Blonde on Blonde*

## Literature
**Who Walk in Darkness** Chandler Brossard (1952)
**And the Hippos Were Boiled in Their Tanks** William S Burroughs/Jack Kerouac (unpublished; an extract appears in *Word Virus*, the William Burroughs Reader)
**Junky** William S Burroughs (1977)
**Kaddish and Other Poems** Allen Ginsberg (1961)
**Walking Home at Night** Allen Ginsberg – in *Collected Poems 1947-1980* (1985)
**Howl and Other Poems** Allen Ginsberg (1956)
**An Oral History of the World** Joe Gould (unpublished)
**Go** John Clellon Holmes (1980)
**This Is the Beat Generation** John Clellon Holmes (the *New York Times* article appears in many Beat Generation anthologies)
**The Autobiography of LeRoi Jones/Amiri Baraka** LeRoi Jones (1984)
**How I Became Hettie Jones** LeRoi Jones/Amiri Baraka (1990)
**On the Road** Jack Kerouac (1957)
**The Subterraneans** Jack Kerouac (1958)
**Desolation Angels** Jack Kerouac (1965)
**Vanity of Duluoz** Jack Kerouac (1968)
**Last Exit to Brooklyn** Herbert Selby Jr (1964)
**Palimpsest** Gore Vidal (1995)

## Others
### Chelsea Hotel
*222 West 23rd Street, between Seventh & Eighth Avenues (212 243 3700).*

### Columbia University
*Between Broadway & Amsterdam Avenue & 114th to 120th Streets (212 854 1754).*

### General Theological Seminary
*175 Ninth Avenue, between 20th & 21st Streets (212 243 5150).* **Open** gardens noon-3pm Mon-Fri; 11am-3pm Sat. **Admission** free.
Take a walk or, in summer, a guided tour.

# Perfume creek

John Waldman

Catch the eerie beauty of Brooklyn's Gowanus Canal before it becomes the Venice of New York.

---

**Start:** Carroll Street subway station, Carroll Gardens, Brooklyn
**Finish:** Hamilton Street Bridge, Carroll Gardens, Brooklyn
**Time:** 1-2 hours
**Distance:** 3 miles/4.5km
**Getting there:** subway trains F or G to Carroll Street station
**Getting back:** subway trains F or G from Smith Street-9th Street station
**Note:** this is not a canalside walk, but involves visiting the canal bridges at regular intervals. It is relatively short, and might tie in with Phillip Lopate's walk, *Bridge the Gap.*

---

You don't have to hold your nose any more. The once legendarily polluted New York Harbor has enjoyed a Lazurus-like environmental resurrection. Although the harbour experienced almost every form of insult mankind has imposed on $H_2O$, its 1,500 square miles require considerable time, and, better yet, a ship, to fully appreciate how this network of bays and straits was sundered and how recovery efforts have allowed it to regain an alien, but nonetheless, workable, ecological functionality. But for those wishing to take the measure of the harbour on foot, there is a place, located, surprisingly, in the heart of Brooklyn – the Gowanus Canal, aka 'Perfume Creek' and 'Lavender Lake', for long the most contaminated waterway among many in the city of New York.

The Gowanus Canal's history is a microcosm, but in conveniently concentrated form, of much of what the broader harbour endured. The canal was preceded by Gowane's Creek (named after a Mohawk chief) in the 1600s – a pristine estuary noted for its oysters, said to be as large as dinner plates and so numerous as to become Brooklyn's first export to Europe. These shellfish were so highly regarded that a Dutch traveller who had already sampled the famous Chesapeake Bay oysters called those from Gowane's Creek, better, in fact, 'the best in the country'.

The headwaters of the creek were dammed in the late 1600s to create mills for grinding locally grown corn. With a grain surplus, the residents of Gowanus petitioned the governing council of New Netherlands for construction and dredging rights for a canal. African slave labourers dug a trench that was six feet deep and 12 and a half feet wide, with a footpath for pulling vessels. In 1776, the Gowanus Canal was integral to the Battle of Long Island, the first bloodshed that occurred in the Revolutionary War. Retreating patriots crossed Gowanus Creek and the surrounding marshlands, burning all the bridges behind them, thus halting the British advance.

The Gowanus Canal was brought nearer to its modern dimensions in the mid-1800s when it was extended northward to Douglass Street, and dredged, widened and lined with bulkheads fronting loading docks. The canal quickly became a major depot for midwestern grain carried along the Erie Canal, and for coal. The area was

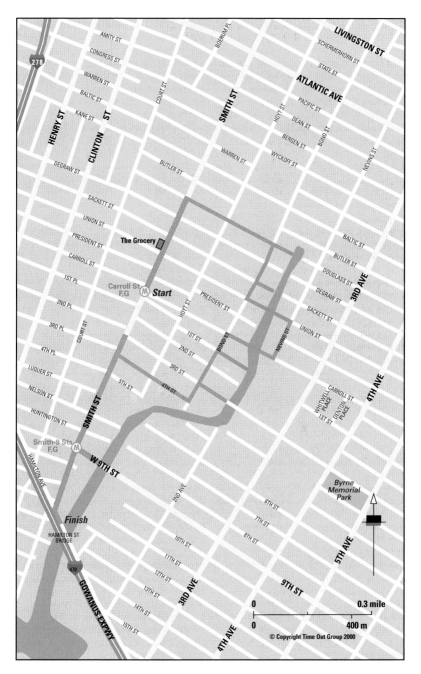

industrialising and, although prints from as late as 1867 still showed schooners moored in pastoral vistas near Gowanus Bay, by 1880, factory and sewage wastes had transformed the waterway into a 'repulsive repository of rank odors' that were noticeable up to a mile away.

By World War I the Gowanus was the busiest commercial canal in the United States. Much of the timber, sand and brownstone that built Brooklyn passed through the 1.8 miles of Gowanus Bay and the Gowanus Canal. And their banks were lined with an ecological firing squad of slaughterhouses, foundries, stone yards, cement makers, paper mills, flour mills, steel mills, soap factories, glue factories, pottery works, oil refineries, gas houses, and other fouling enterprises.

As if that wasn't enough, an annual 40 million gallons of human waste from the surrounding neighbourhoods also flowed, untreated, to the canal, where it would sit and stagnate in the dead-end ditch. So vigorously did this sewage decompose that, according to the *New Yorker* writer Joseph Mitchell, sightseers would visit the canal to view the black, bubbly water where the 'rising and breaking of sludge bubbles makes the water seethe and spit'. The nickname 'Lavender Lake' stems from the dye works that brightened its waters with the various colours of each day's production; 'Perfume Creek' is an obviously sarcastic response to eau de Gowanus. Thomas Wolfe in *You Can't Go Home Again* (1934) provided an especially keen account of its odours and the attitude of fait accompli of the local nostrils: 'And what is that you smell? Oh that! Well, you see, he shares impartially with his neighbors a piece of property in the vicinity; it belongs to all of them in common, and it gives to South Brooklyn its own distinctive atmosphere. It is the old Gowanus canal, and that aroma you speak of is nothing but the huge symphonic stink of it, cunningly compacted of unnumbered separate putrefactions. It is interesting to try to count them. There is in it not only the noisome stenches of a stagnant sewer, but also the smells of melted glue, burned rubber, the smoldering rags, the odors of a boneyard horse, long dead, the incense of putrefying offal, the fragrance of deceased, decaying cats, old tomatoes, rotten cabbage, and prehistoric eggs.

'And how does he stand it? Well, one gets used to it. One can get used to anything, just as all these people do. They never think of the smell, they never speak of it, they'd probably miss it if they ever moved away.'

The canal's waters became so noxious that wooden boats were brought into it to kill off barnacles clinging to their sides. Health workers found malaria and typhoid bacteria in the soupy mix. (Modern surveys also found traces of salmonella, tuberculosis, hepatitis, cholera and gangrene). But despite its intense and alarming odours, the poor people of the neighbourhood did not always comprehend its dangers: a few mothers even carried their asthmatic children to the canal's bridges to inhale what they believed were life-giving vapours. Some improvement in conditions occurred early in the 20th century via a wholly artificial but nonetheless reasonably effective engineering solution. On 21 June 1911, a young woman tossed carnations on the water in front of 350 dignitaries to inaugurate a flushing system, which included a 12-foot-wide tunnel under the Brooklyn streets from Upper New York Bay. The tunnel was fitted with an enormous bronze propeller salvaged from a ship. The flow created by this apparatus took the edge off the odours well into the 1960s until the propeller shaft broke when a worker dropped a manhole cover on it. Some locals suspected sabotage, because it was well known that longshoremen didn't like the current, which made handling barges more difficult. The system wasn't repaired, because city engineers concluded that nearby sewage treatment plant upgrades would reduce

Brooklyn chic can be found on **Smith Street**.

# Perfume creek

stroll through the increasingly fashionable neighbourhood of Carroll Gardens from the Carroll Street station. Take the Smith Street-President Street exit from the subway, and head north. This stretch of Smith Street has seen an influx of restaurateurs from Manhattan relocating on or around this emerging strip, with Grocery, Banania and Sur among the more notable. Now is the time to take refreshment, for hereafter the opportunities are few, and have little to recommend them.

Turn right at Douglass Street and follow it three blocks to the very end. An iron fence prevents full intimacy with the canal but one can view a flow of relatively clean water energetic enough to dislodge a regular series of oil globules that float to the surface and radiate in iridescent rainbow colours (the diver didn't get it all). A recent visit of mine happened to coincide with a water quality sampling by New York City. Although the dead low tide revealed a bottom in places covered with rotting paper and sludge, water clarity measured a Caribbean-like (by canal standards) three and a half feet.

The Gowanus is best explored from its western side, which appears to have the safer streets. Because so much of the canal is fronted by industry on dead-end thoroughfares, it is (with one exception) necessary to walk back to the major north/south avenues of Bond Street and Smith Street to approach new vistas.

Sackett Street, two blocks south of Douglass Street, is where a fellow felt compelled to go for a swim in June 1999, perhaps to celebrate the canal's suddenly somewhat improved water quality. The next day he was being treated surgically in a medical centre for a rare form of flesh-eating bacteria picked up from the canal through a cut on his hand. The physician said that had he waited any longer for treatment he would have faced amputation.

Around the next corner is Union Street, which runs across the first crossing on

the stench of the once-again ponded canal. But the engineers miscalculated and the canal instead grew riper. The city occasionally provided a quick and temporary fix by dumping truckloads of chlorine into the canal as a disinfecting shock treatment.

Although the community began pressuring the city in the late 1960s to reactivate the flushing system, it wasn't mended until very recently, in May 1999. Some local dredging had to be performed at the outflow area prior to turning the flow on; the final stages even included a diver who manually vacuumed oil deposits from the canal bottom. But the benefits were immediate: life returned, most prominently, blue claw crabs, striped bass, bluefish and waterfowl.

The head of the canal at Douglass Street, where the current from the flushing tunnel emerges, is an excellent place to begin a walking tour of the Gowanus. It can be reached via a short

Commercial depots and water towers provide the sunset view from **Union Street Bridge**.

the canal; the views from this modern bridge are purely commercial, featuring oil depots and parking lots. In 1989, a boy fell off this bridge and simply disappeared into the muck. Despite the close confines, divers in special protective suits were never able to find the body, lending credence to the Brooklyn lore that the Mafia holds an especial appreciation for the canal as a place to dispose of its homicide victims. Yellow viewing boxes attached to the railings reflect attempts by community groups such as, in this case, Place in History, to encourage local interest in the canal and its surroundings.

You can cross the bridge and double-back two blocks further south to the funky, ancient Carroll Street Bridge, which was featured in the 1985 movie *Heaven Help Us*. Built in 1889, it is a retractile one-way bridge (the oldest of only four left in the US), which rolls back horizontally to allow ships a 36-foot wide gap to pass. Clad with boards and only a

single lane wide, its most famous feature is a sign of uncertain vintage that states: 'Any Person Driving over this Bridge Faster than a Walk will be Subject to a Penalty of Five Dollars for Each Offence.'

I have been most impressed not by the broader panorama here but by the view downward from the bridge's north-east corner. Below lies a monumental pile of shopping carts, hubcaps, bicycles, wheelbarrows, assorted auto parts and Christmas trees, best visible at low tide. Covered in algae reminiscent of verdigris, the heap resembles an extemporaneous but weathered copper sculpture.

First Street is one block south of Carroll Street. Its terminus at the canal now includes a houseboat home for the first person to actually live on the Gowanus. The bulkhead it is tied to sports a makeshift veranda and garden with stacks of discarded wooden pallets serving as statuary, but don't explore too close on account of the Rottweiler. Note the twin towers of the World Trade Center in the distance – Manhattan and its high life is not far away.

The Third Street Bridge, in the modern drawbridge style, is bordered to the north by the hedgerows of the canal razor wire protecting a telephone company installation. One can listen to rock being crushed by a gravel company whose mounds tower along the canal's east side, not far from a short side-canal said to be filling in and reverting toward marsh – a remarkably long distant ecological memory here. Looking further afield again here, one sees the towering dome-topped clock tower of the Williamsburg Savings Bank to the north-east. Built in 1929 in anticipation of Brooklyn developing a skyline to match that of downtown Manhattan, such development never materialised, and the tower now stands majestic, and isolated.

The stretch that now follows shows a different face of Smith Street, overshadowed as it is by the rising, curving cement and steel construction that carries the subway over the canal, a monstrosity mirrored by the expressway further south.

The Gowanus widens somewhat at the Ninth Street Bridge, which is an aluminium-clad vertical lift structure. The lengthy reaches that can be viewed to its north and south offer the canal's typical rich industrial mix, including oil tanks. A famous oil mishap occurred in January 1976 when 30,000 barrels seeped into the canal from a fire at an oil terminal. Local residents recall it as 'the day the Gowanus Canal burned' with a five-alarm fire with flames that reached 100 feet high and raged for a day and a half.

One long block further is the Hamilton Street Bridge, the canal's final crossing before reaching Gowanus Bay, and the final point on the walk. Above it is the arching viaduct of the Gowanus Expressway, one of the worst highways in America. Most of the time the 140,000 cars and 10,000 trucks per day merely do a crawl on this anything but an expressway, raining soot below. Stench and soot mix here with the odours from a nearby fish-smoking plant.

Downstream of the Hamilton Street Bridge the canal widens further and

The retractile **Carroll Street Bridge** is one of only four left across the whole country.

Signs of life on the **Gowanus** – this houseboat represents the canal's first human resident.

merges with Gowanus Bay, a section better explored by boat. Indeed, boaters are becoming more numerous on the canal as the Brooklyn Center for the Urban Environment now offers guided shipboard 'postapocalyptic' tours that complement personal walking adventures. Moreover, a canoeing club has formed, the Gowanus Dredgers, a name chosen to reflect their advocacy for deepening the canal (the last dredging occurred 25 years ago) so as to improve it for recreational and commercial uses. The chances of spotting canoeists should steadily increase; in 1999 there were two active members, 20 are expected in 2000, and the club's goal is to raise the number to 200.

Gowanus Bay contains the remains of the Isbrandtsen shipping line pier and the Port Authority's Grain Terminal, and various other, mostly defunct commercial enterprises. Because it is nearer Upper New York Bay its water quality has always been better than the canal's and some fishing and crabbing is done off its bulkheads (although a shark

ran up the canal in 1950 and was murdered there for no apparent reason by a policeman's bullets in front of hundreds of bystanders). Recently, two anglers snagged a large suitcase they thought might contain bundles of cash. Imagine their horror when they found only human body parts and not all from the same person.

The best future use of the Gowanus Canal has been debated. There are those who would like to see it filled and those who imagine it as the eventual 'Venice of New York'. Regardless, to appreciate the Gowanus Canal today one must keep its historical transformations in mind, to realise that its now otherwise unremarkable industry is a relic, a faint echo of a no-holds-barred commercial strangulation of an innocent water body. But there is a certain charm to it, albeit macabre, beneath the blight. Ten years ago a Master's student writing about the canal found what I believe is the necessary perspective when he wrote: 'From an environmental standpoint the canal is a nightmare. Yet, at the same time, the area possesses the eerie beauty that one finds among ruins.'

And, as for all heavily urbanised systems, environmental recovery is precarious, but particularly here, given its reliance on a giant dialysis machine. In spring 2000, a 14-foot piece of drifting timber jammed the propeller and halted the flushing system, and the canal began to stagnate. It has since been repaired, but the incident serves as a reminder as to how rapidly postapocalyptic can become apocalyptic again.

## Eating & drinking

### Banania
*241 Smith Street, at Douglass Street, Carroll Gardens, Brooklyn (718 237 9100).* **Open** 5.30-11pm Mon-Thur; 5.30-11.30pm Fri; 10.30am-3pm, 5.30-11.30pm Sat; 10.30am-3pm, 5.30-11pm Sun. Bright and pleasant eaterie serving superb French-American food – perfect for brunch.

### The Grocery
*288 Smith Street, between Union & Sackett Streets, Carroll Gardens, Brooklyn (718 596 3335).* **Open** 6-10pm Mon-Thur; 6-11pm Fri, Sat. Top-notch American cuisine.

### Restaurant Saul
*140 Smith Street, between Bergen & Dean Streets, Boerum Hill, Brooklyn (718 935 9844).* **Open** 6-11pm daily. A sophisticated bistro, worth the walk.

### Sur
*232 Smith Street, between Butler & Douglass Streets, Carroll Gardens, Brooklyn (718 875 1716).* **Open** 5.30-11pm Mon-Thur; 5.30-midnight Fri; 11am-4pm, 5.30-midnight Sat; 11am-4pm, 5.30-11pm Sun. An Argentine version of a classic bistro – the South American specialities draw a loyal local, and chic, crowd.

### Sweet Melissa Patisserie
*276 Court Street, between Butler & Douglass Streets, Cobble Hill, Brooklyn (718 855 3410).* **Open** 8am-10pm Mon-Thur, Sun; 8am-midnight Fri, Sat. Tuck into impeccable pastries in a soothing back garden.

## Literature & film
**You Can't Go Home Again** *Thomas Wolfe* (1934)

**Heaven Help Us** aka **Catholic Boys** (Michael Dinner, 1984, US).

## Organisations

### Brooklyn Center for the Urban Environment
*The Tennis House, Prospect Park, Brooklyn (717 788 8500).* **Open** 8.30am-5.30pm Mon-Fri; open at weekends for gallery shows, call for details.

### Gowanus Canal Community Development Corporation
*515 Court Street, between West 9th & Huntington Streets, Carroll Gardens, Brooklyn (718 858 0557).*

### Hudson River Foundation
*40 West 20th Street, between Fifth & Sixth Avenues (212 924 8290).*

### Place in History
*543 Union Street, Studio 1B, Gowanus, Brooklyn (718 625 1122).*

The F train runs over **Smith** and **9th Streets**.

# Visions of early New York

Edwin G Burrows

First Manahatta, then New Amsterdam, finally New York.

**Start:** Castle Clinton, Battery Park
**Finish:** Trinity Church, Broadway
**Time:** 2-3 hours
**Distance:** 2 miles/3km
**Getting there:** subway trains 1 or 9 to South Ferry station, or trains 4 or 5 to Bowling Green station, followed by short walk
**Getting back:** subway trains 4 or 5 from Wall Street station
**Note:** some of the cafés and restaurants are closed at the weekend.

Although it no longer bristles with cannon, the southern tip of Manhattan – much enlarged by centuries of landfill – is the birthplace of New York. Here, 375 years ago, the Dutch West India Company founded a fur trading post called New Amsterdam. Positioned at the confluence of the Hudson and East rivers, it was the ideal vantage point for controlling the movement of ships through the magnificent harbour below. In 1626, the Company 'purchased' the entire island of Manahatta from the local Lenape Indians for 60 guilders' worth of trade goods, which historians in the 19th century

**Peter Minuit** bought Manhattan for trinkets valued at the now legendary sum of $24.

# Visions of early New York

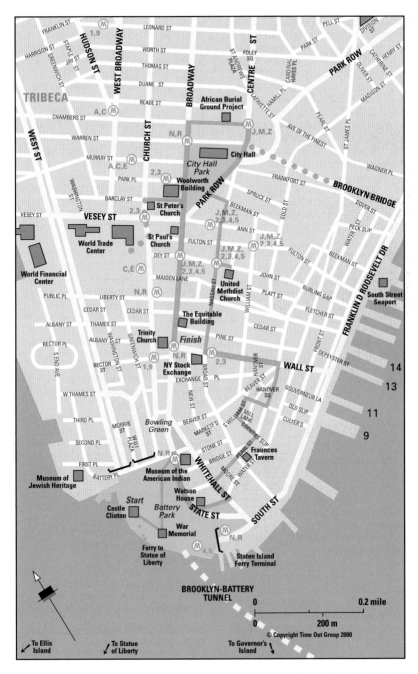

valued at the now legendary sum of $24. The Duke of York's men drove away the Dutch in 1664 and gave the town a new name, New York, after which it thrived on overseas trade, privateering and piracy. Washington's defeat in the Battle of Long Island (1776), fought just across the East River in Brooklyn, led to seven turbulent years of military occupation. Evacuation Day, marking the final departure of His Majesty's forces in 1783, was long celebrated by residents with as much fervour as the Fourth of July.

*Walk to Castle Clinton National Monument, in the south-west corner of Battery Park.*

When conflict with Great Britain erupted again during the Napoleonic Wars, the city rushed to construct new harbour fortifications. Completed in 1811, Castle Clinton stood 300 feet offshore (underscoring the fact that virtually all of today's park rests on made land). With Castle Williams, still standing just across the harbour on Governor's Island, Castle Clinton was intended to discourage another British attack on Manhattan. The British never showed up, the guns were removed, and the fort became a concert hall named Castle Garden. In 1855, Castle Garden became the 'Emigrant Landing Depot', where about eight million immigrants to the United States were processed before it closed in 1890. Now a National Monument, the little museum inside has excellent scale-model dioramas depicting the Battery's history. Tickets for the excursion boats to Ellis Island and Liberty Island may be purchased inside.

New York is first and foremost a city of immigrants, and no site conveys the scope and complexity of the immigrant experience better than Ellis Island, successor to Castle Garden as the principal point of entry into the country. Between 1892 and 1924 more than 12 million newcomers descended on this tiny plot of land – 1.3 million in 1907 alone, mainly Russian Jews and Italians. By 1910, 40 per cent of the city's 4.8 million inhabitants were foreign born. Though repeatedly enlarged to handle the burgeoning numbers of people passing through its doors, the heart of the Ellis Island complex remained the great registry room where inspectors weeded out paupers, criminals, 'mental defectives' and the chronically ill. Prompted by a nativist backlash, Congress adopted a quota system in 1924 that effectively shut the door to further immigration for the next 40 years. Year by year, Ellis Island was abandoned to the elements, though the main building has now been restored. A visit to the immigration museum there is both exhilarating and heartbreaking.

Since Congress abandoned the quota system in 1965, New York has again become a prime destination for immigrants – 80 per cent of whom now arrive from Asia, the Caribbean and Latin America, although sizeable numbers have also arrived from the Middle East, Africa and the former Soviet Union. This time around they usually have to pass muster with the Immigration and Naturalisation Service at airports and highway checkpoints.

Earlier generations of immigrants knew they had reached America when they passed the Statue of Liberty on Bedloe's Island (from 1956 known as Liberty Island). Designed by Frederick-Auguste Bartholdi and assembled over a metal framework designed by Gustave Eiffel, the statue was dedicated in 1886. Its evocative power as symbol of New York and immigration was assured by 'The New Colossus', the poem by Emma Lazarus that deftly turned a commemoration of Franco-American friendship during the American Revolution into a welcoming beacon for refugees:

Immigrants at **Ellis Island** in 1905, hoping not to be weeded out as paupers, criminals, 'mental defectives' or the chronically ill.

*Give me your tired, your poor*
*Your huddled masses yearning to*
*breathe free*
*The wretched refuse of your*
*teeming shore*
*Send these, the homeless, tempest-*
*tossed to me*
*I lift my lamp beside the golden*
*door!*

Whether or not you choose to visit Ellis Island and the Statue of Liberty, take some time to explore Battery Park. Look for the Netherlands Memorial flagpole, the East Coast War Memorial and the statue of the Italian explorer Giovanni da Verrazano (in New York his name is spelled with only one 'z'. Go figure, as the locals say.)

*Make your way out of Battery Park*
*toward the intersection of Battery Place*
*and State Street.*

Under both Dutch and British rule, a massive earthwork fortress loomed over what is now the north-east corner of Battery Park. The fort came down soon after the American Revolution, and its site is currently occupied by the ornate Beaux Arts Custom House (1907).

Prior to the adoption of the national income tax in 1913, a large part of the federal government's revenue was collected here because more foreign goods entered the United States through New York than any other port. That is no longer the case, alas, and in recent decades the city's ancient connection to the sea has become more and more attenuated.

The custom offices moved out in the 1970s, and the building now houses – ironically, perhaps – the National Museum of the American Indian. (The heavily symbolic statuary on its façade is the work of Daniel Chester French, who also contributed the seated figure of Abraham Lincoln to the Lincoln Memorial in Washington, DC.)

*Cross State Street to the plaza in front of*
*the Custom House.*

Directly facing the Custom House lies a half-acre oasis known as Bowling Green Park, the southern terminus of one of New York's most famous thoroughfares, Broadway. Extending to the northern end of Manhattan, 17 miles distant, Broadway follows the course of an old Indian trail that ran along the crest of Manhattan's original hills (one source of the landfill used to enlarge the island's shoreline). The Dutch settlers built crude huts in the broad, flat clearing that marked the foot of the trail. This area later served variously as New Amsterdam's cattle market (thus nearby Marketfield Street), as a parade ground for soldiers in the fort, and as the site for lawn bowling, a favourite pastime of English and Dutch inhabitants alike. Bowling Green was formally laid out as a park in the 1730s for the enjoyment of nearby residents (lower Broadway having become one of the city's choicest residential neighbourhoods). The park's iron fence, erected in 1771, originally enclosed a gilt statue of King George III. On 9 July 1776, following a public reading of the Declaration of Independence, an angry crowd of patriots knocked off the fence's decorative crowns and demolished the statue. The pieces were melted into musket balls for the use of rebel troops. A rather peculiar recent addition to the park is the statue *Charging Bull* that was placed at the north end in 1989.

*Walk back down State Street alongside the*
*Custom House, crossing Bridge and Pearl*
*Streets, to No.7, the red-brick house with*
*the unusual curved porch.*

No.7 State Street, designed by John McComb, was an 1805 addition to the house next door that anchored an entire row of private residences in the so-called Federal style – all the rage among prosperous New Yorkers after the Revolution because it combined neo-classical elegance with republican simplicity. The building, traditionally known as the Watson House, is now the rectory of the Shrine of Elizabeth Seton, who founded the first order of nuns in the United States and was canonised as America's first saint in 1975.

*Swing around the corner of State Street.*

On your right is Peter Minuit Plaza, named for the director of the Dutch West India Company who purchased Manhattan from the Indians in 1626. The flagpole commemorates the 23 Jewish refugees who fled Brazil and came to New Amsterdam in 1654, probably the earliest Jewish settlers in the City. The plaza itself marks the approximate location of the southern tip of Manhattan when New Amsterdam was founded. The West India Company built a wharf here for the ships that came to collect pelts for the Amsterdam market. During the next couple of centuries, the city's waterfront would expand relentlessly up the East River side of Manhattan; not until the advent of steamships in the mid-19th century would significant development occur along the Hudson River shore. Visible on the other side of the plaza is the Staten Island Ferry terminal. The ferry costs nothing, but the views of lower Manhattan are priceless – take a ride if you have some extra time to kill.

*Turn left (north) into Whitehall Street. Walk one block on Whitehall to Pearl Street, and turn right.*

Pearl Street followed the original Manhattan shoreline and was so named because of the heaps of mother-of-pearl shells left there by Native Americans who came to dig for clams and oysters. It is hard to imagine today, but early European explorers and travellers marvelled at the natural abundance of Manhattan and surrounding islands – great hardwood forests full of chattering birds, freshwater streams teeming with fish that could be taken by hand, noisy flocks of 40-pound wild turkeys, herds of deer and giant lobsters. Even at the end of the 19th century, gun-toting New Yorkers came down to the Battery to hunt ducks. The ducks are gone now, and the only hunters to visit this part of town look for prey inside the NASDAQ stock exchange on the corner of Pearl and Whitehall.

*Walk along Pearl, past Moore Street, to the corner of Pearl and Broad. Look – but don't walk – north (left) along Broad Street.*

When New York was still New Amsterdam, the Dutch dredged out a sluggish tidal creek to make a canal that reached from the East River up to Exchange Place, where the ferry to Long Island docked. Handsome brick residences sprang up along the canal, their stepped gables and tile roofs redolent of old Amsterdam, while merchants gathered to swap news and conduct business at the foot of a bridge that crossed the mouth of the canal (its location now recalled by nearby Bridge Street). In 1676, choked with refuse and effluvia, the canal was filled in and transformed into one of lower Manhattan's widest streets.

*Cross Broad Street to Fraunces Tavern.*

On the south-east corner of Pearl and Broad stands one of the Financial District's best-known landmarks, the yellow-brick Fraunces Tavern. The 1719 original was built by Stephen De Lancey, a Huguenot merchant whose family later acquired property north of the city where Delancey Street now runs. Samuel Fraunces bought it in 1763 and opened the Queen's Head Tavern, a favourite watering hole of patriots as relations between Great Britain and the colonies deteriorated. Twenty years later, following the British evacuation of the city in 1783, George Washington chose Fraunces Tavern for a tearful farewell

The southern tip of Manhattan c1850 – **Castle Garden** can be seen off-shore...

dinner with his officers. The present building is a 1907 reconstruction, mostly conjectural, though it affords a pretty good idea of the Georgian-style splendour enjoyed by New York's great merchants in the 18th century. The museum upstairs has a fine collection of artefacts, prints and maps relating to the history of lower Manhattan.

*Continue along Pearl Street, past Coenties Slip on the right and Coenties Alley on the left.*

Coenties Slip – the origin of the name is disputed – was once an inlet of the East River where merchants could load and unload. In 1641, near the corner of Pearl Street and Coenties Alley, the Dutch built a large stone public house with a jail in the basement to accommodate the town's alarmingly large number of troublemakers. In 1653 it became the first Stadt Huys, or City Hall, and continued to serve in that capacity until the end of the 17th century, when a new City Hall was erected at Broad and Wall. Construction of offices facing

Broad Street uncovered the foundations of the Stadt Huys; look for the archaeological exhibit under the arches on the south-west corner of Coenties Alley and Pearl.

*Turn left into Coenties Alley and look to the right down Stone Street.*

Stone Street gets its name from the fact that it was the first in New Amsterdam to be paved – with cobblestones – and 30 years after the West India Company first set up shop on Manhattan, a detail that serves as a useful reminder of the narrow, often muddy footpaths endured by early residents. The 'revitalisation' project currently under way will preserve the commercial buildings that sprang up along Stone Street in the 19th century.

*Continue up Coenties Alley to South William Street. Turn right into South William and walk to Mill Lane.*

South William was once known as Mill Street because it passed the site of a mill famous in the city's early history. In its

... but by c1890 **Manhattan** has caught up with it, as the island grows with landfill.

upper room, among other things, the Jewish refugees from Brazil conducted religious services in the 1650s and the last Director-General of New Amsterdam, Peter Stuyvesant, signed the articles of capitulation to the English in 1664.

*Proceed along South William, past Mill Lane, to the corner of South William and Beaver Street.*

Beaver Street, which runs left (west) to Bowling Green and right (east) to Wall Street, immortalises the animal whose luxurious pelts lured the Dutch West India Company to Manhattan – and would be quickly hunted to near-extinction by local Indians eager to trade for blankets, iron tools and firearms. Delmonico's Restaurant, straddling the corner of South William and Beaver Street, is a reincarnation of the eaterie founded in 1827 and arguably the most celebrated restaurant in the United States until its closing a century later.

*Turn right, past Stone Street, into Hanover Square.*

From the second half of the 18th century to the early 19th, Hanover Square was the city's business centre (named in honour of King George I, the German prince who became the first British sovereign of the House of Hanover in 1714). Because of its proximity to the waterfront – then only a block away on present-day Water Street – respectable merchants built residences in or near the square, among them a certain William Kidd, whose home faced the square on Pearl Street. Perhaps early New York's most famous pirate (though not the only one), Captain Kidd was hanged in London in 1701; perdurable legend has it that he buried a great treasure out on Long Island before imperial authorities caught up with him. On the south side of the square, occupying the block between Stone and Pearl, is India House (1854), originally a bank, then home of the Cotton Exchange, and now a luncheon club for businessmen. The little park in the centre of the square has a statue of Abraham DePeyster, a

Huguenot-appointed mayor by the British at the end of the 17th century.

Hanover Square's fortunes dimmed after 1835, when a terrible fire broke out on Pearl Street and spread rapidly across town, consuming 650 buildings before it could be contained three days later.

*Follow Pearl Street north toward Wall Street.*

By the middle of the 17th century, a fierce struggle for commercial supremacy had erupted between England and the Netherlands. In 1653, fearing an attack from New England, the Director-General of New Amsterdam, Peter Stuyvesant, ordered the construction of a wooden stockade across the island of Manhattan on the northern edge of town. Never tested in battle (the Duke of York's forces arrived by sea ten years later), the stockade was torn down in 1699 and replaced by a corridor soon known as Wall Street. Its presence is a reminder that New Amsterdam occupied only a very small corner of Manhattan – one-eighth of

a square mile – and that the city's history, then as now, was intimately tied to the ebb and flow of international affairs. Also worth noting is the fact that in 1711, close by the intersection of Pearl and Wall, the city established a market for the purchase and sale of slaves. Slave labour had already become an essential component of the municipal economy, and the number of slaves in and around the city grew steadily. By the middle decades of the 18th century, more than one out of every five residents of the city was enslaved.

*Turn left up Wall Street toward Hanover Street.*

Opposite the end of Hanover Street to the left, on the building at 74 Wall Street, is a plaque marking the site of the home of Edward Livingston, scion of a prominent Revolutionary-era clan; the important point, however, is that Wall Street remained a pre-eminently residential quarter until the early decades of the 19th century. No.55 Wall Street, the large building with the imposing bronze doors

View of **Wall Street** from the corner of Broad Street c1860 – money in the making.

and the double row of columns – Ionic below, Corinthian above – is the former Merchant's Exchange building (1842), now occupied by the upscale Regent Hotel. A pioneering example of Greek Revival architecture, it replaced an earlier exchange destroyed in the 1835 fire. The upper row of columns, added at the beginning of the 20th century, conceals a lovely central dome still visible from the inside. Directly across the street at 48 Wall is the Bank of New York, founded back in 1784 by Alexander Hamilton, an emigrant from Nevis in the West Indies who engineered New York's recovery from the devastation of the Revolution. A bit further up the street, at 40 Wall, is the skyscraper built in 1929 for the Bank of the Manhattan Company – founded in 1799 by Aaron Burr. Five years later, the legendary rivalry between Hamilton and Burr led to a duel in which Burr shot Hamilton dead. Blazoned across the front of 40 Wall today is the name of Donald Trump, only the most recent ego to set up shop on Wall Street.

**New York Stock Exchange**, 1903.

*Continue on Wall, past William, to the intersection of Wall, Broad and Nassau.*

New York's second City Hall opened in 1701 on the north-east corner of Wall and Nassau, replacing the old Dutch Stadt Huys on Pearl Street. After the Revolution it was extensively renovated for the new federal government, and George Washington took the oath of office as first President of the United States on its balcony in 1789 – hence the statue of Washington that has gazed presidentially over Wall Street since 1883. The present building, another fine example of Greek Revival architecture, went up on the site in 1842. Now the Federal Hall National Memorial, its magnificent interior rotunda is used for historical exhibits.

Directly opposite, at 23 Wall, stands the Morgan Guaranty Trust Company building (1913) – heart of JP Morgan's financial empire. In 1920, an anarchist bomb exploded outside the building, killing 33 people and injuring hundreds. Scars from the blast can still be seen in the exterior walls along Wall Street.

On the south-west corner of Broad and Wall is the New York Stock Exchange building (1903). Stock trading began on Wall Street only a few years after Washington's inauguration. As the pace of business quickened – fuelled primarily by speculation in railroad securities after the 1830s – the exchange occupied various sites on the street. By 1865, when it moved to its present address, the concentration of banks, insurance companies and brokerage houses in its vicinity had made Wall Street synonymous with American capitalism. The pandemonium on the trading floor can be observed from the visitors' gallery.

*Glance down Broad Street, remembering the old Dutch canal, then head north on Nassau, past Pine and Cedar, to Liberty Street.*

Chase Manhattan Plaza (1960), on the east side of Nassau Street, is the home of the Rockefeller fortune. The fifth basement boasts a vault the size of a football field that reputedly holds $50 billion in securities. On the north side of Liberty looms the Federal Reserve Bank of New York (1924). Designed in the Florentine 'palazzo' style, this is the bank for banks. Its vaults contain more gold than Fort Knox or any other place in the world – $136 billion worth (1990 prices), representing more than ten per cent of all the gold mined throughout history.

*Keep going up Nassau, crossing Maiden Lane. Turn right down to 44 John Street, the John Street Methodist Church.*

The first Methodist church in America was erected on this site in 1760. The present structure, which dates from 1841, has many handhewn beams from the original building.

*Retrace your steps to Nassau Street and continue along Nassau one block to Fulton Street.*

The Nassau Street Pedestrian Mall is a busy but fairly tacky strip of fast-food joints, T-shirt vendors, discount electronic stores, and other dubious establishments. Fun for bargain hunters, perhaps, but don't forget to look up and take in the many elegant old commercial buildings hidden behind the kitschy storefronts. Note especially the green and pink pile holding down the north-west corner of Fulton and Nassau.

*If time allows, you might head east on Fulton down to the South Street Seaport and Fulton Fish Market – an attempt, only partially successful, to preserve the East River waterfront as it was in the 19th century. If time is short, continue up Nassau Street, across Ann Street, and turn left (west) on Beekman Street.*

The red-brick office building on the south-west corner of Fulton and Beekman is the Temple Court (1882), which as the name suggests was intended to serve the city's burgeoning number of lawyers. Across from it, on the north-west corner of Fulton and Beekman, stands the dazzlingly ornate Potter Building (1883). Its terracotta façade conceals an early example of the structural steel framework that would later be employed in the construction of skyscrapers.

The intersection of Beekman and Park Row marks the approximate centre of 'newspaper row', a string of buildings that in the 19th century housed the offices of New York's once-numerous daily newspapers – as many as 19 in 1893 alone. Only two survive, one of which, the *New York Times,* was published in 41 Park Row. In 1904, the *Times* moved far uptown to Longacre Square, renamed Times Square.

*Cross Park Row to the recently refurbished park occupying the triangle between Park Row and Broadway.*

Presiding over this rare bit of greenery is New York's third and present City Hall. Designed by John McComb (Castle Clinton) and Joseph Mangin, a French architect who worked on the Place de la Concorde in Paris, it was completed in 1811 and immediately recognised as one of the finest neo-classical buildings in the country. Unfortunately, the current administration does not welcome visitors.

*Walk around the Park Row (east) side of City Hall to Chambers Street, noting the Brooklyn Bridge (1883) on the right. If time allows, a stroll across the bridge offers a spectacular panorama of lower Manhattan.*

The tall building to the east is the Municipal Building (1914). Prior to 1898, New York City consisted of Manhattan and portions of the Bronx. In that year, however, an act of the state legislature created 'Greater New York' by consolidating Manhattan, all of the Bronx, Queens, Brooklyn and Staten Island into one super-city with five 'boroughs'. Designed by the famous architectural firm of McKim, Mead & White, the 35-storey Municipal Building testifies to the greatly enlarged scale of municipal government brought about by Consolidation. The gilt statue on top is of *Civic Fame*. The heavily ornamented building at the north-west corner of Chambers and Centre Streets is the Surrogate's Court (1911), another monument to municipal expansion said to be a pared-down copy of the Paris Opéra.

Directly behind City Hall, currently barely visible under walls of scaffolding, is the notorious 'Tweed' Courthouse (1874). Costing more than the US Capitol in Washington or the Houses of Parliament in London, this is the building on which the infamous 'ring' organised by Boss William Tweed made millions after the Civil War.

*Walk west (left) along Chambers Street, past the Tweed Courthouse.*

At the time of the American Revolution, this was the northern edge of the city – much larger than it had been when the Dutch were in charge and Wall Street marked the upper limit of settlement, but still a far cry from the vast, pulsing metropolis that would engulf upper Manhattan in the century to follow. Today's City Hall Park was then an open field known as the Common. It was the scene of parades, military drills, public executions and political demonstrations. Where the Tweed Courthouse now stands were barracks occupied by His Majesty's redcoats. Directly across Chambers Street was the so-called 'Negro Burying Ground', recently rediscovered and excavated by archaeologists. Beyond sprawled the rural seats of rich city merchants and government officials, interspersed with small farms, orchards, pastures and woody glades.

*Continue west on Chambers Street toward Broadway. Stop at the corner of Chambers and Broadway.*

Frank W Woolworth counting his dimes in the romanesque lobby of the **Woolworth Building**.

If ever there was a holy of holies for New York shoppers, it is the north-east corner of Chambers and Broadway. There, in 1846, a Scottish immigrant named AT Stewart erected his Dry Goods Emporium, the first department store in the United States. Also known as the Marble Palace, it employed a staff of 2,000 and catered to the elite, whose carriages jammed Broadway (hence 'carriage trade' as a synonym for wealthy customers). When the elite moved further uptown, abandoning lower Broadway to trade and commerce, Stewart followed them. The *New York Sun* was published here from 1917 to 1952 (note the street clock with the motto: 'The Sun, it shines for all.'). The building now houses municipal offices.

*Cross to the west side of Broadway and head back downtown, passing City Hall and the park on your left.*

Stop in front of the Woolworth Building, which occupies the block between Park Place and Barclay Street. While Manhattan is renowned today for its skyscrapers, they are a recent imposition on the urban landscape, historically speaking. Until the early years of the 20th century, few buildings in the city exceeded five or six storeys in height, and when people imagined its future growth they thought horizontally, not vertically. This changed abruptly on the eve of World War I. Businessmen like Frank W Woolworth, founder of a successful chain of five-and-dime stores, started to advertise their corporate prowess by erecting fantastically tall buildings supported by an internal steel skeleton. The 1913 Woolworth Building remains one of the most beguiling examples of the new form. Designed by Cass Gilbert to resemble the Houses of Parliament in London, its 60-storey neo-Gothic façade is a marvel of gargoyles, spires and flying buttresses. Go inside for the dazzling Romanesque lobby of pure gold leaf, rich marble and a

turquoise mosaic ceiling. Look for the series of carved figures under the cross-beams. Among them are architect Gilbert (with a model of the building) and Woolworth (gleefully counting nickels and dimes). Little wonder that this was immediately dubbed 'the Cathedral of Commerce'. It also ranked as the world's tallest building until completion of the uptown Chrysler Building in 1930.

*Turn west into Barclay Street and walk down to the corner of Church Street.*

The south-east corner of Church and Barclay is occupied by St Peter's Church (1836). Freedom of worship for Roman Catholics was not secure in New York until after the adoption of the first state constitution in 1777, which among other things disestablished the Church of England and prohibited religious qualifications for public office. St Peter's, founded in 1785, was the first Roman Catholic parish in the city. The present building is yet another good example of the Greek Revival style that was all the rage in the early 19th century.

*Time permitting, this is an opportune moment to continue down Church Street for a closer look at the twin towers of the World Trade Center. The view from the observation deck is breathtaking in good weather. Alternatively, go back up Barclay Street to Broadway and turn downtown again.*

As you go, try to visualise lower Broadway as it was 150-odd years ago lined with fashionable brick residences, not office buildings.

*Cross Vesey Street and stop at St Paul's Chapel.*

Completed in 1766, St Paul's is Manhattan's only surviving pre-Revolutionary building (everything else,

Dutch and English alike, has succumbed to fire or the wrecking-ball). Built by Trinity Church to serve its uptown parishioners, St Paul's is a close copy of London's fashionable St-Martin-in-the-Fields (the colonial gentry of New York, even those with Dutch antecedents, took their political and cultural clues from the British). George Washington and other notables had pews here. Note that the Broadway entrance is actually the back of the church: the front was originally meant to look out over the Hudson.

*Stroll a few more blocks down Broadway to Thames and take in the Equitable Building across the street at 120 Broadway.*

The Equitable Building (1915) holds a special place in the architectural history of New York, not because of its height (a mere 40 storeys) but because it occupies every square inch of its site and rises straight up from the sidewalk like a medieval fortress. Its construction triggered a wild controversy, critics warning that Manhattan pedestrians would never see

the sun if such monstrosities were allowed to proliferate. In response, the city enacted its first zoning law, requiring that future skyscrapers could use only a portion of their sites – the higher they rose, the less ground they could cover.

*Continue down Broadway to Trinity Church.*

Three Anglican churches have stood on this site at the head of Wall Street. The first, erected in the 1690s, symbolised the vigorous assertion of British law and culture in New York after the Glorious Revolution brought William and Mary to the throne (among the residents who chipped in for its construction was Captain Kidd, about to begin his career as a pirate). A stronghold loyal to the crown in the turmoil that preceded the Declaration of Independence, Trinity was destroyed by a terrible fire that engulfed a third of the town in 1776 – deliberately set, it has been alleged, by patriots forced to abandon New York after their recent defeat in the Battle of Long Island. Its

**Trinity Church** and its graveyard lend some tranquillity to the financial fracas all around.

replacement was demolished in the 1830s to make way for the present structure, designed by the famous architect Richard Upjohn and completed in 1846. Though disestablished after the Revolution, the parish was not stripped of its substantial real estate holdings on the west side of Manhattan, now worth untold millions of dollars. In the churchyard lie the graves of Alexander Hamilton, Robert Fulton, Albert Gallatin, William Bradford and other New York notables. The Soldier's Monument (1852) commemorates the thousands of Americans who perished in British prisons during the Revolution.

*Either catch the subway just north of the church on Broadway, or resume walking downtown on Broadway toward Bowling Green and the Battery, the starting point of the walk.*

# Eating & drinking

## Bayard's
*1 Hanover Square, between Stone & Pearl Streets (212 514 9454).* **Open** 3.30-10.30pm Mon-Sat. A stunning setting in the India Club for creative French food with an American accent, a formal atmosphere and an impressive bill.

## Burritoville
*20 John Street, between Broadway & Nassau Street (212 766 2020).* **Open** 11.30am-midnight Mon-Thur, Sun; 11.30am-1am Fri, Sat. Fast and cheap self-service café.

## Cosí Sandwich Bar
*55 Broad Street, between Beaver & Exchange Streets (212 344 5000).* **Open** 7am-9pm Mon-Thur; 7am-7pm Fri; 11am-4pm Sat. In the perfect sandwich, it's not just the filling that matters, but the bread. At Cosí, they know that. A *TONY* 100. **Branch:** 54 Pine Street, at William Street (212 809 2674).

## Delmonico's
*56 Beaver Street, at South William Street (212 509 1144).* **Open** 7-10am, 11.30am-10pm Mon-Fri. A smart Continental-style restaurant – the homemade pastas are among the highlights.

## Fraunces Tavern Restaurant
*54 Pearl Street, at Broad Street (212 269 0144).* **Open** 7am-9.30pm Mon-Fri. An American melting-pot menu where Washington once ate.

## Kokura Japanese Restaurant
*19 South William Street, between Broad & Beaver Streets (212 482 8888).* **Open** 11.30am-9.30pm daily. A restaurant with a sedate milieu that encourages both eating and hanging out.

## Rosario's
*38 Pearl Street, between Whitehall & Broad Streets (212 514 5763).* **Open** 8am-3pm Mon-Fri. Sturdy Southern Italian, justifiably popular for breakfast and lunch.

# Buildings

## Bank of New York
*1 Wall Street, at Broadway (212 495 1784).* **Open** 8.30am-4pm Mon-Fri.

## City Hall
*1803-12 City Hall Park, between Broadway & Park Row (Mayor's office 212 788 3000; tours 212 788 6865).* **Open** for tour parties of 13 only – 2wks notice required.

## Federal Hall National Memorial
*26 Wall Street, at Nassau Street (212 825 6888).* **Open** 9am-5pm Mon-Fri.

## Federal Reserve Bank
*33 Liberty Street, between William & Nassau Streets (212 720 6130).* **Open** by appointment only, arranged at least 2wks in advance.

## Municipal Building
*1 Centre Street, at Chambers Street (212 669 2400).* **Open** 8.30am-4pm.

## NASDAQ Stock Exchange
*33 Whitehall Street, at Pearl Street (212 363 6510).*

## New York Mercantile Exchange
*1 North End Avenue, at Vesey Street (212 299 2499).* **Open** 9am-5pm Mon-Fri. **Admission** free.

## New York Stock Exchange
*20 Broad Street, at Wall Street (212 656 5168).* **Open** 9am-4.30pm Mon-Fri. **Admission** free.

## Surrogate's Court
*31 Chambers Street, at Centre Street (212 374 8233).* **Open** 9am-5pm Mon-Fri.

## Tweed Courthouse
*52 Chambers Street, between Broadway & Centre Street (no phone).* Closed for renovation.

## Woolworth Building

*233 Broadway, between Park Place & Barclay Street (212 233 2720).* **Open** 7am-7pm daily.

## World Financial Center & Winter Garden

*West Street, to the Hudson River, Vesey Street to Albany Street (212 945 0505).* **Admission** free.

## World Trade Center

*Church Street to West Street, between Liberty & Vesey Streets (212 323 2340/groups 212 323 2350).* **Open** *Tower 2 Observation deck/rooftop promenade* (open weather permitting) *Sept-May* 9.30am-9.30pm daily; *Jun-Aug* 9.30am-11.30pm daily. **Admission** $13; $6.50-$11 concessions; free under-6s.

# Churches

## John Street United Methodist Church

*44 John Street, between Nassau & William Streets (212 269 0014).* **Open** 11.30am-3pm Mon-Fri; by appointment Sat.

## St Paul's Chapel

*211 Broadway, between Fulton & Vesey Streets (212 602 0874).* **Open** 9am-3pm Mon-Fri, Sun.

## St Peter's Church

*16 Barclay Street, at Church Street (212 233 8355).* **Open** phone for details.

## Shrine of Elizabeth Ann Seton

*7 State Street, between Pearl & Whitehall Streets (212 269 6865).* **Open** 7am-5pm daily.

## Trinity Church Museum

*Broadway, at Wall Street (212 602 0872).* **Open** 9-11.45am, 1-3.45pm Mon-Fri; 10am-3.45pm Sat; 1-3.45pm Sun; closed during concerts.

# Museums

## Fraunces Tavern Museum

*54 Pearl Street, at Broad Street (212 425 1778).* **Open** 10am-4.45pm Mon-Fri; noon-4pm Sat, Sun. **Admission** $2.50; $1 concessions; free under-6s. **No credit cards**.

## Museum of American Financial History

*28 Broadway, at Beaver Street (212 908 4110).* **Open** 10am-4pm Tue-Sat. **Admission** $2 donation.

## National Museum of the American Indian

*George Gustav Heye Center, US Custom House, 1 Bowling Green, between State & Whitehall Streets (212 668 6624).* **Open** 10am-5pm Mon-Wed, Fri-Sun; 10am-8pm Thur. **Admission** free.

## The Statue of Liberty & Ellis Island Immigration Museum

*Statue of Liberty Ferry, departing every half hour from Gangway 4 or 5 in Battery Park at the southern tip of Manhattan (212 363 3200).* **Operating** 9am-5pm; 3.30pm last trip out. Extended hours July-Aug. **Admission** $7; $6-$3 concessions; free under-3s. Purchase tickets at Castle Clinton in Battery Park. It is worth noting that the boat visits both sites – you cannot simply visit one site.

# Other

## African Burial Ground Project

*290 Broadway, between Duane & Reade Streets (212 432 5707).* **Open** 9am-5pm Mon-Fri.

## Battery Park

*Between State Street, Whitehall Street & Battery Place.*

## Department of Parks & Recreation

*888 NY PARKS/212 360 2774.*

## Fulton Fish Market

*South Street, at Fulton Street (212 487 8476).* **Open** 9am-3pm daily. **Tours** *Apr-Oct* 6am on 1st and 3rd Thur of the month. **Tickets** $10 (reservations required).

## The New York Times

*229 West 43rd Street, between Seventh & Eighth Avenues (212 597 8001).*

## The Regent Wall Street Hotel

*55 Wall Street, between William & Broad Streets (212 845 8600).*

## South Street Seaport

*Water Street to the East River, between John Street & Peck Slip (for information about shops and special events, call 212 732 7678).*

## Staten Island Ferry

*South Street, at the foot of Whitehall Street (718 727 2508).* **Open** boats depart every 30min, 24hrs daily. **Tickets** free.

# The exile tour

Valerie Stivers

From the Russian delights of Brighton Beach to Coney Island's Freak Bar, this is a seaside jaunt with a funfair finale.

---

**Start:** Brighton Beach subway station, Brighton Beach, Brooklyn
**Finish:** Surf Avenue, Coney Island, Brooklyn
**Time:** 2-3 hours
**Distance:** 4 miles/6km
**Getting there:** subway trains D or Q to Brighton Beach station
**Getting back:** subway trains B, D, F or N from Coney Island-Stillwell Avenue station
**Note:** Astroland (the funfair) has variable opening and closing times depending on the season and weather (see listings).

---

I moved back to Manhattan from Moscow in the spring of 1998 – skinny, homeless, and in need of a doctor who spoke English. Russia had literally made me sick, and the pills and injections to cure no-one-knew-what were causing brilliant and cavernous nightmares. I should have been glad to leave, instead of mooning and taking photos of the trains and the highway between hot sweats. Moskva, in the nominative case, Moskvye in the prepositional, Moskvoo in the dative, and so forth. I was totally in love, love-hate, the unrequited kind you don't get over. Leaving felt like going into exile instead of out of it.

Inevitably it turned out that no American doctors knew what I had either, and I got stuck in NYC, having not said goodbye or bought a single souvenir. Why didn't I come back with chocolate from the formerly state-owned Krasny Oktyabr (Red October) brand?

There was the 'Alyonka' variety, with a Socialist Realism illustration of a female toddler; 'Kuzya, Alyonka's friend' later got his own candy bar, though his twinkle-eyed Aryan illustration seems too old to bond with Alyonka. And best of all, the Nasha Marka, which opens to reveal a teeny bar of every kind of Krasny Oktyabr chocolate.

There were other things, too. I could have brought some of the dry, sweet poppy-seed rolls available in the entrance of every Moscow metro. I should have returned with the music of Boris Grebenshchikov's group, Akvarium, which sounds like Bob Dylan played by musicians with classical music backgrounds and has been touted as the most influential rock band of the former Soviet Union. It was these and other nameless nostalgias that got me on the endless D train (no Moscow to Petushki, no Yellow Arrow, but still far) out to Brighton Beach, New York's largest Russian community.

Brighton Beach sits on the same five-mile long, semi-detached strip of land as another New York oddity, Coney Island (the famed locale of early-20th-century amusement parks Luna Park, Dreamland and Steeplechase). Here, the Russian community begins to mix with the carneys and residents of a huge low-income housing project. This tour of two of New York's farthest-out destinations will take you through the many post-Soviet delights of Brighton Beach to the gimcrack attractions of Coney Island, ending up at the Freak Bar – where all exiles should land, in the end.

Historically, Brighton Beach was a low-

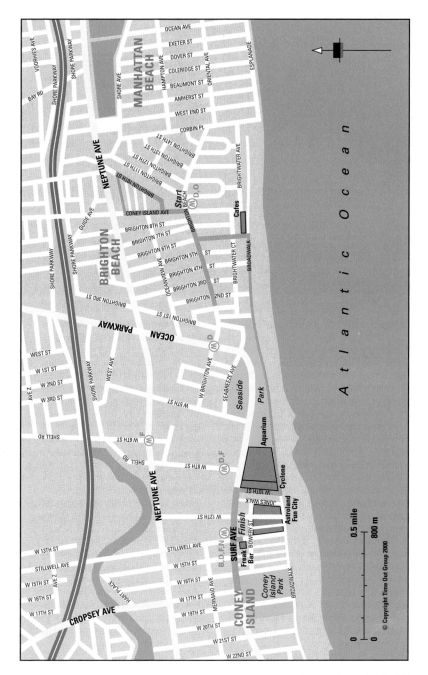

The de-Russification of Brighton Beach is evident on and around **Brighton 10th Street**.

cost destination for Jews fleeing Eastern Europe in the 1920s and then German occupied territories in the 1930s and '40s. In the mid-'60s, the Soviet Union eased restrictions on Jewish emigration. The Russian Jews came in droves, spurred by Russian anti-Semitism. By the mid-'70s, Brighton Beach was a thriving, Russian-speaking residential community. The last wave, this time mainly of non-Jews, came when the USSR collapsed in '91. Today, the Brighton El train casts golden bars of light across shady, central Brighton Beach Avenue; old men sell tins of caviar on the street corners; Russian is the lingua franca; and businesses thrive selling everything from Russian teas to videos.

Getting off the train at the Brighton Beach stop puts you on Brighton Beach Avenue. At first, it looks like any middle-income region in the New York boroughs – overhead train tracks, sidewalks fronted by a clutter of awnings; overweight women wearing too much make-up. There's not much to evoke Moscow's dusty, poplar-lined streets or colossal boulevards. However, if you head west down the

avenue's southern side, the neighbourhood's character will begin to emerge. Everyone around you is speaking Russian! 'Idi suda,' (come here), young mothers call to their children. Ancient, bent-over babushkas, accompanied by husbands in their dotage, carry shopping bags. Handsome Slav boys dressed in Armani-esque black outfits (with black leather jackets in winter or black leather sandals in spring) stroll along projecting a mafia 'tude, regardless of whether they're really waiters or cab drivers or whatever; the real Russian mob is no longer based here.

About halfway down the avenue, stop into No.230; the English part of the sign says 'Books Music Video' and, in the top right-hand corner of the yellow awning, 'St Petersburg Publishing' (Dom Knigi St Petersburg). This is one of many superbly stocked Russian-language media outlets. Amuse your friends with videos of your favourite American films dubbed into Russian; pick up an original from a great Russian director; or buy a contemporary movie (*Brat,* written and directed by Aleksei Balabanov, is a beautifully shot film about modern St Petersburg street life). Those of you daunted by the march of cyrillic across the spines of books, movie boxes, and CD cases shouldn't be afraid to ask the teenage clerks for help – they all speak English. Music must-haves include anything by Akvarium (*Dyeti Dekabrya, Acoustica*), and a newish recording called *Ivan Kypala*, in which traditional folk songs, sung by babushkas from the countryside north of Moscow, are laid over modern beats.

Strolling on the **boardwalk**, down by the sea.

Cross to the north side and head east back up the street; it's time to tackle Russia's notorious food. If you aren't familiar with the cuisine, imagine the feast laid out for the collector of dead peasants, in the Gogol novel *Dead Souls*: 'Chichikov turned around and saw the table already laden with mushrooms, pirozhki, savory dumplings, cheesecakes, pancakes thick and thin, open pies with all kinds of fillings: onion filling, poppy-seed filling, smelt filling and who knows what else.'

Such things are still available. Some of them are even tasty. At Brighton's best-known grocery, M & I International (just

south of Brighton 2nd Street) fizzy, salty, imported Georgian mineral water (Borjomie brand) sells for $1.99; a deli counter holds heaping bowls of pre-prepared salads – beets in mayo, cabbage in a pungent vinaigrette; and, at a stand in the centre of the main floor, packages of thick, spongy and slightly sour brown bread are heaped next to powerful Russian ryes.

But don't fall for International's pirogi. The best I've had in Brighton Beach (though they're nothing compared to those served in Moscow's Krisis Genre) are back up the western side of Brighton Beach

Wave upon wave of local families come to enjoy the seaside delights on **Brighton Beach**.

Avenue at a stand (manned by a Russian-speaking Mexican) outside the Bread Basket store. They're greasy, delightfully chewy, and stuffed with meat, cheese, potato or cabbage. Each one is the size of an athletic sock and costs only 50¢. You can also get the poppy-seed rolls here. Any of these foods immediately transports me to my local Moscow grocery. Friends whom I've inflicted Russian food upon seem to favour the pirogi and breads over the salads. Everyone steers clear of the jellied meats, pickled apples and other traditional, but less accessible fare.

The cheapness of Brighton's street snacks is offset by its pricey restaurants. This strip is famous for several big, gaudy restaurant-clubs that are regularly packed with the wealthier Brightoners, American men throwing bachelor parties, and gawking tourists. You'll see one, the National, on your left. Check out the menus in Russian and English hung on the slick black façade. Further up the street, the Exclusive Deli carries the Krasny Oktyaber chocolates (behind the register),

along with Russian staples similar to those at International. Eating greasy food and drinking salty water may have you ready to sit and have a real drink. But if you'd still like to walk a while, continue up the street to Coney Island Avenue, then follow it left (north). Your first right, on to Brighton 10th Street, reveals quirky, residential Brighton-slice-of-cake-shaped houses squeezed into the corner by the train tracks. Continuing down Brighton 10th Street to, oh, maybe Brighton 10th Path, Brighton 10th Terrace or Brighton 10th Court (a left on any of these will take you back to Coney Island Avenue) can demonstrate the changing face of the neighbourhood. Instead of Russians, you'll begin to see the Asians, Middle Easterners and Mexicans who are part of a widely reported trend toward the de-Russification of Brighton Beach. Slavic immigration has fallen off in recent years (everyone eligible has already come, some say). Furthermore, successful immigrants and their children from the first wave are moving out. On the drowsy residential side lanes off Brighton 10th, groups of Indian children play in the

No parking, but plenty of screaming, as masochists ride the wooden roller coaster, **Cyclone**.

street, and the Muslim call to prayer floats from open windows.

The original Russian immigrants, many of whom were from Odessa on the Black Sea, felt at home in Brighton in part due to its proximity to the ocean. To get there, return to Brighton Beach Avenue, and take Brighton 6th Street east; go up the ramp, on to the country's most celebrated boardwalk. Five miles of elevated wooden slats border a wide, camel-coloured beach studded with wire-mesh trash cans. The boardwalk, put down in the 1920s and named after the Brooklyn Borough President of the time, Edward J Riegelmann, stretches west from Brighton to the private residential community of Seagate on the island's westernmost tip. To the east lies a cluster of Russian restaurants and, in the blue distance, the embankment of Manhattan Beach, a wealthy neighbourhood now known for its nouveau-riche Russian population.

The restaurants to your left – Tatiana, Moscow Café, the Winter Garden – have similar menus and equivalent high prices. The food is delicious: sour bread to dip in borscht; blini with caviar; salty, oily tomato and cucumber salads; but you're really paying for the seat on the boardwalk. At the Tatiana Restaurant and Nightclub (not to be confused with the next-door Tatiana Café), heavy tablecloths cover al fresco tables garnished by fake flower arrangements and equipped with sun umbrellas. Moderately hostile/ condescending service will make anyone who's visited the mother country feel right at home. As will the glitzy indoor details such as the waterfall and fishtank floor. Warning: this will be your last opportunity for food not of the cotton-candy and hot dog variety.

After taking a rest at Tatiana, head west down the boardwalk. You'll notice the Russian crowds giving way to amusement-seeking Manhattanites and black and Hispanic residents of the high-rise housing looming off to your right.

This is the area most people mean when they say 'Coney Island', though technically the entire spit, from Manhattan Beach to Seagate, is Coney Island. The area (which was once separated from the mainland by a river) entered English-speaking history as Gravesend, a quaint English farm community founded in 1643 by religious dissenter Lady Deborah Moody. This it remained until the 1840s, when the first inn to take advantage of Gravesend's glorious beaches, the Coney Island House, began to draw tourists (Washington Irving, Herman Melville and Walt Whitman slept here). The tourists kept on coming, and the infrastructure to amuse them grew. Before the roads were paved, there was a hotel in the shape of an elephant (the Elephant, billed as the Colossus of Architecture), with a cigar store in one 60-foot-in-circumference front leg, and spiral staircases – one for guests to go up, the other to go down – in the hind legs. By the early 1900s, Coney Island supported three lavish amusement parks. The book *Good Old Coney Island*, by Edo McCullough, nephew of the park's Steeplechase founder, sums it up in the opening line: 'For three-quarters of a century Coney Island has been the most famous seaside resort in the world.'

Of course, those words were written in 1957, when Coney Island was already deep in a slump that it still hasn't recovered from. One of the parks, Dreamland, burned to the ground in 1911 and was not rebuilt. Luna Park burned and then closed in 1946 (the New York Aquarium stands on its remains), and Steeplechase shut its doors in 1964, leaving only the desiccated skeleton of its parachute jump, which was modelled after an exhibit at the 1939 World's Fair, and is unmistakable on the horizon.

On the boardwalk from Brighton Beach, you'll see the New York Aquarium on your right, and then soon after, the gaudy storefronts of Coney Island's remaining 'fun zone'. Although this seedy strip does thriving business in modern gimmicks (a machine where you can 'morph' your picture with that of your mate to determine what your 'child' will look like, for example) there are a few genuine historical landmarks. Turn right on West 10th Street to take a spin on the Cyclone, the country's oldest rollercoaster, and one of the few remaining that's wooden and uses only a chain-pull up an initial incline and then gravity, as a means of propulsion.

After the ride, those of you who've managed to hold on to your lunch, and your nerve (the Cyclone does not, shall we say, take the corners gently), can wander among the fun zone's many newer rides, games and amusements. The other historical landmark ride is the Wonder Wheel ferris wheel. When you've been sufficiently shaken up, exit the fun zone past the Cyclone (you should be at the corner of West 10th and Surf Avenue), and go west on Surf. The northern side of this street is lined with an incredible array of truly junky junk shops and Russian furniture stores. My best (and only) finds have happened in a nameless warren on the corner of Surf and Henderson, which advertises '$1 any item' but does not, in fact, sell everything for $1 (entrance next to the Bengal Grocery).

Nathan's Famous Hot Dogs, dominating the corner of Surf and Stillwell, is primarily famous for being famous (how American!), and for having a confusing queue policy, where you stand in one line for burgers, another for seafood, and so forth. Hopefully, you've filled up on Russian food and can bypass Nathan's for a Surf Avenue institution known as the El Dorado 'bump your ass off' bumper cars. Spectators line up on one side of a black wire cage, catching the beat of the booming dance music and watching their friends go round. Above the El Dorado is the Surf Art Exchange, a Russian-owned gallery with a great view of the fun zone and the sea. Paintings such as the one of

Lenin with a buxom, naked red lady on his lap may seem puerile, but if a painter had done this in pre-glasnost Russia, it would have meant a death sentence, or at least an 'opportunity' to help populate Siberia.

Like Vladimir Illyich, the next stop on our tour is also a remnant of a lost world. One block beyond Nathan's on Surf Avenue, the fun zone turns to wasteland, best represented by the surreal hulk of the old Astroland rollercoaster, surrounded by a high chainlink fence, topped off with barbed wire and sitting on a lot strewn with broken glass, panties and syringes. The coaster is being overgrown by weeds, and its spectral beauty may not be long for this world – a minor-league baseball stadium is currently under construction nearby.

Astroland does not invite lingering, but back on West 12th Street, just off Surf, there's a Freak Bar that does. To top off your day spent mooching through NYC's edge cities, grab a stool at this hideaway inside the 'Sideshow by the Seashore'. Corona goes for $3, there's an old eight-track player, and for company you're likely to get freaks like Izzy the tattooed man at the bar next to you. Afterwards, it's but a short stumble to the Stillwell Avenue B, D, F, N stop, and a train home. Of course, if this was a train in a Russian novel of the Moscow-Petushki/Yellow Arrow ilk, you'd never get home. You'd end up in Brighton Beach again. But if you've at all gotten the bug of the place, that'll happen anyway.

## Eating & drinking

### Bread Basket
*307 Brighton Beach Avenue, between Brighton 3rd & Brighton 4th Streets, Brighton Beach, Brooklyn (718 368 1336).* **Open** 8am-9pm daily.

### Four Eleven Brighton Deli
*411 Brighton Beach Avenue, between Brighton 4th & Brighton 5th Streets, Brighton Beach, Brooklyn (718 368 3001).* **Open** 8am-9pm daily.

### Freak Bar
*1208 Surf Avenue at Stillwell Avenue, Coney Island, Brooklyn (718 352 5159).* **Open** 2-8pm Mon; 2-9pm Fri; 1pm-midnight Sat, Sun.

**Nathan's Famous** is *so* famous that it has an annual hot-dog eating competition.

### M & I International

*237 Brighton Beach Avenue, between Brighton 1st & Brighton 2nd Streets, Brighton Beach, Brooklyn (718 646 1225).* **Open** 8am-10pm daily. All the cues in this bustling market point to Russia.

### Nathan's Famous

*1310 Surf Avenue, at Stillwell Avenue, Coney Island, Brooklyn (718 946 2202).* **Open** 8am-2am Mon-Thur, Sun; 8am-3am Fri, Sat. The mother of all hot-dog stands.

### National

*273 Brighton Beach Avenue, between Brighton 1st & Brighton 2nd Streets, Brighton Beach, Brooklyn (718 646 1225).* **Open** 8pm-3am Fri, Sat; 7pm-1am Sun (shows 10.30pm). Opt for the 'Russian banquet' for a series of national dishes.

### Primorski

*282 Brighton Beach Avenue, between Brighton 2nd & Brighton 3rd Streets, Brighton Beach, Brooklyn (718 452 4451).* **Open** 11am-2am daily.

### Tatiana

*3152 Brighton 6th Street, Brighton Beach, Brooklyn (718 891 5151).* **Open** noon-midnight daily.

### Volna

*3145 Brighton 4th Street, Brighton Beach, Brooklyn (718 332 0341).* **Open** 11am-11pm daily.

### Winter Garden Restaurant

*3152 Brighton 6th Street, Brighton Beach, Brooklyn (718 934 6666).* **Open** noon-midnight Mon-Thur, Sun; noon-1am Fri, Sat.

## Entertainment

### Astroland

*1000 Surf Avenue, at West 8th Street, Coney Island, Brooklyn (718 372 0275).* **Open** *summer* noon-late (weather permitting); *winter* phone for details. **Tickets** $1.75 single for kiddie rides. **No credit cards.**

### New York Aquarium

*Surf Avenue, at West 8th Street, Coney Island, Brooklyn (718 265 3405).* **Open** *summer* 10am-6pm daily; *winter* 10am-5pm daily. **Admission** $8.75; $4.50 concessions. **No credit cards.**

## Literature & film

**Brat** (*Brother*) (Aleksei Balabanov, 1997, Russia)
**Dead Souls** Nikolai Gogol (1842)
**Good Old Coney Island** Edo McCullough (1957).

## Shopping

### Surf Art Exchange

*1220 Surf Avenue, Coney Island, Brooklyn (718 265 3972).* **Open** noon-5pm Tue-Sun.

# Hoop, skip and jump

Robert Heide & John Gilman

Independent galleries and Museum Mile: compare and contrast.

---

**Start:** Gansevoort Street, Meatpacking District
**Finish:** Burger Heaven, East 53rd Street
**Time:** 3hrs-all day
**Distance:** 5 miles/8km
**Getting there:** subway trains A, C or E to 14 Street-Eighth Avenue station
**Getting back:** subway trains E or F from Fifth Avenue station
**Note:** this is a walk in two distinct areas (Chelsea and upper Fifth Avenue), and needs a subway or bus ride from the end of one to the start of the other. Each half is really a walk in itself: the first is a tour of the independent galleries in Chelsea, the second through the museums of Fifth Avenue. The second part also coincides with some of Lee Stringer's walk, *Down and Out and Up Again.*

---

Rounding the corner of Christopher Street and Hudson in Greenwich Village and heading up Eighth Avenue to the Chelsea art galleries we spot Hoop in his Millennium Time Machine Art Van. Hoop, whose fantastic art creations on wheels have been written about in several issues of the *New York Times*, offers us a lift in his way-out vehicle to Chelsea's border with the Village, where we are to begin our gallery walk. His Art Van is covered with clocks and watches on one side and tin cans on the other and has two fronts with grilles and lights to confuse the issue of coming and going. We agree to meet up later in front of the Sonnabend

Gallery where he had been thinking of parking his show-and-tell moveable art exhibit and hanging out anyway.

Amidst excited cries from astonished passersby of 'What is it?' and 'What time is it?' and 'Which way is it going?', Hoop drops us off in Gansevoort Street in the Meatpacking District. This is the city's wholesale butchers' district where big wooden signs such as 'Schuster Meat Corp, specialists in boneless beef cuts and pork butts' hang alongside meathooks on overhead rails.

The area, in the north-west corner of the Village, and rubbing against the West Side Highway and the Hudson River, is a jumble of cobblestoned streets filled with meat trucks and the smell of blood. As such it has attracted a lively nightlife that includes transsexual, or transgender, as well as actual female hookers, decadent late-night clubs and bars like Hogs and Heifers where bikers expect their 'galfriends' to hang their bras inside on stuffed deerheads and mounted bison heads. Architects' offices, restaurants, art, antique and furniture galleries have transformed the area into New York's up-and-coming real-estate discovery. Florent, a sort of upscale French diner, hosts an annual Bastille Day affair in mid-July that often features charming wooden guillotines, straw-strewn streets, live goats, an outdoor dining area offering up crêpes suzettes and other French delicacies, Piaf-like singers, can-can girls and gender-bender Marie Antoinette lookalikes.

At Washington Street we notice the beginning of the rusted-out and abandoned Westside freight train trestle

# Hoop, skip and jump

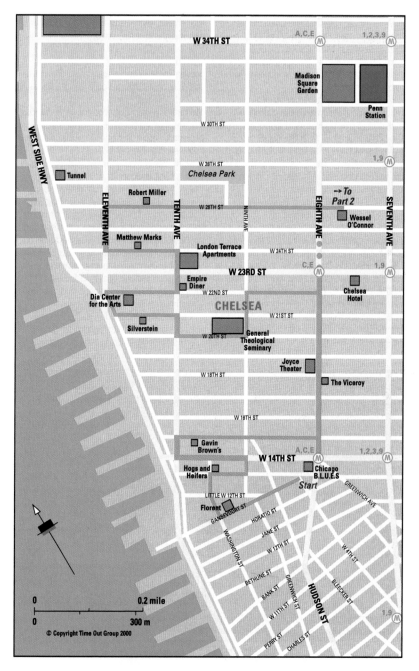

W 34TH ST

A,C,E     1,2,3,9

Madison
Square
Garden

Penn
Station

WEST SIDE HWY

W 30TH ST

W 28TH ST

Chelsea Park

1,9

Tunnel

Robert Miller

→ To
Part 2

W 26TH ST

ELEVENTH AVE

TENTH AVE

NINTH AVE

EIGHTH AVE

SEVENTH AVE

Wessel
O'Connor

Matthew Marks

London Terrace
Apartments

W 24TH ST

C,E    1,9

Empire
Diner

W 23RD ST

Chelsea
Hotel

W 22ND ST

Dia Center
for the Arts

CHELSEA

W 21ST ST

Silverstein

W 20TH ST

General
Theological
Seminary

Joyce
Theater

W 18TH ST

The Viceroy

W 16TH ST

Gavin
Brown's

A,C,E    1,2,3,9

Hogs and
Heifers

W 14TH ST

Chicago
B.L.U.E.S

Start

GREENWICH AVE

LITTLE W 12TH ST

Florent

GANSEVOORT ST

HORATIO ST

W 4TH ST

JANE ST

WASHINGTON ST

W 12TH ST

BETHUNE ST

BANK ST

GREENWICH ST

HUDSON ST

BLEECKER ST

W 11TH ST

1,9

PERRY ST

CHARLES ST

| 0 | 0.2 mile |
|---|----------|
| 0 | 300 m |

© Copyright Time Out Group 2000

that originally began near Canal Street for hauling refrigerated trains. Today it twists between buildings and forges straight up to 32nd Street, and will reappear regularly in our wander through West Chelsea.

Walking along the quiet streets, we reach 14th Street, where the galleries begin in earnest. Dozens of Soho galleries, unable to compete with the retail store invasion of their cast-iron buildings and cobbled streets, have defected to the post-industrial Chelsea hinterland. Drawn by the large, light and airy garage and warehouse spaces, the streets west of Ninth Avenue boast a feast of independent galleries. The latest in cutting-edge art from all over the world – shocking, amusing, bizarre, pointless and plain weird – is displayed in the skylit cavernous spaces that are worth the visit in themselves. Come here when they're closed, however, and the ribbed metal shutters hide any real sign of the creativity on display, and the area has a ghostly air. Trendy shops and restaurants have followed in the wake of the art movement, signalling the rising tide of gentrification in the area.

Head west along 14th Street to the Cynthia Broan Gallery currently presenting a group show called *Pet Show 2000*, centred around pets and including a wall of 'lost pet' flyers collected by Michael Dickas. The wonder of pets from the point of view of their owners is projected into a variety of media including knitwear for dogs. The logo for this show is an abstract man following after his dog with a pooper-scooper in hand – the same image you will find on city posts, poles and streetlamps as you let your dog lead you astray. A few pets are brought in by their owners, but they seem uninterested in the goings-on. There's a hot-dog barbecue stand outside the gallery – now that hot dog you are eating may in itself be declared a work of art. In fact these red 'dogs' were bought just next door at the Old Plymouth Beef Company.

The most cutting-edge gallery in this area is Gavin Brown's enterprise just around the corner on West 15th Street. This youth-cult art centre has a lower

Clocks away! – **Hoop** and his **Time Machine** make an exhibition of themselves.

The Westside freight track overlooks the carcass deliveries in the **Meatpacking District**.

eastside feel to it. Londoner Gavin Brown's original gallery was near the Holland Tunnel; and it is where Billy Name, Andy Warhol's assistant and the man who photographed the Silver Factory scene, was shown just after a silver metal chest filled with his own early lost negatives was rediscovered following Warhol's death. Today an installation by Spencer Sweeney has a metal window frame with smashed glass and curtains with an automotive pattern on them. These are being blown by an electric fan outside the window meant to simulate the wind. On the inside floor of the window are shards of broken glass and a brick someone must have thrown that has the word 'NERDS' painted on it. The work is entitled *I Hate Fucking Nerds*. Gavin Brown's attracts a mostly hip young crowd who appear to be rich, skinny and starving. They drift into the chic gallery bar where they sip exotic pink cocktails in long-stemmed glasses.

Walking east to Eighth Avenue, we briefly turn south a few steps to check out the talent and show times at the Chicago

B.L.U.E.S. where a dozen different headliners appear every month, including heavies like Sweet Georgia Brown, Tommy Castro, Popa Chubby, Ernie Williams and the Wildcats.

We resume our walk north up Eighth Avenue into the lively and thriving Chelsea district (so named in 1750 by Captain Thomas Clarke after London's Chelsea Hospital), which today has a large, visible and fashion-conscious gay population. The Avenue, between 14th and 23rd, is a hotbed of shops, bars, clubs and restaurants, all serving the residential crossover blocks that radiate east to Seventh Avenue and west as far as the Hudson River. We pass Cajun at 16th Street, where they serve New Orleans Cajun food and on Monday nights host an oyster bar and acts such as the famous Vince Gioriano and His Nighthawks Orchestra, playing original 1930s-style hotel dance band arrangements in the Leo Reisman *Coconut Grove* style. Foxtrot, anyone?

Gay men's fashion shops like p chanin, Bang Bang and Camouflage abound. We stop for an 'Atom Bomb' cocktail, one of

Girls on film – cutting-edge shows are a regular feature of **Gavin Brown's enterprise**.

the specials at Flight 151 Bar and Restaurant, which is decorated with World War II memorabilia. Ask the bartender, a seasoned vet, to make you a 'Pearl Harbor Zombie'.

Cooled off and dizzy, we wander a few steps south and into the Chisholm-Larrson Gallery to check out the fantastic selection of vintage (mostly early 20th-century) posters advertising everything from travel junkets to food, wine and deco dancers. On the south-east corner at 18th Street is the splendiferous Viceroy, noted for its original turn-of-the-century bar, comfortable round booths and newer deco wall sconces. It was a favourite of once local resident Shirley Stoler, who liked to sip Brandy Alexanders or Grasshoppers there. Shirley, the flame-haired overweight star of the American film classic *The Honeymoon Killers* and Lina Wertmüller's *Seven Beauties* (she played the sadistic Nazi commandant), was a friend to all in this Chelsea neighbourhood until she passed away.

The 'Atom Bomb' drink took its toll so we postpone a toast to the ghost of Shirley

at the Viceroy and continue on up the avenue to the landmark art moderne-style Joyce Dance Theater. Once a grungy movie house called the Elgin where *Pink Flamingoes* and *El Topo* were first shown to the LSD-soaked crowds at midnight screenings, it's now an intimate dance venue that has attracted the finest choreographers in the business from Doug Elkins to Merce Cunningham.

Havana Chelsea, almost opposite, is the stop-off point for a frothy papaya drink and what is considered the best Cuban sandwich in New York. Another good choice for lunch on the avenue is the Bendix Diner at the north-west corner of 21st Street. The Eighth Avenue Kitchen Market is a take-out place for the best in prepared foods and Mexican groceries. The Big Cup Tea and Coffee Shop can lay claim to be the main lounge-around meeting ground for the cruising gay men of Chelsea, alongside Rawhide, which attracts those who are into leather.

Continuing our walk up to 23rd Street, we stop to glance westward to the London Terrace Apartments, one of the most desirable and grandiose residential complexes in the city, offering tenants a nautical art deco swimming pool on the roof as just one of its advantages; and east to the Bauhaus-style apartment complex of yellow brick; and to the Chelsea Hotel, a landmark built in 1884 and on the National Register of Historic Places, which features fancifully ornate wrought-iron balconies. The Chelsea was home at one time or another to a variety of notables including Dylan Thomas, Thomas Wolfe, O Henry, Virgil Thompson, and Sid Vicious and Nancy Spungen.

Backtracking to 22nd Street, we head west towards Ninth Avenue, noting the typical brownstone architecture of the area, the houses dating from the 1830s through the 1890s. These tree-lined residential streets of Chelsea are noted for their gardens and lush flowers, so we walk down to the General Theological Seminary of the Episcopal Church. This imposing Gothic Revival building complex, constructed between 1883 and 1902, surrounds a central quadrangle at historic Chelsea Square. The Seminary property, donated by Clement Clarke Moore, author of the famous poem 'Twas the Night Before Christmas', has over 32,000 square feet of lawn, 60 trees and 35 flower beds, and is considered a true oasis in the heart of New York City.

On Tenth Avenue we cut up to 21st Street and head west to return to the gallery trail. Silverstein, is exhibiting strange-looking, greenish-white painted life-size earthen mice grouped on the floor, reminiscent of Ray Johnson, the famed collagist. Back in the '60s, his dead animal happenings would involve Johnson delivering dead rats sprayed gold; or sometimes he would let dozens of live white mice loose in a scared friend's apartment. Also at the Silverstein show is *Between Grains of Sand and Microchips*, glass sculptures by Donald Lipski, Kiki Smith and Yoko Ono. 'Japanamation' is of special concern at this gallery.

Opposite, the Bonakdar Jancou Gallery is a vast skylit gallery in what seems like a cement bunker. It exhibits odd, and often disturbing, pieces – currently huge haunting canvasses by Carla Klein. The outside of the two-storey building, probably constructed in the 1920s, features cement relief architectural details of wheels with wings indicating that the premises were formerly a taxi garage.

Turning north up Eleventh Avenue, we pass the Chelsea piers and the Chelsea Sports Center on the Hudson River. Stretching from 17th Street to 23rd, it offers a golf club, bowling and other sports activities, including equestrian, a yacht basin and other amenities. This stretch also offers a view of the Department of Corrections' highly embelished (brick with terracotta) art deco prison on the West Side Highway at 20th Street; as a prison, it's best viewed from the outside only. Little deco made it into the jail cells anyway.

We then head east along 22nd Street, noting the rock street sculptures every

Cor blimey, the **London Terrace Apartments**.

few yards, to the pioneering Dia Center For the Arts. This non-profit Chelsea institution was until 1993 the area's only major claim to art, and is a mainstay of the arts community. It has long-term installations by major contemporaries, and poetry readings (Amiri Baraka and Jayne Cortez have read here), and is worth a visit not least for Dan Graham's glasshouse on the roof.

Just beyond is the Sonnabend Gallery at 536 West 22nd Street. Gallery director Antonio Homem shows us through the great white gallery, and the cylindrical outdoor sculpture garden. Sonnabend opened in Paris in 1963, was in Soho for many years and had its celebrity-studded inaugural exhibition in May 2000, a retrospective of its 40 years – the likes of Andy Warhol's four coloured *Campbell's Soup Can* (1965), Gilbert and George's *Blood and Piss* (1996), *Raw War* by Bruce Nauman (1972), and Jeff Koons' *Pot Rack* (2000) that, alas, is already sold for $250,000. The gallery's list of artist is impressive – James Rosenquist, Haim Steinbach, Roy Lichtenstein and Robert Rauschenberg among them. At this point an authorial note might be of interest. Co-author of this walk, Robert Heide, gave Andy the idea at the Silver Factory in the 1960s to continue to paint his soup cans and Marilyns, only changing and varying the use of colour: in other words, a Marilyn with a fuchsia face and orange hair or a green and purple soup can, et cetera. This was in reply to Andy's persistent and annoying question: 'What'll we do next?' Andy's obsession with the repetition of image coupled with his profound sense of Zen emptiness caused him to remark, 'Oh, gee, yeah,' as he embraced the free-floating idea. And this became a major shift in his work.

The Pat Hearn Gallery (at No.530) has long been in the vanguard of the New York art world, whether here, or in her East Village and Soho spaces that preceded her move to Chelsea. The *Nocturnal Dream Show*, Sheyla Baykal's

1970s photos of the Angels of Light (a camp high-drag glitter show that performed in New York, San Francisco, and Europe), is featured today. The late Baykal, protégé of the late great Peter Hujar (we hope these two are clicking away somewhere in the Great Beyond), photographed Vietnam War protests, the Fugs in performance, John Vaccaro's Theater of the Ridiculous, and Eric Broaddus (the costume and book artist) – Baykal's images of an alternative theatre are wondrous in themselves.

On the corner of 22nd and Tenth Avenue we hit upon the fabled Empire Diner, one of the first of the creative reuses of the great American diner. The black and white enamel and chromium roadside architectural gem was moved from a location in New Jersey (the diner capital of the US) to this corner of Chelsea. We pass the glamorous Empire to turn left into West 24th Street – look back eastward for a fine view of the block-square 1920s London Terrace Apartments complex rising above the continuous freight train trestle.

West 24th is a busy gallery street, dizzy with large, bright spaces. Metro Pictures has a group show, the highlight of which was a Cindy Sherman oversized cibachrome colour photograph of herself as a grotesque. At Matthew Marks' glass-fronted converted garage is the exceptional exhibit entitled *Weegee: Distortions*. Weegee, whose real name was Arthur Fellig, was a freelance photojournalist for New York tabloids in the 1930s. Weegee memorabilia, snapshots, postcards, letters and some of his books (*Weegee's World*, *Naked City*, *Naked Hollywood* and *Weegee's Creative Camera*) were exhibited beside late 1940s and early 1950s portraits of Salvador Dali, Mao Tse Tung, Marilyn Monroe and the three faces of Andy Warhol, all distorted and wavy as in a fun-house mirror.

The Andrea Rosen Gallery can be relied upon to show the young heroes of the decade, and of the years to come too, no doubt – currently, Julia Scher, the artist who is in the forefront of work investigating systems of technology (she pioneered work in surveillance technology). Her eerie eliptical sculptures incorporate microwave ovens – small orange men are trapped within, trying to find a way out of their terrifying mechanistic environment.

At Eleventh Avenue, we walk up toward 26th Street, dropping into the Art Resources Transfer, which today shows a major retrospective by Patricia Broderick. Her muted colour gauche-on-paper artworks have the same immediate sense of warmth, charm and depth as Patsy herself, as she is called by friends. Tributes to her late TV star husband James, famed one-eyed aviator Wiley Post, and to the late Jim Carruthers are highlights and very moving personal pieces. Yes, she is also known as actor Matthew's mother, but the message here is that Patsy shines through in herself and in her work as an artist and woman to be reckoned with.

Just north of here on 27th Street are clubland's Twilo and Tunnel discos. We've attended a good number of parties here – the Tunnel's scale and decor particularly are worth a visit.

Swing east down 26th for the last two galleries on this part of the tour. Robert Miller at No.524 used to be a 57th Street stalwart but has relocated to join the throng in Chelsea. But he has brought with him a fine collection of work – Lee Krasner, Robert Mapplethorpe and Bruce Weber have been featured here. As we head east we drop in on the Wessel & O'Connor Gallery between Seventh and Eighth Avenues. It's really a photography gallery, and doesn't normally feature painting, but today is clearly an exception. Mark Beard, a Chelsea resident and artist with a theatrical penchant for the absurd, is showing here. He invented a fictional painter he calls Bruce Sargeant, who has produced some provocative super-size, ornately framed homoerotic portraits with

an Edwardian flair. Sargeant, apparently, met his untimely demise in a wrestling accident in 1938. Beard promises to include other new 'artists' in his next show including a lesbian modernist, a Viennese expressionist and a Beaux Arts teacher, all presumably – and conveniently – deceased.

As if on cue, Hoop turns up as we emerge from the gallery, to chauffeur us to the Conservatory Gardens in the northern end of Central Park, the next stop on this culture-vulture trail.

From here, the walk moves to the top of Fifth Avenue, near 103rd Street station. You could of course walk there, but it is a fair distance, so it is probably best to go east by bus (the M23 on 23rd Street), or by subway (the E train), and then change to the 6 train to continue north.

We take the Hoop Art Van the scenic route uptown, along the FDR Drive. We're going to track the museums of Fifth Avenue's Museum Mile (and some more besides), from north to south. The stretch is an exhausting and remarkable monument to human creativity – sculpture, paintings, photography, design, furniture, and of course the architectural splendour of the buildings themselves. We have our favourites, where we linger, and others we pass by, but as a whole they cater for such an eclectic range of tastes, exciting even the least curious of people, that it's a case of each to their own. Enjoy.

Heading into the Hispanic section of East Harlem we wend our way to 104th Street at Fifth Avenue where we stop in front of the magnificent Vanderbilt Gate to Central Park, across from El Museo del Barrio. The ornate wrought-iron gate came from one of the Vanderbilt estates. Passing through the great gates we descend a graceful staircase to a formal hedge-framed half-acre lawn, flanked by rows of Japanese lilac and crab apple trees. Beyond is a circular pond and fountain, with a semicircular arbour above. It's the central Vanderbilt

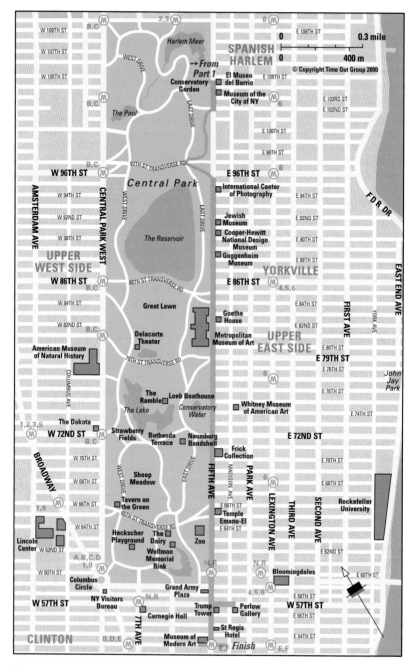

Conservatory Garden, and it is beautiful on a summer's day. The Perrenial Garden to the south, called the 'secret' garden, features zinnias, day lilies, roses, petunias, hollyhocks, giant ferns and wildflowers. A friendly, elderly park volunteer points out the Barnett Fountain Group and pool, which had been given to the children of the city in 1924. The North Garden is formal and maze-like with circular pathways that lead to the central art nouveau fountain of bronze nude nymph-like women. Beyond, on the other side of the high garden fence, you see the Harlem Meer, a small lake in the north-east corner of Central Park.

Exiting Vanderbilt Conservatory Garden the way we came in, we cross Fifth Avenue and head into El Museo del Barrio, passing two plexiglass cows in the courtyard, one painted and signed by Eliza Jimenez. These are but two of 500 such cows, individually painted and corporate-sponsored, appearing in unexpected places on the streets and in plazas around the city during the summer of 2000. The lobby of the museum is adorned with colourful terracotta tiles featuring 1920s children at play. Perched on the edge of Spanish Harlem, the museum devotes itself to the works of Hispanic artists, as well as supporting community events such as the annual, and lively, Mexican Day of the Dead.

As we emerge, we see Hoop parked on Fifth Avenue. We leave him surrounded by questioning gawkers as we walk south a block to the Museum of the City of New York, where several exhibits showcase the vast history of the city. *New York Songs of the City* has selections of sheetmusic and songbooks from the last century featuring splendid artful pop culture graphics on their covers. Tin Pan Alley songs were played at home on the upright, on the phonograph and on the radio, in the movies, and eventually on TV. All of America joined in along with stars like Al Jolson, Kate Smith, Ruth Etting and Vaughn de Leath, a lady dubbed 'the first crooner' whose soft voice spared radio tubes, that were said to break when tenors such as Caruso sang on air.

We decide to reenter the Park at 102nd

Bronze nudes find a way to cool off in the **Vanderbilt Conservatory Garden**, Central Park.

Street and walk along the hilly lawns, an unbroken pastoral pleasure, until the transverse (the road that crosses east and west across the Park) directs us back on to Fifth Avenue proper. Just south is the East 96th Street Children's Playground, certainly worth a stop if you have youngsters.

The International Center of Photography is in a building that was formerly the home of Willard Straight, founder of the *New Republic*. Georgian and Federal architecture were incorporated in this attractive 1913 building. The Center is particularly strong on news and documentary photography, with a huge library collection of biographical and photographic files. We view an exhibition of shocking blow-ups called *Deeds of War*, featuring atrocities in Rwanda, Afghanistan, Indonesia, South Africa and Eastern Europe. The young and the old, starving, skeletal and crippled children of Romania, the Balkans, Chechnya and other blighted regions. The Center's Daguerrian Gallery featured beautifully displayed and dimly lit (as in the days of gaslight) old daguerrotypes of African Americans by daguerreotypist Augustus Washington (1821-75) – a haunting peek into a long-ago private domain of personal treasures.

We dip into the Jewish Museum, an eclectic collection of artefacts (most rescued from Europe prior to the outbreak of World War II), all housed in the 1908 Warburg Mansion, but we're eager to reach the Cooper-Hewitt National Design Museum of the Smithsonian Institution. This is a place we authors have lectured at; we also contributed *objets de* pop culture, such as diner cups and electrical appliances, to several of their fine exhibitions. Now the only museum in the US devoted to historical and contemporary design, it's in one of the great mansions of New York, whose owner, industrialist Andrew Carnegie, had asked for a simple, roomy house; his architects came up with a 64-room Georgian-style mansion. We step out of the great double doors and down the grand staircase to the garden across from the park, where events are often held for the public. (One summer here they had a wonderful exhibit of new designs for tents, that were all erected and displayed on the lawn.) The Cooper-Hewitt is also host to groups such as the New York Art Deco Society, which holds annual meetings and programmes on a variety of deco interests.

Leaving the Cooper-Hewitt garden, we cross through the museum and out on to 91st Street and once again on to elegant Fifth Avenue. We pass by the Engineer's Gate at 90th Street, and the National Academy of Design, an honorary organisation of artists that maintains a museum and a school of fine arts. Its museum is one of the foremost collections of 19th- and 20th-century American art.

Our next stop is the Guggenheim, a Frank Lloyd Wright creation. Glorious and inspiring, an art work in itself, the circular building sits back in an airy and spacious plaza. It has been reported that Wright constructed it to withstand the effects of an atomic bomb. The Guggenheim is planning to expand, building an extravagant new gallery downtown on the South Street Seaport, an architectural fantasy to rival the one recently opened in Bilbao. A huge model of the building – all towers, wavy metal roofing and open plazas – is on show in one of the tower rooms. However, because we are getting vertigo on the Guggenheim ramps, we decide to slip out. Leaving the lobby the first thing we notice, looking south through an arched and tinted window, is Hoop's Art Van, parked on 88th Street, the serene white museum a perfect setting for the gaudy artmobile; clearly Hoop is following closely on our trail. People are taking pictures of it from inside and out.

Our next stop, the elegant Goethe-Institut New York/German Cultural Center, has an exhibit about the *New*

Looking south across Central Park from the roof garden of the **Metropolitan Museum of Art**.

*York City Centennial Project* by Alan Sonfit. Sonfit's *Time Landscape* is a favourite place of ours in Greenwich Village. In place since 1965 at the corner of Houston Street and LaGuardia Place, it's a fenced re-creation of an indigenous New York forest, left as it would have been, untended.

The experience of walking up the palatial steps at the Metropolitan Museum, one of New York's and the world's great landmark buildings and which some architects have compared to an august courthouse, is exhilarating. Inside the Great Hall, with its marble columns and vaulted ceiling, an information kiosk directs visitors to what they fancy, which at the Metropolitan could be practically anything. To the right is the Temple of Dendur and all things Egyptian; to the left are the splendid halls (newly refurbished) of Greek and Roman art. Beyond, there's an impressive European collection (post-Impressionists to the fore), whole rooms of tromp l'oeil marquetry reconstructed from Urbino, a huge room housing a life-size façade of an

18th-century mansion, and an excellent Islamic art collection. The treats go on and on. The roof garden has a contemporary sculpture installation and is a tremendous place to take in the breathtaking views and the vast scope of Central Park. The Metropolitan is an institution that requires visits over and over again; it is always an eye-opener, as well as an education.

A thunderstorm that has been threatening all day finally breaks and heavy rains pour forth as we make our way down the steps and across the street to the shelter of the Stanhope Hotel's outdoor café. Sipping a bone-dry martini or some other concoction below blue awnings here allows you to contemplate the Met from across the avenue.

Hoop shows up outside the smart, chic hotel with its classic bar room and elegant lobby; and, once again, the Time Machine caused a stir. He orders a Bloody Mary cocktail before taking off for New Jersey to make a mashed potato creamed corn and meatloaf supper for his mother.

We jump on the Fifth Avenue bus and

Gardens, galleries, Goya, Gainsborough – there's quite a G-force at the **Frick Collection**.

get off on 72nd Street to take in the Frick. The Frick is not part of the annual official Museum Mile celebration. The outstanding, astounding Frick Collection is housed in an imposing mansion with adjoining formal gardens. This great New York mansion, bequeathed and maintained as one of the finest small museums in the world, was constructed in 1914 in the 18th-century European style for Henry Clay Frick, one of Carnegie's co-industrialists. The fanciful building features an indoor garden court and reflecting pond, and gallery upon gallery filled to the brim with world-class art and furniture including James Whistler, Goya, Anthony Van Dyck, a pensive self-portrait by Rembrandt, and then the Turners, Veroneses, Vermeers, Gainsboroughs. Of particular note is the Antoine Fragonard room for Madame Du Barry, and in a separate hallway Marie Antoinette's commode and secretary are exquisite to behold. In another room François Boucher canvasses painted for Madame de Pompadour's library in Chartres depict idealised rosy-cheeked

children at various kinds of simple play.

Leaving the Frick we decide to make a stop – after once again boarding the Fifth Avenue bus – at the Katharina Rich Perlow Gallery in the Fuller Building, where the work of David Ahlstead is on show. There are 25 galleries in the Fuller Building, which is itself an outstanding example of art deco architecture from 1929, depicting construction workers in its motifs.

Walking and skipping down the Avenue 'like a couple of swells who stay in the best hotels' (as sung by Judy Garland and Fred Astaire in *Easter Parade*), we pass the colourful Warner Brothers store, the three-storey Disney flagship store and the new Brooks Brothers superstore. Here's the recently restored gem of a hotel, the St Regis, where Joe Dimaggio and Marilyn Monroe had their honeymoon. The Old King Cole bar room here has an original Maxfield Parrish mural of King Cole and his courtiers; it was here that the Bloody Mary was invented.

Our final museum destination is the

Museum of Modern Art, MoMA for short. Holding possibly the finest 20th-century collection in the world, it is also famous for its film restorations and archives. The Modern is always screening something special and unusual – sometimes well-known classics, at other times films not shown anywhere since their original release. We decide to stay for the screening of Fellini's *La Dolce Vita*, which neither of us have seen since its 1960 release. So we settle back into the dreamy black and white decadence of buxom blonde Anita Ekberg and Marcello Mastroianni, who seemed always to be having one kind of identity crisis or another (at least on film).

Once the picture is over and we find ourselves outside again, we cross to the on to Burger Heaven 53rd Street (halfway between Fifth and Madison) for a burger and a cup of coffee. Leaving the concrete, glass and steel skyscrapers in Midtown we head back to Greenwich Village, where the buildings are low and you can see the sky above.

## Eating & drinking

### Big Cup

*228 Eighth Avenue, between 21st & 22nd Streets (212 206 0059).* **Open** 7am-1am Mon-Thur, Sun; 7am-2am Fri, Sat. Loungey, neighbourhoody gay coffeeshop – ideal for reading the papers.

### Bendix Diner

*219 Eighth Avenue, at 21st Street (212 366 0560).* **Open** 8am-midnight daily. Popular '50s-style diner with the staples – try the desserts.

### Burger Heaven

*9 East 53rd Street, between Fifth & Madison Avenues (212 752 0340).* **Open** 7am-8pm Mon-Fri; 8am-7pm Sat; 9.30am-5pm Sun. Top ground-beef burgers in a sleek futuristic setting.

### Cajun

*129 Eighth Avenue, at 16th Street (212 691 6174).* **Open** 11am-11pm daily.

### Empire Diner

*210 Tenth Avenue, at 22nd Street (212 243 2736).* **Open** 24hrs daily; closed 4am Mon-8am Tue. The essence of preserved Americana, best sampled at night, when it glows.

### Flight Bar & Restaurant

*151 Eighth Avenue, between 17th & 18th Streets (212 229 1868).* **Open** 11am-4am daily.

### Florent

*69 Gansevoort Street, between Greenwich & Washington Streets (212 989 5779).* **Open** 9am-5am Mon-Thur, Sun; 24hrs Fri, Sat. French cuisine draws punters throughout the night.

### Havana Chelsea

*188 Eighth Avenue, between 19th & 20th Streets (212 243 9421).* **Open** 8am-10pm Mon-Sat; noon-9.30pm Sun. Hole-in-the-wall Cuban diner with a big heart.

### Hogs & Heifers

*859 Washington Street, at 13th Street (212 929 0655).* **Open** 11am-4am Mon-Fri; 2pm-4am Sat, Sun. *Deliverance* extras and genuine rednecks in this redlit dive.

### Melrose Café, Stanhope Hotel

*995 Fifth Avenue, between 80th & 81st Streets (212 650 4700).* **Open** 11.30am-10pm daily.

### Rawhide

*212 Eighth Avenue, at 21st Street (212 242 9332).* **Open** 8am-4am Mon-Sat; noon-4am Sun.

### The Viceroy

*160 Eighth Avenue, at 18th Street (212 633 8484).* **Open** 11.30am-midnight Mon-Wed; 11.30am-1am Thur, Fri; 9am-1am Sat; 9am-midnight Sun. The decor and food strike a French bistro pose with an American accent.

## Chelsea galleries

### Andrea Rosen Gallery

*525 West 24th Street, between Tenth & Eleventh Avenues (212 627 6000).* **Open** *Sept-June* 10am-6pm Tue-Sat. *July, Aug* 10am-6pm Mon-Fri.

### Art Resources Transfer

*210 Eleventh Avenue, at 25th Street (212 691 5956).* **Open** *Sept-July* 11am-6pm Tue-Sat. *Aug* 11am-6pm Tue-Fri.

### Bonakdar Jancou Gallery

*521 West 21st Street, between Tenth & Eleventh Avenues (212 414 4144).* **Open** 10am-6pm Tue-Sat.

### Chisholm-Larrson

*145 Eighth Avenue, between 17th & 18th Streets (212 741 1703).* **Open** *Sept-May* 11am-7pm Mon-Fri; 11am-6pm Sat; 1-5pm Sun. *June-Aug* 11am-7pm Tue-Fri; 11am-5pm Sat.

### Cynthia Broan Gallery

*423 West 14th Street, between Ninth &
Tenth Avenues (212 633 6525).* **Open** noon-6pm
Tue-Sat.

### Dia Center for the Arts

*548 West 22nd Street, between Tenth & Eleventh
Avenues (212 989 5566).* **Open** *mid-Sept-mid-
June* noon-6pm Wed-Sun.

### Gavin Brown's enterprise

*436 West 15th Street, between Ninth &
Tenth Avenues (212 627 5258).* **Open** 10am-
6pm Tue-Sat.

### Matthew Marks

*523 West 24th Street, between Tenth &
Eleventh Avenues (212 243 0200).* **Open**
*winter* 10am-6pm Tue-Sat; *summer* 10am-6pm
Mon-Fri.

### Metro Pictures

*519 West 24th Street, between Tenth & Eleventh
Avenues (212 206 7100).* **Open** *Sept-May* 10am-
6pm Tue-Sat. *June, July* 10am-6pm Tue-Fri.
Closed Aug.

### Pat Hearn Gallery

*530 West 22nd Street, between Tenth &
Eleventh Avenues (212 727 7366).* **Open** 11am-
6pm Tue-Sat.

### Robert Miller

*524 West 26th Street, between Tenth & Eleventh
Avenues (212 980 5454).* **Open**. *Sept-May* 10am-
6pm Tue-Sat. *June-Aug* call for hours.

### Silverstein

*520 West 21st Street, between Tenth
Avenue & West Side Highway (212 929 4300).*
**Open** *winter* 10am-6pm Tue-Sat; *summer* call for
hours.

### Sonnabend Gallery

*536 West 22nd Street, between Tenth & Eleventh
Avenues (212 627 1018).* **Open** *Sept-June* 10am-
6pm Tue-Sat. *July, Aug* 11am-5pm Tue-Fri.

### Wessel & O'Connor Gallery

*242 West 26th Street, between Seventh & Eighth
Avenues (212 242 8811).* **Open** *Sept-May* Tue-
Sun 11am-6pm. *July, Aug* 11am-6pm Mon-Fri.
*June* 11am-6pm Tue-Sat.

## Clubs & theatres

### Chicago B.L.U.E.S.

*73 Eighth Avenue, between 13th & 14th Streets
(212 924 9755).* **Open** call after 5pm for details.

### Joyce Theatre

*175 Eighth Avenue, at 19th Street (212 242
0800).* **Open** *box office* noon-7pm Mon-Sat; noon-
6pm Sun. **Other location:** Joyce Soho, 155
Mercer Street, between Houston & Prince Streets
(212 431 9233).

### Tunnel

*220 Twelfth Avenue, at 27th Street (212 695
4682).* **Open** 10pm-6am Fri; 11pm-noon Sat;
10pm-4am Sun.

### Twilo

*530 West 27th Street, between Tenth &
Eleventh Avenues (212 268 1600).* **Open** hours
vary with event.

## Museum Mile

### Cooper-Hewitt
### National Design Museum

*2 East 91st Street, at Fifth Avenue (212 849
8400).* **Open** 10am-9pm Tue; 10am-5pm Wed-
Sat; noon-5pm Sun. **Admission** $5; free 5-9pm
Tue, under-12s at all times. **No credit cards.**

### El Museo del Barrio

*1230 Fifth Avenue, between 104th & 105th
Streets (212 831 7272).* **Open** 11am-5pm
Wed-Sun. **Admission** $4; $2 concessions. **No
credit cards.**

### Goethe-Institut/
### German Cultural Center

*1014 Fifth Avenue, at 82nd Street (212 439
8700).* **Open** *library* noon-7pm Tue, Thur; noon-
5pm Wed, Sat. *Gallery* 10am-7pm Tue, Thur;
10am-5.30pm Wed; 10am-4pm Fri; noon-5pm Sat.
**Admission** free.

### Jewish Museum

*1109 Fifth Avenue, at 92nd Street (212 423
3230).* **Open** 11am-5.45pm Mon, Wed, Thur, Sun;
11am-8pm Tue. **Admission** $8; free 5-8pm Tue,
under-12s at all times. **No credit cards.**

### International Center
### of Photography

*1130 Fifth Avenue, at 94th Street (212 860
1777).* **Open** 10am-5pm Tue-Thur; 10am-8pm
Fri; 10am-6pm Sat, Sun. **Admission** $6; $4
concessions; voluntary contributions 5-8pm Fri.

### Metropolitan Museum of Art

*1000 Fifth Avenue, at 82nd Street (212 535
7710).* **Open** 9.30am-5.15pm Tue-Thur, Sun;
9.30am-8.45pm Fri, Sat. **Admission** *suggested
donation* $10; $5 concessions; free under-12s. **No
credit cards.** No pushchairs on Sundays.

## Museum of the City of New York

*1220 Fifth Avenue, at 103rd Street (212 534 1672).* **Open** 10am-5pm Wed-Sat; noon-5pm Sun. **Admission** *suggested donation* $5; $4 concessions; $10 family ticket. **No credit cards.**

## National Academy of Design

*1083 Fifth Avenue, at 89th Street (212 369 4880).* **Open** noon-5pm Wed, Thur, Sat, Sun; 10am-6pm Fri. **Admission** $8; free 5-8pm Fri, under-5s at all times. **No credit cards.**

## Solomon R Guggenheim Museum

*1071 Fifth Avenue, at 88th Street (212 423 3500).* **Open** 9am-6pm Mon-Wed, Sun; 9am-8pm Fri, Sat. **Admission** $12; $7 concessions; free under-12s; voluntary donation 6-8pm Fri.

# Other museums & galleries

## Frick Collection

*1 East 70th Street, at Fifth Avenue (212 288 0700).* **Open** 10am-6pm Tue-Sat; 1-6pm Sun. **Admission** $7; $5 concessions; under-10s not admitted, 10-16s must be accompanied by an adult. **No credit cards.**

## Katharina Rich Perlow Gallery

*13th Floor, The Fuller Building, 41 East 57th Street, between Madison & Park Avenues (212 644 7171).* **Open** 10am-6pm Mon-Fri (phone to confirm).

## Museum of Modern Art

*11 West 53rd Street, between Fifth & Sixth Avenues (212 708 9400).* **Open** 10.30am-5.45pm Mon, Tue, Thur, Sat, Sun; 10.30am-8.15pm Fri. **Admission** $9.50; $6.50 concessions; free under-16s; voluntary donation Fri. **No credit cards.**

# Parks

## Department of Parks & Recreation

*888 NY PARKS/212 360 2774.*

# Shopping

## Bang Bang

*147 Eighth Avenue, between 17th & 18th Streets (212 807 8457).* **Open** 11am-10pm Mon, Wed, Fri; 11am-11pm Thur, Sat; noon-8pm Sun.

## Brooks Brothers

*666 Fifth Avenue, at 53rd Street (212 261 9440).* **Open** 10am-8pm daily.

## Camouflage

*141 Eighth Avenue, between 16th & 17th Streets (212 741 9118).* **Open** noon-7pm Mon-Fri; 11.30am-6.30pm Sat; noon-6pm Sun.

## Disney Store

*Fifth Avenue, at 55th Street (212 702 0702).* **Open** 10am-8pm Mon-Sat; 11am-7pm Sun.

## Kitchen Market

*218 Eighth Avenue, between 21st & 22nd Streets (212 243 4433).* **Open** 9am-10.30pm Mon-Sat; 11am-9.30pm Sun. This narrow store is chock-full of Mexican goodies – including *nopales* (cactus leaves) and San Francisco-style burrito.

## p chanin

*152 Eighth Avenue, between 17th & 18th Streets (212 924 5359).* **Open** noon-9pm Mon, Tue, Sun; noon-10pm Wed; noon-11pm Thur-Sat.

# Literature & film

**Weegee's World** Weegee with Miles Barth, Ellen Handy, Alain Bergala (1997)
**Naked City** Weegee (1945)
**Naked Hollywood** Weegee with Melvin Harris (1953)
**Weegee's Creative Camera** Weegee with Roy Ald (1959)
**The Honeymoon Killers** (Leonard Kastle, 1969, US)
**Seven Beauties** (Lina Wertmüller, 1975, It)
**Pink Flamingoes** (John Waters, 1972, US)
**El Topo** (Alexandro Jodorowsky, 1971, Mex)
**La Dolce Vita** (Federico Fellini, 1960, It/Fr)

# Others

## Sports Centre at Chelsea Piers

*Pier 60 (212 336 600).* **Open** 6am-11pm Mon-Fri; 8am-9pm Sat, Sun. **Admission** day membership $35.

## Chelsea Hotel

*222 West 23rd Street, between Seventh & Eighth Avenues (212 243 3700).*

## General Theological Seminary

*175 Ninth Avenue, between 20th & 21st Streets (212 243 5150).* **Open** *gardens* noon-3pm Mon-Fri; 11am-3pm Sat. Free. You can walk through the grounds of the seminary (when open) or take a guided tour in summer (call for details).

## St Regis Hotel

*2 East 55th Street, between Fifth & Madison Avenues (212 753 4500).*

# You gotta have park

Maitland McDonagh

Come down by the Riverside.

---

**Start:** West 125th Street subway station
**Finish:** Eleanor Roosevelt statue at West 72nd Street
**Time:** 4-5 hours
**Distance:** 4.5 miles/7.5km
**Getting there:** subway trains 1 or 9 to 125th Street station
**Getting back:** subway trains 1, 2, 3, or 9 from 72nd Street station
**Note:** there is a possible detour to the American Museum of Natural History, and/or the Children's Museum of Manhattan. It should be noted, however, that this is already a long walk. Despite the length, it is suitable for children, because much of it is set in a park. Some of this walk coincides with *Town and Gown*, Rachel Wetzsteon's walk.

---

Manhattan's public parks are a welcome respite from the sensory overload that comes with living in this dense, noisy and infuriating city. Riverside is the second-largest in Manhattan (after limelight-hogging Central Park), and shares the same architect, Frederick Law Olmstead. Designed in 1880, Riverside is a relatively narrow strip of green that snakes some four and a quarter miles down Manhattan's West Side, from 158th down to 72nd Street; one day, if real-estate mogul Donald Trump has his way, it may stretch further south. It's unfortunate that most of the park's 323 acres are cut off from the Hudson River by the abominable West Side Highway, but that doesn't stop

skaters, dog walkers, bird watchers, tai chi practitioners, gardeners, runners, sunbathers, bike riders, squirrel feeders, tennis players, picnickers, ball players and people who just like to laze around outdoors from enjoying its curved expanse and tranquil beauty.

This is a hearty walk and can be done in either direction, but I recommend starting at the top; Riverside Park is built along a series of rolling slopes, and if you're headed downtown, you're mostly walking downhill. You can do this walk at any time of year, but during the winter there's not much point in visiting the deserted lower portion of the park, and the winds along Riverside Drive, which blow right off the Hudson River, are harsh.

To start uptown, take the subway to the 125th Street station. This is one of the few elevated platforms in Manhattan; the train comes above ground at 122nd Street, and by the time it reaches the 137th Street stop, it's gone back under. Head downstairs and make a right on Tiemann Place (named after 19th-century mayor Daniel Tiemann), then a left on to Claremont Avenue. Walk a block and a half on Claremont, and immediately past International House (a residence for graduate students from all over the world), take the steps up to Sakura Park.

This small park was named in honour of some 2,000 Japanese cherry trees donated by the Committee of Japanese Residents of New York (sakura means cherry blossom) to NYC parks in 1912. Cherry trees flower in the spring, and the slightest breeze sends showers of small pink petals cascading to the ground. At the top of the steps to the right is a large, stone Japanese lantern,

# You gotta have park

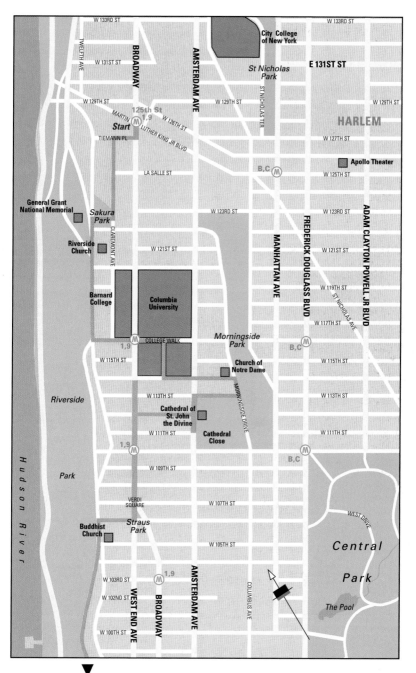

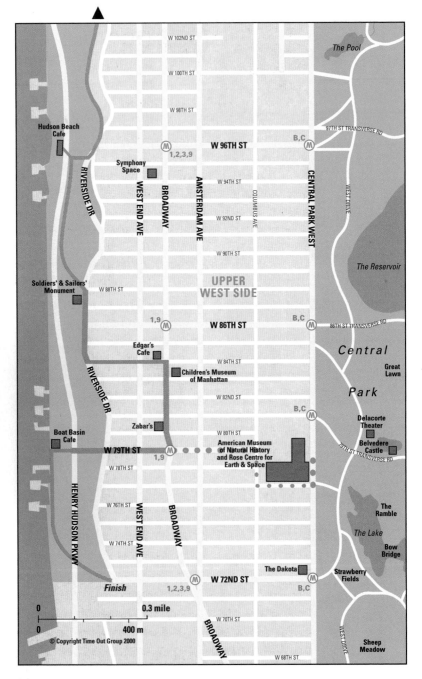

The railtrack rides overhead at **125th Street station**, delivering people to the world below.

donated by the city of Tokyo and dedicated on 10 October 1960 by then Crown Prince (now Emperor) Akihito. Once you're in Sakura Park – which locals call Cherry Park – you can see Grant's Tomb. Head for it by crossing Riverside Drive.

It's a feeble but long-standing New Yorker's idea of fun to ask some unsuspecting fool who is buried in Grant's Tomb, then cackle triumphantly: 'Nobody!' Strictly speaking, it's a mausoleum and not a grave, so no one's actually buried there. But entombed within are the 18th President of the United States, Ulysses S Grant, and his wife Julia. Back when New York City phone numbers started with exchanges (think *Pennsylvania 6-5000*), the exchange up here was Monument: Grant's Tomb was the monument. Grant was a pivotal figure during America's only civil war (1861-5), which ended when Confederate General Robert E Lee surrendered to him. Grant later served two terms as president (1868-76), and lived in New York City from 1881 to 1884. When he died in 1885, his family decided to inter him in New York rather

than Washington DC, the traditional resting place of national heroes. The mausoleum – one of the largest in the world – was erected in 1897, and was at one time among the most popular tourist attractions in New York City. Its interior houses a small museum, and the monument is surrounded on three sides by free-form, vaguely Gaudi-esque benches covered with colourful mosaic tile work. They're completely out of sync with the conventional style of the monument itself and were added in 1973; the mosaics were done by local children under the supervision of the CityArts Workshop. I grew up nearby; my sisters and I all contributed our artistic efforts (we also used to sit on the eagles that flank the entrance). Opinion on the benches is bi-polar: some hate their blobby silhouettes and child-like imagery, others are charmed. During the 1970s and '80s the memorial was sadly neglected, and in 1994 a group of Grant's descendants went complaining to a federal judge, citing its defacement by urine stains, garbage, litter and graffiti. Illinois legislators suggested bringing Grant's remains home to the state where he was born. This sabre-rattling had the desired effect, and the place is now immaculate.

You don't have to look far for the massive Riverside Church; it's right across Riverside Drive and towers over the neighbourhood. A taxi driver once snorted, as I told him to make a right at the church, 'You Americans – anyplace else in the world they'd call that thing a cathedral.' Built over the course of three years, its architecture inspired by the 13th-century French cathedral of Chartres, Riverside Church opened in 1930 and can seat 2,500; it's an interdenominational house of worship, so come one, come all. It's famous for its commitment to social activism and community outreach, and hosts a series of performing arts events. Riverside Church is chock-a-block with the usual stained glass, gargoyles and statues of saints; oddball details worthy of

The last resting place of **Ulysses S Grant** and his wife had its heyday as an attraction 100 years ago. It's nice and quiet now.

note include a slightly macabre carving of Nobel Peace Prize-winning medical missionary and theologian Dr Albert Schweitzer (1875-1965) holding a human heart (he's in a grouping of statues on the façade of the church's south wing), and three small columns topped by carvings of dopey-looking animals and humans with phones clutched to their ears (it's at the north end of the Corridor of American Churches, just by the public phones on the first floor). Created long before telephones were cut loose from their moorings, this prescient sculpture seems aimed straight at boors who use their cell phones everywhere. Riverside's 20-storey bell tower houses a 74-bell carillon that chimes on the quarter hour between the hours of 11am and 4pm; the view is spectacular, and you'll never know just how loud church bells really are until you stand next to them – remember, this church owns a 20-ton bass bell.

Exit the church on the Riverside Drive side, and stroll down to 116th Street. Make a left, and straight ahead, at the top of a two-block hill, you'll see the main entrance to Columbia University. Columbia was founded in 1754, as King's College, by royal charter of England's King George II; its mission was 'the instruction and education of youth in the learned languages and liberal arts and sciences'. It's the oldest institution of higher learning in New York state (fifth oldest in the US) and occupied three other Manhattan locations before moving to the Morningside Heights campus in 1897. The campus is bisected east to west by College Walk, which takes you past Low Memorial Library (which now houses offices and the Visitor's Center rather than books) and its statue of the Alma Mater on the north, and the Butler Library on the south; Columbia's world-famous School of Journalism is also on the South Campus. The prettier portion of the campus lies north, up the steps that flank Low. This area of the campus also houses Pupin Hall, where Columbia scientists began

'That's right... Gargoyle, **Riverside Church**...'

At Morningside and 114th Street, make a right and walk to 113th Street. You'll pass the old entrance to St Luke's Hospital (now St Luke's/Roosevelt Hospital Center); the hospital was founded in 1846, and the handsome Morningside entrance was, at the time of writing, shrouded in construction scaffolding. I strongly advise against a detour into Morningside Park to your left, which may be the most notoriously crime-ridden park in Manhattan.

Cross 113th Street and make a right: you're walking along the north end of the grounds of the Episcopal Cathedral of St John the Divine, which can be entered from Amsterdam Avenue. In addition to being the largest cathedral in the world (the nave is 601 feet long), St John's is famous for the fact that more than 100 years after construction started, it remains unfinished. This has earned it the nickname 'St John's of Perpetual Construction'. The cornerstone was laid in 1892 and the main structure opened in 1941, three weeks before Japanese planes bombed Pearl Harbor and America's consequent entry into World War II brought construction to a halt. The cathedral's twin towers were unbuilt, and its incomplete decorative elements remained untouched until 1979, when cathedral management began training unemployed neighbourhood residents as stonemasons to carve saints and grotesques. In 1982, construction resumed on the towers; it stopped again in the early '90s and the one more-or-less finished tower remains covered with scaffolding. At present, the cathedral is three-quarters finished, with no completion date in sight.

The church includes numerous chapels and bays, many with unusual themes. The seven Chapels of the Tongues pay tribute to immigrant groups, while the Communications Bay in the nave honours the mass media. Other bays contain memorials to sacred geometry, fallen firemen and victims of genocide; one contains a huge hunk of quartz crystal.

conducting atomic research in 1925, and the lovely St Paul's Chapel; between the brick-paved paths and the lush landscaping, you'd hardly know you were smack dab in the middle of Manhattan. The wide lawns and benches offer a pleasant opportunity to sit back and savour the uncanny quiet.

Come out on 114th Street (head for the Butler Library to find a path out), make a left and walk across 114th Street, whose south side is lined with brownstones housing Columbia fraternities. Between Amsterdam Avenue and Morningside Drive you'll come across the side gallery of the Roman Catholic Grotto Church of Notre Dame. The gallery, with its curved row of slender double columns, is usually open and looks on to a pretty little flower garden and a statue of the Virgin Mary. The church itself, built in 1910, has its main entrance on Morningside Drive and is almost always closed; a shame given that there's a stone replica of the grotto at Lourdes behind the altar.

The lovely grounds are patrolled by screaming peacocks; there's a rose garden, and another dedicated to plants mentioned in the Bible. My favorite sight, however, is the macabre *Peace Fountain* sculpture that supposedly celebrates the triumph of good over evil: you wouldn't know it to look at the giant crab monster and severed head. It's especially creepy at night, when it's floodlit.

Events worth noting include the celebration of the Feast of St Francis of Assisi, patron saint of animals, with a 'Blessing of the Animals' at an 11am mass on the first Sunday in October (his feast day is 4 October) – everything from house cats to circus elephants wind up on the steps; and on the first and third Saturdays of the month there's a tour to the top of the cathedral (be warned: it involves climbing up 124 feet of spiral stone stairs). It's also a haven of community activity – St John's hosts music events, silent films with organ accompaniment, dance programmes and art exhibitions.

When you're done, walk west along 112th Street. On the downtown side of the street, around the middle of the block between Broadway and Amsterdam Avenue, you might want to step into Labyrinth Books, an independent shop specialising in works of a scholarly nature.

On the north-east corner of Broadway, a pop-culture landmark awaits. If you've ever watched *Seinfeld*, you'll know that neon sign anywhere: it's Tom's Restaurant, the exterior of the joint where Jerry and the gang spent countless hours yadda-yadda-yadda-ing about nothing. The interior of the real Tom's looks absolutely nothing like the TV interior, which was shot in a California studio and is a whole lot nicer than the real thing. That guy you've seen on TV selling CDs from a stand on the corner is often there, and there's probably a poster in the window for Kramer's Reality Tour. Once

Run the gauntlet of the bell tower to see Midtown Manhattan arrayed before you from the top of **Riverside Church**.

the across-the-hall neighbour of *Seinfeld* co-creator Larry David, Kenny Kramer claims that he inspired the show's nutty Cosmo Kramer. His three-hour bus tour takes in a variety of *Seinfeld*-related locales, with running commentary from the man himself. I've never taken it, but it's reputed to be pretty entertaining. Back to Tom's: before *Seinfeld*, it was immortalised in Suzanne Vega's *Tom's Diner* ('I am sitting/In the morning/At the diner/On the corner'). Vega grew up on 102nd Street and attended Barnard College, across the street from Columbia. People come from around the world to have their pictures taken in front of the place; since the food is undistinguished, the coffee is nasty and, frankly, the staff are often rude, you might want to move on once you have your snapshot.

Cross Broadway and walk north to the West End restaurant between 113th and 114th Streets. You wouldn't know it from the current outdoor café, airy interior and smoke-free atmosphere, but this was once the hangout of Beat icons Jack Kerouac (*On the Road*), Allen Ginsberg (*Howl*) and William S Burroughs (*Naked Lunch*). Back in the 1940s it was a dark, cheap bar, the ideal venue for hard-drinking, cash-poor, angel-headed hipsters. Ginsberg and Kerouac were both former Columbia students: football-scholarship student Kerouac dropped out and joined the Navy during his sophomore year; after leaving the service he moved in with a girlfriend who was still at Columbia and who introduced him to aspiring poet Ginsberg, who'd been expelled for writing obscenities on his dorm window, and to neighbourhood eccentric Burroughs. The rest is legend: take a look inside and imagine them bellied up to that dark-wood bar, smoking and drinking and versifying. The West End (which, after being bought by the owner of Greenwich Village landmark The Village Gate, was for a while called the West End Gate) remains a popular destination for Columbia students and locals.

A few yards towards the north lies

Mondel Chocolates, one of a handful of independent candy makers left in New York City. On a nice day you could find it with your eyes shut by the smell of chocolate wafting out the open door. Run by members of the Hungarian immigrant Mondel family since it opened in 1944, this tiny shop specialises in handmade white, dark and milk chocolates in fanciful shapes. On Mother's Day, Valentine's Day and other major candy-giving holidays, the line of customers stretches out the door. Take your candy and do an about-turn. Walk back down Broadway, past the West End and down to 107th Street.

Get ready, *Titanic* buffs: this is the north end of Straus Park, a triangular patch of green at the point where Broadway and West End Avenue merge. A wealthy, elderly couple, Ida and Isidor Straus, were returning to New York from Europe in 1912; it was their misfortune to be aboard the *Titanic*. Though offered preferential lifeboat seating because of his age, Isidor refused; Ida stood by her man, handing her lifejacket and expensive necklace to her maid. The Strauses had lived for many years in a house overlooking what was then called Bloomingdale Park; in 1915 a memorial fountain was unveiled, and the park renamed in their memory.

At 106th Street, make a right, walk to the elevated part of Riverside Drive and turn left. Just before 105th Street you'll see a large statue of a Japanese man. He is Shinran Shonin (1173-1262), founder of the Jodo Shinshu Buddhist sect, and the building is a Buddhist temple founded in 1938. This statue once stood in Hiroshima; it survived the atomic bomb blast and was moved to New York in 1955.

At 104th Street, cross Riverside Drive into the park; there's a staircase between 104th and 103rd Streets that leads to the lower level of the park. Follow the path to the right on to the paved Promenade, cross the Promenade and go down one more flight of stairs by an open-air café. You're at the optimistically named

Hudson Beach Volleyball courts, where nets are set in oversized sandboxes and players often don beach gear. Overlooking the courts is the Hudson Beach Café, featuring casual food with a vaguely Mexican accent, plus Pina Coladas and Margueritas. Olé! There are also public restrooms here, worth mentioning because they're few and far between in New York City. Take advantage. (To the north is a soccer/baseball/softball field and beyond that a skateboard/rollerblade course, one of ESPN's extreme sports locations.)

Now walk south along the Promenade until it leads you back up to Riverside Drive at 96th Street. From 95th to 92nd Street between Riverside Park and the apartment buildings across the street is Joan of Arc Park, a small plot of green that's home to a statue of the Maid of Orléans. The pedestal includes stones from the cathedral where she was imprisoned before her martyrdom in 1431. Go have a look, or simply cross 96th Street and walk back down into the lower level of Riverside Park at 95th. Follow the path to the Community Garden at 91st Street (you may have seen it in *You've Got Mail*; it's where Tom Hanks and Meg Ryan kiss). On most nice weekend days, neighbourhood gardeners will be there pruning and weeding. At the south end of the small garden, make a left and walk up the curving, sloping path that will lead you to the Soldiers and Sailors Memorial Monument on the upper level of Riverside Park at 88th Street. This Civil War monument, dedicated in 1900, includes three cannons that point towards the Hudson River.

Stay up by the road and head south along the shaded sidewalk to make a left across Riverside Drive on to 84th Street. You're now on Edgar Allan Poe Street. When the street signs went up in 1980, Poe's middle name was misspelled 'Allen', but the embarrassing error was quickly corrected. Poe lived for a little more than a year (1844-5) at Brennan Mansion, on 84th between Broadway and West End

The imposing statue of **Shinran Shonin** survived Hiroshima, and now guards a temple.

Avenue; while in residence, he wrote *The Raven*. The Alameda apartment building and Café Edgar's (both 255 West 84th Street) now occupy the Brennan site; there's a plaque dedicated to Poe at the end of the building closest to Broadway, but you have to look way up to see it.

On the corner of Broadway and 84th Street, turn right and walk south. If you're with children, turn left down 83rd Street to the Children's Museum of Manhattan. Less a museum in the traditional sense than an educationally oriented play space, it offers a wide variety of kid-friendly activities, from painting and puppet shows to the interactive 'Body Odyssey' and a working TV studio.

Back on Broadway, now crowded with shops, head south for the world-famous Zabar's food and housewares emporium between 80th and 81st Streets. Founded in 1934, its specialities include such traditional Jewish comfort foods as pickled herring, lox, cream cheese, rugelach and pastrami, but it also carries an international selection of gourmet foods and coffee. It's the place to go for

offbeat kitchen items, espresso machines, fondue sets, teapots and cookware at discounted prices. It's also a world-class scene: if you want to see that notorious New York pushiness up close, try getting a number at the deli counter. Directly across the street is H&H bagels; many New Yorkers swear that H&H's bagels have Zabar's bagels beat dead to rights. You may have to conduct a taste test.

Consider yourself at a crossroads when you see the First Baptist Church of New York at 79th Street and Broadway. If you were to turn left and walk to Central Park West, you'd find yourself at the American Museum of Natural History, founded in 1869 to encourage and develop 'the study of Natural Science' by both professionals and laymen. This is where Ross of TV's *Friends* works. Originally housed in a section of the arsenal building inside Central Park, the cornerstone for the museum's present location was laid in 1874 by President Grant. It's one of the largest natural history museums in the world, and anyone who grew up in New York gets an intense nostalgic rush looking at its dusty dioramas of African wildlife. Which is not to say that the museum itself is a museum piece; its permanent collection includes a rearing, 50-foot Barosaurus skeleton; the four-and-a-half-billion-year-old Ahnighito meteorite, the largest ever retrieved from the earth's surface; a 94-foot replica of a blue whale that hangs overhead in the Hall of Ocean Life; and a mineral and gem collection that includes the famous Star of India, the largest blue star sapphire in the world. Pretty spiffy.

Right next to the museum is its sister institution, the newly opened (February 2000) Rose Center for Earth and Space. The Rose Center sits on the site of the old Hayden Planetarium, and looks uncannily like a square Lucite paperweight with a globe inside, blown up to Brobdingnagian proportions. The sphere contains two theatre spaces; the top half houses the Space Theater, which kicked off with the *Passport to the Universe* show, a virtual voyage through the universe narrated by Tom Hanks. The bottom half houses the Big Bang Theater, which features an elaborate show on the origins of the universe. The emphasis throughout is on interactivity and attention-grabbing presentations. The recently renovated 79th Street subway station is a handsome gateway to the museum: between the mosaics of poison dart frogs on the floor and the dinosaur fossil reliefs embedded in the walls, it's one of the system's handsomer stops.

If you've made the detour, try to stop into Maxilla and Mandible, on Columbus Avenue between 81st and 82nd Streets. Founded in 1983, M&M sells objects that appeal equally to those with scientific interests and those with a macabre bent. Its ever changing stock includes shells, mounted insects, African porcupine quills, ostrich eggs, small fossils (trilobites and the like) and bones – from teeth to complete skeletons. How do they get those bones so clean? The

knowledgeable and helpful staff are a little cagey, but it's been reported that there's a very large vat of maggots in the basement. In 1999, a fossilised human skull of considerable scientific value was found by M&M's staff in a recently purchased collection. Although the original was returned to paleoanthropologists in Indonesia, where it originated, the shop sells a museum-quality reproduction. But I'd suggest saving all this for another trip: Broadway to Central Park West is a hike, and you could easily spend hours in the Natural History Museum and the Rose Center.

Back at 79th Street and Broadway. Make a right and walk to Riverside Drive, then cross over to the park and follow the path under the bridge, down some stairs, through a short tunnel, and you'll emerge at the Boat Basin Café, run by the same company as the Hudson Beach Café uptown. Through the café and there's another flight of stairs to the right, which will take you down to the 79th Street Boat Basin itself (note: more restrooms). Boats can dock here overnight or indefinitely; there's a hardy community of New Yorkers who live on houseboats year round. The boat basin is one of the few places in Riverside Park where the West Side Highway doesn't cut you off from the river, and the northernmost pier is sometimes open to the public; it's a very soothing place to sit on a hot afternoon. Families of mallards swim at the water's edge. When you're tired of all this natural serenity, head south alongside the Hudson River. There's a ball field that runs parallel to the south end of the marina – walk past it, and keep going past a second set of public conveniences (an embarrassment of riches!). Take a left and head up the long and winding road that will lead you through a short tunnel and out of the park at 72nd Street. (At the time of writing, there was construction going on that will, among other things, build a

**Riverside Park** snakes down the Upper West Side – an opportunity for sun and shade.

staircase leading directly from the lower level of the park to the tunnel.)

The last site you'll see is a bronze statue of former First Lady Eleanor Roosevelt (1884-1962) encircled by a curving walkway. Roosevelt, the wife of President Franklin Delano Roosevelt (who served from 1933 to 1945), was politically active in her own right and as a delegate to the United Nations her efforts helped secure the passage of its Universal Declaration of Human Rights in 1948. The statue was unveiled in 1996, and if you'd like to end your walk with a little feminist seethe, you can meditate on the fact it was the first statue of an American woman ever commissioned for a New York City park.

# Eating & drinking

## Boat Basin Café

*West 79th Street, Riverside Park (212 496 5542).* **Open** *May-Sept* noon-midnight Mon-Fri; 11am-midnight Sat, Sun. *Oct-Apr* closed. A stone amphitheatre overlooking the moored boats on the Hudson river, this summer retreat is devoted to burgers and beer.

## Edgar's Café

*255 West 84th Street, between Broadway & West End Avenue (212 496 6126).* **Open** 11am-1am Mon-Thur, Sun; 11am-2am Fri, Sat. Elaborate salads and diabolical desserts amid the spirit of Edgar Allan Poe.

## H&H Bagels

*2239 Broadway, at 80th Street (212 595 8003).* **Open** 24hrs daily.

## Hudson Beach Café

*West 105th Street, Riverside Park (917 567 2743).* **Open** 8-11am, 3-10pm Mon-Fri; 8am-11pm Sat, Sun.

## Mondel Chocolates

*2913 Broadway, between 113th & 114th Streets (212 864 2111).* **Open** 11am-7pm Mon-Sat; 11am-6pm Sun.

## Tom's Restaurant

*2880 Broadway, at 112th Street (212 864 6137).* **Open** 6am-1.30am Mon-Wed, Sun; 24hrs Thur-Sat. A diner frequented by Columbia University students and *Seinfeld* fans, who come for the standard burger and milkshake fare.

## The West End

*2911 Broadway, between 113th & 114th Streets (212 662 8830).* **Open** 11am-3am (varies) daily. The wide draught selection still draws students from Columbia University. It holds readings and live music – jazz at the weekends.

## Zabar's

*2245 Broadway, at 80th Street (212 787 2000).* **Open** 8am-7.30pm Mon-Fri; 8am-8pm Sat; 9am-6pm Sun. Rafts of Jewish delicacies, fabulous displays of coffee, bread and cheese in this New York landmark.

# Churches & temples

## Church of Notre Dame

*405 West 114th Street, at Morningside Drive (212 866 1500).* **Open** church opens half an hour before the daily masses at 8am and noon.

## First Baptist Church of New York

*West 79th Street, at Broadway (212 724 5006).* **Services** 6.20pm Wed; 10am Sat; 9am Sun.

## The New York Buddhist Church

*331-332 Riverside Drive, between 106th & 105th Streets (212 678 0305).* **Open** 11am Sun; all other visits by appointment only.

## Riverside Church

*490 Riverside Drive, at 122nd Street (212 870 6700).* **Open** 9am-4pm daily. *Bell tower* 11am-4pm Tue-Sat; 12.30-4pm Sun.

## Cathedral of St John the Divine

*1047 Amsterdam Avenue, at 112th Street (212 316 7490).* **Open** 7am-6pm Mon-Sat; 7am-8.30pm Sun. **Services** 8am, 8.30am, 12.15pm, 5.30pm Mon-Sat; 8am, 9am, 9.30am (Spanish), 11am, 7pm Sun.

# Museums

## American Museum of Natural History/Rose Center for Earth & Space

*Central Park West, at 79th Street (212 769 5000/recorded information 212 769 5100).* **Open** 10am-5.45pm Mon-Thur, Sun; 10am-8.45pm Fri, Sat. **Admission** *suggested donation* $8; $4-$5 concessions. **No credit cards.**

## Children's Museum of Manhattan

*212 West 83rd Street, between Broadway & Amsterdam Avenue (212 721 1234).* **Open** 10am-5pm Tue-Sun. **Admission** $5.

Bucketloads of olives, baskets of bread, beanbags of coffee – visit **Zabar's** food fest.

## General Grant
## National Memorial

*Riverside Drive, at 122nd Street (212 666 1640).*
**Open** 9am-5pm daily.

## Shops

### Labyrinth Books
*536 West 112th Street, between Amsterdam
Avenue & Broadway (212 865 1588).* **Open** 9am-
10pm Mon-Fri; 10am-8pm Sat; 11am-7pm Sun.

### Maxilla & Mandible
*451 Columbus Avenue, between 81st & 82nd
Streets (212 724 6173).* **Open** 11am-7pm Mon-
Sat; 1-5pm Sun.

## Film, literature & music

**You've Got Mail** (Nora Ephron, 1998, US)
**Howl and Other Poems** Allen Ginsberg (1956)
**Naked Lunch** William S Burroughs (1959)
**On the Road** Jack Kerouac (1957)
**The Raven** Edgar Allan Poe (1845)
**Tom's Diner** Suzanne Vega from *Solitude
Standing* (1987)

## Others

### Columbia University
*Between Broadway & Amsterdam Avenue &
114th to 120th Streets (212 854 1754).*

## Kramer's Reality Tour
*starts at Pulse Theater, 432 West 42nd Street
(outside US 212 268 5525/within US 1-800
KRAMERS).* **Tour** noon Sat, Sun. **Tickets** $37.50.

## Parks

### Department of
### Parks & Recreation
*888 NY PARKS/212 360 2774.*

### Joan of Arc Park
*Riverside Drive, West 91st Street to West 95th
Street.*

### Morningside Park
*West 110th Street to West 123rd Street,
Manhattan Avenue to Morningside Drive.*

### Riverside Park
*Riverside Drive to Hudson River, West 72nd
Street to Clair Place.*

### Sakura Park
*Riverside Drive, Claremont Avenue to West
122nd Street.*

### You Gotta Have Park
*Parks throughout the city (212 360 3456).* An
annual celebration of New York's public spaces
held in May, with free events in the major parks
of all five boroughs.

# My Corona

Peter Zaremba

Flushed with the success of World's Fairs and Beatles concerts, whatever happened to Queens?

**Start:** Main Street and Roosevelt Avenue, Flushing, Queens
**Finish:** Shea Stadium, Flushing Meadows-Corona Park
**Time:** 3-4 hours
**Distance:** 4.5 miles/7.5km
**Getting there:** subway train 7 or Long Island Railroad to Flushing Main Street station
**Getting back:** subway train 7 or Long Island Railroad from Willets Point-Shea Stadium station
**Note:** avoid doing this on a Monday. Since it ends at Shea Stadium, it could precede a visit to watch the Mets.

**Main Street**, Flushing – Far Eastern energy.

Queens, the city's largest borough, doesn't lend itself easily to the strolling tourist. Even to other New Yorkers it's a sprawling *terra incognita*. The term 'Queens' itself is mostly used by sitcom scribblers and newcomers, implying a false illusion of a unified entity. Mail here is addressed neither to Queens, nor to New York, New York, but to the names of old villages and locales that for centuries were widely separated by empty spaces of fields and meadows. Only the 20th-century pressure for housing filled in the blanks, at the same time erasing most of what had been before.

One exception is Flushing, which preserved a good hunk of its long history prior to reinventing itself as one of the city's premier Asian centres. The town was settled by Quakers in 1645 and named in honour of the Dutch city where many English dissenters had found refuge prior to deciding to take their

chances in the New World. As an English town in a Dutch province, Flushing set off on its course as a place unto itself. The movement for American independence received a lukewarm reception throughout the region, and Flushing voted 4-1 against even sending a delegate to the Continental Congress. Likewise, the town overwhelmingly voted against incorporation into the City of New York in 1894. It was incorporated anyway. Even so, Flushing managed to hang on to its identity as a prosperous Long Island town, complete with its own Main Street, through most of the 20th century.

# My Corona

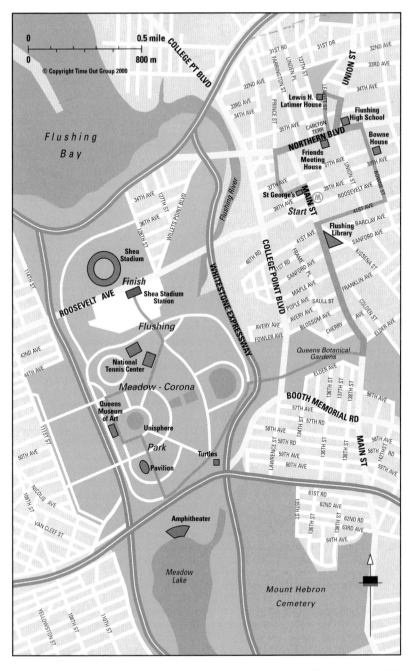

I was a relatively late arrival. My family moved to a quiet corner of Flushing in 1968, in time for me to celebrate my 13th birthday in a big old frame house with three porches and a widow's walk. Travelling out to Flushing via the No.7 train, we emerge at the corner of Roosevelt Avenue and Main Street to begin our walk. Jets boom low overhead on their way to the nearby runways of La Guardia Airport, and all sorts of commercial and bus traffic roars along the street. By the time I had left Flushing for the bright lights of 'the city' in the mid-'70s, Main Street was in serious decline. Now in many ways it's unrecognisable, having been completely revitalised with Far Eastern energy. On the north-west corner once stood the Clam Bar, hangout in the late '60s for a gang called the Skells. Due to normal gang life attrition, their menacing presence has vanished, and the site is now occupied by a one-hour photo lab. Across Roosevelt Avenue there was another haunt called the Sundowner Pub, but it's impossible to place its exact location amid the busy new Asian beauty shops and Hong Kong-style bakeries. As we've got a lot of ground to cover, we should drop into one, like King's Queens Bakery, for a quick breakfast. There are fresh red bean and taro buns to be had for a matter of cents, as well as Horlicks, which will be reassuringly familiar to British visitors. Thus fortified we can begin by turning left on Main Street and heading north. Despite its metamorphosis into a sort of Chinatown without the misery, Flushing still bears many of the hallmarks of an older small-town America. On the east side of Main Street at the corner of 39th Avenue rises the art deco Chamber of Commerce Building, built of yellow and orange brick enlivened with polychrome ceramic trim. Opposite this is the austere modern façade of the Queens County Savings Bank.

Crossing 39th Avenue places us in front of St George's Episcopal-Anglican Church, constructed in 1854 of native schist. Until very recently its slate-covered steeple was the tallest thing in downtown Flushing. The parish was organised in 1704 and is proud of the royal charter it received from George III in 1765. Despite the town's rampant Loyalism, parish vestryman Francis Lewis was an outspoken advocate of separation from England. He became one of the signatories of the Declaration of Independence, an affront for which he and his family suffered grievously. If the church happens to be open, go in. It's a cool and serene spot for a bit of meditation, or a temporary respite from the incessant noise outside.

From the church we can continue north for a few steps and then turn left at 38th Avenue, heading west along the wall of the church grounds. At the rear of the church we pass a mulberry-shaded burying ground filled with weathered stones. At the corner we can turn right and again head north on Prince Street. Flushing has had a strong African-American presence since its earliest days, and this was once the heart of the black community. Now the street has been largely given over to automotive repair shops, but here and there we can spot a holdout 19th-century residence, isolated and in much need of repair (which it shall most likely never receive). Approaching 37th Avenue we can look off to our left and in the distance see a fine Federal-style clocktower. This wasn't the site of any momentous historical event, but the factory of a long defunct zipper company. After we cross 37th Avenue we pass the modernist building of the Ebenezer Baptist Church, the second oldest black congregation in Flushing, dating from the 1850s. Much to the parishioners' credit, the old chapel was allowed to continue standing alongside the new church when it was dedicated in 1971. Continue down to the corner. Ahead were once the William Prince Nurseries, after which the street is named. Even in colonial times Flushing was noted for its nurseries, and despite the frenzied efforts of builders there are still many fine specimens of exotic trees to be seen along the streets.

At the next corner we turn right on to traffic-laden Northern Boulevard. Designated State Highway 25A, this was for a long time the main route along the north shore of Long Island. The ill-fated Nathan Hale was said to travel by here on his covert mission during the Revolution, and F Scott Fitzgerald describes Gatsby and his cortege passing this way making for their Long Island estates. Ignoring the traffic as best we can, we head into what was the core of the old village of Flushing.

Main Street terminates at the hulk of the former RKO Keith's Theater where I saw the blacksploitation epic *Mandingo*... twice. Once 'The North Shore's Finest Movie House', it's now abandoned and disgracefully stripped of its marquee, but in these multiplex days there isn't much use for silent-era movie palaces. Crossing the end of Main Street, we should immediately cross halfway to what's left of Flushing Park, greatly reduced by the constant widening of the boulevard. There used to be a much-loved cast iron fountain dedicated to Neptune on this spot, but it disappeared in the scrap-metal drives of the last World War. The circle marking its outline in the pavement was erased during recent 'renovations' of the park. Now the first thing you see is the Spanish American War Memorial, one of the few monuments in the city to this particularly unsavoury conflict. A sign notifies us that the park was renamed in honour of Daniel Carter Beard, Flushing resident and father of the American scouting movement. Walking along the narrow mall, I can't help but cast a glance to the south side of the boulevard, where excavating machines are tearing a gaping hole where once stood the notorious '60s and early '70s teen night spot the Bee Hive. Soon there will be some indistinguishable business on the site, but as youths we were warned away from here with lurid tales of spiked cocktails and incipient

drug use. As soon as we were able, we talked our way in, and were well pleased to learn that the stories were true.

A few feet further on the south side of the street stands the appropriately sober wood-shingled Friends' or Quakers' Meeting House, dating from 1694. As the sign notes, this extraordinary building has been in continuous use as a house of worship with the exception of the years 1776-83, when it was utilised as a military hospital and prison by the British Army. True to the Quakers' non-violent philosophy, I received counselling here as a possible conscientious objector during a later conflict (despite the Quakers' good intentions, I dutifully showed up in the tow of my mother to register at the local draft board). Behind the Meeting House there remains a beautiful rural graveyard, which provided a wonderfully romantic hideaway for passionate youth.

Directly in front of the Meeting House, isolated on an island in the boulevard, is the town's Civil War Monument. However indifferent the town might have been to the cause of independence, abolitionist feelings ran high here. Flushing responded forthrightly during the bloody conflict and the all-too-many names of casualties memorialised on the obelisk are entirely those of volunteers.

We cross Northern Boulevard to the monument, taking care to avoid becoming a casualty too. As we do so we notice another curiosity, a stone watering trough dating from 1909. It's been filled with concrete to guarantee its never being used for its original purpose of slaking the thirst of overworked draught animals and it was knocked askew during recent renovations of the park. At least now someone is attempting to use it as a flower planter.

Completing our crossing of the boulevard brings us to the old Flushing Town Hall, located at the corner of Linden Place. This brick neo-romanesque structure was finished just in time for the Civil War (1862), and the town's volunteer companies mustered here to depart for the carnage. Many notable people spoke here, from Frederick Douglass to PT Barnum and his diminutive buddy Tom Thumb. After Flushing's incorporation into the City of New York, the building ceased to function as a town hall, and eventually was abandoned. In 1970, as a student volunteer, I became involved in a laughable attempt to restore the decrepit structure as the grandiosely titled Flushing Anthropological Museum. Under the aegis of a 'curator' and his comic sidekick, I unwittingly shifted a 'collection' of dubious African masks from one impossibly decayed room to the next, until the curator and his assistant departed from the scene, never to return. Luckily the Town Hall was eventually restored and is again serving as a venue for cultural affairs.

Beyond the Town Hall on Northern Boulevard we see the pink marble World War Memorial. I don't know if the Angel's sword is broken by intent or accident, but the effect is just as good. Behind the memorial rise the crenellated mock-castle towers of the State Armory. In keeping with its original purpose, the Armory now houses something called the North Queens Police Task Force. Let's turn left at the corner and head north on Leavitt Street. As we pass, glance up Carlton Place at the narrow lane's rows of early 20th-century homes for an idea of what this area looked like before 'urban renewal'. When we cross 137th Street, we can see a pleasant frame house sitting alone, surrounded by gardens and a formidable chain-link fence. This was the home of electrical pioneer Lewis H Latimer, moved here in 1988 to spare it the fate of hundreds of similar houses in Flushing. The self-educated son of runaway slaves, Latimer developed the carbon filament that greatly enhanced the practicality of the first electric light bulb, and drew up the plans for the patent of Alexander Graham Bell's first telephone.

Cross Levitt Street in front of the house and turn right up 34th Road, which is lined with run-down pre-war apartment buildings. We'll turn right again at the end of the block on to Union Street and proceed to the corner with Northern Boulevard. To the left across 35th Avenue we see Flushing High School, where I posed as a student from 1970 to 1973, until they gave me a diploma to get rid of me. This venerable institution was founded in 1875, the first free public secondary school in what is now New York City. The present beige-coloured structures and tower date from 1913 and have a nice pseudo-Oxfordian air about them. The Ramones may have gone to 'Rock and Roll High School' in Forest Hills, but Flushing was attended by Andy Shernoff, who popularised the term 'punk rock' in his fanzine *Teenage Wasteland* and whose group the Dictators released what many consider to be the first LP of the genre. Passing before its imposing front, we can see that the school is set back behind fine old trees, including a large weeping beech that you can spy as we reach the eastern end of the campus. According to school lore, this land was deeded for its construction on the proviso that this tree never be cut down. If this is true, I can imagine the Board of Education's legal department staying up many a sleepless night trying to figure out a way to rid themselves of the expansion-stymying tree.

If we continued east on Northern Boulevard we would eventually be stopped where the island ends at Orient Point, some 100 miles distant. Instead we'll turn right across the boulevard, at the beginning of Bowne Street. On the corner, also built of buff brick, is the YMCA. Constructed in 1906, it's still going strong, and as the Village People so astutely observed, 'you can stay there'. If you're in need of lunch, the Kum Gang San Restaurant is just a few doors down, where a Korean barbecue, a waterfall and other wonders await you.

Relics of old Flushing – the **Kingsland Mansion** and Weeping Beech (top) and **Bowne House**.

As we walk south on the west side of Bowne Street we come to a large irregularly shaped stone marking the site of the 'Fox Oaks' under which George Fox, the founder of the Society of Friends or Quakers preached in 1672. There are still oaks here, magnificent trees that form a leafy canopy over the street. At the next corner, 37th Avenue, we'll turn left, crossing Bowne Street and into the Margaret Carman Green, a shady retreat for chatting retirees and recovering drug addicts. Walking straight ahead, we exit the small park and see a pale yellow wooden house to our left. This is the Kingsland Homestead, built in 1774 and originally situated atop a pleasant knoll several blocks east of its present site. The house was moved here in 1968 when the knoll was removed to make way for a less than essential shopping centre. It's now the HQ of the Queens Historical Society. Right behind the house is the landmark Weeping Beech. This colossal tree was grown from a shoot brought from Belgium in 1847 by Samuel Parsons, whose Flushing nurseries also supplied the trees for Central and Prospect Parks. The main trunk died in 1997, but a ring of auxiliary trunks live on. Until the Kingsland Homestead was parked next to it, you could make a complete circuit of the immense tree, but now we must retreat back through the green to Bowne Street.

We make a left at the street and there crouched behind a stone farm wall we find an old English 'salt box' house.

Unlike the Kingsland Mansion, the Bowne House is right where it's been since 1661, making it the oldest existing structure in Queens. Its builder, John Bowne, came to prominence in 1662, when Quakers secretly met at his house and in woods nearby. Contrary to Flushing's charter of 1645 (which promised 'Liberty of Conscience'), and the Flushing Remonstrance of 1657, the Dutch governor Peter Stuyvesant fined Bowne for harbouring these disturbers of the peace. Bowne refused to pay, and was banished to Holland. His trial and acquittal there, and subsequent return to Flushing, signalled the culmination of a long struggle for freedom of worship in the town.

Continuing down Bowne Street we cross 38th Avenue. On the opposite corner there's a large boulder dumped here by the ice age glaciers. It bears the dates 1620-1920, commemorating the 300th anniversary of the landing of the Pilgrims at Plymouth, Massachussetts. A beautiful New England-style Congregational Church of their brethren once stood here, but it fortuitously burned down in the early '70s to make way for the high-rise nursing home we now see.

As we approach the corner of Roosevelt Avenue we pass the sombre red-brick Reformed Church to our left, the established religion of New Netherlands that Bowne and his friends had run afoul of.

I can't bear to go any closer to my old neighbourhood, so after crossing over the sunken tracks of the Long Island Railroad, we leave Bowne Street by turning right on to 41st Avenue. We pass between rows of '60s-era apartment buildings that give way to a jumble of old and new after we again cross Union Street. There's a row of not-so-bad new businesses running along on our right – at least the builder had the decency not to tear down the trees that line the street.

At this point a growing thirst reminds me that my favourite taverns, in fact every tavern, has vanished. However, just before plunging once again into the frantic bustle of Main Street, the sharp eye is rewarded with the most welcome sight of Kelly's Pub. Perhaps it's been overlooked by the forces of change due to its minuscule size, but the survival of this 1930s bar, in a form more Irish than ever before, seems no less remarkable than that of the Bowne House.

After a few $1.50 mugs of beer the thought of escaping on the transportation bonanza waiting just a few steps away on Main Street might seem tempting.

Despite some evidence to the contrary, water quality in the **Flushing River** is improving.

However, there's a lot left to see and who knows when we'll be this way again. Are you still with me?

We continue on 41st Avenue towards the Long Island Railroad station and turn left at the corner. This is the start of Kissena Boulevard, also laden with eateries such as a branch of the reputable Vietnamese restaurant Pho Bang, and the intriguing ABC American Cooking, which serves up 'Hong Kong Style' versions of classics like lobster thermidor and chicken Maryland. On the narrow triangle of land formed by the intersection of Kissena and Main stands the new, glass-walled Flushing Library (1998), a very creditable piece of postmodern architecture. In the basement, there's a modest display on the library's history and the Remonstrance, but the original document they once proudly preserved has been removed to Albany. Crossing in front of the library and down the granite steps we are again on Main Street. Turning left, we soon pass Sanford Avenue, where we can look left at the white-columned portico of the Windsor School, housed in the type of mid-19th-century mansion that was until recently common in this area. The congregation of the Flushing Free Synagogue met here until the construction of the adjacent brick temple in 1917. As we cross Sanford Avenue we are met with more columns, those of the dignified Federal-style Flushing Central Post Office (1932). At the corner, there's a plaque affixed to a maple-shaded boulder honouring the postal workers of the town who fell in World War II. Inside the lobby we can mail any postcards picked up along the way, or have a look at the WPA murals of north Queens communities including one depicting Plains Indians on horseback in neighbouring Corona (were they lost?). Although no one at the post office now recalls it, a specimen of the postage stamp issued to commemorate the 300th anniversary of the Flushing Remonstrance was once displayed here.

From here it's all downhill (literally) as we pass oriental fruit stalls and sidewalk food vendors on our trip down Main Street. The Far East goes out with a bang at the corner of Franklin Street in the form of the lavish East Lake Restaurant, which grew from a typical roadside diner. The tanks of exotic wok-bound fish in its foyer make it seem a little like an aquarium. After this, the flavour of Main Street turns distinctly South Asian, with halal meat markets and the sweet scents from the Indian shops perfuming the air. If it's hot enough, you can grab a kulfi from the sidewalk freezer in front of the House of Spices. Restaurants like the Choopan Kabab House do a brisk business catering skewers of meats and pilaf to a growing Afghani population. We pass successive cross-avenues named in alphabetical order for the trees and shrubs that flourished here when it was the site of Parson's vast nurseries: Blossom, Cherry, Dahlia…

Since the Latimer House was conveniently moved for us there's no need to proceed to Holly Avenue. Instead, at Elder we say goodbye to Main Street. Unlike other Main Streets that are withering across the country, it has transformed itself and thrived. Here we turn right and enter the gates of the Queens Botanical Gardens, which has its origins in the Gardens on Parade exhibit of the 1939-40 World's Fair. It occupies part of the corridor of parkland following the former course of Ireland's Creek, a tributary of the Flushing River that still runs beneath us as a storm sewer. Long ago my mother lent her two green thumbs to the gardens as a volunteer. I never bothered to come to admire her work, so this is also my first time here. We proceed through the visitors' centre, where no one remembers her, and straight along the path to the Bee Garden on our left. Satisfied that our little friends are working hard enough, we look to our right. Here we can discern a statue sadly hidden in the brush at the rear of the Wedding Garden, one of the 19th-century religious sculptures loaned to the garden by the Brooklyn Museum in the hope that they would never be given back.

Before we ponder the poignant scene much further, let's exit the garden by the gate thoughtfully provided for us here and proceed along the path to our right through the Arboretum. Following the path through the orchards and field, we come upon a pedestrian bridge that will carry us over College Point Boulevard and into Flushing Meadows, the city's most used park and site of two World's Fairs. Appropriately, we enter by having to walk beneath the rumbling traffic of the elevated Whitestone Expressway, one of no fewer than six highways that slice through the park's 1,200 acres.

Thirty-five years after the last World's Fair closed, the park still has the look of the former site of something important. Ahead on Fowler's Path lies a large reflection pool fed by piping the Flushing River underground, flanked by two lofty flagpoles that are relics of the 1939-40 Exposition. Before reaching the pool, we'll turn left on Avenue E. We follow it along as it makes a broad arc, somewhere passing over the river as it flows beneath us marking the ancient boundary between Flushing and Newtown. If you like, we can cut across the field on our left to where the river emerges. The large turtles that sink into its murky waters at our approach signal a definite improvement in the water quality. This less than prime corner of the fairgrounds was the site of me and my sister's favourite exhibit, the Best Living Pavilion, three floors of salesmen pushing miracle stain-removers, and amazing nozzles that would give you dozens of glasses of soda from a single bottle.

Further on, the river widens into some large man-made lakes where a classmate of mine was knocked unconscious with an oar and drowned during a school outing in 1968. I wasn't present then and won't go there now. Instead we stay on Avenue E

until it ends at 3rd Street and make a left. This brings us to the Long Island Expressway, a terminally clogged artery servicing the endless suburbia stretching eastward. With the park's flat unloveliness all around us, it's evident that our schools of landscape design aren't turning out any Frederick Law Olmsteds these days. No one seems to mind and, to be fair, the entire place was reclaimed from a despoiled marsh, the 'valley of ashes' described by F Scott Fitzgerald in *The Great Gatsby*. We travel on with the Expressway to our left until we reach an overpass leading to the lakes. Rather than take the overpass we head right at its base and after a few hundred feet arrive at the site of the Vatican Pavilion (1964-65). Luckily, the memorial takes the form of a large stone sofa and we can sit down. Inscriptions note the visit of Pope Paul VI (I waved) and the exhibition here of Michelangelo's *Pietà*, which I was lucky enough to admire before additional work was done upon it by a mad Hungarian artist.

Sitting here we face the massive concrete towers of the dangerously deteriorating New York State Pavilion. Now barricaded and closed, it was once the scene of rock concerts, including a riotous coupling of the MC5 and the Stooges on the night of 29 August 1969.

From here we have no trouble finding our way along 2nd Street to the Unisphere, the 140-foot-high stainless-steel globe that was the symbol of the 1964-65 fair. Surrounded by a still functioning fountain, it's fared far better than the New York State Pavilion, but was also the focus of much teenage ferment in the ill-omened summer of 1969.

Bearing left around the fountain we see the former New York City Pavilion, the only surviving structure from the 1939-40 fair. Now the Queens Museum, it houses contemporary art exhibits, a roller rink and, more interestingly, a huge, regularly updated scale model of the entire city. The building was the seat of the United

Nations until the present headquarters were completed in 1950.

Turning right at this building we head north on 1st Street and soon find ourselves amid the cedars of the Israel-America Friendship Grove. A tablet here, at the start of Yitzhak Rabin Walk, recalls that the United Nations sanctioned the creation of the Jewish state while in session in Flushing on 29 November 1947. We hit North Boulevard and make another right.

On our left is the USTA National Tennis Center, the overblown complex that replaced the much classier West Side Club in nearby Forest Hills as the home of the US championship games (US Opens). Its centrepiece is the Arthur Ashe Stadium, a much more fitting tribute to the tennis great than wedging his statue in among those of a lot of Confederate generals. The stadium dwarfs the former Singer Bowl, another leftover of the last fair, where Jimi Hendrix, The Doors and the Jeff Beck Group made sensational appearances in the summer of '68. In solar oven-like heat I sweltered through the summer of '73 as the foreman of a mutinous crew of pot-smokers readying the bowl for its rededication as Louis Armstrong Stadium. Things had changed and there followed a mercifully short series of concerts featuring the likes of Edgar Winter and Sly Stone.

Following the perimeter of the tennis centre, we make a left on Avenue A, which soon brings us to the plaza that served as the main entrance for millions of fair-goers awed by yesterday's vision of tomorrow. The plaza is decorated with fair-themed mosaics, including one listing the contents of the time capsule buried during the last fair. I could lead you on one last detour around the pitch 'n' putt golf course to our right, and then we could have an Ecuadorian dinner under the trees, cross the dam that made the reclamation of the meadows possible and see an ersatz waterfall with dyed blue water. But it's been a long haul.

In front of the plaza is a broad ramp that will carry us over the train yards and bus depot that somehow also

The creation – the huge **Unisphere** under construction for the 1964-65 World's Fair...

... in **Flushing Meadow Corona Park**
where it still dominates the skies

muscled in on park land. The depot is named in honour of Casey Stengel. In 1962 the beloved Stengel was hauled out of much-deserved retirement to manage the new Metropolitan Ball Club, whose dazzling ineptitude on the field caused him to despair, 'Can't anyone here play this game?' Dead ahead of us is their home, Shea Stadium, first of the so-called 'cookie cutter' stadiums and for my money the worst ballpark in the major leagues. I'll never forgive the fact that the historic Polo Grounds in Harlem were demolished when the Mets moved to Shea and I've been so reluctant to enter the stadium that I turned down the chance to see the Beatles there with my sister on 15 August 1965 (the Fab Four would appear there once again on 23 August 1965).

From up on the ramp there's a nice view of Flushing, which now has its own skyline as well as the unusual double-decked drawbridge that carries the No.7 train into town. It's just a few more steps to the Shea Stadium station and a train back to Manhattan, or you can jump on the Long Island Railroad, which will breeze you back to Penn Station in less than 15 minutes. I'll say my farewells here; after all, as I said, who knows when we'll be back this way again.

# Eating & drinking

### ABC Hong Kong Style American Cooking
*41-13 Kissena Boulevard, at Main Street, Flushing, Queens (718 461 1313).* **Open** 11am-2.30am daily.

### Choopan Kabab House
*43-27 Main Street, Flushing, Queens (718 539 3180).* **Open** 11.30am-11.30pm daily. Afghani cuisine.

### East Lake
*42-33 Main Street, at Franklin Avenue, Flushing, Queens (718 539 8532).* **Open** 9am-2am daily.

### House of Spice
*42-75 Main Street, at Blossom Avenue, Flushing, Queens (718 539 2214).* **Open** 9.30am-8pm daily.

### Kelly's Pub
*136-11 41st Avenue, between Main Street & Kissena Boulevard, Flushing, Queens (718 359 9668).* **Open** 8am-4am daily.

### King's Queens Bakery
*135-46 Roosevelt Avenue, at Main Street, Flushing, Queens (718 888 9311).* **Open** 24hrs daily.

### Kum Gang San
*138-28 Northern Boulevard, at Union Street, Flushing, Queens (718 461 0909).* **Open** 24hrs daily. The best Korean barbecue this side of Seoul. Don't play safe with just the marinated beef, strike out to the seafood options.

### Pho Bang
*41-07 Kissena Boulevard, at Main Street, Flushing (718 939 5520).* **Open** 10am-10pm daily. Try one of 16 soups in this popular Vietnamese restaurant, and cap it all with a traditional sweet coffee.

# Accommodation

### Flushing YMCA
*138-46 Northern Boulevard, at Bowne Street, Flushing (718 961 6880).* **Open** *office* 8am-9pm Mon-Fri; 9am-4pm Sat; 11am-4pm Sun.

# Gardens & parks

### Corona Park
*Between Northern Boulevard & Jewel Avenue.*

### Department of Parks & Recreation
*888 NY PARKS/212 360 2774.*

### Queens Botanical Garden
*43-50 Main Street, Flushing (718 886 3800).* **Open** *Apr-Oct* 8am-6pm Tue-Fri; 8am-7pm Sat, Sun; *Nov-Mar* 8am-4.30pm Tue-Sun; closed Mon except legal holidays.

# Museums & galleries

### Bowne House
*37-01 Bowne Street, between 37th Avenue & Northern Boulevard, Flushing, Queens (718 359 0528).* **Open** under renovation until at least 2001, but there are still tours available – phone for details.

### Flushing Town Hall
*137-35 Northern Boulevard, at Linden Place, Flushing (718 463 7700).* **Open** 9am-5pm Mon-Fri; noon-5pm Sat, Sun.

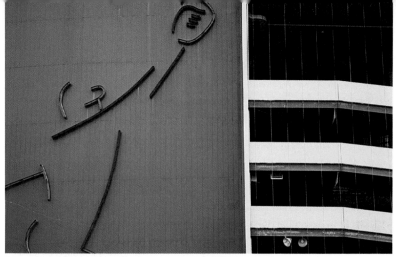

Despite being boycotted by the author in 1965, **Shea Stadium** survives to this day.

### Kingsland House/Queens Historical Society/ Weeping Beech Park

*143-35 37th Avenue, at Parsons Boulevard, Flushing (718 939 0647).* **Open** 2.30-4.30pm Tue, Sat, Sun. **Admission** $3. **No credit cards**.

### Lewis H Latimer House

*34-41 137th Street, at Leavitt Street, Flushing (718 961 8585).* **Open** open to public summer 2000.

### Queens Museum of Art

*New York City Building, Flushing Meadows-Corona Park (718 592 9700).* **Open** 10am-5pm Wed-Fri; noon-5pm Sat, Sun. **Admission** *suggested donation* $4; $2 concessions; free under-5s. **No credit cards**.

## Public services

### Flushing Central Post Office

*136-23 Main Street, at Franklin Avenue, Flushing (718 321 6822).* **Open** 8.30am-8.30pm Mon-Fri; 8.30am-5pm Sat.

### Flushing Library

*41-17 Main Street, at Kissena Boulevard, Flushing (718 661 1200).* **Open** 10am-8pm Mon; 1-8pm Tue; 10am-6pm Wed; 10am-6pm Thur, Fri; 10am-5pm Sat.

## Religion

### Bowne Street Community Church

*143-11 Roosevelt Avenue, at Bowne Street, Flushing, Queens (718 359 1553/0758).* **Open** *service* 10am Sun.

### Ebenezer Baptist Church

*36-12 Prince Street, between 36th Road & Northern Boulevard, Flushing (718 353 6236).* **Open** 11am-1pm Sun.

### Free Synagogue of Flushing

*41-60 Kissena Boulevard, between Sandford Avenue & Main Street, Flushing, Queens (718 961 0030).* **Open** *services* 8.15pm Fri.

### Friends' Meeting House

*137-16 Northern Boulevard, between Main & Union Streets, Flushing (718 358 9636).* **Open** by appointment only.

### St George's Episcopal-Anglican Church

*135-32 38th Avenue, at Main Street, Flushing (718 359 1171).* **Open** 11.30am-1.30pm daily.

## Stadiums

### Shea Stadium (New York Mets)

*123-01 Roosevelt Avenue, at 126th Street, Flushing (718 507 8499).* **Open** *information & tickets* 9am-5.30pm Mon-Fri. **Tickets** $12-$30.

### USTA National Tennis Center (US Open)

*Flushing Meadow (718 760 6200/tickets 888 673 6849).* **Date** late Aug-early Sept. **Tickets** $33-$69 day tickets.

## Literature & film

**The Great Gatsby** F Scott Fitzgerald (1925)
**Rock 'n' Roll High School** (Allan Arkush, 1979, US)

# Rock & roll shopping spree

Anna Sui

One-stop shopping for all your pop-style needs.

> **Start:** Fifth Avenue at 12th Street
> **Finish:** Fressen restaurant on West 13th Street
> **Time:** 1-2 hours
> **Distance:** 1 mile/2km
> **Getting there:** subway train F to 14th Street station.
> **Getting back:** subway trains A, C or E from 14th Street station.
> **Note:** most shops in this area open around 11am and close around 8pm, Sundays included.

I'm known as a major shopaholic. Of course I have my favourite high-fashion haunts all over town, but when I need a quick fashion fix sometimes I just go right around the corner from my apartment to 8th Street. I live in the West Village and some of my favourite venues for downtown rock style are located right here.

Before we start on our tour of some of my secret neighbourhood favourites, let's get our bearings. Looking downtown you will see the Washington Arch, designed in 1889 by Stanford White for the centenary of George Washington's inauguration. It marks the central entrance to Washington Square Park (where Henry James' *Washington Square* is set) and the centrepiece of the New York University district. NYU dormitories and offices are sprinkled all around this area. On the corner here you will find the tiny Forbes Magazine Galleries, the legacy of the company's founder, Malcolm Forbes. This

eccentric collection displays a mix of 200 objects by the Russian court jeweller Fabergé (including a dozen Fabergé eggs; the Kremlin only has 11!); 12,000 toy soldiers in elaborate dioramas; a large model boat collection, and a wide-ranging selection of original Presidential correspondence dating from George Washington to Ronald Reagan. This small museum is not usually crowded and is always a hit with everybody.

The beautiful First Presbyterian Church between 11th and 12th Streets was built in 1844 in the perpendicular Gothic style. It was modelled after the Church of St Saviour in Bath, England, although the tower is a replica of Magdalen College tower in Oxford.

Continue down to 8th Street, and turn right. The long block between Fifth and Sixth Avenues (called Avenue of the Americas to confuse you) has traditionally been one of the main thoroughfares of Greenwich Village bohemia from the 19th century through the hippie heyday of the 1960s and on until today. In 1914, sculptor Gertrude Vanderbilt Whitney (Gloria Vanderbilt's aunt) set up an art studio here at No.8 West 8th Street. She also founded the Whitney Museum of American Art at this location in 1931 (it moved to its present site on Madison Avenue in 1954). The building is now used by the New York Studio School. Classes in drawing, painting and sculpture are held here. They often hold open life-drawing classes in the evening that anyone can attend.

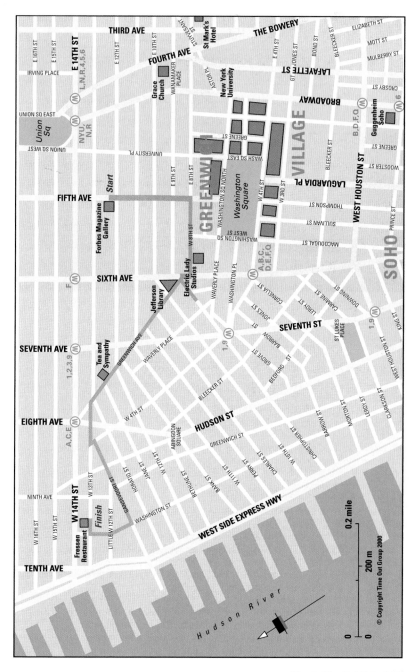

**Enz** on West 8th Street – packed with fashion accessories, including Sid Vicious's boots.

Cross the street and head for Nos.27 and 29, the first stops on this shopping spree. You will notice this block specialises in inexpensive, trendy Club Kid-wear and classic rock-and-roll gear. Here you will find lots of cheap shoe stores, Indian import emporiums and 'head shops' full of rock T-shirts, punky studded belts and wristbands, silver heavy metal skull rings and rave-style plastic jewelry – catering to all the Pop Music Tribes – mixed among tattoo parlours, fast food joints and comic book stores.

I discovered L'Impasse quite by accident (upstairs at No.29). At first look, the shop seemed to blend-in with the rest of the street, but at closer inspection, an elevated sensibility is definitely at play here. I imagine rap star divas like L'il Kim and Foxy Brown shop here. It stocks the most over-the-top selection of flashy colours, slinky fabrics and all the pastel fur, fluorescent snakeskin or spangled spandex you could ever want – in the trampiest Barbarella halters, tube-tops and mini-skirts, not to mention wild glitter make-up, wigs in primary colours

and disco feather boas. It's just so much fun. Last Christmas I bought a pale lavender rabbit-fur halter-top for Naomi Campbell here.

Next door, Petit Peton stands out as my favourite among the deluge of shoe stores traditionally found on this block. It specialises in the most outrageous bejewelled, feathered and pink mink mules (and the highest spike heels!) that go from glam rock to streetwalker. They also currently have a small selection of men's shoes with all the up-to-the-minute Techno-details, square toes and startling colours you won't find everywhere.

Further along at No.61 is Funhouse, two floors of everything any self-respecting Goth kid needs – from velvet Renaissance Fair dresses to black satin vampire capes and ruffled poet shirts. Don't forget to stock up on white kabuki makeup and black lipstick.

Opposite at No.48 is Enz. Among the wealth of fashion accessories on display is a pair of boots that belonged to Sid Vicious, visible behind the counter. Continue west on the south side. At No.52

**Electric Lady Sound Studios**, founded by Jimi Hendrix in 1970 and still in use today.

is the location of Jimi Hendrix's recording studio. Electric Lady Sound Studios was founded by him in 1970 and is still in use. In 1992 I did a photo shoot here with Naomi Campbell for *W Magazine* in the bathrooms, whose stalls are still decorated with original psychedelic magazine collages from the 1970s. One of the studios here has an adorable mural of two blonde girls at the control panel/sound board of a spaceship navigating through a rainbow sky. Hendrix also kept an apartment in back, even though he lived nearby. The building's owners have recently removed the original barrel-shaped brick exterior that used to jut out into the street. The current studio's management (along with the New York Landmark Society and Hendrix fans) tried to save this eccentric detail, since the building would have been eligible for landmark status this year, but to no avail. Some of the hundreds who have recorded here include: Aerosmith, the Beastie Boys, Chuck Berry, Blondie, Lou Reed, David Bowie, The Clash, Cher, Miles Davis, Alice Cooper, Joan Jett, the Rolling Stones, Kiss,

T Rex, The Ramones and Talking Heads.

Next door at No.54, TLA Video is in the space that used to be the 8th Street Theater (don't bother looking, there's nothing left) but this is where they originally played midnight shows of *The Rocky Horror Picture Show* and wild costumed, interactive audiences used to line up on the sidewalk. The tradition carries on at the Cinema Village on weekend nights.

Negotiate your way across Sixth Avenue to Christopher Street to find my absolute favourite perfume shop, Aedes de Venustas (at No.15, downstairs). This is one of those hidden, chic neighbourhood shops that specialises in the most wonderful high-end scented candles, soaps, pot-pourri and bath/skin-care products you can imagine. I always stock-up on Agraria 'bitter orange' incense and Mariage Freres 'Himalayan rose' scented candles. Treat yourself! Further along is Amalgamated Home (two locations at Nos.9 and 19), known for *Wallpaper\** magazine-style furniture, decorative arts and hardware. Opposite, Matt McGhee (at

No.22) has gorgeous old-world hand-blown Christmas ornaments all-year-round and, retracing your steps to Greenwich Avenue, you'll pass Geppetto's Toy Box (at No.10), perfect for way-above-average dolls, books and teddy bears for the kids.

Back at Greenwich Avenue and ahead of you across the street is the back of our architecturally beautiful Public Library (it was once voted America's fifth most beautiful building). Built in 1907, it was originally the Jefferson Market Courthouse. Where the community garden now grows there used to stand an art deco-style women's prison (torn down in 1974). The remaining building was also scheduled to be torn down but thankfully was saved by the efforts of concerned local residents, including poet ee cummings, and was converted into a public library in 1961.

Turn left and continue west on Greenwich Avenue. These blocks between Sixth and Seventh Avenues harbour a few more cool shops. I'm always scouring flea markets and vintage shops for inspiration.

Star Struck at No.47 is a great venue for both women's and men's clothes. They have a good eye, especially for the 1950s through the 1970s – great denim, cowboy shirts and circle skirts – and so are a good resource for those interested in the current swing dance craze.

In a film-obsessed town like New York, there are of course several excellent video rental/retail shops. Among those in-the-know (like Martin Scorcese), World of Video is considered a top-notch favourite. It specialises in classics, cult and world-cinema choices along with all the current titles. The staff are friendly and knowledgeable.

Across the street is Bangally African Expo. While working on one of my collections I began looking to Africa for inspiration. My research led me here, to one of the best importers of African goods in New York. I'm currently fascinated by multicoloured leather goods from the Tuareg tribes of the Sahara Desert in Niger. I love the intricate cut-out appliques and fringes in mixes of celedon green and blood red. They also specialise

**Geppetto's Toy Box** on Christopher Street, chock-full of toys, teddies, books and dolls.

in gorgeous textiles, clothing and the best
assortment of glass beads.

Further along at No.48, Tibet Kailash is
my favourite importer of shawls, jewellery
and textiles. This small shop has the best
colour selection of luxurious pashmina
shawls, plus those beautiful Pakistani
wedding shawls with flowers embroidered
on wool. All summer I wear their cotton or
silk embroidered Indian *kurta* tops.

Further along at No.66 is Be Seated –
pop in for Mexican Day of the Dead
figurines, Indonesian batik fabric, kilim
pillow-covers from Turkey and the most
unusual baskets. Across the street is Our
Name Is Mud, where model Kirsty Hume
once had a fun birthday party – we sat at
tables and painted glazes on blank
ceramic cups or plates and picked them
up several days later after they were
fired. I painted hot-rod flames on my cup
and saucer and still admire it on my
kitchen shelf.

Now that we've exhausted ourselves
shopping let's get something to eat. Cross
Seventh Avenue to a stretch of Greenwich
Avenue with some popular inexpensive
eateries. For the expatriate English
community and anglophile New Yorkers,
Tea and Sympathy (at No.108) offers
British home cooking: apple, stilton and
walnut salad, bangers and mash, treacle
pudding with custard and ginger beer. I
recently heard that they're opening a third
shop on this block featuring a take-out
fish and chips counter. Across the street
Benny's decor has the look of a rec room
circa 1975 and is full of NYU students
enjoying Cal/Mex burritos the size of your
thigh at great prices. (They both offer
take-out at separate storefronts.)

If you really want to splurge, take a
short walk through the little park at the
end of Greenwich Avenue, across Eighth
Avenue and on to Gansevoort Street. This
is the Meatpacking District. Very early in
the morning (when you're tripping home
from some nightclub) you can still see the
arrival of whole carcasses of beef
delivered to the warehouses in this

**Public Library** – saved from demolition.

neighbourhood, and the smell of raw meat
still infuses the air throughout the heat of
the day. Late at night these cobblestoned
streets are full of transvestite hookers and
the denizens of nearby S&M bars. These
blocks are also the host of newly hip
restaurants, art galleries and shops – a
wander down Gansevoort Street passes
the ever popular French diner Florent and
the Gansevoort gallery. Of the fashionable
shops cropping up all over this area, a
particular favourite of mine is Breukelen
at 68 Gansevoort Street. I had seen some
adorable pop-art handbags they carried in
some magazine and had to have one. The
shop mainly carries chic objects for the
modern home.

Beyond Washington Street you come to
the Hudson River and a view across to
New Jersey, but I tend to turn north on
Washington and then on to 13th Street to
my absolute favourite restaurant, Fressen.
It specialises in what's freshest in the
market that day and only uses organic,
free-range ingredients. The decor is very

**Tea and Sympathy** – home from home.

Scandinavian Zen modern, a relaxing conclusion to this tour of my favourite neighbourhood shops and restaurants. I urge you to develop your own tour.

## Eating & drinking

### Benny's Burritos
*113 Greenwich Avenue, at Jane Street (212 727 0584).* **Open** 11.30am-11pm Mon-Fri, Sun; 11.30am-midnight Sat. Delivers some of the best Cal-Mex in Manhattan – huge burritos.

### Benny's Burritos To-go
*112 Greenwich Avenue, between 12th & 13th Streets (212 633 9210).* **Open** 11.30am-11pm Mon-Fri, Sun; 11.30am-midnight Sat.

### Carry On Tea and Sympathy
*110 Greenwich Avenue, between 12th & 13th Streets (212 807 8329).* **Open** 11.30am-10pm Mon-Fri; 9.30am-10pm Sat, Sun.

### Florent
*69 Gansevoort Street, between Greenwich & Washington Streets (212 989 5779).* **Open** 9am-5am Mon-Thur, Sun; 24hrs Fri, Sat. French cuisine draws punters throughout the night – a *TONY* 100.

### Fressen
*421 West 13th Street (no sign), at Washington Street (212 645 7775).* **Open** 6pm-midnight Mon-Thur; 6.45pm-1am Fri, Sat. Creative American fare in an arresting setting – the 1999 *TONY* winner for best decor.

### Tea and Sympathy
*108 Greenwich Avenue, between 12th & 13th Streets (212 807 8329).* **Open** 11.30am-10pm Mon-Fri; 9.30am-10pm Sat, Sun. A taste of the UK, and a fine one at that.

## Film & music

### Electric Lady Sound Studios
*52 West 8th Street, between Fifth & Sixth Avenues (212 677 4700; www.electricladystudios.com).*

### World of Video
*51 Greenwich Avenue, between Charles & Perry Streets (212 691 1281).* **Open** 11am-10pm Mon-Thur; 11am-11pm Fri, Sat; noon-9pm Sun.

### Cinema Village
*22 East 12th Street, between Fifth Avenue & University Place (212 924 3363/box office 212 924 3364).*

## Museums & public buildings

### First Presbyterian Church
*12 West 12th Street, at Fifth Avenue (212 675 6150).* **Open** 12.15-12.45pm Mon, Fri.

### The Forbes Magazine Galleries
*62 Fifth Avenue, between 12th & 13th Streets (212 206 5548).* **Open** 10am-4pm Tue, Wed, Fri, Sat (hours subject to change). **Admission** free.

### New York Studio School
*8 West 8th Street, between Fifth & Sixth Avenues (tour information 212 777 0742/class information 212 673 6466).*

## Shopping

### Aedes De Venustas
*15 Christopher Street, between Sixth Avenue & Waverly Place (212 206 8674).* **Open** noon-8pm Mon-Sat; 1-7pm Sun.

### Amalgamated Home
*9, 13 & 19 Christopher Street, between Sixth Avenue & Waverly Place (212 255 4160).* **Open** noon-8pm Mon-Sat; 1-7pm Sun.

### Bangally African Expo

*30 Greenwich Avenue, between West 10th & Charles Streets (212 627 6489).* **Open** 11am-9pm daily.

### Be Seated

*66 Greenwich Avenue, between Sixth & Seventh Avenues (212 924 8444).* **Open** 11am-7pm Mon-Fri; 11am-6pm Sat.

### Breukelen

*68 Gansevoort Street, between Greenwich & Washington Streets (212 645 2216).* **Open** 11am-7pm Tue-Sun.

### Enz

*48 West 8th Street, between Fifth & Sixth Avenues (212 475 0997).* **Open** 11am-9pm Mon-Sat; noon-8pm Sun.

### Funhouse

*61 West 8th Street, between Fifth & Sixth Avenues (212 674 0983).* **Open** 11.30am-9pm Mon-Thur; 11am-9pm Fri, Sat; noon-8pm Sun.

### Geppetto's Toy Box

*10 Christopher Street, at Gay Street (212 620 7511).* **Open** 11am-8pm Mon-Thur, Sat; 11am-10pm Fri; 1-7pm Sun.

### L'Impasse

*29 West 8th Street, upstairs between Fifth & Sixth Avenues (212 533 3255).* **Open** 11am-9pm Mon-Sat; noon-8pm Sun.

### Matt McGhee

*22 Christopher Street, between Sixth Avenue & Waverly Place (212 741 3138).* **Open** noon-7pm Tue-Sat.

### Our Name Is Mud

*59 Greenwich Avenue, between Seventh Avenue & 11th Street (212 647 7899).* **Open** 1-8pm Mon, Tue; 1-10pm Wed; 1-11pm Thur, Fri; 11.30am-8pm Sat; 11.30am-7pm Sun.

### Petit Peton

*27 West 8th Street, between Fifth & Sixth Avenues (212 677 3730).* **Open** 11am-9pm Mon-Sat; noon-8pm Sun.

### Star Struck

*43 Greenwich Avenue, between Sixth & Seventh Avenues (212 691 5357).* **Open** 11am-8pm Mon-Sat; noon-7pm Sun.

### Tibet Kailash

*48 Greenwich Avenue, between Sixth & Seventh Avenues (212 255 9572).* **Open** 11am-8pm daily.

Savour the smells of dinners-to-be along West 13th Street in the **Meatpacking District**.

# Flea market fun

## Kim Deitch

Weekend bargain-hunting in the parking lots off Broadway.

---

**Start:** corner of Grand Street and Broadway
**Finish:** 'The Grand Bazaar', West 25th Street between Sixth & Seventh Avenues
**Time:** 1 hour-all day
**Distance:** 2 miles/3km
**Getting there:** subway trains J, M, Z, N, R or 6 to Canal Street station
**Getting back:** subway train F from 23rd Street station
**Note:** most of the flea markets are only open on Saturdays and Sundays, and offer the best bargains in the morning. The Strand Bookstore is open daily.

---

## Eating & drinking

### Gramercy Tavern
*42 East 20th Street, between Broadway & Park Avenue South (212 477 0777).* **Open** noon-2pm, 5.30-10pm Mon-Thur; noon-2pm, 5.30-11pm Fri; 5.30-11pm Sat; 5.30-10pm Sun. *Tavern* **Open** noon-11pm Sun-Thur; noon-midnight Fri, Sat. A 1999 *TONY* winner – a welcoming upscale restaurant.

### Pamela's Café
*683 Broadway, at 3rd Street (212 529 1778).* **Open** 8am-11pm daily. Dependable, reasonably priced soups, salads and sandwiches.

### Pete's Tavern
*129 East 18th Street, at Irving Place (212 473 7676).* **Open** 11am-2am Mon; 11am-3am Tue-Sat; 11am-2am Sun. A well-preserved fossil of what New York taverns used to be, serving burgers and Italian basics.

### Punch
*913 Broadway, between 20th & 21st Streets (212 673 6333).* **Open** noon-11.30pm daily. American food with a world-cuisine twist.

### Sal Anthony's
*55 Irving Place, between 17th & 18th Streets (212 982 9030).* **Open** noon-9.30pm daily. A variety of generous, well-prepared Italian dishes, and an extensive list of daily specials, draws a regular Italian clientele.

### Yama
*122 East 17th Street, at Irving Place (212 475 0969).* **Open** noon-2.20pm, 5.30-10.20pm Mon-Thur; noon-2.20pm, 5.30-11.20pm Fri, Sat. Good, fresh sushi in what was once the home of Washington Irving.

## Bookshops

### Strand Book Store
*828 Broadway, at 12th Street (212 473 1452).* **Open** 9.30am-10.30pm Mon-Sat; 11am-10.30pm Sun. *Rare Books* **Open** 9.30am-6.20pm Mon-Sat; 11am-6.20pm Sun.

## Flea markets

### Annex Antiques Fair & Flea Market
*Sixth Avenue, between 25th & 26th Streets (212 243 5343).* **Open** 9am-5pm Sat, Sun.

### The Garage
*112 West 25th Street, between Sixth & Seventh Avenues (212 243 5343).* **Open** 9am-5pm Sat, Sun.

### The Grand Bazaar
*25th Street, between Sixth Avenue & Broadway. (no phone).* **Open** 6am-5pm Sat, Sun.

### Soho Antique Fair & Collectibles Market
*Grand Street, at Broadway (212 682 2000).* **Open** 9am-5pm Sat, Sun.

## Literature & music

**The Caballero's Way** O Henry (1907)
**Felix the Cat** Paul Whiteman from *The Paul Whiteman Collection* (1987).

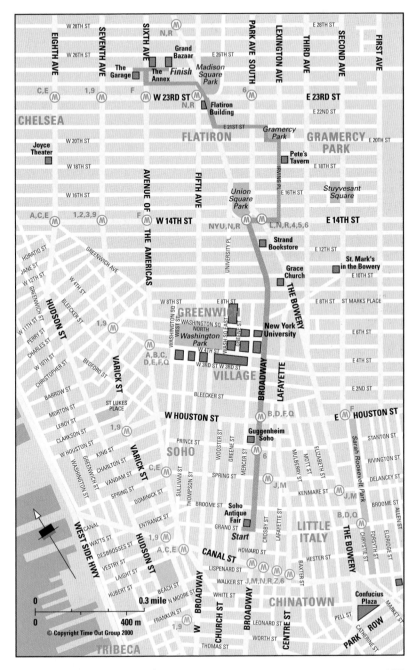

# Jagged symmetries

Victor Bockris

From the fashionable wealth of Upper East Side to the magical mix of Eighth Avenue.

---

**Start:** Third Avenue at East 69th Street
**Finish:** Biography Bookshop, West 11th Street
**Time:** 2-3 hours
**Distance:** 3 miles/4.5km
**Getting there:** subway trains B or Q to 68th Street-Hunter Street station
**Getting back:** short walk to subway trains 1 or 9 from Christopher Street station
**Note:** this walk overlaps with some of William Boyd's walk, *Up Madison, Down Lexington,* and some of Robert Heide and John Gilman's *Hoop, Skip and Jump.*

---

I start on the corner of 69th Street and Third Avenue because I particularly like the carriage houses on the north side of 69th between Third and Lexington. They are beautiful examples of this type of architecture. They have big doors for garages. On the other side of the street is a classic 1950s high-rise apartment building, about 35 storeys high with terraces. It reminds me of a giant birthday cake. It's an absolutely gorgeous day in New York, it's 25 April 2000, the cherry blossoms are blooming in the trees and there are flowers everywhere. This is my New York.

At the corner of 69th and Lexington I'm looking south down Lexington toward the large slab of stone buildings that are Hunter College. I see a lot of students walking around. Although this part of the Upper East Side is not as grand as when you get closer to Madison Avenue, it's still

nice. Two rather interesting crosswalks on different storeys connect the buildings on the East and West side of Lexington. Looking beyond them are the skyscrapers of midtown. Gazing north I'm looking in the direction of Andy Warhol's old house at 79th and Lexington, where his best friend and manager Fred Hughes – one of the great heroes in the history of New York City – now lives. The next block of 69th Street is fairly similar to the previous one in that you have Hunter College on the left and a continuation of carriage houses and townhouses on the right. Most of these houses appear to be relatively unchanged. One of the major entrances to Hunter College is in the middle of the block on the south side of the street.

Park Avenue is twice as wide as any of the other streets. It has two lanes uptown and two lanes downtown divided by a median that sports a row of beautiful trees, blossoming now with the short-lived cherry blossoms, and a nice lawn. There are rectangles of extraordinarily beautiful tulips at each end and small bushes create a wall along each side. To get the best view down Park stand on the corner by 700 Park Avenue. From there you see the grand sweeping view down to the MetLife Building and Grand Central Station. Look north at the majestic line of apartment buildings that stretch up to the nineties and beyond. They are all 15 to 20 storeys high. This is one of the great views in New York and riding down Park Avenue is one of the great cab rides, too. It's one of those images of travel that fill the city; so much of New York is about going somewhere. The nature of the city is travelling.

# Jagged symmetries

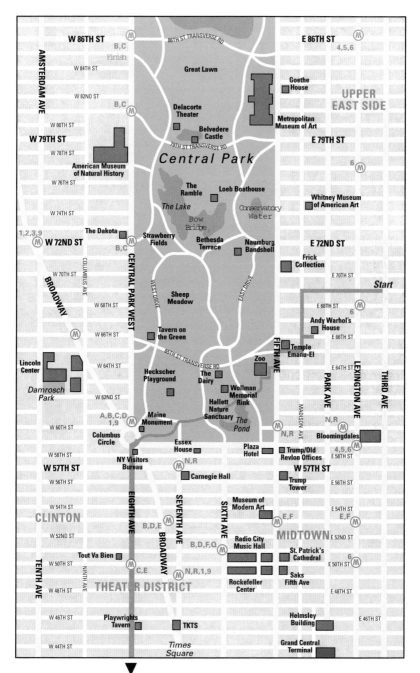

W 86TH ST B,C
Finish
86TH ST TRANSVERSE RD
E 86TH ST
4,5,6

AMSTERDAM AVE

W 84TH ST

Great Lawn

Goethe House

UPPER EAST SIDE

W 82ND ST B,C

Delacorte Theater

Metropolitan Museum of Art

W 80TH ST

W 79TH ST

W 78TH ST

Belvedere Castle

79TH ST TRANSVERSE RD

E 79TH ST

American Museum of Natural History

*Central Park*

6

W 76TH ST

The Ramble

Loeb Boathouse

Whitney Museum of American Art

W 74TH ST

*The Lake*

*Conservatory Water*

The Dakota

*Bow Bridge*

1,2,3,9 W 72ND ST B,C

Strawberry Fields

Bethesda Terrace

Naumburg Bandshell

E 72ND ST

COLUMBUS AVE

Frick Collection

W 70TH ST

CENTRAL PARK WEST

E 70TH ST

*Start*

BROADWAY

Sheep Meadow

WEST DRIVE

EAST DRIVE

E 68TH ST

6

W 68TH ST

Andy Warhol's House

E 66TH ST

W 66TH ST

Tavern on the Green

Temple Emanu-El

FIFTH AVE

65TH ST TRANSVERSE RD

Lincoln Center

W 64TH ST

Heckscher Playground

The Dairy

Zoo

E 64TH ST

PARK AVE

LEXINGTON AVE

THIRD AVE

*Damrosch Park*

W 62ND ST

Wollman Memorial Rink

Hallett Nature Sanctuary

MADISON AVE

A,B,C,D 1,9

Maine Monument

*The Pond*

N,R

W 60TH ST

Columbus Circle

Essex House

Plaza Hotel

N,R

Bloomingdales

Trump/Old Revlon Offices

4,5,6

W 58TH ST

NY Visitors Bureau

N,R

E 58TH ST

W 57TH ST

Carnegie Hall

W 57TH ST

Trump Tower

E 56TH ST

W 56TH ST

EIGHTH AVE

W 54TH ST

Museum of Modern Art

E 54TH ST

CLINTON

SEVENTH AVE

SIXTH AVE

E,F

E,F

W 52ND ST

B,D,E

Radio City Music Hall

E 52ND ST

BROADWAY

B,D,F,Q

St. Patrick's Cathedral

MIDTOWN

Tout Va Bien

NINTH AVE

W 50TH ST

C,E

N,R,1,9

Saks Fifth Ave

6

E 50TH ST

TENTH AVE

W 48TH ST

THEATER DISTRICT

Rockefeller Center

E 48TH ST

W 46TH ST

Playwrights Tavern

TKTS

Helmsley Building

E 46TH ST

W 44TH ST

*Times Square*

Grand Central Terminal

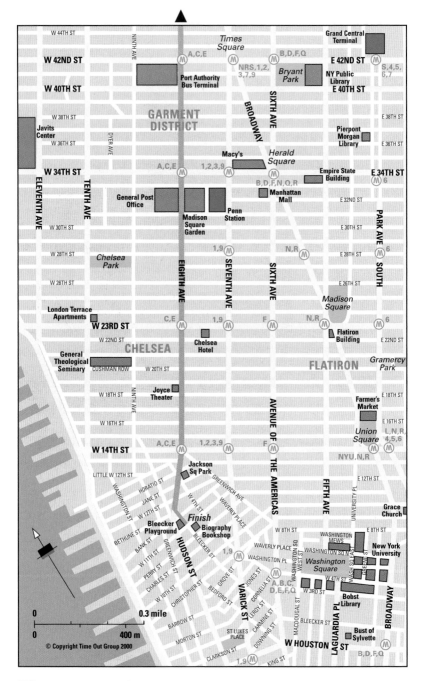

W 44TH ST
W 42ND ST
W 40TH ST
NINTH AVE
Times Square
A,C,E
Port Authority Bus Terminal
NRS,1,2, 3,7,9
Bryant Park
B,D,F,Q
Grand Central Terminal
E 42ND ST
NY Public Library
E 40TH ST
S,4,5, 6,7

W 38TH ST
GARMENT DISTRICT
DYER AVE
BROADWAY
SIXTH AVE
E 38TH ST
Pierpont Morgan Library
W 36TH ST
E 36TH ST

Javits Center
W 34TH ST
ELEVENTH AVE
TENTH AVE
A,C,E
Macy's
1,2,3,9
Herald Square
B,D,F,N,Q,R
Manhattan Mall
Empire State Building
E 34TH ST
6

General Post Office
Madison Square Garden
Penn Station
E 32ND ST
PARK AVE SOUTH

W 30TH ST
E 30TH ST

W 28TH ST
Chelsea Park
1,9
SEVENTH AVE
SIXTH AVE
N,R
E 28TH ST
6

W 26TH ST
EIGHTH AVE
E 26TH ST
Madison Square

London Terrace Apartments
W 23RD ST
C,E
1,9
F
N,R
Flatiron Building
6
E 22ND ST

W 22ND ST
CHELSEA
CUSHMAN ROW
Chelsea Hotel
FLATIRON
Gramercy Park

General Theological Seminary
W 20TH ST

NINTH AVE
Joyce Theater
W 18TH ST
AVENUE OF THE AMERICAS
Farmer's Market
E 18TH ST

W 16TH ST
E 16TH ST

W 14TH ST
A,C,E
1,2,3,9
F
Union Square
L,N,R, 4,5,6

NYU,N,R

LITTLE W 12TH ST
Jackson Sq Park
GREENWICH AVE
FIFTH AVE
UNIVERSITY PL
E 12TH ST
Grace Church

WASHINGTON ST
HORATIO ST
JANE ST
W 12TH ST
WAVERLY PLACE
W 8TH ST
WASHINGTON MEWS
E 8TH ST
New York University

BETHUNE ST
BANK ST
Finish
W 4TH ST
Bleecker Playground
Biography Bookshop
WAVERLY PLACE
WASHINGTON SQ N
WASHINGTON PL
Washington Square
WASHINGTON SQ E
GREENE ST

W 11TH ST
GREENWICH ST
HUDSON ST
BLEECKER ST
1,9
JONES ST
A,B,C, D,E,F,Q
W 4TH ST

PERRY ST
W 3RD ST

CHARLES ST
GROVE ST
BEDFORD ST
CORNELIA ST
Bobst Library
BROADWAY

W 10TH ST
CHRISTOPHER ST
VARICK ST
LEROY ST
MACDOUGAL ST
LAGUARDIA PL
Bust of Sylvette

0        0.3 mile
0        400 m
BARROW ST
MORTON ST
ST LUKES PLACE
CARMINE ST
DOWNING ST
BLEECKER ST
W HOUSTON ST
B,D,F,Q

© Copyright Time Out Group 2000
CLARKSON ST
1,9
KING ST

The block between Park and Madison Avenues on 69th is a classic Upper East Side block with a number of quite beautiful mansions, most of them about five storeys high. As I approach the corner of 69th and Madison Avenue, I am always struck by the whiteness of the pavements and the colourful boutiques and restaurants. Across from me on the north-west corner of Madison is what was once the Westbury Hotel, which looks like it's lost its individuality in a rather dull renovation. I used to visit the drug smuggler Tom Sullivan there. He had three suites in a row that he rented for at least $1,000 a day to plan his smuggling operations in South America. It was fascinating to watch him spread his maps out on the floor. I remember taking William Burroughs and Terry Southern up there and how impressed they were by his generosity. He's dead now. He killed himself in hospital when he realised he had ruined his life.

Turning left I am walking down Madison Avenue. From 72nd Street to 62nd Street, Madison Avenue offers the greatest selection of clothes shops for men and women in America. When I first moved to New York, if I got depressed, I just zipped up here on the subway and walked these ten blocks. The feeling of wealth and the beautiful people walking around straightened me out in 15 minutes. On the east side of the street I come to Dolce & Gabanna, probably the most expensive of all. I always find their clothes to be incredibly funny. More like a costume than clothes. Today they've got a pair of camouflage pants with an ugly snakeskin jacket for women and a very ordinary-looking blue blazer with a pair of fat beige pants for men. It's so bad it's embarrassing. Next is Donna Karan; she's got a new building here on the same block but it's under construction. Gianni Versace's shop is next. He's sporting a black man's suit with double-breasted lapels on a single-breasted jacket. I mean, so what? Max

Mara occupies the building that used to be Halston's beige bunker-like headquarters at the corner of Madison and 68th. I did my first published interview with Halston in *People Magazine* in 1973. He was a great artist, equal in his domain to Warhol.

I'm crossing to the 68th Street block of Madison. The next shop is Kenzo. Kenzo is my favourite designer here. He always has something a little bit more interesting for men than anybody else. Today he has outdone himself with a lovely medium grey double-breasted suit with high short lapels, three buttons. It's the sort of suit I've been thinking of designing for the last five years. Kenzo always has good lapels on his jackets and you can tell they're well cut and would fit nicely. I would definitely buy this suit.

The Gardenia Restaurant and Café at 796 Madison is the only coffeeshop for at least ten blocks going south, so if you're walking down here and you want a cup of coffee, stop at the Gardenia between 67th and 68th.

Standing on the north-east corner of Madison and 67th offers a view of the most beautiful part of Madison Avenue, the stretch between 67th and 62nd Streets. The buildings are lovely. Nothing goes above 12 storeys, so there's a lot of sky and you're also looking towards the skyscrapers of Midtown.

I am turning left on 66th Street to nip up the block and check out Andy Warhol's house at 57th East 66th. It's a five-storey Georgian mansion with two columns framing double black doors. It has a nice little oval plaque in a dull red on it that reads, 'The pop artist Andy Warhol, 1928-1987, best known for his silk screens of cultural icons including Jackie Kennedy, Marilyn Monroe, Chairman Mao, and Campbell's soup cans, lived here from 1974 to 1987. The founder of *Interview Magazine* and the producer of undergound films such as *Chelsea Girls* (1966) and *Trash* (1970) predicted "everybody will be world famous for fifteen minutes".' That's a pretty good summation of Andy's career, although he directed *Chelsea Girls*. The windows are barred on the ground floor. There's also a stairway leading down to the basement, a tradesmen's entrance to the kitchen, which used to be the province of his Filipino maids, Aurora and Aurora. Walking back now, retracing my steps to the corner of Madison, this is the way Andy would come every morning when he left his house, turning left on Madison to walk to the last Factory at 33rd Street between Madison and Fifth. It's a very lovely walk; he used to stop at his favourite antiques shops and hand out copies of *Interview* and get a dose of fame. New York is full of ghosts. So many people I've known over the years are dead but live on in their work.

One of the nice things about this neighbourhood is how clean it is. The pavements are really clean. There's not a scrap of litter to be seen anywhere. Everybody dresses in a nice way. No one looks raggedy here. All the women look extremely rich. They could really be on TV or in a movie. Of course, on Madison Avenue one is focusing one's eyeballs not so much on the buildings as the shop windows. The striking Giorgio Armani building on the north-west corner of 65th and Madison is a large white building of four or five storeys taking up half the block. There's nothing particularly inviting in its windows at the moment. I don't know why people get carried away. The clothing is so ordinary. There are much more interesting things to be found by the shopper with the will to investigate. These are shops for lazy people who think a label will make them look good. Somebody should design a suit made out of labels.

I'm going to walk down 65th Street between Madison and Fifth to the park. This is my favourite block because it's got the Cambridge Chemists; they have the anti jet-lag formula kit available here. A lot of the local people travel and

constantly have jet-lag. It's got a very inviting window. Oh, perfumed drawer lining paper. I'd like some of that. Very nice. Here's the Music Box shop, it's one of these little shops up here you wouldn't find anywhere else.

These rich people all look so happy. Of course, they may be terribly depressed. You can't tell. Money doesn't always drive away depression, but make-up does – that's why the Cambridge Chemists is really the most important shop.

There's an enormous amount of construction at 65th and Fifth Avenue, which is characteristic of New York. They're always tearing down something, or building something, or cleaning something, or hiding something. Maybe it's all an elaborate ruse for a big heist and the construction workers are really thieves. I'm turning left on Fifth walking down the avenue now between 65th and 64th; 834 Fifth Avenue is a classic apartment building of the kind that stretch up Fifth Avenue in an endless boring line up into the nineties. Dull looking, expensive-looking, prohibitive.

Obviously it's a truism to say that light makes an enormous amount of difference to the way one looks at and responds to anything, but I'm particularly struck by this in New York. I have a feeling that the light in New York is seductive. The light as it reflects off the glass skyscrapers in Midtown; the light in the early morning in Central Park as the mist rises out of the water and dew-swept lawns; the light on the Hudson River, the light in your eyes… Reminds me of a story about a guy who was pulled over for speeding by a policeman who said, 'Where's the fire buddy?' to which he responded, 'In your eyes, officer,' which floored the cop, who let him go immediately. But that was a long time ago.

I leave the almost uniformly grey, elegant apartment buildings that line Fifth Avenue for the beautiful Arsenal Building, which is inside Central Park opposite the zoo entrance to the park on the corner of

Reflection, by **Calvin Klein**.

64th and Fifth. This is one of the best ways to enter Central Park, defined by two sets of wide steps facing the Arsenal Building. This building, almost a block long, is the headquarters of the Parks Department. It looks like a small fortress, with turrets at each end and two in the centre where the portcullis would have been. A friend of mine, Gerard Malanga, used to work here. He had a very nice office in a turret on the roof. I turn left, go round the Zoo Gallery and now I am walking on a lovely 30-foot-wide modern cobblestone-style walkway that runs through the centre of the zoo. There are open-air cafés on both sides. I pass out through the entrance to the zoo defined by a column on each side of the path. I usually come here before anything's open, when there's no one around, which is nice because it's so quiet and beautiful. But it's interesting now, with places opening up more. I notice a lot of schoolchildren in large groups going on a tour of the zoo, surprisingly quiet. Dangerous combination, children and zoos. How often have you heard the story of the little girl who got eaten by the lion or the little boy who threw his peanut butter and jelly sandwich into the cage, went in after it and found himself being mothered by a gorilla? Only last week some stupid person thrust their arm through the bars of a zoo out west only to have it neatly severed at the shoulder by a pissed-off tiger. How would you like to be locked up in a fucking cage all your life? There's nothing humane about it. They should put them all on drugs. At least then they'd have something to look forward to – their morning shot!

It's about 65 degrees and a gentle breeze wafts by. April in New York. One expects to see Audrey Hepburn walking along. Instead, a depressed-looking man on a bench, head in his hands, is either trying to sleep or to work something out. I suppose the homeless spend a lot of time in the park during the summer. It's strange how few of them you see. I've been through here early in the morning and I've never seen any homeless people. I think they congregate further north from here, this low end of the park being too busy for them.

Another 15 yards past the zoo entrance I turn right on to a rougher cobblestone road leading up a gentle incline to a two-lane road that curves through this section of the park and which is a wonderful bicycle route during the weekend when cars aren't allowed here. I make a right and take the first left-hand turn off of it on to a narrow path.

I'm always surprised by how empty the park is. New York is such a crowded city, with a population of over ten million, yet walking in the park around 10am I see nobody. One of the nice things about the park is you can wander off the paths anytime – walk to my left on the grass down to the water, there, if you want to. This path is lined with old, tall black elegant electric lamps. I'm turning left and walking over a small bridge that goes across the water, which extends from the bottom part of the park; it's a very peaceful, very beautiful man-made lake with swans and ducks. There are people sitting on benches reading the paper by the water. This is probably one of the most peaceful places in New York to sit in the early morning. If I was living in the nearby Plaza Hotel I would certainly come here in the spring and summer months to read my paper and drink my coffee.

As I'm walking I'm pretty much going along the southern end of the park, parallel to 59th Street, and I can see the great hotels that line Central Park South (aka 59th Street), starting with the Plaza, the most famous one probably, where the Beatles and the Rolling Stones first stayed when they came to New York, making it world famous to another generation. I once tried to get a job as the room-service waiter on the midnight to 5am shift at the Plaza, but on reflection I was afraid too many of the guests would want to have weird sex…

They didn't give it to me because they couldn't figure out why I wanted it. They thought something was wrong. And I guess they were right, because essentially I would

Take tea at the Palm Court, **Plaza Hotel**.

have done it to write about it. God knows you see more than anything being a room-service waiter between midnight and 5am. Champagne ordered up to the room, you know, that kind of thing, yessirree Bob.

I'm walking past a pretty thick clump of trees to my left. To my right, looking down the hill, is the slowly melting Wollman Skating Rink, which is really something to see in winter, particularly in the early mornings, when there are maybe only five or six people on the ice and they're all experts. They're all skating up a storm. It makes me think of Oxana Bayoul, the wonderful skater from Serbia who came here under such tragic circumstances and won a championship six years ago. Whenever I look at the rink I think of Oxana. What a marvellous thing it is to be able to skate.

You can also ride horses in Central Park. I've done that. That's really lovely. The Claremont Stables, up on West 67th just off the park. You ride across a block of road then you enter the park, and you

can gallop along some of the paths they have there. Something always goes wrong, of course, when you go with a group of people. Somebody always gets freaked out, a horse rushes off across the park, dragging her with him. It's quite funny to watch.

After approximately 50 yards the path inclines up to a water fountain (where I take a drink) at the edge of another two-lane road. I cross the road and turn left, walking along the bicyclists' and joggers' path as it follows a gentle curve to my right, heading south-west.

I think walking is the best way to see a city. I remember Burroughs once saying, 'I'm sort of partial to walking. The way to walk is just to lean forward.' It's certainly better than running, there's no question about that. I think you're watching interior movies when you're running. Now I can see the line of hotels along Central Park South. The great Essex House in the middle there, where Muhammad Ali used to stay, the St Mortiz down at the end. My favourite is still the Plaza. Tea in the Palm Court Lounge, very romantic. I've taken a number of my girlfriends there. It's a good place to be seen. You have to have the right clothes, the right look. When I was young, I had the right look for anything, now I only have it for writing. I guess as you get older you have the right look for certain things.

Why do we New Yorkers not appreciate every inch of New York, I mean Manhattan, it's just so wonderful. I can't believe I haven't walked on every block, shaken hands with every statue, glanced into every laundromat. I wonder how much of it has to do with how we increasingly live our lives through other people, via this devouring of newspapers and magazines about celebrities, and seeing what they did. One doesn't *play* basketball, one reads about one's favourite team, just as after a while one doesn't get married but reads about it. When I think of New York I think of Truman Capote and Fred Astaire, Andy Warhol, Grace

Kelly, Cary Grant; I think of films, I think of magic, I think of tap-dancing down Fifth Avenue. I don't think of myself. And actually I've had a lot, I mean hundreds, probably thousands of classic New York experiences. Shooting uptown in a cab to a party, grabbing a bunch of people and going to a great restaurant and then on to a party on a boat, taking a ferry across to Staten Island with a girl. We used to take cabs and smoke really strong grass and share it with the cab driver, which was insane because we'd be tearing up the West Side Highway and you come to that part where there's a big truck suspended in the air as part of an advertisement but you don't realise that and you think you're driving in the sky…

This city has changed, man. You know, if you get caught smoking a joint in the streets of New York you have to spend the night in jail. There's no way to get out of it unless you're very rich and you know people, but obviously you can get out of jail, get out of anything, if you're very rich and know people. If you're just a regular schmo with a big schlub body and you're caught doing that, it means you're gonna sleep on the cold cement floor of the big house using a bucket to piss in.

Of course, now that the mayor has been caught with his pants down, porking his best friend for the last ten years while his wife, who's actually more beautiful than the mistress… forget it. He has such a pinched face it's hard to imagine him kissing anybody, he looks like he'd cut into them. That's why he's the mayor of New York. He's tough as nails and proud of it. He never walks anywhere. He gets carried.

I come to a corner, where the road is intersected by a left-hand curve, which leads out of the park at Sixth Avenue. This is where you begin to see the horses and carriages coming out now. Most of them park along 59th Street. I've seen five or six of them go by. It's a pretty reasonable thing to do. It's not that expensive. Of course, they go very slowly. It's another way to see the leaves float by.

Central Park is a wonderful place to go bicycle riding, too. I'm pretty sure that on weekends they close it to traffic. It's just for joggers and bikers and walkers and lovers and hustlers and rapists and clowns. Well, hell, this is New York, we're not going to pretend anything. Save me from those who would pretend everything is fine when everybody in the room wants to kill each other.

As I approach, 50 yards away from the exit from the park at Columbus Circle, the cacophany of the city grows slowly in my ears, the sound of trucks, buses, the sound of hammering, jackhammers going into the pavement, cutting up the sidewalk, the sound of building, tootings of horns, blaring radios and voices muttering and screaming and shouting. I always look forward to this part because it is going to take me to the head of Eighth Avenue and I'm going to walk down the entire stretch of Eighth Avenue, from top to bottom. I love Eighth Avenue. It boils with life.

Now here we are, walking out of the park and into Columbus Circle. Columbus Circle is really quite a remarkable place; it has an enormous, magnificent white stone plinth, on top of which is the large, bright shiny golden statue of someone who reminds me of Boadicea, standing on three horses waving her arms. There's a plaque here desciibing it. 'In Memoriam, the USS *Maine*, destroyed in Havana Harbor on February 15, 1898. This tablet is cast from metal recovered from the USS *Maine*.' Whoa. That's impressive, isn't it? That's something to write home about. Here's a pigeon taking a bath. There's a nice little place you can get a coffee. Here's another little plaque.

Standing here, facing away from in front of this great statue at the big roundabout that is Columbus Circle. There's a wonderful silver globe to my right, next to one of the tallest office buildings in Manhattan. Columbus Circle itself is centred around a big roundabout with a tall thin column with a full-sized figure atop it. I'm crossing Broadway now and in the

The city sounds grow as **Columbus Circle** approaches.

middle of Columbus Circle one of the unusual buildings to my left is what used to be the Huntington Hartford Museum. Huntington Hartford was a miserable old bastard who inherited massive amounts of money from the A&P supermarket chain. And he just spent it being miserable. He paid people to have sex. He actually paid my girlfriend to have sex once, and that's why I don't like him. He's one of those people who looked like an absolute monster by the time he died. He turned into an absolute monster. He had every possibility to have a wonderful life, but he just caused trouble for people. He was an adolescent. He always complained about how hurt he was. Listen, I wouldn't be hurt if I had 50 million dollars. I wouldn't be hurt *at all*.

Well, now I'm back on my favourite avenue, Eighth Avenue. Trucking down Eighth Avenue, it's a sort of Grateful Dead Avenue. Fifty-seventh is one of the big cross-streets of Manhattan, going from one river to the other. You can see both rivers if you run up and down it, you can see the horizons over them. Again, I'm walking under the scaffolding here, down Eighth Avenue, between 57th and 56th.

Horses and carriages going to Central Park to drive people around. I must say the horses in those carriages look pretty well taken care of. About 15 years ago a horse did keel over here. The owner tried to say it was on drugs but that didn't stand up and he was drummed out of the business. Now he runs a bus company. Shits always rise, it's a law of physics.

Lot of cars now. All exactly the same. Cars have totally lost their character in America. They all look exactly the same. Like the people. It really is a communist country. They would like everything to look the same. Andy was so right about that. They love uniforms. I think one of the best things you could do in America would be to institute a uniform clause in schools, because children would get along much better if they all wore the same clothes. Instead of having a fucking fit deciding what to wear, because it might

not be cool enough. Can you believe this? Schoolchildren are deciding if they look cool enough before going to school. That's a lot of peer pressure when you're eight.

It's a magic moment of quietness on Eighth Avenue now, as I walk down the lower 50s. Suddenly the city is blanketed in silence and then it all starts up again. The sunlight just makes so much more difference when you're walking down the street. The sun is bouncing off everything. It creates a kind of miniature light show of your own, so it's really a little bit like watching a rock show with or without a light show. I remember once when I was trying to get Blondie to sign up to make a documentary for the BBC, I took Nigel Finch, the director, to Howard Johnson's between 52nd and 51st for a drink to discuss the progress we made because at that point Debbie and Chris were living on 58th Street and we had just come from their apartment. He looked around and said to me, 'This is the worst place I've ever been in my life.' And it was. It is hard to describe the effect of places like Howard Johnson's and McDonald's. They give me the feeling I used to have of being in a very boring geometry class in high school.

One of the really impressive office buildings on Eighth Avenue is in this block between 50th and 49th, taking up the whole block on the west side of the street. It's called, appropriately enough, Worldwide Plaza. I think I went there once to deliver some material to Glenn O'Brien. He does work with Calvin Klein, and for Island Records, and I think he's just coming back from Cannes where they showed his *Downtown 81* film, which I'm very keen to hear about. It's a wonderful little film he made about life in downtown New York in 1981 starring Jean-Michel Basquiat, co-starring Walter Stedding, with appearances by a large number of people from the scene. An outstanding performance by James Chance. Really reminding you of just how sharp that period was.

All packed up and ready to go – the tenements on **Eighth Avenue** look doomed.

To me the symmetry between Madison Avenue in the 60s and Eighth Avenue in the 40s is one of the great examples of that jagged New York symmetry people speak about. But it really is, this is the other side of the coin, you know. And of course, to be honest, I would love to live on Madison Avenue in the 60s, there's such a wonderful air there of contentment, safety and a sharpness, but I have to come down to Eighth Avenue to keep myself awake. Because it gets very dull up there. Being safe isn't all it's cracked up to be. Where's the adventure?

On the west side of the street, very old apartment buildings, about nine or ten storeys tall, over a bunch of miscellaneous shops, photo shops, gift shops, restaurants, cleaners, a residential neighbourhood on that side of the avenue, on this side it's a kinda tourist trap. It's very interesting, isn't it? Rosa's Place. The Engine 54 Ladder Four Battalion Nine Fire Department – very attractive-looking, squat bunker-like building over enormous red garage doors from which fire engines come belting out.

A building on Eighth Avenue that is boarded up and a whole row of buildings next to it, old tenement apartment buildings, they're all obviously about to be knocked down and turned into some kind of super-expensive sealed high-rise or something. Such loud cars, such loud horns, I can hardly hear myself… People can't stand stopping in New York. It's in their natures to keep moving. It's the nature of the city to move. I like what Stephen Crane wrote about New York. He was writing about the Lower East Side, of course, but he wrote that the mindset of living in New York was like living in a state of war. I think that was probably truer when he wrote it in 1860 than it is now. Walking past an open parking lot, just a guy sitting on a little stoop there. He'll be happy to park your car but it will cost an arm and a leg. Ten dollars an hour at least. Kind of a nice old building on the corner of what they call Restaurant Row and Eighth Avenue, just a typical apartment building with dormer windows all along the top and a nice little turret in the corner. I rather like it. Yeah, 46th

Street is Restaurant Row. That's because there are a whole lot of restaurants in there, a lot of very nice little restaurants, particularly French ones. Tout Va Bien being particularly good. Well, listen, nobody who lives in New York cooks, that's ridiculous. We eat out, man. Or we eat in. But we don't cook. You never smell cooking smells, not in my part of the woods anyway. Most of us just don't eat. The air in New York is so full of nutrients, and it has, of course, all the things you need to live.

Actually this is a very interesting neighbourhood, because to the west of me, between Eighth and the river, you have a population made up largely of people who work in restaurants, waiters, cooks, subcooks, busboys, managers, maître d's, the whole bit. And so you have a hodgepodge of different nationalities living in what is not a particularly expensive area. While looking to the left it is a whole different world because you are now looking towards the Midtown office area, and the theatre district. Anyway, we're right at the centre. Pretty gift shops selling cheap ties, hats, lots of open-air tourist shops, restaurants, car parks.

The Playwright Tavern is between 46th and 45th. I always wanted to go here, pretend I was Shakespeare or something, let's see if they have anything... John Millington Synge, Patrick Cavanagh, Brendan Behan, Samuel Beckett, Sean O'Casey, they're all on the menu. James Joyce – is he a playwright? They haven't got their names on the dishes. They should have the James Joyce Burger. How about the Beckett Burger? I'll take a Beckett cheeseburger and a Joyce to go. Here's Daniella Trattoria Ristorante, breakfast, lunch and dinner. What do they have for breakfast in Italy? Probably cold pasta. David Byrne likes cold pizza for breakfast.

The season's main event, *Kiss Me Kate*, that's at a theatre on 45th Street. Going to the theatre appears to me to be an almost completely dead art.

Something that's just so separate from the world I live in. I feel like I don't know anybody who's been to the theatre in the last 20 or 30 years, and yet they claim they're selling out all the time and doing great business there. Mind you, there are very few, if any, original plays.

Forty-third Street is Leon Davis Street. And here's the Times Square subway station. Of course, you can get the Eighth Avenue subway here, it'll take you straight down Eighth Avenue, underneath where we're walking, and it'll shoot you down to 14th Street in eight minutes. The subway is one of the most efficient subways in the world. The Moscow subway is the cleanest; Paris subway is very colourful. The two greatest illusions in America are that size and speed are important in ratio: the bigger something is the better it is, the fastest something is the better it is. Those two things are so undeniably untrue that it's remarkable that they still hold up. But Americans are impressed by speed and size.

Standing at the corner of 42nd Street and Eighth Avenue. In the distance you can hear a jackhammer, underneath me you can hear the subway – buh buh buh buhh, it does have a beat to it, the bebop beat – and it's very noisy, trucks, buses, oddly enough, no voices. People don't talk much in the street, they tend to keep to themselves, but you've got to stand on this corner for a few minutes. First of all, the big ads 60 by 40 feet on the walls. There's a big sign that says 'Win or go home' that has the Knicks on it, our wonderful basketball team, led by my hero Latrell Spreewell. On the south-west corner where the bus terminal is you've got an enormous live TV screen, about ten by 12 feet. Way down to my right there's some really lovely, very tall, 40-storey apartment towers that are for artists. Tennessee Williams had a place there because it has a swimming pool. Of course, there's a long waiting list, but once you get in you get a place there cheaply, relatively cheaply, and they're nice, too.

There's usually a spare seat at the **Port Authority Bus Terminal** on 41st Street.

I'm walking down the block between 42nd and 41st with the Port Authority to my right – buses coming from San Francisco, or LA, buses from Chicago or Houston, it's quite an exciting place to hang around if you've got any eyes. It's one of the notorious places in the city because lots of young teenagers, runaways, come in on buses, so you have a lot of pimps and oddball people waiting around the Port Authority. You also have a lot of police.

There's a vast difference between Eighth Avenue below 42nd and Eighth Avenue above 42nd. Now you've got these guys cleaning shoes out on the street here, between 42nd and 41st, there are at least two active shoe-shine setups, something you don't see very often these days. This is your classic, old-fashioned friendly shoe-shine guy. He's trying to get as much out of you as he possibly can. He's got all the equipment. Brushes, the cans of polish.

And now we get into a strikingly different Eighth Avenue below 42nd Street. This is the scrappiest, the dirtiest,

the funniest part of the avenue. Great juxtapositions between sex video shops and then this very wonderful hat shop, Knox, and a very good camera shop, Eighth Avenue Electronics. Now if Kenzo is my favourite Madison Avenue shop then Generations at 616 Eighth Avenue must be my favourite Eighth Avenue clothes shop for men. There is a perpetual sale and they have suits selling for $120, $100 or less. It's really, really a good deal. They have wonderful things here. I highly recommend this shop.

Above, as I said, it's a tourist area and a residential area. But now it's a kind of boiling area full of God knows what. Mostly shops. Some nice outdoor food stands, video shops you can go in, obviously largely pornographic; pawnbrokers on the other side of the street – this is a neighbourhood you would describe as bustling. Now I'm knocking into people, not paying attention.

I'm looking forward to having a big breakfast, too, at my favourite Village café, Bonbonierre, but we'll get there, quite a ways to go yet. Now we're in the

Garment District. The garment district is a little bit of a puzzle. It's characterised by a lot of men wheeling around a contraption on which clothes are hung on a rail and the rail has got wheels so you can move like 40 dresses across the street fast. I love these chaps who are constantly pushing these clothes from one place to another. A lot of these shops that you pass are wholesale and they have just bolts of fabric in the window. There are one or two places where you can buy things extraordinarily cheaply if you look carefully and watch. This is my favourite shoe shop where I'm going to get a pair of shoes. Actually they have the exact boot that I want, yep, there it is. It's 550 Eighth Avenue. It's called Mike's Shoe Plaza. That's a good place to go if you want to get your classic Beatle boots.

I'm not walking as fast as I intended to. It's interesting, you see, what happens on Eighth Avenue, there's just so much going on that you sort of constantly find yourself slowing down to check things out, plus there are so many people and you can't move that fast, you have to stop at lights, you have to jostle for position, you don't want to bump into people too much. And you gotta cut across the street against the light. You've gotta be on your toes.

I'm crossing with the light at what is called West 36th Street and Eighth Avenue. And here's my favourite cheap clothes shop, Mr Joe at 500 Eighth Avenue, where you can get things for a couple of dollars. Let's see if they've got anything of interest today. Well, they've got some very nice dresses for three dollars, you see, you can actually buy here a nice sort of black dress with flowers on it for $2.99. It's very, very reasonable. If they had a small one I would take it. And keep it until I find the person it fits. I think I found her last night. Most men don't like to buy women's clothes, it makes them uncomfortable. I love to buy women's clothes for them. Particularly for someone who really appreciates it.

All right, moving along now, opposite us is the old New Yorker Hotel, which used to be quite a grand hotel, close to Penn Station. And people used to meet there in the cocktail lounges. The outside of the building is the same, it's just dirty, it hasn't been cleaned or anything. It's lost it's charm, but it's a good memory. Crossing 34th and Eighth Avenue, coming up on Madison Square Garden. Madison Square Garden, inside, is remarkable. I went to see a big basketball game there about a month ago. On the other side of the street you have one of the outstanding buildings in New York, the large public post office building, between 33rd and 32nd taking up the whole block on the west side of Eighth Avenue. It's got these wide lovely steps, about two-thirds of the block, a row of steps leading up to, I'd say, about 25 large Roman columns that are at least four or five storeys high. It's a magnificent building, built in the old grey/white slab brick period, whenever the hell that was, it's an imperial type of building with the flag flying, centre, over the top and a nice white mast. They don't do anything with it, it just sits there. They don't clean the top, they don't make it special.

The subway is beneath me. I'm actually walking on the grating, underneath which subway cars are travelling at this moment, and cars are hooting their horns and people are making noises with pushcarts, even some conversation. It's lower Eighth Avenue, between 34th and 23rd Streets, a whole other area than the previous ones. It's made up largely of small local shops, hardware stores, pubs, liquor stores, delicatessens, cleaners, and it's sort of a residential neighbourhood off to the west and an office neighbourhood in the blocks to my east. It's also the dirtiest neighbourhood we've walked through so far. There's more crap on the streets here than there is anywhere else we've been so far today. I don't find it so displeasing, it's just part of the thing. The people are dressed very much in relation to the

The **Post Office Building** in all its classical glory – it just sits there while life speeds by.

**Chris Stein, Jed Johnson, Debbie Harry** and **Andy Warhol** – an evening out in 1980.

neighbourhood, too. A lot of people in jeans here, jeans and T-shirts, patchworks, a lot of people wearing sneakers.

On the west side of Eighth Avenue between 29th and, well, going down at least four blocks, you've got an enormous project, cheap apartments, especially made for the habitation of poor people, probably hard to get into. They're over 20 storeys high, with terraces, nice-looking from the outside, but you can imagine what a hell it is inside maintaining all those toilets, all those systems, and getting water up to all those levels. I think it would be a difficult place to live, frankly.

Here's an enormous Rite Aid, taking about, oh, a third of the block, and right on the next corner you've got a CVS Pharmacy taking up half the next block, right next to each other. I guess it just underlines the fact that the third biggest business in the United States is the drug business, the pill business. I have to say that to me probably the murkiest and most evil business in America is the drug business. The majority of people in the

United States are probably addicted to prescription drugs. The obvious story is that the drug companies, noticing how much money was made by illegal drugs in the 1970s, jumped on it with the attitude, well, if you're a bunch of people who want to get hooked, get hooked to us. Of course, their drugs aren't anything like as good but they seem to work for a lot of people.

Standing on the corner of 23rd and Eighth Avenue and looking to my left down to the Chelsea Hotel, which is almost to Seventh Avenue, and looking to my right the London Terrace Apartments building, where many interesting people live. I visited there a few times. It's a lovely building with a wonderful swimming pool. I was thinking of living there myself but it's just too expensive, $4,000 a month for a large two-bedroom apartment.

The people who stay at the Chelsea will come down here to Eighth Avenue to have breakfast or get coffee. Two blocks down is a really nice place, the Big Cup at 228 Eighth Avenue. It has armchairs and coffee tables and couches. You can really relax there and have your coffee and some kind of pastry.

Now this area, from 22nd, going down to about 12th Street, is my favourite part of Eighth Avenue. This is a good place to live. From my point of view, I would say second to the Village as a place to live – it's purely residential, but you've also got a number of interesting art galleries, restaurants, and going further west, some very nice houses. It has all those terrific 24-hours-a-day Korean delicatessens where the food is so clean it sparkles.

One of the problems of New York is that you can't really live here if you're a failure, it's a city for people who are here to make it and you either are striving to make it or you've made it. To not be striving, to have failed, I don't know, how

easy that would be, how hard that would be? The Beats started at the position of being failures, but they made to fail very successful for themselves. But certainly people who you meet in New York are largely here to achieve something. Of course, a lot of people have made it and then fallen from the positions that they achieved and are trying to remake it, and that's actually, I think, one of the most interesting places to be at.

I've seen a number of people succeed at that recently, Debbie Harry being an outstanding example with the re-formation and great success of Blondie, she really got back up there again. And she really worked hard to do that. I can tell you, I really admire that woman enormously, apart from liking her. I mean,

**William Burroughs** puts in a call on the corner of 23rd Street after dinner at the Chelsea.

Debbie's probably one of the best people I've met in New York, really, she's such a soulful person and she's really been through it all, my God, does she know it back and forth.

One of the best things about this part of Eighth Avenue is the restaurants. Here's a couple of brasseries, the Rocking Horse Café, a Mexican restaurant. There are some good clothes shops, too. Camouflage is the best one, that's on the west side of the street, a little bit further down.

The Joyce Theater is across the street. The Joyce Theater used to be the Elgin, a great old movie house where we used to come to double features in the afternoon. They always had really good films. It's now a successful dance theatre. There's a row of restaurants in the block. Liquor stores – once you're in residential neighbourhoods there is a liquor store on almost every block. I once thought it must be terribly hard to stop drinking in New York because the liquor stores are there and they're so inviting looking, you know. Flashing red neon signs. The people are always so glad to see you, watching you die.

Aahh! A beautiful old checker cab just spun by. You don't see those very often. People renovate them, they look wonderful. p chanin, a little clothes shop. And my favourite shoe shop, Giraudon. Nice Italian restaurants, Japanese restaurants, banks, parking lots. What a wonderful place New York is. It's a feast of a city. It has everything. If you want to understand New York, see Manhattan from above. Take a helicopter ride. When I say New York I always mean Manhattan. I'm a bit of a snob about that because I know that Brooklyn has lovely neighbourhoods, but New York to me is Manhattan and you don't need anything else. The other neighbourhoods don't add anything you don't have here.

I always say that one of the most striking things about this walk is going through the different neighbourhoods. There is no more abrupt change than from where I am now at the corner of 14th Street and Eighth Avenue and walking just one block from here, to 13th, in the Village. One of the things that is most striking when you come into the Village is the sound level, it just becomes much quieter, almost immediately, and this is largely because apart from Eighth Avenue, you're not allowed to drive trucks through the Village. It's so quiet.

And here we have the first of a series of little parks, Jackson Square Park, 2.27 acres, a triangular park, right where Horatio Street reaches the head of the triangle with Eighth Avenue. Horatio Street is one of the great streets in the Village, where Bebe Buell and Todd Rundgren lived and gave great parties many moons ago. Little has changed in the Village, except the population. It used to be a predominantly gay area. Now it's much more mixed and there are a lot more young children running about, screaming and yelling and throwing fits, cursing at their parents as American children learn to do at a young age from watching television.

Almost to the end of Eighth Avenue now, this is just a lovely residential neighbourhood, you have the Art Bar, the laundromat, the magazine shops, that's a sign of an expensive residential neighbourhood when you see the kinds of magazines they have. West 4th Street, you're looking, to the left, at the Corner Bistro, a famous bar that's been there since, you know, since the '40s, I believe, and you're looking at a little delicatessen on the right-hand corner but right in front of you, you're looking at a really lovely street – it's tree lined, and it's mostly consistent houses that are about four storeys high and in every block there's at least one restaurant, or bookshop, or flower shop, or hairdresser or that kind of thing. And the people here are also quite different, they look more poetic.

Now I'm entering the strip between Jane Street and 12th and we're coming up on Bonbonierre, which is my favourite place to have breakfast. Crossing West 12th, on Eighth Avenue, you're looking to your right straight down 12th towards the river, and across another one of the beautiful triangular little parks. Along here on the left a nondescript apartment building. But the most striking effect of walking into this part of the Village is the fact that now no buildings can be taller than 12 storeys so you're looking at a lot of sky. Also one of the most remarkable things I've just noticed for the first time now is the fantastic bright slanted silver roof on one of the houses at the junction of where Hudson meets Eighth, above the old Bus Stop Café. It must have some solar use.

Now this is really a delightful promenade, walking from the head of Bleecker Street as it bends south. To my right is the Bleecker Playground, which is closed off to all but those attending the children. It's a very nice area, for very young children mostly. It's another one of

the great little City of New York parks that is run from the Arsenal Building. You've got the dulcet sounds of children's voices floating up from the playground, and where that ends, it's fenced off with a nice iron fence. Then you've got a very rare thing in New York, a seating area, just simply here, to the right of the pavement. A large seating area containing some 20 dark green benches, long enough to seat eight people in a row, shaded by 14 trees. It's just a beautiful area. The statue here says *The Family*, 1979, by Chaim Gross, native to the City of New York in honour of Edward Koch, the mayor from 1978 to 1989. Edward Koch was a very good mayor, he was the mayor who policed this area and made sure it was safe for gay people, because when I moved here in 1976 we had just had the truck murders and gay bashing was a serious problem.

Anyway, I'm now coming up on my favourite bookshop of all, the Biography Bookshop at Bleecker and 11th. How lucky I am to live in a neighbourhood that has a biography bookshop. Apart from carrying my own books, they have a very good selection and often they'll have a table out here with books on sale. For example, Miles's book on Burroughs is on sale for $6.98 in hardback. Actually it looks like it's been snapped up. There were two copies here yesterday. *Easy Riders, Raging Bulls* by Peter Biskind, one of my favourite books, is out, and they actually have in stock my books on Warhol and Richards, Cale and Blondie and so on and so on. Oh, *Notes from the Underground*, I have to buy this. This is right up my street. And also it's a great-looking book. I'm going to come back and get that. No you're not. You're going to get it right now.

## Eating & drinking

### Art Bar
*52 Eighth Avenue, between Jane & Horatio Streets (212 727 0244).* **Open** 4pm-2am Mon-Thur, Sun; 4pm-3am Fri, Sat. Neighbourhood bohos frequent this dive scene.

**Biography Bookshop** – a lifetime's reading.

### Big Cup
*228 Eighth Avenue, between 21st & 22nd Streets (212 206 0059).* **Open** 7am-1am Mon-Thur, Sun; 7am-2am Fri, Sat. Loungey, neighbourhoody gay coffeeshop – idealy for reading the daily papers.

### Bonbonierre
*28 Eighth Avenue, at 12th Street (212 741 9266).* **Open** 7am-4.30pm daily.

### Bus Stop Cafe
*597 Hudson Street, at Bethune Street (212 206 1100).* **Open** 6am-11pm daily.

### Corner Bistro
*331 West 4th Street, at Jane Street (212 242 9502).* **Open** 11am-4am Mon-Sat; noon-4am Sun. One of the tastiest jaw-stretching burgers at this smoky tavern. A *TONY* 100.

### Daniella Ristorante
*320 Eighth Avenue, at 26th Street (212 807 0977).* **Open** noon-3pm, 5-10pm Mon-Fri; 5-10pm Sat, Sun. Closed Sundays in summer. Don't judge by appearances – Daniella's conjures up robust North Italian food with a French twist.

### Gardenia Café
*797 Madison Avenue, between 67th & 68th Streets (212 628 8763).* **Open** 7am-10pm daily. Unpretentious setting for salads and sandwiches.

### The Palm Court
*The Plaza Hotel, 768 Fifth Avenue, at 59th Street (212 546 5350).* **Open** 6.30am-midnight daily. Classic tea for two in sumptuous surroundings.

### Playwright Tavern & Restaurant
*732 Eighth Avenue, between 45th & 46th Streets (212 354 8404).* **Open** 9am-4.30am daily.

### Rocking Horse
*182 Eighth Avenue, between 19th & 20th Streets (212 463 9511).* **Open** 11.30am-11pm Mon-Thur, Sun; 11.30am-midnight Fri, Sat. A packed, colourful dining room serving fine *nuevo Mexicano*.

### Rosa's Place
*303 West 48th Street, between Eighth & Ninth Avenues (212 586 4853).* **Open** noon-11.45pm daily.

### Tout Va Bien
*311 West 51st Street, between Eighth & Ninth Avenues (212 265 0190).* **Open** noon-3pm, 5-11.30pm Mon-Sat; noon-3pm, 5-10pm Sun. French country food in this adorable little 50-year-old bistro.

## Hotels

### Essex House
*160 Central Park South, between Sixth & Seventh Avenues. (212 484 5100).*

### Howard Johnson Plaza Hotel
*851 Eighth Avenue, at 51st Street (212 581 4100).*

### New Yorker Hotel
*481 Eighth Avenue, between 34th & 35th Streets (212 971 0101).*

### The Plaza Hotel
*768 Fifth Avenue, at 59th Street (212 759 3000).*

### Milford Plaza
*270 West 45th Street, at Eighth Avenue (212 869 3600).*

## Parks

### Central Park Wildlife Center
*Fifth Avenue, at 64th Street (212 861 6030).* **Open** 10am-5pm Mon-Fri; 10.30am-5.30pm Sat, Sun. **Admission** $3.50; 50¢-$1.25 concessions; free under-3s. **No credit cards.**

### Claremont Riding Academy
*175 West 89th Street, between Amsterdam & Columbus Avenues (212 724 5100).* **Open** 6.30am-10pm Mon-Fri; 6.30am-5pm Sat, Sun. **Rental** $35 per hour, lessons $42 a half hour. Introductory package for first 3.5 hours, $100.

### Department of Parks & Recreation
*888 NY PARKS/212 360 2774.*

### Loeb Boathouse
*The Lake, near Fifth Avenue & East 17th Street (212 517 4723).* **Open** *May-Oct* noon-4pm Mon-Fri; 11am-4pm Sat, Sun. *Boat hire* $10 per hour plus $30 deposit; $30 per half-hour for chauffeured gondola (only at night). **No credit cards.**

### Wollman Memorial Rink
*Midpark at 62nd Street (212 396 1010).* **Open** 11am-6pm Thur, Fri; 11am-8pm Sat, Sun. *Skating* **Open** *mid-Oct-end Mar* 11am-3pm Mon, Tue; 11am-9.30pm Wed, Thur; 11am-11pm Fri, Sat; 11am-9pm Sun. **Admission** $7; $3 concessions. *Skate rental* $3.50.

# Shopping

## Emporio Armani
*601 Madison Avenue, between 57th & 58th Streets (212 317 0800).* **Open** 10am-8pm Mon-Fri; 10am-7pm Sat; noon-6pm Sun.

## Biography Bookshop
*400 Bleecker Street, at 11th Street (212 807 8655).* **Open** 11am-10pm Mon-Thur; 11am-11pm Fri, Sat; 11am-7pm Sun.

## Cambridge Chemists
*21 East 65th Street, between Madison & Fifth Avenues (212 734 5677).* **Open** 9.30am-7pm Mon-Fri; 10am-5pm Sat.

## Camouflage
*141 Eighth Avenue, between 16th & 17th Streets (212 741 9118).* **Open** noon-7pm Mon-Fri; 11.30am-6.30pm Sat; noon-6pm Sun.

## DKNY
*655 Madison Avenue, at 60th Street (212 223 3569).* **Open** 10am-7pm Mon-Wed, Fri, Sat; 10am-9pm Thur; noon-6pm Sun.

## D&G
*825 Madison Avenue, between 68th & 69th Streets (212 249 4100).* **Open** 10am-6pm Mon-Wed, Fri, Sat; 10am-7pm Thur.

## Eighth Avenue Electronics
*620 Eighth Avenue, between 40th & 41st Streets (212 575 5614).* **Open** 9.30am-7.30pm daily.

## Generations
*616 Eighth Avenue, between 39th & 40th Streets (212 398 2374).* **Open** 9.30am-7pm Mon-Sat; 11.30am-6pm Sun.

## Gianni Versace
*647 Fifth Avenue, between 51st & 52nd Streets (212 317 0224).* **Open** 10am-6.30pm Mon-Sat.

## Giraudon
*152 Eighth Avenue, at 17th Street (212 633 0999).* **Open** 11.30am-11pm Mon-Sat; 1-7pm Sun.

## Mr Joe
*500 Eighth Avenue, between 35th & 36th Streets (212 279 1090).* **Open** 9.30am-8pm Mon-Sat; 11am-6pm Sun.

## Kenzo
*805 Madison Avenue, at 68th Street (212 717 0101).* **Open** 10am-6.30pm Mon-Wed, Fri, Sat; 10am-7pm Thur.

## Knox Hats
*620 Eighth Avenue, between 40th & 41st Streets (212 768 3781).* **Open** 10am-7pm Mon-Sat; 10am-5pm Sun.

## Max Mara
*813 Madison Avenue, at 68th Street (212 879 6100).* **Open** 10am-6pm Mon-Wed, Fri, Sat; 10am-7pm Thur.

## Mike's Shoe Plaza
*550 Eighth Avenue, between 37th & 38th Streets (212 921 8218).* **Open** 10am-7pm Mon-Fri; 11am-6pm Sat; noon-6pm Sun.

## p chanin
*152 Eighth Avenue, between 17th & 18th Streets (212 924 5359).* **Open** noon-9pm Mon, Tue, Sun; noon-10pm Wed; noon-11pm Thur-Sat.

## Rita Ford Music Boxes
*19 East 65th Street, between Madison & Fifth Avenues (212 535 6717).* **Open** 9am-5pm Mon, Wed, Fri, Sat; 9am-6pm Tue, Thur.

# Venues

## Joyce Theatre
*175 Eighth Avenue, at 19th Street (212 242 0800).*

## Madison Square Garden
*Seventh Avenue, at 32nd Street (212 465 6741).*

# Film & literature

**Chelsea Girls** (Andy Warhol, 1967, US)
**Trash** (Paul Morrissey, 1970, US)
**Easy Riders, Raging Bulls** Peter Biskind (1998)

# Others

## General Post Office
*421 Eighth Avenue, between 31st and 33rd Streets (212 967 8585).* **Open** 24hrs daily. Free.

## Hunter's College
*695 Park Avenue, between East 68th Street & Lexington (212 772 4000).*

## Port Authority Bus Terminal
*40th-42nd Streets, between Eighth & Ninth Avenues (212 564 8484).*

## Staten Island Ferry
*South Street, at the foot of Whitehall Street (718 727 2508).* **Open** boats depart every half hour, 24hrs daily. Free.

# Salons and saloons

Marion Meade

About town and around the table with Dorothy Parker.

**Start:** Algonquin Hotel, West 44th Street
**Finish:** Algonquin Hotel, West 44th Street
**Time:** 2-3 hours
**Distance:** 2.5 miles/4km
**Getting there:** subway trains B, D, F or Q to 42nd Street station
**Getting back:** subway trains B, D, F or Q from 42nd Street station
**Note:** this is a circular walk, and coincides with some of the same area, and era, as Minda Novek's walk, *Tall Town*.

In the summer of 1919, two theatrical press agents decided to throw a luncheon to welcome home the *New York Times* drama critic from the Great War. Several dozen journalists showed up at the Algonquin Hotel, where they proceeded to tease Aleck Woollcott about his combat experiences, which had been fought at a safe distance behind the front lines. Such a terrific time was enjoyed by all that afterward one of the guests politely remarked, 'Why don't we do this every day?' And that was the accidental birth of the fabled Algonquin Round Table, the literary salon that has been compared, inaccurately in my opinion, to the Bloomsbury Group in London. By no means were the Algonquin writers the most important, or most intellectual, in our publishing firmament, certainly not in the category of giants like Hemingway and Fitzgerald. The Round Table was simply a handful of friends – a dozen or so humorists, critics and playwrights – who liked each other's company and so met every day for lunch and heated conversation. Why the name? Well, they ate at a large round table in the Rose Room, the hotel's dining room right off the lobby. It may seem odd that a bunch of talkative exhibitionists should be of interest to folks outside of New York City. But they had loony personalities and exceptional talent for self-promotion – and being irreverent and often malicious didn't hurt matters either. In their heyday, the whole mad, wired Algonquin crowd – Robert Benchley, George S Kaufman, Franklin P Adams, Aleck Woollcott – came to personify everything Americans considered clever and sophisticated.

The queen of the Algonquin Round Table was Dorothy Parker, one of the shrewdest and most elegant satirists of the 20th century. Demure in appearance and manner, a perfect little lady, Mrs Parker, as she preferred to be addressed, was renowned for her scathing wit in both writing and conversation. Hearing that a friend had hurt her leg on a trip to London, she responded coolly, 'She probably injured herself sliding down a barrister.' When told that Calvin Coolidge was dead, she promptly fired from the hip, 'How can they tell?' Katharine Hepburn's acting, she wrote, 'runs the gamut of emotions from A to B.' A remark that Clare Booth Luce was invariably kind to her inferiors caused her to murmur, 'And where does she find them?' My personal favourite is a caustic review of a science book that was written 'without fear and without research'. Everything considered, her patter sounds remarkably fresh after 75 years.

Although outwardly successful, Mrs

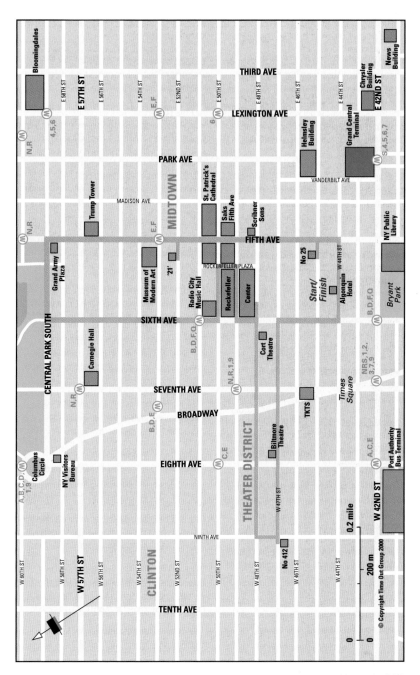

Parker's private life was a mess. She wrote poems that were masterpieces of irony and brilliant short stories like 'Big Blonde', her dark portrait of a good-sport party girl, but that was not the whole story. There were self-destructive relationships and a half-dozen suicide attempts. Numbing herself with an ocean of booze, she survived two marriages, countless lovers, and a monumental writer's block.

A native New Yorker, Dorothy Rothschild Parker began her life on the Upper West Side as the daughter of a wealthy clothing manufacturer. At the turn of the century, summer vacationing at the Jersey shore, she would ask other children, 'What street do you live on?' – never what town or city. That people lived anywhere except New York never occurred to her.

During her 73 years she resided, worked or played all over Manhattan. Still, the most logical place to begin a Dorothy Parker walk has got to be the Algonquin Hotel at 59 West 44th Street, one of the city's most famous literary landmarks. A plaque just outside the entrance announces that here is the site of the legendary Round Table 'where such acid tongued wits as Dorothy Parker, Robert Benchley, and Alexander Woollcott traded barbs and bon mots daily over lunch'. Not only has Parker endured as the most famous member of the Round Table, but the hotel was also her home at various times, a less well-known fact. To Parker, never a domestic person, hotels were the perfect answer to most of life's problems, because they meant never having to cook, make your own bed or be alone. All she needed, she once joked, was a hotel room with a bed to lay her hat and a few friends. Even though the 'Gonk' was her favourite hotel, she seldom paid her rent because she felt the establishment should be flattered to have her there.

Not so long ago, Times Square resembled a honky-tonk amusement park. Its transformation in recent years, little short of fantastic, has left some Midtown streets practically unrecognisable. Not West 44th Street, especially the single block between Sixth Avenue (aka the Avenue of the Americas) and Fifth Avenue, which is much as it was in Parker's day.

This particular block, packed with prime real estate, is the home of New York clubs: the New York Yacht Club, Harvard Club, Penn Club, New York City Bar Association and the General Society of Mechanics and Tradesmen. Also preserved, however, are some significant sites from Dorothy Parker's early history.

Leaving the Algonquin, make a left and walk toward Fifth, past the Hotel Iroquois and the red-brick Harvard Club designed by McKim, Mead and White in 1894. Next door at Nos.19-25 is an ordinary office building whose ground floor flies the tomato-red awnings of an Italian restaurant and a sports club. The upper floors of this, the Berkeley Building, once housed the editorial offices of the Condé Nast publishing company. In 1915, Dorothy Rothschild got her first job in publishing, writing saucy photo captions for *Vogue* magazine. Subsequently moving over to *Vogue*'s sister publication, *Vanity Fair*, she contributed light verse and humorous articles. In 1918, she replaced PG Wodehouse as drama critic, quite a coup for an unknown writer who was only 25 and female.

Cross to the other side of the street and double back toward Sixth Avenue because another magazine associated with Parker has also left its footprints in this block. The office building at No.28 bears a Literary Landmark plaque that reads, 'The *New Yorker*, founded in 1925, two blocks north of this site, occupied several floors of this building from 1935-1991.' Listed are a dozen writers, including James Thurber and John Updike, but curiously there is no mention of Parker,

who as one of the magazine's founding writers helped to create what would become known as 'New Yorker Style', particularly the short essays called 'casuals'. If you cut through the lobby to the building's south entrance, at 25 West 43rd you'll notice an identical plaque, again with no reference to Parker and her Round Table friends, without whose unpaid contributions the magazine would never have survived. The New Yorker in the past ten years has moved twice, to 20 West 43rd and now to the shiny Condé Nast office tower at 4 Times Square.

A bit further down the block at 44 West 44th is the upscale Royalton Hotel, a windowless wonder with a futuristic Star Wars-style interior. The renovated Royalton is owned by Ian Schrager of Studio 54 fame, but in Parker's day, the hotel was a fleabag. Parker's best friend was the puckish humorist Robert Benchley, who did his writing in a room at the Gonk but found the three-ring circus atmosphere too distracting. Almost opposite was the Royalton, a place sufficiently unappetising, he decided, so that Dottie and the other party-loving Round Tablers would never think of roaming across the street and bothering him there. (He was wrong.)

Keep heading west to the corner of Sixth Avenue and imagine yourself back in Jazz Age Times Square, a bustling, claustrophobic village of low office buildings, lofts and high-stooped brownstones. Narrow side streets were congested with theatres and restaurants and cellar speakeasies, where the bars were lined with bottles of Canadian Scotch just off the boat and little dishes of orange slices and lemon peel for the Whiskey Sours, Old Fashioneds and Tom Collinses. At 1120 Sixth Avenue, between 43rd and 44th Streets, you'll notice the unimpressive Hippodrome office building and parking garage. But back then it was the real Hippodrome, an indoor stadium that presented circuses and other theatrical extravaganzas and touted itself as 'The World's Largest Playhouse'. Avenue of the Americas, then Sixth Avenue, was cast into perpetual gloom by an overhead railroad. The tracks of the elevated trains were directly above the sidewalks and the trains almost touched the buildings on either side.

One of the most poignant remarks about Manhattan Island was written by Parker in 1964: 'As only New Yorkers know, if you can get through the twilight, you'll live through the night.'

Let's retrace Parker's footsteps as she leaves the Algonquin at twilight one evening and plunges into the Times Square throngs, on her way to her aisle seat on an opening night at the Biltmore. During any theatrical season in the '20s, there were no fewer than 70 theatres in which roughly 250 shows might open. Parker's trail takes her north under the El tracks on Sixth Avenue to the intersection of 47th Street, where she heads west along the side street. Crossing Broadway and Seventh Avenue, she arrives at the Biltmore Theater, at the corner of West 47th Street and Eighth Avenue (now opposite the Brooks Atkinson Theater). Right now the venerable Biltmore is a ruin, sadly deserted and boarded up, although its ghostly marquee is still visible. Parker spent many an evening at theatres such as the Biltmore, the Garrick, and the Selwyn – almost all of them intact but whose names have been changed. Parker so loved the theatre that she would write several Broadway plays of her own (Close Harmony and The Ladies of the Corridor among them). By the same token, she could be a merciless critic whose wicked reviews sometimes sounded a show's death knell. After sitting through a dreadfully boring turkey, she recommended that audiences best come prepared with knitting. 'If you don't knit, bring a book.'

**Broadway** and Times Square in the '20s and early '30s were a bustling congestion of theatres, restaurants and speakeasies.

From the Biltmore it's a short walk to your next stop on West 47th Street. Travelling west of Eighth Avenue takes you off the beaten track to a neighbourhood called Clinton but traditionally known as Hell's Kitchen, once a notorious area of tenements and warehouses, headquarters for hoodlum gangs with names like the Hudson Dusters. In 1923, when Hell's Kitchen was still a sinister place, editor Harold Ross and his wife Jane Grant purchased a double house between Ninth and Tenth Avenues and began making plans to publish a new humour magazine. At No.412 you'll find a ramshackle four-storey building with a green door and peeling dark grey paint, the spot that was the real birthplace of The *New Yorker*. From the outset, Parker and her Round Table friends were in on the discussions, helping Ross find a name for his magazine and then keeping the fledgling publication afloat with free contributions. Parker was also a frequent visitor to after-theatre parties at the house, where the gregarious Aleck Woollcott lived for a time with Ross and Grant. The house had no electricity and each room was heated with a potbelly stove. It is now a Literary Landmark with a plaque declaring that Ross used to tell his writers 'if you can't be funny, be interesting', and recording the factoid that the 1923 housewarming was attended by Dorothy Parker, Harpo Marx and George Gershwin. She did indeed attend the party, and so did Scott Fitzgerald and Edna St Vincent Millay who recited her poems. Parker and playwright Charles MacArthur (*The Front Page*) rented a merry-go-round and gave rides to the neighbourhood children. More on the *New Yorker* later.

Your next stop is the Rockefeller Center. Walking east on 48th Street, stop to look at the Cort Theater, at No.138, where Parker attended many a first night from her aisle seat. One of the oldest and most beautiful of Broadway theatres, it was built in 1912 for a producer named John Cort and remains one of the few old houses to retain its original name.

Continue to the corner of Sixth Avenue and West 48th Street, where you'll see the Simon & Schuster Building. Cross the avenue and walk a few doors east on 48th Street until you reach No.61, a side entrance of the publishing company. On this site once stood a four-storey brownstone that housed Boni & Liveright, one of the most historic firms in American publishing. Horace Liveright was a dynamic entrepreneur who threw fabulous parties on the awning-covered roof garden and was said to keep a home-made still and a 'casting couch' in his private office. Parker's first two volumes of bestselling poetry, *Enough Rope* (1926) and *Sunset Gun* (1928), were published by Liveright, whose roster of blue-chip authors included Eugene O'Neill, Theodore Dreiser, Ernest Hemingway, Anita Loos, Sherwood Anderson and William Faulkner. In fact, there was hardly a major American writer alive in the '20s whom Liveright didn't publish. For all his brilliance, however, Liveright went bankrupt in 1930 and died three years later at the age of 46.

Now walk back to Sixth Avenue, head north, and turn right on to West 49th Street and the heart of the Rockefeller Center. The area between Fifth and Sixth Avenues, extending from 48th to 52nd Streets, was in the '20s a jumble of decaying row houses and small shops. Between 1931 and 1940, 11 acres were razed and 14 buildings constructed (18 today) in order to create 'a city within a city', one of the outstanding architectural achievements in the world. In the short block between Sixth and the skating rink on the Lower Plaza were the former sites of two speakeasies that Parker and Benchley frequented almost nightly.

Although the sale of alcohol was banned in 1920, Prohibition created more

Some of Parker's favourite gin mills were razed to the ground to make way for this 'city within a city', the **Rockefeller Center**.

Although on a different site now, the '21' club was one speakeasy that survived Prohibition.

drinkers than ever and triggered the opening of hundreds of illegal bars and clubs in Midtown. During these years, Parker's lifelong problem with alcohol began. Her hangovers, she joked, were so historic that they 'ought to be in the Smithsonian under glass.'

Halfway up the block on the north side of 49th Street you will see the 70-storey General Electric Building at 30 Rockefeller Plaza, the home of NBC Studios and the Rainbow Room. On this spot was Tony Soma's, Parker's favourite gin mill. (Tony Soma was the maternal grandfather of actress Anjelica Huston.) Tables at Tony's were covered with red checked cloths. Bootleg booze was served speakeasy-style

in white china mugs, and food was pretty much limited to steak sandwiches. When a Tony's bartender one night asked what she was having, a grim Parker answered, 'Not much fun.' She suffered from suicidal depressions and made several attempts to end her life. One of her poems, 'Resume', rates the various methods of committing suicide, an example of the way she used highly personal experiences as raw material for her writings.

Opposite Tony Soma's at 42 West 49th was another of Parker's favourite hangouts, Jack and Charlie's Puncheon Club, operating from a brownstone with an iron grille gate and tiny speakeasy peephole. Catering to the Harvard and

Yale crowd, it is said to have served the best black market Scotch available. When the 49th Street row houses were demolished, Tony's closed for good, but Jack and Charlie's reopened on West 52nd Street as the '21' Club. Today the exact site of the Puncheon Club can be pinpointed as somewhere between Christie's and the street-level studio of NBC's *Today* show.

Returning to Sixth Avenue, we have eight blocks' worth of gawking time before the next Parker site. Keep walking straight uptown past Radio City Music Hall, the New York Hilton and the Harley Davidson Café. Keep in mind that in the '20s, you would have been walking under the El tracks and risking cinders and soot from the trains falling on your head. On the north-east corner of Sixth Avenue and West 57th Street you can't miss a gold and gilt-trimmed medical office building whose ground floor is occupied by a sporting goods store and a stationer's. Eighty years ago, this was a three-storey commercial building nestled next to the El train and tenanted mainly by artists.

Parker and her husband Eddie rented an apartment there, and when they separated in 1922 she stayed on alone. Across the hall was the studio of Neysa McMein, an important illustrator at whose nightly alcohol-soaked open houses the Round Table people liked to congregate (she had installed a still in her bathroom). For Parker this lively building at 57 West 57th Street meant both wonderful parties and frightening memories. It was here one night in 1923 that her miseries eventually caught up with her and she tried to kill herself. After ordering dinner from the Swiss Alps restaurant downstairs, she slashed both wrists with an old razor blade of her husband's.

But back to happier times. Continue up Sixth Avenue for two more blocks and take a right at Central Park South. Keep an eye out for the Park Lane Helmsley Hotel (No.36). On this spot, actually at 38 West 59th, stood a brownstone where

Parker used to visit her friend Scott Fitzgerald and his new wife Zelda shortly after their marriage in 1920.

You are now approaching the Plaza Hotel, one of the city's most magnificent landmarks, a 19-storey French Renaissance chateau built in 1907. In the lobby is the famed Palm Court, where afternoon tea is served to the accompaniment of violins and a harp. It was here in the Palm Court on a Sunday afternoon in 1920, when the streets of New York were piled with snow, that Parker had been summoned to tea by the editor of *Vanity Fair*. On the table there was a bowl of mossy red roses, but this was plainly not a cosy social occasion. One of Parker's unkind reviews had caused extreme pain to Broadway impresario Flo Ziegfeld, and so over the china teacups, Mrs Parker learned that her services would no longer be required. If she wished, she could write little things from home. Even though she left the Plaza boiling mad that January afternoon, her dismissal turned out to be a blessing in disguise because she soon embarked on her real career of poet, short story writer, and later screenwriter.

Emerging from the Plaza, you could turn north on Fifth and walk 15 blocks uptown to East 74th Street. A few doors in from Central Park is the Volney, which looks like a typical East Side co-operative apartment house. Fifty years ago, however, it was a residence hotel, inhabited almost entirely by elderly widows. Parker was inspired to write (with Arnaud D'Usseau) *The Ladies of the Corridor*, which played on Broadway in 1953. The Volney was Parker's last home, the hotel where she lived with her poodle, Troy, and a nurse-companion, and where she died of a heart attack on 7 June 1967.

But this detour uptown is out of your way and personally I don't think it's really worth the hike. Instead, let's stick with the young Dorothy Parker and head back downtown on Fifth Avenue. On the corner of 57th Street, pause to take a peek in the windows of Tiffany & Co. One of Parker's most charming short stories, 'The Standard of Living', evokes delicious memories of Parker and her dear friend Robert Benchley when they worked together at *Vanity Fair* in 1919, a pair of struggling young writers still trying to make names for themselves. In the story, however, it is two window-shopping stenographers who amuse themselves by fantasising how they would spend a million dollars. Finally one day the girls can't resist entering a Fifth Avenue jewellery store, where they are shocked to learn that a string of pearls costs a quarter of a million dollars. If Tiffany's was not the inspiration for 'The Standard of Living', then surely it must have been Cartier, another grand jewellery establishment five blocks down the avenue on the corner of 52nd Street. When you reach Cartier, cross Fifth Avenue and go down West 52nd Street for a look at the present day '21' club, which is one of the few speakeasies to survive from the Prohibition era. It is now a high-class establishment (lunch for two, with wine, will run to about $150), but has some charming cast iron jockeys with horse owners' names beneath spread along the ornate balcony.

While there is no trace of Parker at '21' now, at least one of the Round Table celebrities is here in spirit because a plaque in the bar is dedicated to Robert Benchley. It simply says 'Robert Benchley – His Corner'.

Go back to Fifth and continue downtown on the final leg of your walk. After passing the Gothic towers of St Patrick's Cathedral and the Channel Gardens flower beds of the Rockefeller Center, both located at 50th Street, note the handsome building at 597 Fifth, between 49th and 48th Streets. Currently occupied by the United Colors of Benetton store, this was originally the home of Charles Scribner's Sons, the prestigious book publisher of Hemingway, Fitzgerald and Wolfe. The company name can still be seen chiselled into the ornate façade, and

high on the south-facing wall. Scribner's still exists – it's a subsidiary of Viacom Inc – but its glory days are long over. At 45th Street, make a right. A quick walk to No.25 will allow you to check out the *New Yorker*'s very first home, the dinky Central Building now surrounded by hardware and electronic stores. Don't look for a landmark plaque here. During its ten years in this location (1925-35), the *New Yorker* evolved from a sophomoric humour rag into one of the most successful literary magazines in publishing history. But at first it was, in the words of James Thurber, 'the outstanding flop of 1925'; unpaid contributors expected its demise at any moment. Unenthusiastic, and always a great procrastinator, Parker had little motivation to turn in work. A grumpy Harold Ross blew his stack. 'I thought you were coming into the office to write a piece last week. What happened?' 'Somebody was using the pencil,' Parker explained sorrowfully.

Only yards away is City Noodle, several steps down the culinary ladder from '21', but one of Midtown's unsung Chinese restaurants serving generous portions of good cheap food. Except to refuel here, I don't see any reason to linger.

To get back to the Algonquin, continue one further block south on Fifth and take a right. The hotel had a $5.5-million dollar facelift in 1998, but it is still possible to soak up plenty of Victorian atmosphere. (A house cat roams the premises.) The best place to enjoy a drink is the oak-panelled lobby, where you can sit on a dusty-looking velvet sofa among the potted palms and ring the tabletop bell to summon waiters in grey and red waistcoats. Other first-floor spots include the Oak Room and the romantic Blue Bar. The celebrated Rose Room is gone but its replacement, the Round Table Room, is dominated by a huge round table; lunch

The Gothic towers of **St Patrick's Cathedral** stand proudly opposite the Channel Gardens of the Rockefeller Center.

for two with wine is about $60. Upstairs, the hallowed hallways have been papered with *New Yorker* cartoons, and on each room door is a plaque with a quip from Dorothy Parker or one of the Round Table wits.

Parker supposedly used to live on the second floor but by this time exact locations are impossible to confirm. I can tell you this much, however: in 1932, in residence with her dachshund Robinson, she overdosed on sleeping powders and summoned help by throwing out the window a glass that shattered below on 44th Street. So I figure the room must have been on a fairly low floor. Today, on the 11th floor, the hotel has confected a two-room Dorothy Parker suite, which is pleasantly decorated with memorabilia: autographed letters, photographs of the writer as a glamorous young woman and a mature woman with her poodle, and a movie poster for *Sweethearts*, a sentimental Nelson Eddy/Jeanette MacDonald musical she co-wrote in 1938.

If you decide to book the Dorothy Parker suite, you will have to shell out $579 per night, the same as for the hotel's other suites, but the off-peak rate is a steal at $279. I can just imagine Parker, who was born with a built-in bull-detector, howling with laughter over those room rates. Late in life she seems to have enjoyed making fun of the Round Table and its ten-year lunch, which she dismissed as 'just a lot of people telling jokes and telling each other how good they were'. Even so, the Gonk survives as one of Manhattan's most beloved literary institutions. If the essence of Mrs Dorothy Parker lingers anywhere, this has got to be the place.

# Eating & drinking

### '21'
*21 West 52nd Street, between Fifth & Sixth Avenues (212 582 7200).* **Open** noon-2.30pm, 5.30-10.15pm Mon-Thur; noon-2.30pm, 5.30-11pm Fri; 5.30-11pm Sat; 5.30-10.15pm Sun. Former speakeasy and hallowed haunt of old-boydom retains its classic American dishes.

### Blue Bar
*Algonquin Hotel, 59 West 44th Street, between Fifth & Sixth Avenues (212 840 6800).* **Open** 11.30am-12.45am Mon-Sat; noon-12.45 Sun.

### City Noodle Shop
*15 West 45th Street, between Fifth & Sixth Avenues (212 768 1629).* **Open** 10.30am-10pm daily.

### Harley Davidson Café
*1370 Sixth Avenue, at 56th Street (212 245 6000).* **Open** 11.30am-midnight Mon-Fri; 11.30am-1am Sat, Sun.

### Oak Room
*Algonquin Hotel, 59 West 44th Street, between Fifth & Sixth Avenues (212 840 6800).* **Open** 7-11pm Tue-Thur (show 9pm); 7pm-1.30am Fri, Sat (shows 9, 11.30pm).

### The Palm Court
*The Plaza Hotel, 768 Fifth Avenue, at 59th Street (212 546 5350).* **Open** 6.30am-midnight daily. Classic tea for two in sumptuous surroundings.

### Round Table Room
*Algonquin Hotel, 59 West 44th Street, between Fifth & Sixth Avenues (212 840 6800).* **Open** 7am-10am, 11.30am-2.30pm, 5-10.30pm daily. Standard American meat, fish and pasta dishes in this legendary New York institution.

### Torre di Pisa
*19 West 44th Street, between Fifth & Sixth Avenues (212 398 4400).*

# Clubs

### General Society of Mechanics & Tradesmen
*20 West 44th Street, between Fifth & Sixth Avenues (212 840 1840).*

### Harvard Club of New York City
*27 West 44th Street, between Fifth & Sixth Avenues (212 840 6600).*

### New York City Bar Association
*42 West 44th Street, between Fifth & Sixth Avenues (212 382 6600).*

### New York Yacht Club
*37 West 44th Street, between Fifth & Sixth Avenues (212 382 1000).*

### Penn Club
*30 West 44th Street, between Fifth & Sixth Avenues (212 764 3550).*

# Hotels

### Algonquin
*59 West 44th Street, between Fifth & Sixth Avenues (212 840 6800).*

### Park Lane Helmsley
*36 Central Park South, between Fifth & Sixth Avenues (212 371 4000).*

### The Iroquois
*49 West 44th Street, between Fifth & Sixth Avenues (212 840 3080).*

### New York Hilton
*1335 Sixth Avenue, between 53rd & 54th Streets (212 586 7000).*

### The Plaza Hotel
*768 Fifth Avenue, at 59th Street (212 759 3000).*

### Royalton
*44 West 44th Street, between Fifth & Sixth Avenues (212 869 4400).*

# Theatres & studios

### Brooks Atkinson Theater
*256 West 47th Street, between Broadway & Eighth Avenue (212 719 4099).*

### Cort Theater
*138 West 48th Street, between Sixth & Seventh Avenue (212 239 6200).*

### NBC
*30 Rockefeller Plaza, 49th Street, between Fifth & Sixth Avenues (212 664 3700).* **Open** *tours* 8.30am-5.30pm Mon-Sat; 9.30-4.30pm Sun. **Admission** $17.50, $15 concessions. Under-6s not admitted.

### Radio City Music Hall
*Sixth Avenue, between 50th & 51st Streets (212 247 4777).* **Open** *tours* 10am-5pm Mon-Sat; 11am-5pm Sun. **Admission** $15; $9 under-12s.

# Shops

### Cartier
*653 Fifth Avenue, at 52nd Street (212 446 3459).* **Open** 10am-6pm Mon-Fri; 10am-5.30pm Sat.

### Christie's
*20 Rockefeller Plaza, at 49th Street, between Fifth & Sixth Avenues (212 636 2000).* **Open** 9.30am-5.30pm Mon-Fri.

### Tiffany & Co
*727 Fifth Avenue, at 57th Street (212 755 8000).* **Open** 10am-6pm Mon-Wed, Fri, Sat; 10am-7pm Thur.

### United Colors of Benetton
*597 Fifth Avenue, at 48th Street (212 593 0290).* **Open** 10am-7pm Mon-Sat; 10am-5pm Sun.

# Publishers & publications

### The New Yorker
*4 Times Square, West 42nd Street, between Sixth Avenue & Broadway (212 286 5611).*

### The New York Times
*229 West 43rd Street, between Seventh & Eighth Avenues (212 597 8001).*

### Condé Nast Publications
*4 Times Square, West 42nd Street, between Sixth Avenue & Broadway (212 286 2860).*

### Simon & Schuster
*1230 Sixth Avenue, between 48th & 49th Streets (212 698 7000).*

# Film & literature

**Enough Rope** Dorothy Parker (1926)
**The Front Page** Charles MacArthur & Ben Hecht (1928)
**Here Lies: The Collected Short Stories of Dorothy Parker** Dorothy Parker (1939)
**Not So Deep As a Well: Collected Poems** Dorothy Parker (1936)
**Sunset Gun** Dorothy Parker (1928)
**Sweethearts** (WS van Dyke, 1938, US)

# Others

### Rockefeller Center
*48th to 51st Streets, between Fifth & Sixth Avenues (212 632 3975).* **Admission** free. *Tours* self-guided tours are available at the GE Building, 30 Rockefeller Plaza (the north-south street between Fifth and Sixth Avenues).

### St Patrick's Cathedral
*Fifth Avenue, between 50th & 51st Streets (212 753 2261).* **Open** 7am-8.45pm Mon-Fri, Sun; 8am-8.45pm Sat. *Tours* 9-11am, 1.30-4.30pm Mon-Fri. Call for tour dates and times. **Services** 7am, 7.30am, 8am, 8.30am, noon, 12.30pm, 1pm, 5.30pm Mon-Fri; 8am, 8.30am, noon, 12.30pm, 5.30pm Sat; 7am, 8am, 9am, 10.15am, noon, 1pm, 4pm, 5.30pm Sun.

# Bridge the gap

Phillip Lopate

Take pleasure in wandering through a peaceful urban community that actually works.

**Start:** Brooklyn Bridge
**Finish:** Smith Street, Brooklyn
**Time:** 3-4 hours
**Distance:** 7.5 miles/12km
**Getting there:** subway trains 4, 5 or 6 to Brooklyn Bridge-City Hall station; trains J, M or Z to Chambers Street station
**Getting back:** subway trains F or G from Bergen Street station
**Note:** this walk offers spectacular views of the Manhattan skyline, so it is worth choosing a clear day. It could be followed by John Waldman's walk, *Perfume Creek*.

When out-of-towners ask me for activity tips in New York, I offer the usual ideas – the Frick Collection, a walk down Broadway – followed by 'Hey, why don't you come over to Brooklyn?' I am apt to be met with a frown, an abashed confession that they've never been to Brooklyn, and the clear suggestion that they're not about to start now. Too bad: Brooklyn is fascinating. (Of course, I grew up in it and might be prejudiced.) Though the borough has its share of handsome civic, cultural, recreational and commercial structures, what's most compelling about it is its residential neighbourhoods, where real people live. I'm not saying real people don't live in

**Brooklyn Bridge** and the views it offers are stunning – a true suspension of belief.

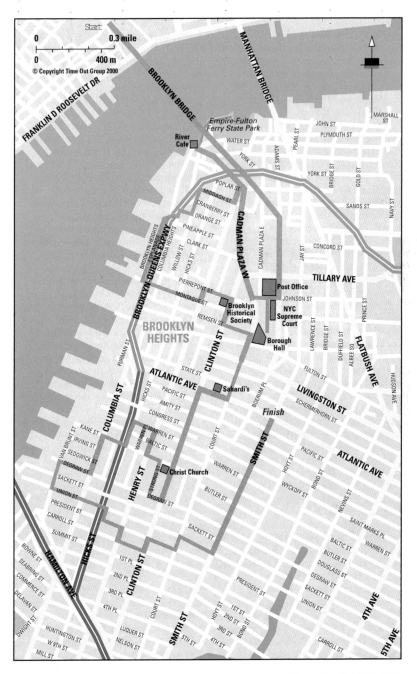

Start

0                0.3 mile

0           400 m

© Copyright Time Out Group 2000

FRANKLIN D ROOSEVELT DR

BROOKLYN BRIDGE

MANHATTAN BRIDGE

MARSHALL ST

Empire-Fulton Ferry State Park

River Cafe

JOHN ST

PLYMOUTH ST

WATER ST

PEARL ST

ADAMS ST

YORK ST

YORK ST

YORK ST

BRIDGE ST

GOLD ST

NAVY ST

POPLAR ST

MIDDAGH ST

CRANBERRY ST

ORANGE ST

PINEAPPLE ST

CLARK ST

WILLOW ST

HICKS ST

SANDS ST

CADMAN PLAZA W

CADMAN PLAZA E

JAY ST

CONCORD ST

Brooklyn Heights Esplanade

COLUMBIA HEIGHTS

PIERREPONT ST

MONTAGUE ST

REMSEN ST

Brooklyn Historical Society

Post Office

NYC Supreme Court

JOHNSON ST

TILLARY AVE

LAWRENCE ST

BRIDGE ST

DUFFIELD ST

ALBEE SQ

PRINCE ST

HUDSON AVE

FLATBUSH AVE

BROOKLYN HEIGHTS

FURMAN ST

CLINTON ST

Borough Hall

STATE ST

FULTON ST

LIVINGSTON ST

SCHERMERHORN ST

COLUMBIA ST

HICKS ST

ATLANTIC AVE

PACIFIC ST

AMITY ST

CONGRESS ST

Sahardi's

BOERUM PL

COURT ST

Finish

PACIFIC ST

HOYT ST

BOND ST

ATLANTIC AVE

KANE ST

IRVING ST

VAN BRUNT ST

SEDGWICK ST

DEGRAW ST

SACKETT ST

UNION ST

PRESIDENT ST

CARROLL ST

SUMMIT ST

WARREN ST

BALTIC ST

HENRY ST

STRONG PL

Christ Church

DEGRAW ST

WARREN ST

BUTLER ST

WYCKOFF ST

NEVINS ST

SAINT MARKS PL

WARREN ST

BALTIC ST

BUTLER ST

DOUGLASS ST

DEGRAW ST

SACKETT ST

UNION ST

SACKETT ST

HAMILTON AVE

HICKS ST

BOWNE ST

SEABRING ST

COMMERCE ST

DELAVAN ST

DWIGHT ST

HUNTINGTON ST

W 9TH ST

MILL ST

1ST PL

2ND PL

3RD PL

4TH PL

CLINTON ST

COURT ST

LUQUER ST

NELSON ST

SMITH ST

5TH ST

PRESIDENT ST

HOYT ST

1ST ST

2ND ST

3RD ST

4TH ST

BOND ST

CARROLL ST

4TH AVE

5TH AVE

Manhattan, but they often look as if they're waiting for a casting call, or a psychiatric social worker: as soon as you cross over to Brooklyn, the dress becomes more casual, not to say zhlubbier, the walk slower, the accent thicker, the sky higher and more expansive. Brooklyn is the Texas of New York.

The best way to enter is by strolling over the Brooklyn Bridge, that masterpiece of engineering and aesthetic eclecticism (steel cables slung like piano wires over a Gothic wall) by the Roeblings, father and son. Since its opening in 1883, it has become one of New York's beloved landmarks, providing breathtaking views of the whole port area. It was Washington Roebling's inspiration, in a city where the street is the essential unit, to turn the bridge into a sort of boulevard, by providing a central boardwalk raised above the traffic. You catch the pedestrian entrance in Manhattan at Chambers Street, by the Municipal Building, where you merge into the stream of walkers, joggers and bicyclists. Those who tire may pause by the monument plaques in the centre, meanwhile holding on to any headgear in the strong breeze.

Follow right to the end of the central walkway and walk past the side of the turreted, castle-like US Post Office, a Romanesque Revival building with magnificent stonework and deep parking bays, on one block and turn right, along the front entrance of the Post Office, to Cadman Plaza. This is the large, open public space that welcomes you to Brooklyn: free of cars, it invites busy office workers to cut across, and idlers to loll on the benches, taking in the triple-decker black fountain, the Brooklyn Borough Hall (a Greek Revival hôtel de ville, with a golden figure of Justice on top), the columned Brooklyn Municipal Building in the background, the ornate, restored subway kiosk that now holds an elevator for the disabled or lazy, and, on any clement day, tented stalls that proffer

earrings, African masks, handbags, shifts, votive candles, baseball caps, even Oriental massage. The grassy, flowered part of Cadman Plaza is called Columbus Park, and holds the requisite statue of the Genoan navigator at one end, and a pedestalled Henry Ward Beecher, Brooklyn's 19th-century abolitionist preacher, surrounded by grateful black children, on the other. (His church sermons were so popular that Beecher ferries swollen with devotees would cross over from Manhattan each Sunday. That is, until the love-scandal involving him with a parishioner's wife brought him down.)

Alongside the plaza stands the New York State Supreme Court, a long horizontal building, very 1950s, with white-framed windows that suggest square portholes, done by the same architectural firm, Shreve, Lamb & Harmon, that gave us the Empire State Building. This part of downtown Brooklyn is awash in bulky courthouses, fiercely barred jails, bail bondsmen, reluctant jurors, summons-respondents and criminals' loved ones, looking lost, clutching papers with the scribbled address of some judicial chamber. Brooklynites often have bad associations with these buildings.

Yet the courthouses did much to stabilise the area until prosperity returned, in the form of Metrotech (a nearby campus of speculative office buildings) and the Marriott Renaissance Plaza, the first new hotel to rise in Brooklyn in over half a century.

We could stride deep into the heart of Brooklyn from Cadman Plaza, but I have another suggestion. First let's double back and explore the historic area down by the East River, the Fulton Ferry District, which is so important to Brooklyn's past and future. Follow Cadman Plaza West alongside the park, and follow the side of the bridge (where it changes its name to Old Fulton Street), past a choppy, nerve-racking zone of Brooklyn-Queens Expressway off-ramps and parkways.

Thrusting glass towers and decaying brick warehouses – they're both on view at **DUMBO**.

Stop in at the Anchorage, an art gallery located in the Brooklyn Bridge innards, if it happens to be open; if not, cross over to Front Street. You will be standing in front of a quaint cast-iron white palazzo, once a bank, now the home of the Tin Room Café.

Across the street is the area's most architecturally impressive building: Eagle Warehouse, by Brooklyn's great architect, Frank Freeman. The 1893 storehouse, now converted to condominiums, has the brooding look of a Roman prison fortress, Castel Sant Angelo, say, with its projecting cornices and meticulously thin brickwork. Ah, the golden age of American masonry (predominantly the work of poor Italian immigrants). If you look around quickly at the Brooklyn waterfront skyline, you can see a few more muscular, striking old high-rises, one bearing the name Sweeny Manufacturing Company Building, another the Clock Tower (an early reinforced-concrete loft building, also turned into condos). Together, they convey the romance of that era, when the ships brought everything in the world to the Fulton Ferry loading docks. Once the Brooklyn Bridge opened, the area declined in importance.

Proceed down the hill, past Patsy Grimaldi's, said to have the best pizza in New York (coal-brick oven, fresh ingredients, red-checkered tablecloths, low acoustic-tiled ceiling and loud Sinatra). You pass by a mélange of old two or three-storey structures that date from the mid-19th century, when this street was a popular thoroughfare for thirsty travellers and dock workers who served the Fulton Ferry.

Wander down to the Fulton Ferry pier. From this point, George Washington and his troops slunk ignominiously out of New York, fleeing to fight another day. The pier has been recently restored and turned into an attractive public space; still standing on it is the simple, lighthouse-like tower that had been used for drying fire hoses. It's locked; someday they'll find a new use for it. To the left is Bargemusic, a floating crate where chamber music of fairly high quality can be heard half the year. To the right is the River Café, a classy restaurant with million-dollar views, where I've eaten only once and keep promising myself to go back, when I'm feeling more worthy. There's a lovely garden attached to it, open to the public. You pass round the garden and to the right and find yourself directly under the brontosauran arch of the Brooklyn Bridge; it feels startlingly theatrical, as if you'd suddenly drifted on to the set of *A View from the Bridge* or *Dead End*. I've seen young Hispanic men on occasion polishing low-riders here, while their girlfriends marked time, chewing gum.

At water's edge, the area between the Brooklyn and Manhattan Bridges, known as DUMBO (Down Underneath the Manhattan Bridge Overpass), has the look of a great urban space still in the process of becoming. It isn't there yet. You pass a ditch littered with garbage, and some city administrative building, fenced off with barbed wire, which I was once told is used as a repository for glass. Then you come upon the Empire Fulton Ferry State Park: modestly designed and landscaped, it consists of a narrow wooden boardwalk, grassy knolls and views of the Manhattan skyline that are to die for. It is clean and well maintained, perhaps because it's under the jurisdiction of New York State, rather than the more hard-pressed City. Just behind the park looms the mysterious, tantalising Empire Stores, a row of post-Civil War warehouses, dark-brown brick, whose arched windows have been boarded up for decades. It's a perennial architectural school project: What would you do with the Empire Stores? Con Edison, the local utility company, had once planned to turn it into a generating plant; the City had thought to relocate the meat market there; a developer had proposed the sort of retail emporium that seems to infest waterfronts everywhere, cotton candy and T-shirts;

Day or night, the **Brooklyn Heights Esplanade** has few rivals for its sweeping skyline views.

local artists had lobbied for subsidised studios. You look at it and think: surely a more civilised city would have figured out by now how to make use of such a promising shell. It has a karmic, Victorian lunacy that resists all intervention.

Someday, 30 years hence, this whole part of waterfront Brooklyn will be transformed into a bright, overly defined public space, edged by private luxury housing, no doubt. Go now, if you have an attraction to the twilight poetry of decay and potential still unrealised.

You should now retrace your steps out of the park, past the River Café, and ascend Old Fulton Street on the Eagle Warehouse side. Peel off at Henry Street, on the right: this will take you to the enchanted backwaters of Brooklyn Heights.

Henry Street intersects with Poplar Street and, one block further along, Middagh Street. On a pleasantly hot, sunny day I can't imagine anything nicer than to stroll back and forth on these tree-lush streets, past the old clapboard cottages or Federal houses with their iron fences, which put me in mind of

Nantucket or New Orleans – in any case, not most people's idea of New York. Middagh Street is particularly rich in wood houses and cultural history, for it was at 7 Middagh (now sadly demolished) that Jane and Paul Bowles, Carson McCullers, WH Auden, George Davis (literary editor of *Harpers Bazaar*) and theatrical designer Oliver Smith set up house, with Richard Wright and Gypsy Rose Lee frequent visitors. Other writers who lived close by in Brooklyn Heights included Thomas Wolfe, Hart Crane (who rented the old apartment of Washington Roebling, from the window of which the invalid engineer had overseen the final stages of the Brooklyn Bridge), WEB DuBois, Arthur Miller, Norman Mailer, Truman Capote and Alfred Kazin. The cosy, comfy atmosphere of the so-called fruit streets (Pineapple, Cranberry, Orange) and the tree streets (Poplar, Willow) give the lie to the notion that creative effort requires suffering.

Indeed, as you ramble through these blocks, down Willow, up Pierrepont, across Columbia Heights, through mysterious little mews such as Love Lane or Grace Court Alley or Monroe Place, I think you will agree that no other area in New York is so harmonious or enjoys such consistent architectural quality. Parts of Greenwich Village or the Upper East Side may come close, but they must absorb regular clashes of visual dissonance at the cross-streets, whereas in Brooklyn Heights everything feels of a piece.

Not that the structures in the Heights are all alike, ranging as they do from modest bungalows to swanky mansions to block-long art deco apartment towers to sober brownstone churches, but everything moves to the same decorous beat, everything fits.

At Orange Street and Columbia Heights you can enter the Brooklyn Heights Esplanade, one of the happiest models for experiencing the water's edge in New York. Overlooking the harbour, and the Statue of Liberty in the distance, above but visually removed from the BQE (Brooklyn-Queens Expressway), the Esplanade exploits one of Brooklyn's greatest assets: its spectacular views of Manhattan. The hexagonal paving blocks, the painted steel railings, the old-fashioned lampposts add up to a superbly well-designed, safe, secure and congenial pedestrian environment. There, you are apt to see young lovers, elderly strollers, mothers with baby carriages, local residents reading on benches – but, oddly enough, no tourists. (Across the water, on the Manhattan side, tourists flock to the much tackier bleachers of the South Street Seaport's Pier 17, where no self-respecting New Yorker would ever be seen.) Part of the pleasure of walking the Esplanade is also facing away from the river, and looking into the backyards of the refined Columbia Heights houses, which make a continuous, civilised streetscape.

Exit the Promenade at Montague Street, and allow yourself to be swept along the popular main shopping street of Brooklyn Heights. If you are hungry, I recommend Teresa's, a capacious, competent diner

whose large menu offers everything under the sun, with special expertise in Polish dishes such as pirogi and kielbasa.

Parallel to Montague Street, a block or so north, is Pierrepont Street, which has many fine mansions and apartment houses worth investigating. I particularly like 84 Pierrepont, at the corner of Henry Street, by that same Frank Freeman who designed the Eagle Warehouse. Here he let his imagination run amok, with castellated protruding curves and turrets, the house unveiling itself to the eye in stages.

Another Romanesque Revival knockout, a block east, is the Brooklyn Historical Society, at the corner of Pierrepont and Clinton Streets, by architect George B Post – a symphony of deep reddish-blackish shades in brick, from 1881. Take Clinton Street a few blocks south to Remsen Street, go left and you will see a few more lovely public buildings from this era: Freeman's St Francis College at 176 Remsen, and the stunning Franklin Building a few doors down, at 186 Remsen, a marvellous combination of rock-face brownstone base and redbrick upper storeys.

At the end of Remsen Street, you will find yourself, amazingly enough, back at Cadman Plaza, facing the Brooklyn Borough Hall. You have been wandering in a circle, and now you are ready to sally forth into deepest Brooklyn. I would take Court Street, the main north/south axis, which is merely an extension of Cadman Plaza East under a new name. Court Street serves the government office workers, the court personnel, the Board of Education's bureaucratic staff headquartered at nearby Livingston Street, and neighbourhood residents. A wide and pleasant thoroughfare, with hardware stores, diners, photocopy shops and video stores at street level and a few storeys' worth of apartments above, its essentially low-built scale has been threatened, so locals feel, by a new, hefty tower between State and Schermerhorn Streets, which holds 12 movie theatres and a Barnes & Noble chain bookstore. The architects, Hardy Holzman Pfeiffer, obviously tried to give the high-rise some zest by stacking three coloured, striped sections on top of each other, but disgruntled residents consider it the ugliest intrusion imaginable. Myself, I welcome the extra movie theatres and bookstore, and in any case don't feel that Brooklyn should be frozen under a bell jar of pre-war quaintness. Brooklyn is not a fragile lily, but a once and future urban centre of robust development. Still, I will change my tune if three or four similar skyscrapers invade Court Street.

As you near Atlantic Avenue, you start to see signs in Arabic indicating the presence of a thriving Middle Eastern community. A turn right on to Atlantic Avenue takes you past Moroccan, Lebanese, Yemeni, Libyan and Jordanian restaurants, as well as the magnificent Sahadi's, an Arabian Nights of an appetiser store – filled with barrels of pistachio nuts, couscous, halvah, dates, dried apricots, spices – to which Arab-Americans and gourmet cooks flock from miles around. (Were you to turn in the other direction, left on Atlantic, you would

encounter blocks of antiques stores, which used to feature bargains and now offer choice, collectable furniture at the expected prices.)

Keep walking west, towards the water. If you turn left on to any of the streets parallel to Court Street, such as Clinton, Henry or Hicks, you will enter the area, just south of Atlantic Avenue, known as Cobble Hill. It is part of that lovely necklace of neighbourhoods that forms Brownstone Brooklyn: Brooklyn Heights, Cobble Hill, Boerum Hill, Carroll Gardens, Fort Greene, Park Slope, miles and miles of residential communities dominated by the classic, cocoa-coloured New York row house, commonly with a staircase, or stoop, leading to the entrance. Novelist Edith Wharton expressed her snobbish disapproval of this essentially middle-class dwelling type by remarking acidly that New York is "cursed with its universal chocolate-covered coating of the most hideous stone ever quarried." Notwithstanding her disdain, the brownstone has stood the test of time brilliantly as a one-family abode, or a one-family with rental apartment income, or a multiple dwelling.

**Sahadi's** is a dazzling blur of Middle Eastern delicacies – an Arabian strip on Atlantic Avenue.

There is no particular reason why a tourist should seek out Brownstone Brooklyn, except for the pleasure of walking through peaceful urban communities that work. In our current era, when city-making seems almost a lost art, planners from all over America would give their eye-teeth to recreate the texture of such functioning neighbourhoods in their locales.

Here it seems effortless: a continuous street wall of brownstone or brick row houses, which provide both home ownership and sufficient density to promote street interaction in a public realm. A walk south along Clinton Street, for instance, will give you a good sense of the varieties that can be squeezed from this simple row house. Many brownstones have elaborate decorative incisions and carved pediments. Some are wide and opulent, mansions built by wealthy merchants; others have narrow fronts, covering no more than two rooms per floor.

Unfortunately, brownstone weathers poorly, and so the façades are often ornamented as well by cracks, chips, scaling. There is also a good deal of artificial brownstone, dyed stucco. If you check out an interesting 1851 church at the corner of DeGraw and Strong Streets, by the distinguished architect Minard Lafever, you can see how the stucco veneer is flaking off the old brownstone, producing a picturesquely leprous façade like a ruined Spanish monastery. Nearby, at the corner of Clinton and Kane, is the much better-preserved Christ Church, by Richard Upjohn, who built Wall Street's famed Trinity Church: this dignified English Gothic structure has Tiffany windows and a façade of cut ashlar – what else? – brownstone.

Getting tired of brownstone? Then head immediately down Henry to Warren Street, turn right to the middle of the block, and discover one of the most magical spaces in New York City. This is Warren Place, an enclosed mews (which

Brownstone stoops decorate **Clinton Street**.

you may enter from the Warren Street side; the Baltic Street side is locked) of exquisite, gingerbread houses on either side of a series of flower gardens and ivy pits, which looks like a movie set of Victorian England. The redbrick façades and black wrought iron gates make for a very pleasing ensemble, and you are brought up short by the plaque informing you that these were built in 1879 as cottages for 'workingmen'. Oh, to be a workingman and qualify! They are part of, and surrounded by, a much larger apartment complex, the Home Buildings, on Warren Street. The design amenities of these handsome, six-storey brick buildings – open balconies, spiral staircase, garden courtyard – are even more amazing when you realise that they were among the first planned low-income housing in the country. The developer Alfred Tredway White, whose enlightened principle was philanthropy plus five per cent, rented out four-room apartments in the 1870s for $1.93 a week.

The Home Buildings occupy all of Hicks Street between Warren and Baltic. It would be heavenly to live in them, were it not for the roar of the BQE, which they face. How I would love to cover this open sore of an expressway (since it's already below grade, it would only cost, say, a half-billion dollars to platform over), which severs Cobble Hill from its western sliver. At least you can walk over the expressway, using one of the cross-bridges at Kane or Sackett or Union Street, to explore that mysterious western part, one or two streets wide: the land that time forgot. Along Columbia Street there are still a few giant forklifts standing, remnants of the working port that, for the most part, died in the 1960s (killed by containerisation and its need for huge back-space).

All this part of Brooklyn used to be dominated by waterfront industries: the humble, aluminium-sided houses were built by Italian longshoremen for their families. If you walk along Union Street, on the sliver side, you still find the old Italian food stores – latticinis and salumerias with awnings advertising fresh mozzarella, and a foccaceria/restaurant called Ferdinando's that has decent, authentic regional food and a tiled-floor ambience straight out of turn-of-the-century Sicily (since 1904, proclaims its painted sign).

Cross over the highway again, along Union Street, to the area known as Carroll Gardens. These streets, too, are rich in Italian greengrocers, delis and bakeries (I recommend the cinnamon roll at Mazzola's). What distinguishes Carroll Gardens most is its layout. The area was developed in 1846, by a land surveyor named Richard Butts, in such a way as to allow for unusually deep blocks, which meant residents could enjoy spacious front gardens as well as backyards. It's a visual treat to walk around these blocks – especially the streets south of Union, namely President, Carroll, First and Second – in springtime and absorb the

bursts of colour from the flowerbeds, or in winter, when the residents of Carroll Gardens outdo each other with their Christmas lights. In this largely Roman Catholic neighbourhood, religion is taken seriously, as one can see from the nativity scenes and bleeding Christ statues on people's front lawns, as well as the periodic processions through the streets. Not for nothing has Brooklyn been called City of Churches: there are splendid, or at least sturdy, examples of church architecture on every other block in Carroll Gardens and Cobble Hill. Carroll Gardens also boasts a surfeit of funeral parlours: you might, for instance, check out the imposing, Greek-columned Guido Funeral Home, on the corner of Clinton and Carroll Streets.

By now you should have doubled back to Court Street and Union. Pause here a moment, taking in the fact that Court Street functions as a class divide: to the west (towards Clinton, Henry and Hicks), the houses are more expensive and desirable; to the east (towards Smith, Hoyt and Bond), somewhat less so. The reason may be not so much architectural as racist: east of Court Street is closer to the Gowanus Houses, a largely African-American public housing project that extends for blocks between Hoyt and Bond Streets, and that has a reputation for crime and squalor. Go and have a look, if you want: chances are, you will see nothing scary, just people hanging out, but the atmosphere of desperate hard luck is palpable, and, looking up at the grimy project towers, you can't help thinking how far we have fallen from the low-income standard set a half-mile away at Warren Place.

Where Union crosses Smith, you ought to wander down Smith Street, back in the direction of Atlantic Avenue, and experience for yourself what has been called the Smith Street Renaissance. Smith and Court Streets, a block away from and parallel to each other, are the main commercial streets through this part of

Hidden away by apartment complexes and the BQE motorway is the **Warren Street** mews.

town. Traditionally, Court Street has been the more important of the two – it is certainly the prettier, wider, more tree-lined. But for some odd reason, in the last few years, following a set of minor improvements that included repaving Smith Street and installing gaslight-era lampposts, it is Smith Street that has boomed, with a slew of ambitious, swinging restaurants that have drawn diners from all over Brooklyn and the other boroughs: Uncle Pho, The Grocery, Smith Street Kitchen, Sur, Saul's, – and a new one opening every month. There are also chic boutiques, arty handbag stores, coffee bars, and other hip shops. It is as though the young, trend-setting entrepreneurs – the sous-chefs and fashion designers fresh out of college who used to open places in the Lower East Side or Soho – have flocked to Smith Street, partly because downtown Manhattan has gotten too expensive, partly because they are taken by the perverse allure of this nondescript, narrow street, which used to hold taverns, brothels and boarding houses for sailors.

I live a half-block away from Smith Street, and have watched the whole phenomenon develop. If nothing else, it is proof that Brooklyn is happening, for better or worse. Gentrification is fanning out everywhere that decent housing

stock already exists. If most of the money is coming from Manhattan, whose real estate values have so skyrocketed as to lure middle-class families and creative youth across the river, so be it.

One is constantly being reminded that Brooklyn used to be the fourth-largest American city, before its amalgamation with the rest of New York in 1898, and would still be fourth largest if counted separately (a concept that makes little sense). The fact is, the current boom is occurring precisely because of Brooklyn's umbilical, bedroom-borough dependence on Manhattan. So, while Brooklyn may become increasingly an option for back-office space, or for new go-getters trying out ideas, it can never hope to compete with Manhattan as a mature metropolis, nor should it try. The charm of Brooklyn is its laid-back, slightly provincial atmosphere, wrapped around a serious, solid residential core.

# Eating & drinking

### Ferdinando's Focacceria

*151 Union Street, between Hicks & Columbia Streets, Carroll Gardens, Brooklyn (718 855 1545).* **Open** 11am-6pm Mon-Thur; 11am-9pm Fri, Sat. Cheap Italian venue that has a loyal following among Carroll Gardens residents – try the arancino special, or the authentic homemade tiramisu for dessert.

## Patsy Grimaldi's
*19 Old Fulton Street, between Front & Water Streets, Brooklyn Heights, Brooklyn (718 858 4300).* **Open** 11.30am-11pm Mon-Thur; 11.30-midnight Fri; noon-midnight Sat; noon-11pm Sun. **No credit cards.** A treasure for lovers of brick-oven-baked pizzas, and a *TONY* 100.

## The Grocery
*288 Smith Street, between Union & Sackett Streets, Carroll Gardens, Brooklyn (718 596 3335).* **Open** 6-10pm Mon-Thur; 6-11pm Fri, Sat. Top-notch American cuisine.

## Mazzola Bakery
*192 Union Street, at Henry Street, Carroll Gardens, Brooklyn (718 643 1719).* **Open** 6am-8pm Mon-Fri; 7am-8pm Sat; 7am-3pm Sun.

## River Café
*1 Water Street, at Cadman Plaza West, Brooklyn Heights, Brooklyn (718 522 5200).* **Open** noon-2.30pm, 6-11pm Mon-Sat; 11.30am-2.30pm, 6-11pm Sun. Dress smart, bask in the view and savour the fine dishes. It's a 1999 *TONY* winner.

## Sahadi Importing Company
*187 Atlantic Avenue, between Court & Clinton Streets, Brooklyn (718 624 4550).* **Open** 9am-7pm Mon-Fri; 8.30am-7pm Sat. The most comprehensive selection of MiddleEastern foodstuffs in New York.

## Restaurant Saul
*140 Smith Street, between Bergen & Dean Streets, Boerum Hill (718 935 9844).* **Open** 6-11pm daily. A sophisticated bistro, worth the walk.

## Smith Street Kitchen
*174 Smith Street, between Warren & Wyckoff Streets, Boerum Hill, Brooklyn (718 858 5359).* **Open** 5.30-10.30pm Mon-Thur; 5.30-10.30pm Fri, Sat; 5.30-10pm Sun. Globally inspired seafood creations.

## Sur
*232 Smith Street, between Butler & Douglass Streets, Carroll Gardens, Brooklyn (718 875 1716).* **Open** 5.30-11pm Mon-Thur; 5.30pm-midnight Fri; 11am-4pm, 5.30pm-midnight Sat; 11am-4pm, 5.30-11pm Sun. An Argentine version of a classic bistro, with, of course, South American specialities.

## Teresa's
*80 Montague Street, between Montague Terrace & Hicks Street, Brooklyn Heights, Brooklyn (718 797 3996).* **Open** 7am-11pm daily. A classic diner serving classic Polish fare.

## Tin Room
*1 Front Street, at Old Fulton Street, Brooklyn Heights, Brooklyn (718 246 0310).* **Open** 11.30am-9.30pm Mon, Wed, Thur; 11.30am-10pm Fri, Sat; 11.30am-9pm Sun. Italian dishes in a light airy indoor space (or garden) with acoustics worthy of the opera and flamenco performances here at weekends.

## Uncle Pho
*263 Smith Street, at Union Street, Carroll Gardens, Brooklyn (718 855 8709).* **Open** 5-11pm Mon-Thur; 5-11.30pm Fri, Sat; 5-10pm Sun. There's a stylish interior to this Vietnamese restaurant.

# Buildings

## Brooklyn Borough Hall
*209 Joralemon Street, Brooklyn Heights, Brooklyn (718 802 3900).* **Open** tours 1pm Tue.

## New York State Supreme Court
*360 Adams Street, Brooklyn Heights, Brooklyn (718 643 8076).* **Open** 9am-5pm Mon-Fri.

# Galleries & museums

## The Anchorage
*Cadman Plaza West, between Hicks & Old Fulton Streets, DUMBO, Brooklyn (212 206 6674).* **Open** times vary, ring for details.

## Brooklyn Historical Society
*128 Pierrepont Street, at Clinton Street, Brooklyn Heights, Brooklyn (718 254 9830).* **Open** noon-5pm Mon, Thur, Sat. **Admission** $2.50; free Mon. **No credit cards.**

# Others

## Bargemusic
*Fulton Ferry Landing, next to Brooklyn Bridge, Brooklyn (718 624 4061).* **Admission** $15-$23. **No credit cards.**

## Christ Church
*326 Clinton Street, Brooklyn Heights, Brooklyn (718 624 0083).* **Open** 9.30am-4pm daily.

## Empire Fulton Ferry State Park
*26 New Dock Street, Brooklyn Heights, Brooklyn (718 858 4708).* **Open** *summer* 8.30am-8.30pm daily; *spring, fall* 9am-6pm daily.

## Guido Funeral Home
*440 Clinton Street, Brooklyn Heights, Brooklyn (718 852 2324).*

# Tall town

Minda Novek

Round and about Damon Runyon's Broadway.

**Start:** 42nd Street, between Broadway & Seventh Avenue
Finish: Duffy Square, West 47th Street at Broadway
**Time:** 2-3 hours
**Distance:** 3 miles/4.5km
**Getting there:** subway trains N, R, 1, 2, 3, 7 or 9 to 42nd Street-Times Square station
**Getting back:** subway trains N, R, 1, 2, 3, 7 or 9 from 42nd Street-Times Square station
**Note:** Times Square is most dramatic at night, but also a busy area during the day – it might be worth aiming to end the walk at dusk or later. Theatre tickets are generally sold through Tele-charge (see listings for details). This walk is in a similar area, and vein, to Marion Meade's walk, *Salons and Saloons*.

Like millions before and since, Damon Runyon came to New York hot on the trail of success. He left Denver in 1910 at the age of 30, giving up a job at the *Rocky Mountain News* and his closest rough companion, liquor, and within a year he had become a sports reporter on William Randolph Hearst's *American*. Runyon grew up in a Colorado steel town, where he spent his youth in frontier-style saloons, newspaper offices and flophouse beds. His career as a journalist took him around the world and his triumphs as a fiction writer brought him entry to Hollywood studios; but in New York, he pretty much kept to his old ways, working, hanging out and often living 'round and about one neighborhood'. In Times Square, the worlds of journalism, theatre, music, sports and crime overlapped in all sorts of interesting ways. It became Runyon's self-appointed beat. The places he frequented became settings for his stories; the 'types' he found there became his characters. As he put it once, looking out over Broadway, 'I took one little section of New York and made half a million dollars writing about it.'

Runyon remained a newspaper reporter throughout his life, covering all aspects of the sporting world, from the athletes and the events, to the managers and gamblers who, often as not, lost money on them. When the need arose, he also wrote about political events and criminal trials. But he's best known today for his short stories, which put a droll spin on the comings and goings of outlaws and others on the make in Prohibition-era Broadway. Runyon brought a new kind of vernacular voice to American fiction through his use of the historic present tense, modelled on the street slang of New York's underworld in the '20s and '30s. Though his work was never countenanced by critics, it's had a long run in the public's affection. His works have been translated into several languages, and there are still some collections in print, as well as volumes of poetry and journalism, but you'll probably find more in libraries than bookstores. A couple dozen films have also been made from the Broadway stories, beginning in the early '30s. The best of these are *The Big Street* (starring Henry Fonda and Lucille Ball), *Lady for a Day* (May Robson), *The Lemon Drop Kid* (Bob Hope), *Little Miss Marker* (Shirley Temple) and *A Pocketful of Miracles*

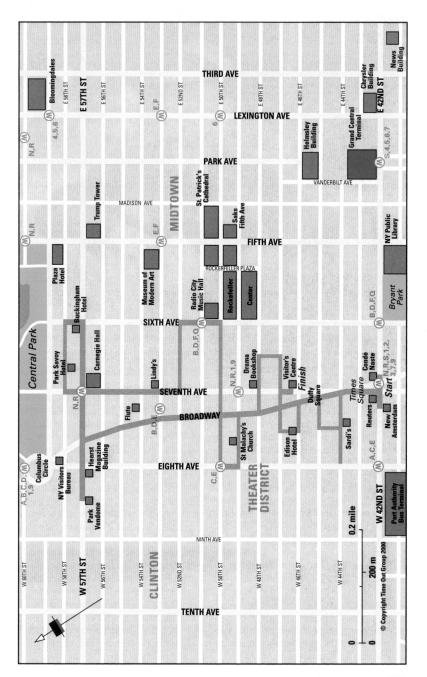

THIRD AVE

E 58TH ST
E 57TH ST
E 56TH ST
E 54TH ST
E 52ND ST
E 50TH ST
E 48TH ST
E 46TH ST
E 44TH ST
E 42ND ST

Bloomingdales

4,5,6

N,R

E,F

6

LEXINGTON AVE

Helmsley
Building

Chrysler
Building

News
Building

PARK AVE

Grand Central
Terminal

S,4,5,6,7

VANDERBILT AVE

Trump Tower

MADISON AVE

MIDTOWN

St Patrick's
Cathedral

Saks
Fifth Ave

N,R

E,F

FIFTH AVE

NY Public
Library

Plaza
Hotel

Museum of
Modern Art

Radio City
Music Hall

ROCKEFELLER PLAZA

Rockefeller

Center

Central Park

Buckingham
Hotel

Park Savoy
Hotel

Carnegie Hall

SIXTH AVE

B,D,F,Q

Bryant
Park

B,D,F,Q

Lindy's

Drama
Bookshop

Visitor's
Centre

Finish

N,R,1,9

Times
Square

N,R,S,1,2,
3,7,9

SEVENTH AVE

N,R

Start

Condé
Naste

Columbus
Circle

A,B,C,D,
1,9

Flute

B,D,E

BROADWAY

Duffy
Square

St Malachy's
Church

Edison
Hotel

Reuters

New
Amsterdam

Sardi's

A,C,E

NY Visitors
Bureau

Hearst
Magazine
Building

EIGHTH AVE

C,E

THEATER
DISTRICT

Park
Vendome

W 57TH ST

CLINTON

NINTH AVE

W 42ND ST

Port Authority
Bus Terminal

0.2 mile

W 60TH ST
W 58TH ST
W 56TH ST
W 54TH ST
W 52ND ST
W 50TH ST
W 48TH ST
W 46TH ST
W 44TH ST

TENTH AVE

200 m

© Copyright Time Out Group 2000

0

0

Short story writer and newspaper reporter **Damon Runyon** had an eye for the gee-gees.

(Bette Davis, Glenn Ford and Peter Falk). *Guys and Dolls*, a musical based posthumously on his Broadway stories, is perhaps the best known today.

Most of the places in Runyon's 'Tall Town', no matter how glimmering, entrenched or notorious, are long gone. The ones still standing need some squinting on your part to look as they once did. The others can be seen now only in the mind's eye. You can step inside a theatre or restaurant to go deeper into the fantasy, but eavesdropping on the chatter of 1920s patrons will require a more sustained effort.

A contemplative walker is likely to be elbowed by the rushing crowd. Mondays – when most of the theatres are dark – are the quietest, Saturdays and Wednesdays are matinée days (the biggest crowds). The walk veers in and out of the ruckus. But the ruckus is authentic too. There have been crowds here for over a century, wired by the electric current, since Times Square was ushered into existence by electricity. Which brings me to the point that Broadway, particularly Damon Runyon's Broadway, is the place people came to experience the night. To get the truest sense of it, come in daylight for the buildings and the honky-tonk feel, then backtrack after dark for the lights and intensity.

Start at the entrance of the Times Square subway station (many trains stop here or nearby). At 42nd Street between Seventh Avenue and Broadway, there are seven corners, all of them crowded. Find a jostle-free patch of sidewalk, then stand your ground. On his first trip to the district, Runyon would have come to this very spot, taking the IRT, New York's first subway line. The station – and thence the square – were named for the tower looming overhead, a new home for the *New York Times* and the second tallest building in New York in 1905.

When it opened on New Year's Eve with fanfare and fireworks, it became the defining landmark for a growing neighbourhood that liked to play with time. Since Runyon's death it has been stripped down, resurfaced and now completely buried beneath billboards. On the south-east corner of 42nd and Broadway, the office building with a mansard roof and a Gap store (hid by scaffolding when I last passed by), was once the luxurious Hotel Knickerbocker built by the Astor family. George M Cohan lived here, and Enrico Caruso, who sang Cohan's song, 'Over There', from his hotel window to the Armistice crowds at the end of World War I.

To the west of the Times Building, across Seventh Avenue, the new Reuters Building has arrived, and to the east, at Broadway, Condé Nast's new headquarters. Runyon might be shocked by the scale of these new towers flanking the old one, but not by the presence of the press.

Theatres make the neighbourhood. The first ones to take hold opened on 42nd Street at the turn of the last century. Hammerstein's Victoria (where Reuters stands) was the kingpin – the vaudeville centre for the city in its day. Its roof garden had a windmill, a monkey grotto, and a cow milked for thirsty patrons.

Cross Seventh Avenue to see two surviving early theatres. Disney has restored the completely art nouveau New Amsterdam Theater to its old glory. Look across to the New Victory, another serious restoration job. The theatre passed through many incarnations, including Minsky's Burlesque and a grind house for B-movies before it got its old stairway and lights back, as they appeared around 1900. Look for the date at the top central window.

An early Broadway hangout for Runyon was Jack Doyle's, a second-storey billiard parlour at 42nd and Broadway, where his Hard Boiled Egg Club met. In 1919, Runyon wrote a series for the *NY American* on world championship boxing

contender Jack Dempsey. He also bet hard on Dempsey to knock Willard out in the first round of the match. When he lost (Dempsey won, but not in that round), he found consolation at Doyle's.

Walk north on Broadway to 1501 (between 43rd and 44th Street), built in 1926 to house Paramount's movie palace and pyramid headquarters. All that's left of the stunning decor are the art deco lobby (check out the elevator doors), and the glass globe and clock at the top of the tower (look from almost anywhere on the first half of this walk to see them). Paramount's Adolph Zukor started in Times Square around the same time as Runyon, when he switched from running nickelodeons to putting stage stars in stage plays on film and set off a new trend of feature-length films.

Look across Broadway to the north-east corner of 43rd Street. Eugene O'Neill was born here in an actors' boarding house. The potent blend of realism and experimentation in his plays shocked audiences and helped foster Broadway's boom in the '20s. He remains a strong presence on Broadway – *The Iceman Cometh* recently came back and *Moon for the Misbegotten* is playing now.

Just beyond the corner, professional gambler Herman Rosenthal was shot down on the sidewalk outside the Hotel Metropole in 1912. The case caused a furore over revelations of police and governmental collusion with the underworld, and brought about the arrest, conviction and capital punishment of the officer who stopped 'Beansie' from spilling the beans to the DA. Runyon's character 'the Brain' was a cross between Rosenthal and Arnold Rothstein, whose deaths marked off two distinct eras in Broadway's underworld.

Turn west on to 44th. By the time Damon Runyon arrived in New York, Times Square was famous as a night-time district for pleasure seekers, with its lobster palaces, cabarets, sporting clubs and theatres. There are many old theatres

**Times Square** now and in the '30s (right) – Runyon's self-appointed beat and final resting place.

still standing, but these – so uncluttered and yet close together – give a sense of theatrical Broadway from Runyon's day. They are the Shubert Theater, Broadhurst and Majestic on the north side of the block; the Helen Hayes (once the Little Theater) and St James on the south. Where the St James now stands, Sardi's Restaurant first opened in 1921. Six years later, it moved to No.234. It remains a place where performers, playwrights, producers and other showbusiness people come to read their reviews, celebrate or commiserate. Autographed caricatures of the clientele, past and present, line the walls.

Next to the Shubert Theater is Shubert Alley, an open passageway that will take you through midblock to 45th Street, where the Music Box, Golden, Royale, Plymouth and Booth theatres are still holding their own. Head east back to Broadway and cross it. The south-east corner is a good place to view the Paramount Building. And at the north-west corner of 44th stood the once most imposing sight on Broadway – the Hotel Astor, opened in 1904. The Astor Bar was a favourite neighbourhood meeting place, before and after Prohibition. Runyon usually played with the names of his characters and locales. When something looked permanent (so he thought!), he didn't play around – the Astor Hotel, the Palace and Madison Square Garden appear under their own names.

Walk up Broadway, to 46th Street and cross to the island of the half-price 'Tkts' Booth. This spot is Duffy Square, named for Father Francis Patrick Duffy, a Hell's Kitchen pastor who served in World War I with 'the Fighting 69th' regiment. Runyon saw little action as a war correspondent, but he had lasting respect for the grunts who did the fighting. From Duffy Square, you can see the Times Square dynamo in full throttle.

Now cross again to the north-west corner of Broadway and the 46th Street side of Howard Johnson's Restaurant. I

Theatres still pack them in on **45th Street**.

can't speak for the meals within this Times Square relic, but I love the food on its outside wall, in painted signs that date back before the postmodern era, even the pop art era, though not to Runyon's day. The picture windows let the diners look out, but they also let you look in. The low lighting at the back bar is as eerie as a Hopper painting and appeals to all sorts of cocktail-hour fans.

Runyon might have sat for hours in a place like this, drinking some of his 30 cups of coffee. Look across the street, at the Richard Rodgers Theater. It was called the 46th Street Theater in 1950, when *Guys and Dolls*, the musical by Frank Loesser and Abe Burrows, first opened. Based on several of Runyon's stories, including 'The Idyll of Miss Sarah Brown', it captured the playful humor in them if not the mordant streak. The film version starred Frank Sinatra as Nathan Detroit, Marlon Brando as Sky Masterson and Jean Simmons as Sarah Brown. Her character was based on real-life Salvation

Army captain Rheba Crawford, known as the Angel of Broadway in the mid-'20s. Her street rallies in front of the Hotel Astor and Gaiety Theater (north-west corner of 46th and Broadway) were so well attended, she was arrested for 'blocking traffic'.

The early career of Archie Leach, a vaudevillian later known as Cary Grant, seems straight out of Runyon too. He lived at the National Vaudeville Artists Club, now the Church of Scientology (No.227), after leaving the English acrobatic troupe he had come to America with. He ran up bills and pounded the hot summer pavements, looking for 'a day's work here and a day's work there'.

You can cut up to 47th Street here by entering the back entrance of the Hotel Edison, the unidentified set of glass doors between the Scientology building and the Lunt-Fontanne Theater. This route will take you directly into the hotel's lobby, with its lovely murals styled after the original art deco look of the Edison (built in 1931). The Edison had many famous residents in the '30s, such as George Burns and Gracie Allen (who lived in hotels all around here), Jack Benny, Moss Hart and Ring Lardner. The Friars Club once held meetings here. The organisation was started in 1904 by press agents trying to protect their domain from ticket-seeking frauds. But it soon grew into a showbusiness enclave with a reputation for 'roasting' its members. They have had several Times Square club houses of their own, but during the Depression they lost their lease and ended up here. Runyon was a regular in the Friars, but was kicked out towards the end of his life after an argument in the club. In 1957, they moved out of the neighbourhood for good to East 55th Street. No women were inducted till 1988, and it's still a mostly male bastion of comical minds.

At the front entrance on 47th Street, you'll find the Café Edison, a place where theatrical meetings still take place informally. The café, also known as the 'Polish Tea Room', has a unique look, kind of like an inverted Wedgwood china cup. Another tenant is the Supper Club, a swing-era re-creation, occupying the

**Café Edison**, on West 47th Street, for sandwiches, burgers and theatrical meetings.

Edison's old ballroom and theatre. At weekends, they have a 17-piece big band and a swing revue.

Head to Broadway and cross to the east side, walk south to No.1560 for the Times Square Visitors' Center, in what was once the Embassy Theater. There are free restrooms here, a currency exchange, lots of tourist assistance and a Hotalings. The out-of-town newsstand with papers from everywhere outside New York is a venerable fixture in the Crossroads of the World. Question: 'Weren't you once at 42nd Street?' Answer: 'Of Course!' I guess a hot-house Hotalings is better than none at all.

Backstep to the Palace. Before diving in to the New Amsterdam, Disney got its feet wet on Broadway with *Beauty and the Beast* at the Palace. The landmarked interior is now home to *Aida*. But from the time it opened in 1913, until vaudeville gave up the ghost, this was the biggest of big-time vaudeville theatres.

Head east towards Sixth Avenue on 47th. Behind the Palace, Beacon of Broadway, were the small-timers who'd washed up on Broadway's rocky strand. Runyon described them in 'Dream Street Rose':

'… In Dream Street there are many theatrical hotels, and rooming houses, and restaurants, and speaks… and in the summer time the characters I mention sit on the stoops or lean against the railings… Many actors… live in the hotels and rooming houses, and vaudeville actors… are great hands for sitting around dreaming out loud about how they will practically assassinate the public in the Palace if ever they get a chance.

Furthermore, in Dream Street are always many hand-bookies and horse players, who sit on the church steps on the cool side of Dream Street in the summer and dream about big killings on the races, and there are also nearly always many fight managers, and sometimes fighters, hanging out in front of the restaurants, picking their teeth and

dreaming about winning championships of the world, although up to this time no champion of the world has yet come out of Dream Street.

In this street you see burlesque dolls, and hoofers, and guys who write songs, and saxophone players, and newsboys, and newspaper scribes, and taxi drivers, and blind guys, and midgets, and blondes with Pomeranian pooches, or maybe French poodles, and guys with whiskers, and night club entertainers, and I do not know what all else…'

You can still see a couple of these old hotels, now housing tourists – the Hampshire and the Rio (now Portland Square); and the church steps are the back end of the Church of St Mary the Virgin (entrance on 46th Street). If you cut through the underpass by the Dish of Salt restaurant and walk back towards Broadway, you'll see Music Row, a solid block of music stores, selling and repairing most of the instruments being played around the city in the Broadway theatres, the East Village clubs and Metropolitan Opera. Do I exaggerate? You decide. These stores are a throwback to when Runyon's 'Roaring Forties' were the home of Tin Pan Alley, New York's centre for songwriters and music publishers, such as Irving Berlin and WC Handy. During the Depression, hundreds of out-of-work musicians, hoping to be hired for the day, congregated on the sidewalk between 47th and 48th Street. As did the Times Square Mendicant Squad, futilely trying to control the tide.

Runyon and every other would-be dramatist in New York since the mid-'20s must have spent time in the small second-floor rooms of the Drama Bookshop on the corner of Seventh Avenue and 48th Street. Crammed to the gills with books, scores and videos on every kind of theatrical art or craft, the store encourages serendipitous thinking.

The Silver Slipper, once at 201 West 48th, was one of the clubs Runyon frequented and wrote about. His favourite performers, Clayton, Jackson and Durante (that's Jimmy), developed a reputation here and his girlfriend Patrice worked as a Spanish dancer. It was one of a string of clubs backed by Owney Madden, the Liverpool tough guy who came to power by way of Hell's Kitchen and Prohibition. At his table, Runyon would eavesdrop on everyone else's conversations, listening for his characters' voices. 'On the Erie' he called it, flicking his ear.

Walk up Broadway to 49th Street. On the north-east corner, Lindy's Restaurant opened in 1921, serving Jewish deli food to show folk. It was Runyon's main hangout, and as Mindy's, the scene of many of his stories. These start with Runyon's ubiquitous narrator sitting in Mindy's, eating his gefilte fish, or chicken soup with matzoh balls, or sturgeon, or standing on the sidewalk out front with the other 'citizens', and then something happens to disrupt the evening's fragile peace. 'The Brain Goes Home' was based on the death of gambler Arnold Rothstein, who conducted business from Lindy's. It begins with him walking the narrator 'up and down Broadway in front of Mindy's' and ends with his demise. My favourite Runyon story, 'A Piece of Pie', has no violence other than overeating, in a food contest that takes place at a big centre table in the second-floor dining room, with three waiters serving each contestant.

During the Depression, Lindy's moved to larger quarters across Broadway at 51st (and closed in the late '50s). Across the street, at 1619, the Brill Building stands out on Broadway as a place that is proud of its past. Songwriters continued working from the building long after Tin Pan Alley shut up shop: Paul Simon, Carole King, Donald Fagen and Walter Becker (pre-Steely Dan) to name a few. Step into its lobby and examine the roster of current occupants, like Broadway Video. In the '30s, the Brill also housed gyms and fight promoters, like Runyon's friend Mike Jacobs. Fight managers and others from the boxing and sporting world would sun themselves and gossip along a stretch of concrete on the 49th Street side known as Jacob's Beach.

**St Malachy's**, the 'Actors' Church', appears in Runyon's stories from the 1930s.

Turn west on 49th Street. At No.224, Runyon had a penthouse 'bachelor' apartment in the almost new Forrest Hotel from the breakup of his first marriage (to Ellen) in 1928 to the late '30s, long after his second one (to Patrice). Made over many times since then, the hotel – now called the Time – is going for a super-cool look in its second-floor lobby, but from across 49th Street, you can still see the old shell. In a turn of events Runyon would have appreciated, a senior citizens' home abuts the Time. In 'The Hottest Guy in the World', the narrator invites Big Jule to sit at his hotel window 'where he can see the citizens walking to and fro down in Eighth Avenue and watch the wagons moving into Madison Square Garden by way of the Forty-ninth Street side, for the circus always shows in the Garden in the spring before going out on the road.'

Actually, the year before Runyon moved in, St Malachy's, the 'Actors' Church' across the street, drew such excited gawkers for the funeral of Rudolph Valentino that people on the Forrest side of the block rented out their window space. The church appears in Runyon's stories from the '30s.

Walk on to Eighth Avenue. Each side of the street is the former site of a once important institution. Madison Square Garden, on the west side of Eighth, was the city's major sports arena from 1925 to the mid-'60s (when it moved further downtown). Runyon's involvement with sport, particularly boxing, brought him often to the Garden. He lost a lot of money here but he made it back with stories about the place. Or maybe vice versa.

Just across from the Garden, Polyclinic Hospital was *the* place for those who took sick in the neighbourhood. Underworld financier Arnold Rothstein was taken there after being shot at the Park Central. It figured often in Runyon's stories, 'The Lily of St Pierre', 'Little Miss Marker' and 'A Piece of Pie' to name a few, since anybody who got shot or took sick in the neighbourhood wound up there, including

Runyon himself. In a 1929 column he wrote: 'With these few lines, I am now shoving off to the Polyclinic to lend my presence to a pastime… known as appendix-snatching.' Doctors 'merely open the windows and the odors of some of the fights creep in and chloroform the patients.' Runyon supposedly wrote his first Broadway story to pay his doctor's bills.

Runyon often wrote of the tenement-lined blocks of Hell's Kitchen (Eighth Avenue and the Hudson River, from 34th to 59th Streets). But for him, the action is only a block or two from his door. In *Lillian*, a drunken nightclub singer finds a kitten as he heads home to his fleabag hotel on Eighth Avenue and 49th Street, 'where he lives quite a while, because the management does not mind actors, the management of the Hotel de Brussels being very broadminded, indeed.' In 'Butch Minds the Baby', the narrator leads his party 'over into West Forty-ninth Street, near Tenth Avenue, where Big Butch lives on the ground floor of an old brownstone-front house, and who is sitting out on the stoop but Big Butch himself. In fact, everybody in the neighborhood is sitting out on the front stoops over there, including women and children, because sitting out on the front stoops is quite a custom in this section. Big Butch is peeled down to his undershirt and pants, and he has no shoes on his feet, as Big Butch is a guy who likes his comfort. Furthermore, he is smoking a cigar, and laid out on the stoop beside him on a blanket is a little baby with not much clothes on.'

Walk up to 50th Street and head back east, past Broadway, to the north-east corner of Seventh Avenue. The Roxy Theater once stood here; the Roxy from which any Roxy you ever heard of sprang. Roxy was the nickname of Samuel Rothafal, the man who created nearly all the movie palaces in Times Square, the

**Radio City Music Hall** – in 1932 the biggest theatre in the world.

Strand, the Rialto, the Rivoli, the Capitol; and this was the one he called 'the Cathedral of the Motion Picture'. 'It's Roxy and I'm Roxy,' he crowed. With over 6,000 seats, ushers in military dress, marble floors and crystal chandeliers, the Roxy was the ultimate palace in the late '20s. 'Don't give the people what they want,' Roxy said. 'Give 'em something better.' Damon Runyon was a movie addict, trying to work a picture into his schedule every day he could, and since the Roxy was on his turf, he must have gone there regularly.

Continue on 50th to Sixth Avenue for a Roxy theatre that's still around. John D. Rockefeller hired Roxy to build a theatre as part of his new Center complex. Radio City Music Hall was the result – a modernist version of the older palaces designed for live spectacles – with an art deco decor, statues, murals and a gigantic stage inspired by a sunset. In 1932, it was the biggest theatre in the world, and few have ever matched it. But during the Depression, stage shows couldn't fill a house that size, so movies were brought in as the mainstay of the show. Runyon had begun to get involved in films himself, selling his stories and working on scripts, even producing. His first big hit was *Lady for a Day* (based on 'Madame La Gimp'), which opened at the Music Hall within its first year of operation. Dozens of film adaptations of his work have followed since.

Turn west on to 52nd Street and walk back towards Eighth Avenue. The plank floors, red-checkered tablecloths and wood panelled walls of Gallagher's Steak House haven't changed much since Repeal. Owners Helen Gallagher and Jack Solomon opened it as a speakeasy in 1927 and then made it into a steakhouse in '33, looking pretty much like this. You can see the prime beef dry-aging from the street. Gallagher was a former Ziegfeld Girl and her partner was a restaurateur with serious connections to the sporting world. Runyon must have loved this place, if not for its steaks then for its wall-to-wall

pictorial history of his world. In two large rooms, there are race horses and jockeys, baseball players and boxers, actors and singers, and politicos, local and national.

There may even be a photo of Runyon up there, but it would take hours of hovering over other people's tables to find him. He's there in spirit. One photo of two men, a jockey and a trainer, is of the famous Earl Sande, photographed here in a Panama hat. Runyon wrote several versions of a poem about Sande during the course of his career. Here are a few lines from one version:

*Kummer is quite a jockey,*
    *Maybe as good as the best.*
*Johnson is not so rocky*
    *When you bring him down to the test.*
*But, say, when they carry my gravy –*
*Say, when I want to win,*
    *Gimme a handy*
    *Guy like Sande*
*Bootin' them hosses in.*

Across the street is Roseland, one of the oldest ballrooms in New York. At its original location on Broadway at 51st, Runyon might have danced in 1924 to Fletcher Henderson's band, with a young Louis Armstrong getting everybody jazzed up, including the other musicians. But Runyon didn't dance.

In 'The Brakeman's Daughter' the narrator speaks of 'dancing with the dolls in the Flowerland dance hall'. Roseland offered 'professional' partners, male and female, for those without. In the '20s and '30s, hundreds of hostesses were available for small change. Ruby Keeler reportedly met Al Jolson while a dancer there. Rudolph Valentino, James Cagney, George Raft, Joan Crawford, Anne Miller, Bill Robinson and Fred Astaire all danced there. But bands are the biggest attraction, from Count Basie to Tito Puente. The current site, opened in 1956, used an old ice skating rink. Roseland is the kind of place that's hard to describe without naming names. More recent headliners include Bruce Springsteen, Alanis Morrisette, Beck, Bob Dylan, David Byrne, Fiona Apple and Marilyn Manson.

I wonder what Runyon – with characters like Harry the Horse, the Lemon Drop Kid and Sammy Downtown – would have made of Roseland's roster of bands: Blind Melon, Foo Fighters, Hootie & the Blowfish, Radiohead, Sex Pistols, and Smashing Pumpkins.

Walk back to Seventh Avenue and north towards 53rd. At 825 Seventh Avenue at 53rd Street, there is place called Lindy's – a chain restaurant that bought the name (and maybe some of the recipes). It's more of a precursor of the theme restaurants that line today's Broadway than an accurate rendition of its past, but you may want to check it out. This requires a great deal of squinting.

Cross Seventh Avenue for a couple of places that are more in keeping with Runyon's Broadway, although not quite that old. The Stage Deli at 53rd Street and the Carnegie Deli at 54th are celebrity-frequented meat palaces where the pastrami and corned-beef sandwiches are gargantuan. They also serve the kinds of Jewish dishes Runyon's narrator ate at Mindy's – matzoh ball soup, gefilte fish and smoked fish. Also like Mindy's they aren't kosher, mixing milk and meat. These places have been in business long enough to be legends in their own right.

Turn west briefly at 54th Street for the Texas Guinan's Club Intime, now the Flute Champagne Bar at basement level. Runyon's Miss Missouri Martin and her Sixteen Hundred Club was based on the unshakeable nightclub entrepreneur Texas Guinan and her 300 Club (once at 151 West 54th). A former motion picture cowgirl, Guinan found her metier in riding the law throughout Prohibition. Every time her club was shut down, another sprang up, often in the same location, like the Club Intime. Runyon didn't seem to think much of Guinan, as all his references to Missouri Martin are cutting.

The current club has a bottle of 1928 Krug from Guinan's day lodged in the floor. Once a month, there is a Prohibition night, when drinks are served in coffee mugs, customers come in 1920s attire, and variations of period music are played.

Head back to Seventh Avenue. The Park Central Hotel (55th-56th Street) was the home of *Daily Mirror* columnist Walter Winchell and family at the time Runyon's first Broadway story was published. The lead character in 'Romance in the Roaring Forties' is one Waldo Winchester, 'a nice looking young guy who writes pieces about Broadway for the *Morning Item*. He writes about the goings-on in night clubs, such as fights… and also about who is running around with who, including guys and dolls. Sometimes this is very embarrassing to people who may be married and are running around with people who are not married, but of course Waldo Winchester cannot be expected to ask one and all for their marriage certificates before he writes his pieces for the paper.' In the story, Winchester has marriage trouble of his own.

Arnold Rothstein, the racketeers' banker, was shot here in 1928, after having dinner with Runyon at Lindy's. Runyon wrote a couple of stories about a Rothstein-like character. He also covered the murder trial for *The American*, commenting in his usual droll manner: 'Arnold would have scarcely believed his ears. He lived in the belief he was widely known. He had spent many years establishing himself as a landmark on old Broadway. It would have hurt his pride like sixty to hear men who lived in the very neighborhood he frequented shake their heads and say they didn't know him.' Based on the fact that defendant George McManus was in room 349, and Rothstein's body was found by the 56th Street service entrance, the judge dismissed the case without letting the jury deliberate!

In a column about the link between sports and the courts, Runyon wrote:

'The trial is a sort of game, the players on the one side the attorneys for the defense, and on the other the attorneys for the State. The defendant figures in it mainly as the prize. The instrument of play is the law... perhaps I might call it the puck, for it is in the manner of hockey more than any other sport that it is jockeyed carefully back and forth by the players... The game of murder trial is played according to very strict rules, with stern umpires called judges to prevent any deviation from these rules... I sometimes wonder if the players feel toward each other the bitterness that they not infrequently express in court, or do they hob-nob all friendly together... as baseball players fraternize after a game in which they have attempted to spike each other.'

Walk to 58th Street and head east from Seventh Avenue to the Park Savoy Hotel. A 21-year-old Marlon Brando lived here in 1944 when he was just warming up on Broadway. He and Runyon, at that time living around the corner, never met, but when the musical *Guys and Dolls* was made into a movie, Brando played Sky Masterson. And sang!

The unimposing building further up the block (No.132) was once the original Stork Club. An extended storefront hides the original basement entrance and flanking stone stairways. The three-storey speakeasy was opened in the late '20s by Sherman Billingsly, a former small-time bootlegger. His none-too-silent partners were three of the most powerful gangsters in New York – Owney 'the Killer' Madden, Big Bill Dwyer and Frenchy De Mange. At the behest of Billingsly's friend, Texas Guinan, Walter Winchell helped make the Stork Club popular by referring to it in his column and his radio show as 'the New Yorkiest spot in New York'.

After years of police protection, the Stork Club was shut down for good. Billingsly moved the club elsewhere. The third location (3 East 53rd Street) was a keeper, lasting till the mid-'60s (way gone

now). Runyon frequented the Stork Club, particularly towards the end of his life when he sat at the permanent table of his new close friend, Walter Winchell. During the Depression, Sherman Billingsly and Frenchy DeMange were both kidnapped by 'Mad Dog' Vincent Coll as part of a territory grab. Runyon used the incident in 'The Snatching of Bookie Bob':

'Now it comes on the spring of 1931, after a long hard winter, and times are very tough indeed, what with the stock market going all to pieces, and banks busting right and left, and one thing and another, and many citizens of this town are compelled to do the best they can... So I am not surprised to hear rumors that the snatching of certain parties is going on in spots, because while snatching is by no means a high-class business, and is even considered somewhat illegal, it is something to tide over the hard times... You must know who you are snatching, because naturally it is no good snatching somebody who does not have any scratch to settle with... maybe the party is not a legitimate guy, such as a party who is running a crap game or a swell speakeasy, or who has some other dodge he does not care to have come out... Such a party is very good indeed for the snatching business, because he is pretty apt to settle without any argument.'

At Sixth Avenue, head to 57th Street. At the Buckingham Hotel on the north-west corner, Runyon lived out his last two sickly years alone, when cancer had moved in on him and his wife had moved out. After major surgery on his throat he could no longer speak. He carried a notepad on his nightly travels, writing out short responses to hold up his end in conversations, and pressing his pen down harder for emphasis. To get hotel room service, he'd tinkle a bell into the telephone as a signal to the front desk.

Walk back on 57th to the Park Vendome, west of Eighth Avenue. Runyon lived here in the '30s with his second wife Patrice, in a luxury, two-storey apartment

**George M Cohan** and sightseers, Duffy Square.

back to Duffy Square – the island at 46th Street. Stand at the feet of George M Cohan, the statue, and look around. The chaotic cartoon spectacle of signs is best seen after dark, when the strobing thrusts of light seem less about America's corporate giants duking it out for our attention, than the contributory energy of the whole moving mass. Rest your gaze on the old Times Building, where the ball still drops every New Year's Eve. It looks tarted up for the evening in its gaudy electric costume.

This is the place I wanted you to see. Many may have died on Broadway over the last hundred years, but only Damon Runyon is 'buried' here. He asked in his will for his ashes be 'scattered over the place I have truly loved and that was so good to me'. World War I pilot Eddie Rickenbacker flew over Broadway in a twin-engine plane in December 1946, dropping Runyon off in Times Square for good.

(though he kept the rooms at the Forrest Hotel, for himself). Back at the corner of Eighth Avenue, a stone's throw away, stands the Hearst Magazine Building. Runyon's employer William Randolph Hearst housed his magazine empire here in 1928. The six-storey fortress guarded by muses was meant as the base for a building twice the size. The architect was Viennese transplant Joseph Urban – also a designer for the Ziegfeld Follies, the Metropolitan Opera and Hearst's own Cosmopolitan Pictures. Runyon often showed up to his second-storey office around 10.30 in the morning, after a night on Broadway. He'd write up his piece and then go home to bed.

If you're feeling done in yourself, the Columbus Circle subway – where many trains meet – has an entrance right at the Hearst Building. If you're up for a bit more, especially if it's getting dark, I'd like to show you the last place Damon Runyon went in Times Square. Head to Broadway or Seventh Avenue, and walk

# Eating & drinking

### Café Edison
*228 West 47th Street, between Broadway & Eighth Avenue (212 840 5000).* **Open** 6am-9.30pm Mon-Sat; 6am-8pm Sun. Good-value high-rise deli sandwiches, Jewish standards and all-American burgers.

### Carnegie Delicatessen
*854 Seventh Avenue, at 55th Street (212 757 2245).* **Open** 6.30am-3.45am daily. For price and sheer size of sandwiches Carnegie's stands alone.

### Dish of Salt
*133 West 47th Street, between Sixth & Seventh Avenues (212 921 4242).* **Open** 11.30am-11pm Mon-Fri; 4-11pm Sat. Americanised versions of Cantonese dishes in a cement-and-glass space.

### Flute Bar & Lounge
*205 West 54th Street, between Seventh & Eighth Avenues (212 265 5169).* **Open** 5pm-4am Mon-Fri; 7pm-4am Sat; 7pm-2am Sun. Champagne is the speciality in this basement bar.

### Gallagher's Steak House
*228 West 52nd Street, between Broadway & Eighth Avenue (212 245 5336).* **Open** noon-midnight daily. Choose your own cuts from the walk-in refrigerator.

## Howard Johnson's

*1551 Broadway, at West 46th Street (212 354 4245).* **Open** 7am-2.45am Mon-Thur, Sun; 7am-3.45am Fri, Sat.

## Lindy's

*825 Seventh Avenue, at 53rd Street (212 767 8344).* **Open** 7am-11.30pm Mon-Thur, Sun; 7am-midnight Fri, Sat.

## Sardi's

*234 West 44th Street, between Broadway & Eighth Avenue (212 221 8440).* **Open** 11.30am-11.30pm Tue-Sat; 11.30am-8.30pm Sun. A mecca for theatre-lovers and thespians alike, offering an eclectic menu, and walls covered in caricatures of Broadway and Off-Broadway luminaries.

## Stage Deli of New York

*834 Seventh Avenue, between 53rd & 54th Streets (212 245 7850).* **Open** 6am-2am daily.

## The Supper Club

*240 West 47th Street, between Broadway & Eighth Avenue (212 921 1940).* **Open** 5.30pm-4am Fri, Sat. A perfect balance between quality food and big band entertainment in the one-time ballroom of the old Edison Hotel.

# Churches

## St Malachy's Catholic Church

*239 West 49th Street, between Broadway & Eighth Avenue (212 581 2910).* **Open** 8am-5pm Mon-Fri. *Mass* 5pm Sat; 9am, 11am Sun.

## St Mary the Virgin

*145 West 46th Street, between Sixth & Seventh Avenues (212 869 5830).* **Open** 11am-7pm Mon-Fri. *Mass* 12.15pm Sat; 9am, 10am, 11am, 5pm Sun.

# Theaters

If no telephone numbers are provided, use **Telecharge**, **Ticketmaster** or **Ticket Central** for information and ticket purchasing (*see* **Information** *below*).

## Booth Theater

*222 West 44th Street, between Broadway & Eighth Avenue.*

## Broadhurst Theater

*235 West 44th Street, between Broadway & Eighth Avenue.*

## Gaiety Theater

*201 West 46th Street, between Broadway & Eighth Avenue (212 221 8868).*

## John Golden Theater

*252 West 45th Street, between Broadway & Eighth Avenue.*

## Helen Hayes Theater

*240 West 44th Street, between Broadway & Eighth Avenue.*

## Lunt-Fontanne Theater

*205 West 46th Street, between Broadway & Eighth Avenue.*

## Majestic Theater

*247 West 44th Street, between Broadway & Eighth Avenue.*

## Music Box Theater

*239 West 45th Street, between Broadway & Eighth Avenue.*

## New Amsterdam Theater

*216 West 42nd Street, between Seventh & Eighth Avenues (212 282 2900).* **Tours** Mon, Tue $10; $5 children.

## New Victory Theater

*209 West 42nd Street, between Seventh & Eighth Avenues.*

## Palace Theater

*1564 Broadway, at 47th Street.*

## Plymouth Theater

*236 West 45th Street, between Broadway & Eighth Avenue.*

## Radio City Music Hall

*Sixth Avenue, between 50th & 51st Streets (212 247 4777).* **Open** *tours* 10am-5pm Mon-Sat; 11am-5pm Sun. **Admission** $15; $9 under-12s.

## Richard Rodgers Theater

*226 West 46th Street, between Broadway & Eighth Avenue (212 221 1211).*

## Roseland Theater

*239 West 52nd Street, between Broadway & Eighth Avenue (212 245 5761/concert hotline 212 249 8870).*

## Royale Theater

*242 West 45th Street, between Broadway & Eighth Avenue.*

## St James Theater

*246 West 44th Street, between Broadway & Eighth Avenue.*

### Shubert Theater
*225 West 44th Street, between Broadway & Eighth Avenue.*

## Hotels

### Buckingham Hotel
*101 West 57th Street, between Sixth & Seventh Avenues (212 246 1500).*

### Hampshire Hotel & Suites
*157 West 47th Street, between Sixth & Seventh Avenues (212 768 3700).*

### Hotel Edison
*228 West 47th Street, between Broadway & Eighth Avenue (212 840 5000).*

### Park Central Hotel
*870 Seventh Avenue, between 55th & 56th Streets (212 247 8000).*

### Park Savoy Hotel
*158 West 58th Street, between Sixth & Seventh Avenues (212 245 5755).*

### Portland Square Hotel
*132 West 47th Street, between Broadway & Sixth Avenue (212 382 0600).*

### The Time
*224 West 49th Street, between Broadway & Eighth Avenue (212 320 2900).*

## Information

For tickets, almost all Broadway and Off-Broadway shows are served by:

### Telecharge
*(212 239 6200).* **Open** 24hrs daily.

### Ticket Central
*(212 279 4200).* **Open** 1-8pm daily. Specialises in Off-Broadway and Off-Off-Broadway.

### Ticketmaster
*(212 307 4100).* **Open** 6.45am-11pm daily.

### Tkts
*Duffy Square, West 47th Street, at Broadway (212 221 0013).* **Open** 3-8pm Mon, Tue, Thur, Fri; noon-2pm, 3-8pm Wed Sat, Sun. Good for significant discounts on ticket prices.

### Times Square Visitors' Center
*1560 Broadway, between 46th & 47th Streets (212 768 1560).* **Open** 8am-8pm daily.

## Literature & film

**Guys and Dolls** Damon Runyon (1931)
**Damon Runyon's Blue Plate Special** (1934)
**Money From Home** Damon Runyon (1935)
**More Than Somewhat** Damon Runyon (1937)
**Furthermore** Damon Runyon (1938)
**Take It Easy** Damon Runyon (1938)
**Runyon à la Carte** Damon Runyon (1944)
**The Three Wise Guys & Other Stories** Damon Runyon (1946)
**The Iceman Cometh** Eugene O'Neill (1946)
**Moon for the Misbegotten** Eugene O'Neill (1952)
**The Big Street** (Irving Reis, 1942, US).
**Guys and Dolls** (Joseph L Mankiewicz, 1955, US).
**Lady for a Day** (Frank Capra, 1933, US).
**The Lemon Drop Kid** (Marshall Neilan, 1934, US)
**Little Miss Marker** (Walter Bernstein, 1980, US)
**A Pocketful of Miracles** (Frank Capra, 1961, US).

## Publishers & publications

### Condé Nast Publications
*4 Times Square, West 42nd Street, between Sixth Avenue & Broadway (212 286 2860).*

### Hearst Magazine
*959 Eighth Avenue, between 56th & 57th Streets (212 649 6990).*

### The New York Times
*229 West 43rd Street, between Seventh & Eighth Avenues (212 597 8001).*

### Reuters
*1700 Broadway, between 42nd & 43rd Street (212 593 5500).*

## Others

### Broadway Video
*9th Floor, 1619 Broadway, at 49th Street (212 265 7600).* **Open** 10am-7pm Mon-Fri.

### Drama Bookshop
*723 Seventh Avenue, at 48th Street (212 944 0595).* **Open** 9.30am-7pm Mon, Tue, Thur, Fri; 9.30am-8pm Wed; 10.30am-5.30pm Sat; noon-5pm Sun.

### Madison Square Garden
*Seventh Avenue, at 32nd Street (212 465 6741).*

# Lofty ambitions

Jason Epstein

Soho welcomes fashionable residents with cast-iron bank accounts.

**Start:** corner of The Bowery and Broome Street
**Finish:** Joe's Dairy, Sullivan Street
**Time:** 1-2 hours
**Distance:** 1.5 miles/2.5km
**Getting there:** subway trains J or M to Bowery Street station
**Getting back:** five-minute walk to Houston Street subway (trains 1 or 9)
**Note:** better in the afternoon, any day of the week, when most of the shops are open.

Soho is the most cosmopolitan neighbourhood within the world's most cosmopolitan city. To grasp its essence try to ignore for a moment its physical expression; its cobblestone streets, its beckoning shop windows, its lovely cast-iron façades and fanciful cornices erected a century and a half ago by ambitious merchants serving the new rich of young America's booming metropolis, bursting with wealth then as now. In this souk of souks ignore if you can the Japanese shoppers, their fists full of $100 bills, their hair dyed the color of rusted steel, rebelling and conforming at once. Try also to disregard the platoons of other young sybarites – Russians, Italians, French, perhaps even Uzbeks and Kurds, the men in their sculpted bodies, the women streaked and tinted, their faces surgically refined and expertly painted, buying $300 bed sheets at Portico on Spring Street or $30 cutlets at Cipriani's on West Broadway or $6,000 sofas at George Smith on Spring Street, to say

nothing of costly adornments at Prada, Vuitton, Dolce & Gabbana and Chanel. Try instead to see Soho simply as money, whether in the form of $3 million lofts, $600 shoes or the $990 toilet seat with brass handles for fastidious lifting available at Waterworks on Broome Street. Remove the money, as the whimsical American economy tends to do from time to time, and Soho will vanish, leaving the 200-year-old streets, the buildings and their lofts as lovely and forlorn as the façades of Petra or the abandoned canals of Venice in winter. But on a fine spring day when money bubbles in green torrents through Soho's narrow streets, across its counters and into the tills of its merchants and restaurateurs, this gilded neighbourhood splendidly reveals America's material soul, a honey pot for getters and spenders.

Unlike Manhattan north of Houston Street whose broad avenues run north and south and its side streets from east to west, following the city's grid pattern established in 1811, Soho's main thoroughfares run east to west beginning at Houston and then Prince, Spring, Broome and Grand. Canal Street, with its jumble of shops selling counterfeits of Soho's costly goods as well as electronic gadgets, machinery and low-cost Chinese imports, marks Soho's nether boundary and the upper boundary of Chinatown, where the shops and restaurants attract a less wordly class of tourists, identifiable by their swivelling heads and puzzled contemplation of street maps and guidebooks, often in minor languages.

Start on the corner of Broome Street and The Bowery, a continuation of Chinatown.

# Lofty ambitions

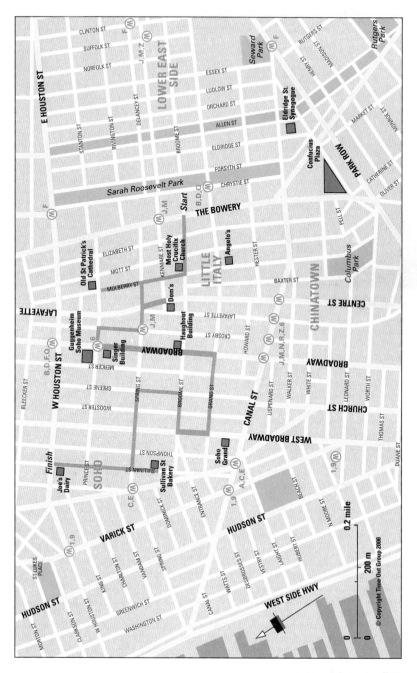

CLINTON ST

SUFFOLK ST

NORFOLK ST

E HOUSTON ST

J,M,Z

F

M

LOWER EAST SIDE

Rutgers Park

RUTGERS ST

MADISON ST

HENRY ST

F

M

ESSEX ST

LUDLOW ST

ORCHARD ST

ALLEN ST

ELDRIDGE ST

STANTON ST

RIVINGTON ST

DELANCEY ST

BROOME ST

Seward Park

MARKET ST

DIVISION ST

Eldridge St. Synagogue

MONROE ST

CATHERINE ST

OLIVER ST

FORSYTH ST

CHRYSTIE ST

Confucius Plaza

PARK ROW

Sarah Roosevelt Park

B,D,Q

M

F

M

Start

J,M

M

THE BOWERY

PELL ST

Columbus Park

Old St Patrick's Cathedral

ELIZABETH ST

MOTT ST

MULBERRY ST

KENMARE ST

Most Holy Crucifix Church

Angelo's

LITTLE ITALY

HESTER ST

BAXTER ST

CHINATOWN

CENTRE ST

LAFAYETTE

Guggenheim Soho Museum

Dom's

Haughout Building

CROSBY ST

HOWARD ST

M

J,M,N,R,Z,6

BROADWAY

Singer Building

M

6

J,M

LAFAYETTE ST

WALKER ST

WHITE ST

LEONARD ST

WORTH ST

W HOUSTON ST

B,D,F,Q

M

MERCER ST

BROADWAY

BROADWAY

CANAL ST

CHURCH ST

BLEECKER ST

GREENE ST

WOOSTER ST

SPRING ST

BROOME ST

GRAND ST

LISPENARD ST

THOMAS ST

Finish

Joe's Dairy

PRINCE ST

SOHO

THOMPSON ST

SULLIVAN ST

Sullivan St Bakery

Soho Grand

WEST BROADWAY

C,E

M

A,C,E

M

1,9

M

DUANE ST

N. MOORE ST

BEACH ST

VARICK ST

DOMINICK ST

ENTRANCE ST

HUDSON ST

1,9

M

1,9

M

ST LUKES PLACE

KING ST

CHARLTON ST

VANDAM ST

SPRING ST

CANAL ST

WATTS ST

DESBROSSES ST

VESTRY ST

LAIGH ST

HUBERT ST

HUDSON ST

MORTON ST

CLARKSON ST

W HOUSTON ST

GREENWICH ST

WASHINGTON ST

WEST SIDE HWY

200 m

0.2 mile

0

0

© Copyright Time Out Group 2000

Soho's deliverance from highwaymen is commemorated outside **Most Holy Crucifix Church**.

Bowery (Dutch for farmstead) was New York's theatrical neighbourhood before the Civil War and until recently its dumping ground for homeless men and women defeated by New York's unforgiving rigours. It is now lined with shops selling restaurant equipment and gaudy residential lighting (O'Lampia at No.155 is an elegant exception) and is on the way to being gentrified.

Turn west along Broome Street towards Mulberry Street. On the south-west corner of Mott and Broome a Chinese shop sells unusual goldfish including a kakaku koi at $980 and, for economisers, Hong Kong Parrot fish at $500. Continue a few paces west, and on your right is a tree facing the entrance to the Most Holy Crucifix church.

This tree, planted some 35 years ago, commemorates the deliverance of the area that now comprises Soho from the lunatic designs of politicians and planners who, in the 1950s, attempted to enhance their power and enrich their patrons by constructing an eight-lane expressway from river to river along the length of the street upon which

you are now standing. This church became the command post of a successful, often bitter, 12-year struggle by the residents, led by Jane Jacobs, the prophet of urbanism, to save the neighbourhood and its gallant cast-iron façades from the expressway that with its access ramps would have obliterated the entire area south of Houston (pronounced *How-ston*) Street – hence SoHo – and north of Canal Street, the upper and lower boundaries of today's Historic District. Faced with the destruction of their premises, the light manufacturers and wholesale distributors who occupied what are now Soho's grand residential lofts moved away. With the defeat of the planners and politicians, the neighbourhood, in 1973, was declared a city landmark, immune from future tampering.

Though it was illegal to reside in these former industrial premises, artists ignored the law and outwitted the housing inspectors by draping their windows at night with blackout curtains. Today these vast lofts are bought and sold for millions, but then artists rented them in whatever condition they found them for a few hundred dollars a month. Paula Cooper, Leo Castelli, Mary Boone, Pace and Larry Gagosian among others opened galleries here showing the work of Jasper Johns, Jennifer Bartlett, Robert Rauschenberg, Erich Fishcl, Richard Serra and John Borofsky, to name only a few.

It was these artists and their galleries that made Soho chic and stimulated the first trickle of money that has since become a flood. The galleries, bars and restaurants where the artists gathered soon attracted visitors from uptown, and the City, faced with a fait accompli and a booming new neighbourhood, agreed that artists could legally occupy their lofts. But as Soho prospered, few of them could afford to remain. By the '90s the artists had left for quieter and less expensive neighbourhoods and by the end of the decade most of the galleries followed. Soho's bohemian period had barely begun before it dissolved in a flood of cash.

Continue west on Broome to the corner of Mulberry Street, formerly the heart of the old Italian neighbourhood known in tourist guides as Little Italy, but now reduced to a three-block stretch of undistinguished tourist restaurants between Broome and Canal. The best (or least bad) of these unremarkable restaurants is the 100-year-old Angelo's on Mulberry just south of Grand, an authentic New York relic. Alternatively, here on the corner of Broome is Caffe Roma, an authentic shard of the old Italian neighbourhood with excellent biscotti. Try the quaresemali.

Turn north up Mulberry, crossing Kenmare, towards Prince Street. Until John Gotti, the notorious leader of the Gambino crime family, was sent to prison in the mid '90s, Mulberry between Kenmare and Prince had been his Manhattan headquarters, patrolled by beefy young men in silver-grey Armani jackets, black turtlenecks, gold chains and surprisingly dainty shoes. Gotti's various premises, with FBI wiretaps removed, are now occupied by ambitious young fashion designers and the Japanese, Korean and Australian restaurants that follow in their wake. Tracy Feith at 209 Mulberry between Kenmare and Prince is a well-known example of the trend.

Continue north to the corner of Prince Street, once a neighbourhood of Irish immigrants where the original St Patrick's Cathedral, long since superseded by the synthetic Gothic structure on Fifth Avenue at 50th Street, stands behind a brick wall, built to protect its cemetery from anti-Irish nativist rioters a century and a half ago. The original church was built in 1815 and rebuilt after a fire in 1868. In 1836 a gang of anti-papist roughnecks marched up the Bowery to attack St Patrick's but desisted when they learned that the Irish had cut loopholes in the brick wall for their muskets and gathered buckets of cobblestones to repel the invaders. Anti-Catholic feeling persisted throughout the 19th century, diminishing as the Irish population prospered and acquired political power. With the election of John F Kennedy in 1960 it had disappeared completely.

Retrace your steps to Spring Street, and turn right towards Lafayette Street, passing on your right Ceci-Cela, a minuscule French pastry shop of surpassing quality, with a few tables in a room at the rear. On the east side of Lafayette to the south where it becomes Cleveland Place is Eileen's 'Special' Cheesecake, a brilliant expression of a famous local delicacy. For handmade sopressatta and other Italian sausages, buffalo mozzarella imported from Naples, and especially fine cuts of beef, lamb and veal at reasonable prices, visit Dom's on the far side of the small triangular park that separates Cleveland Place from Lafayette Street. Dom and his brother Frank have been in the neighbourhood for years but their hearts and sausages, like Dom's accent, are authentically Neapolitan. So are Frank's recipes, which he may be willing to share when he's not busy at his stove.

At Lafayette, you are on the eastern boundary of the Cast-Iron Historic District that comprises Soho. Walk a block to the west along Spring and you will find Balthazar with its red awnings, Soho's most fashionable and probably best restaurant, a plausible rendering of Paris's La Coupole with a well-executed bistro menu. Reserve well in advance if you plan to dine here. Directly across the street is George Smith with its stock of English sofas and chairs, handsome, well made, comfortable. Should you decide to settle in Soho, George Smith offers floor samples at greatly reduced prices several times a year. Turn right up Crosby Street, a cobbled backwater that leads back up to Prince.

By this time you will have exhausted the modest charms of Soho's eastern extension and be ready to plunge into Soho itself. Proceed west towards Broadway, whose handsome ironwork façades, embracing vast street-level store windows, housed the city's most fashionable shops, hotels and theatres from the 1840s until after the Civil War, when they followed the city's great nobles uptown.

On the north-west corner of Broadway and Prince stands a branch of the Guggenheim Museum, where Andy Warhol's *Last Supper* is on permanent display, although the first floor is actually a shop selling posters, reproductions and other museum souvenirs. For the main collection visit the Guggenheim's headquarters at Fifth Avenue and 88th Street in the building designed by Frank Lloyd Wright, whose inverted spiral interior is a major New York artefact and more interesting than the art on display.

Dean and DeLuca at the south-east corner of Prince and Broadway is New York's most elegant foodshop, descended from Giorgio DeLuca's little cheese store that flourished on Prince Street in Soho's bohemian days. The present cheese department, still supervised by Giorgio, is outstanding and the magnificent display of artisanal breads attests to the genius of New York's bakers. The meat here is also superb.

Opposite Dean and Deluca stands the green and rust-red Little Singer Building,

The wall of **St Patrick's Old Cathedral** protected the cemetery from anti-Irish rioters.

one of the more spectacular examples of cast-iron, balconied façades in Soho. It's an L-shaped building (there's a secondary face to the building on the south-west side of Prince) built by the Singer sewing-machine manufacturers, although the original Singer Tower was a still more spectacular structure downtown on Liberty Street until it was demolished in 1970, earning it a place in planning history as the tallest building ever demolished. Next door, the publishers Scholastic, coffers swelling from the success of the *Harry Potter* series, are building an extension to their headquarters, designed by Aldo Rossi to blend into this historic district.

Proceed south on Broadway past Banana Republic, offering casual attire at reasonable prices. On the north-east corner of Broadway and Broome you will find the magnificent Haughwout building with its Palladian façade, one of the first of New York's cast-iron fronts and the precursor of 138 others within the Cast-Iron District. Built in 1857 by a merchant offering china, silver, glass and porcelain, the Haughwout building holds New York's first practical safety elevator. As you proceed south on the west side of Broadway you will pass a number of shops selling inexpensive fabrics, futons and novelties, leftovers from an earlier, less luxurious era, and now being replaced by fashionable shops. Continue along the west side of Broadway to Broome Street where you might pause to look west at the row of cast-iron façades, especially those on the south side of Broome. These are Soho's real treasures and the *sine qua non* of its current revival. The façades were assembled from castings made by New York iron foundries and ordered from catalogues by local architects to create their Florentine fantasies. Try to imagine these façades in their youth, gaily painted. The Roosevelt Building at 480 Broadway between Broome and Grand, erected in 1874 and designed by the fashionable architect

Richard Morris Hunt, is an exquisite, late example of the genre.

Now proceed one block south to Grand Street. On the north-east corner of Broadway and Grand you will see the French Culinary Institute, a handsomely equipped and professionally staffed school for aspiring chefs. Crusty baguettes are sold in its food shop.

Proceed west along Grand Street and you will pass the austere premises of Yohji Yamamoto, the fashionable Japanese designer. If you haven't yet refreshed yourself, Pain Quotidien offers decent baked goods and light meals at communal tables, where milk comes in old-fashioned glass bottles and butter is served in deep bowls, and just north of Grand on Mercer Street you will find Cendrillon, a tiny restaurant featuring South-east Asian dishes. A few hundred feet north of Grand on Greene Street, Kerquelen is the most flamboyant of Soho's shoe stores. Shoe stores abound in Soho – those along Broadway feature utilitarian models, but within Soho itself shoes are displayed and bought as if they were sacred objects.

West Broadway, Soho's main north–south thoroughfare, once the home of its major galleries, is now given over mainly to restaurants and stores offering domestic objects. The SoHo Grand just to the south of Grand Street is one of Soho's two fashionable hotels. (The other is the Mercer, at Mercer and Prince.) Head north up West Broadway. Cipriani, just above Broome Street on the west side, is a Manhattan branch of Venice's Harry's Bar, with a similar clientele and menu and the same three-quarter-scale tables and chairs.

Turn east along Broome towards Broadway again. The Broome Street Bar is a relic of Soho's bohemian past. You will pass the Broadway Panhandler with a vast collection of kitchen equipment at reasonable prices. You may want to stop next door at Waterworks at Broome and Greene to examine the $990 toilet seat and the $90 bath mats on display.

Notice the iron façades along either side of Broome. Though lofts in these buildings are among the world's most costly real estate and large street-level shops currently rent for as much as $80,000 per month, it costs nothing to admire their priceless exteriors. As you proceed along Broome toward Broadway recall that 40 years ago, New York's politicians wanted to destroy this entire area in order to build an expressway, connecting the Holland Tunnel to the west with the Manhattan Bridge to the east, ostensibly to ease cross-town traffic, but in fact to capture a windfall in federal highway funds.

At Greene go north to Spring and turn left again toward West Broadway. Spring is lined with shops offering various luxuries. The Grass Roots Garden at 131 Spring offers what must be the world's most extensive collection of tropical houseplants. L'Occitane at No.146 offers fragrant bath accessories in good-looking bottles.

If by now you have had your fill of fancy shops, you might want to head across West Broadway to Sullivan Street, to the western extension of Soho beyond its official Cast-Iron District boundary. These streets, with their two- and three-storey brick buildings, are architecturally and in community spirit a southern extension of Greenwich Village rather than a true extension of Soho. The Sullivan Street Bakery down to your left is one of New York's best and prices are no more than you would expect to pay for well-made bread. Heading north, you'll pass a couple of worthwhile restaurants. The Blue Ribbon at 97 Sullivan serves excellent oysters. Try for a seat at the bar, for the dining room is always crowded and an hour's wait for a table is normal. As you pass Prince Street you might stop at Raoul's at 180 Prince for a drink at the bar. If you have bought a loaf back at the bakery, however, you might want to walk

on to Joe's Dairy for smoked mozzarella, or simply to stand outside when the smoke rises from Joe's open cellar door on to the street.

# Eating & drinking

## Angelo's of Mulberry Street
*146 Mulberry Street, between Grand & Hester Streets (212 966 1277).* **Open** noon-11.30pm Mon-Thur, Sun; noon-12.30am Fri; noon-1am Sat. Friendly, fun, and with specials as the speciality.

## Balthazar
*80 Spring Street, between Broadway & Crosby Street (212 965 1414).* **Open** 7.30-11.30am, noon-5pm, 6pm-1.30am Mon-Thur; 7.30-11.30am, noon-5pm, 6pm-2.30am Fri; 7.30am-4pm, 6pm-2.30am Sat; 7.30am-4pm, 5.30pm-1.30am Sun. A stunning interior matches first class fare. A *TONY* 100.

## Blue Ribbon
*97 Sullivan Street, between Spring & Prince Streets (212 274 0404).* **Open** 4pm-4am Tue-Sun. A hipsters waffle house, this *TONY* 100 restaurant draws hordes of off-duty chefs.

## Broome Street Bar
*363 West Broadway, at Broome Street (212 925 2086).* **Open** 11am-1.30am Mon-Thur; 11am-2.30am Fri-Sun.

## Caffe Roma
*385 Broome Street, at Mulberry Street (212 226 8413).* **Open** 8am-midnight daily.

## Ceci-Cela
*55 Spring Street, between Mulberry & Lafayette Streets (212 274 9179).* **Open** 8am-7pm Mon-Thur, Sun; 8am-9.30pm Fri, Sat. Luscious pastries in a funky, relaxed setting. A *TONY* 100.

## Cendrillon
*45 Mercer Street, between Broome & Grand Streets (212 343 9012).* **Open** 11am-11pm Tue-Sat; 11am-10pm Sun. For those in search of exotic tastes.

## Cipriani
*376 West Broadway, between Broome & Spring Streets (212 343 0999).* **Open** noon-midnight daily.

## Dean & DeLuca
*560 Broadway, at Prince Street (212 431 1691).* **Open** 10am-8pm Mon-Sat; 10am-7pm Sun. The most sophisticated collection of speciality foods in the city.

Little details adorn the **Little Singer Building** – but it's a mammoth in this 18th-century cast-iron historic district.

### Dom's

*202 Lafayette Street, at Kenmare Street (212 226 1963).* **Open** 8am-8.30pm Mon-Sat; 8am-8pm Sun.

### Eileen's 'Special' Cheesecake

*17 Cleveland Place, at Kenmare Street (212 966 5585).* **Open** 8am-6.30pm Mon-Thur; 8am-7pm Fri; 9am-7pm Sat; 10am-6pm Sun.

### French Culinary Institute

*462 Broadway, at Grand Street (212 219 8890).* **Open** 9am-7pm daily.

### Joe's Dairy

*156 Sullivan Street, between Prince & Houston Streets (212 677 8780).* **Open** 9am-6pm Tue-Fri; 8am-6pm Sat. This is a family affair that has created a loyal following. They even smoke their mozzarella in-house.

### Le Pain Quotidien

*100 Grand Street, at Mercer Street (212 625 9009).* **Open** 8am-7pm daily. This country-style Belgian bakery is the perfect respite from a tiring trudge, featuring the best cinnamon Danish in New York. A *TONY* 100.

### Raoul's

*180 Prince Street, between Thompson & Sullivan Streets (212 966 3518).* **Open** 5pm-2am daily. Reservations requested. Dishes that would satisfy any Parisian, this *TONY* 100 restaurant is a slice of classic Soho. A perfect Manhattan evening of dinner and cocktails.

### Sullivan Street Bakery

*73 Sullivan Street, between Spring & Broome Streets (212 334 9435).* **Open** 7am-7pm daily. Craggy, flour-dusted loaves that crackle apart will tempt you to live on bread alone. A *TONY* 100.

## Churches

### Most Holy Crucifix Church

*378 Broome Street, between Mott & Mulberry Streets (212 226 2556).* **Open** 10am-1pm, 4-7pm daily.

### St Patrick's Old Cathedral

*623 Mulberry Street, at Prince Street (212 226 8075).* **Open** 8.30am-6pm Mon, Tue, Thur-Sun.

## Galleries

### Gagosian

*980 Madison Avenue, at 76th Street (212 744 2313).* **Open** *winter* 10am-6pm Tue-Sat; *summer* 10am-6pm Tue-Fri.

**Branch:** Gagosian Chelsea, 555 West 24th Street, between Tenth & Eleventh Avenues (212 741 1111). **Open** *Oct-June* 10am-6pm Tue-Sat. *Aug, Sept* 10am-6pm Mon-Fri.

### Guggenheim Museum Soho

*575 Broadway, at Prince Street (212 423 3500).* **Open** 11am-6pm Wed-Fri, Sun; 11am-8pm Sat. **Admission** *for both Guggenheim museums* $16; *for Soho only* $8; $5 concessions.

### Leo Castelli

*59 East 79th Street, between Madison & Park Avenues (212 249 4470).* **Open** 10am-6pm Tue-Sat.

### Mary Boone

*Fourth Floor, 745 Fifth Avenue, between 57th & 58th Streets (212 752 2929).* **Open** 10am-6pm Tue-Fri; 10am-5pm Sat.

### PaceWildenstein

*142 Greene Street, between Prince & Houston Streets (212 431 9224).* **Open** *Sept-June* 10am-6pm Tue-Sat. *July, Aug* 10am-5pm Mon-Thur; 10am-4pm Fri.
**Branch:** 32 East 57th Street, between Madison & Park Avenues (212 421 3292). **Open** *Sept-May* 9.30am-6pm Tue-Fri; 10am-6pm Sat.

### Paula Cooper Gallery

*534 West 21st Street, between Tenth & Eleventh Avenues (212 255 1105).* **Open** 10am-6pm Tue-Sat. Call for summer hours.
**Branch:** 521 West 21st Street, between Tenth & Eleventh Avenues (212 255 5247).

### Solomon R Guggenheim Museum

*1071 Fifth Avenue, at 88th Street (212 423 3500).* **Open** 9am-6pm Mon-Wed, Sun; 9am-8pm Fri, Sat. **Admission** $12; $7 concessions; free under-12s; voluntary donation 6-8pm Fri.

## Hotels

### The Mercer

*147 Mercer Street, at Prince Street (212 966 6060).*

### SoHo Grand Hotel

*310 West Broadway, between Grand & Canal Streets (212 965 3000).*

## Shopping

### 38 Aquarium

*371 Broome Street, at Mott Street (212 966 0397).* **Open** 11am-8pm daily.

**The Haughwout** building's cast-iron façade – funded from china, glass and porcelain.

### Broadway Panhandler

*477 Broome Street, between Wooster & Greene Streets (212 966 3434).* **Open** 10.30am-7pm Mon-Fri; 11am-7pm Sat; 11am-6pm Sun.

### Chanel

*15 East 57th Street, between Fifth & Madison Avenues (212 355 5050).* **Open** 10am-6.30pm Mon-Wed, Fri; 10am-7pm Thur; 10am-6pm Sat.

### D&G

*825 Madison Avenue, between 68th & 69th Streets (212 249 4100).* **Open** 10am-6pm Mon-Wed, Fri, Sat; 10am-7pm Thur.

### George Smith

*73 Spring Street, between Broadway & Lafayette Street (212 226 4747).* **Open** 9am-5pm Mon-Fri; 11am-6pm Sat.

### Grass Roots Garden

*131 Spring Street, between Greene & Wooster Streets (212 226 2662).* **Open** 9am-6pm Tue-Sat; noon-6pm Sun.

### Kerquelen

*44 Greene Street, between Grand & Broome Streets (212 431 1771).* **Open** 11am-7.30pm Mon-Thur; 11am-8pm Fri, Sat; 11am-6pm Sun.

### L'Occitane

*146 Spring Street, between Greene & Wooster Streets (212 343 0109).* **Open** 11am-8pm Mon-Sat; noon-8pm Sun.

### O'Lampia

*155 Bowery Street, between Broome & Delancey Streets (212 925 1660).* **Open** 10am-6pm Tue-Sun. Mon by appointment only.

### Portico Home

*72 Spring Street, between Broadway & Lafayette Street (212 941 7800).* **Open** 10am-7pm Mon-Sat; noon-6pm Sun.

### Prada Sport

*116 Wooster Street, between Prince & Spring Streets (212 925 2221).* **Open** 11am-7pm Mon-Sat; noon-6pm Sun.

### Tracy Feith

*209 Mulberry Street, between Spring & Kenmare Streets (212 334 3097).* **Open** 11am-7pm Mon-Sat; noon-7pm Sun.

### Louis Vuitton

*114-116 Greene Street, between Prince & Spring Streets (212 274 9090).* **Open** 11am-7pm Mon-Fri; noon-5pm Sun.

### Waterworks Collection

*475 Broome Street, between Greene & Wooster Streets (212 274 8800).* **Open** 10am-6pm Mon-Sat; noon-6pm Sun.

### Yohji Yamamoto

*103 Grand Street, at Mercer Street (212 966 9066).* **Open** 11am-7pm Mon-Sat; noon-6pm Sun.

# Men of letters

Greg Sanders

Searching for poetic structure in the East Village and Alphabet City.

> **Start:** Astor Place
> **Finish:** Astor Place
> **Time:** 3-4 hours
> **Distance:** 4 miles/6.5km
> **Getting there:** subway train 6 to Astor Place station
> **Getting back:** subway train 6 from Astor Place station
> **Note:** start this walk in the late morning, and avoid visiting the East River Park after dark. This walk has some overlap with Lady Bunny's walk, *The Bunny Hop*; for an exclusively Beat walk, see Barry Miles's walk, *Eyeball Kicks*.

This walk explores the diversity and range of sights offered by the East Village and draws from this amazingly dense neighbourhood some electrical essence of creativity, the same essence that the Beats might have sensed as well. The original Beats, who helped establish the East Village's reputation as New York's counter-cultural, avant-garde centre nearly a half-century ago, consisted largely of four men: Allen Ginsberg, William Burroughs, Jack Kerouac and Gregory Corso. But what has happened to their legacy?

I've lived in the East Village for close to a decade now and even in that relatively short time I've seen dramatic changes. Starbucks, Gap and McDonald's now dot the landscape, stirring up hatred in many who moved here precisely because it seemed to be a last holdout against homogenised consumerism. When I first moved in, crack vials littered the stoop of my building; homeless men sometimes slept in the foyer on cold nights. One looked over one's shoulder when arriving home after midnight. Now I live in the midst of hipdom, an ironically self-referential, fashion-conscious neighbourhood that's exploited its own poverty-stricken past to create a colourful, eclectic present, for better or for worse. That the corruption *fauxhemian* has recently been coined says it all.

One thing is certain – the Beats could never afford to live here now. For a poet or writer just starting out, independent wealth or cash from the folks back home would be necessary. I was an actuary when I first moved here, working for an insurance company on Wall Street. I later quit to commit more time to my writing, a move of questionable sanity.

Start your walk at Astor Place where you will come upon, in the middle of a traffic island, a large cubical sculpture balanced on one of its corners. Called *Alamo*, and created by the sculptor Bernard 'Tony' Rosenthal in 1966, it was permanently installed a year later with the help of a private donor. Surprisingly, it spins on its axis if at least two full-strength adults push against any of its edges in a concerted effort. It is also almost a given that on this same small traffic island, which is bounded by Lafayette Street, Fourth Avenue, Astor Place and East 8th Street, a dozen or so skateboarders and young anarchist types will be gathered beneath and around the cube. These teenagers, mostly from the surrounding suburbs, take advantage of the very short strip of nearly untrafficked asphalt of Astor Place to perform skateboard stunts, many without success. Just south of the cube and about five

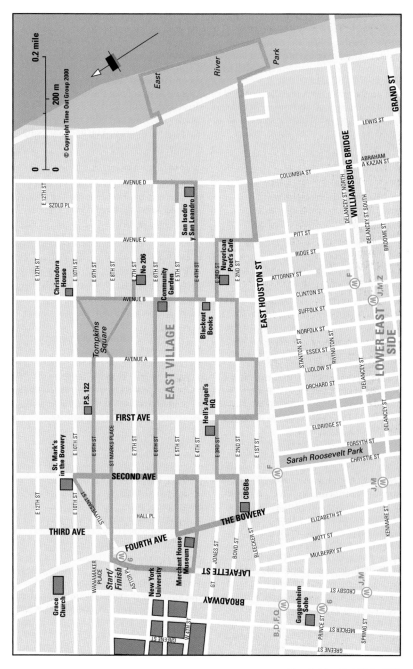

storeys up, you'll see the giant Fischer Music clock. The Fischer Music store, which closed in 1999, was a supplier of sheet music of every genre for just about every instrument in existence, as well as a huge variety of music books.

With the giant clock on your right, you'll be facing east and should be able to see Third Avenue. Walk the short block to Third Avenue, cross the street, and, if you haven't yet had your fill of New York pizza, grab a slice or two at St Mark's Pizza, my favorite pizza joint in Manhattan, partially, I'll admit, because it's just down the block from my apartment. If you get a slice with anything on – try it with fried eggplant (that's aubergine) or fresh tomatoes or pepperoni – they'll sprinkle a bit of extra mozzarella on the slice before throwing it into the oven to heat it up. You are now about five metres from the start of St Mark's Place, the main corridor, *tchachka* capital and requisite entry point to the East Village. Head down it and be aware that this first block is the most obviously touristy, though it still maintains a grungy nostalgia for its seedier past.

There are some good deals to be found if you're shopping for CDs. On the south side you'll see Kim's, a great place for the hard-to-find indie CD or video. Music categories range from 'The Establishment' and 'Sleazy' to 'Krautrock'. Like so many of the music shops along St Mark's, Kim's also carries a good supply of used CDs selling from about $5-$10. A few yards further down, on the north side of the street, you can also check out Joe's CDs (for new CDs enter through the door on the left; for used enter on the right), and a little further down, on the same side of the block, you'll find yet more bargains at 13 St Mark's. I've found some amazing deals in these stores and would suggest checking them out before making the requisite trip to Tower, Virgin or HMV.

Continue across Second Avenue along St Mark's Place, noting that from January to March 1917 Trotsky printed *Novyi Mir*

(*New World*) in the basement of No.77, just prior to leaving for Russia to join the Bolshevik Revolution. The same now horribly re-faced building is also where WH Auden lived from 1953 to 1972. Cafés abound between Second Avenue and Avenue A, mostly on the north side of the street and usually loaded with young couples, platonic and otherwise, leisurely enjoying themselves. You'll undoubtedly notice a high incidence of body piercings, tattoos and dye-jobs among the diners here. You can question the sanity and judgement of the tattooed and pierced, or you can step back, and see it all as a kind of dynamic art show in which the human body is the canvas.

At Avenue A you will be facing the main nexus of the East Village, the 16 patchwork acres of Tompkins Square Park, which was built in 1834. Its 1992 facelift belies its rough past. The park has been the site of numerous riots, demonstrations and skirmishes. In 1877, for example, a peaceful sympathy rally for railroad strikers drew 20,000 participants, who came to hear socialist orators in the park. After two hours the rally was quashed by billy club-wielding mounted police who beat men, women and children without preference, leaving hundreds of casualties in their wake. The more memorable riot took place under Mayor David Dinkins in 1989 when the police, many with their badge numbers and faces obscured, and also indiscriminately wielding billy clubs, cleared the park of squatters and their sympathisers, while also injuring many bystanders and demonstrators as the violence spread through Alphabet City. This was the culmination of many smaller riots and violent disruptions that had taken place in the late 1980s. During the previous years a shantytown had taken root in the park and following the riots, and after the last of the park's homeless were evicted, what remained of their shanties were bulldozed. The park was then closed for three years, during which time a major rehabilitation

Splashing and sleeping are still allowed in **Tompkins Square Park** despite a 1992 facelift.

commenced, much to the chagrin of the homeless, drug dealers and addicts, but to the liking of residents whose property lay adjacent to the park. Still the subject of bitter dispute among many East Villagers, the riots are referred to often as evidence of police brutality and of a department allied with real estate interests and deaf to the cries of the homeless and poor. Many preferred the old Tompkins Square Park, where the reality of the city's social ills were clearly manifested for all to see.

Because of its central location, the park's transubstantiation from a ragged, drug-addled shantytown into a happy, shiny place was a watershed act and a definitive sign that things were seriously changing in Alphabet City. The park is now safe, relatively clean, always policed and closed at night. It still plays host to many free concerts and some of the best fringe events around, and was also the place where Wigstock, the annual festival for New York City's (huge) drag scene, got its start. If you walk east through the park towards Avenue B, you'll come across its most dependable offer of entertainment, the fenced-in, woodchip-strewn dog run. Here dogs, legally unleashed, take their owners to socialise. A good anthropological study can be made of the social etiquette of the dog-owner subculture in Alphabet City. From white kids with pierced eyebrows and matted dreadlocks, or the Armani-clad yuppie, to the rarely spotted old-time radical, it's one of the top spots for people-watching. Not to mention the dogs, full of their own – and possibly more honest – kind of urban freneticism.

At 16 storeys, Christodora House, overlooking the park on the north-east corner of 9th Street and Avenue B, can be seen for blocks away. Built in 1928 to replace its smaller predecessor of the same name, Christodora (a Greek conjunction for 'Gift of Christ') was for much of the past century the cultural centre of the Lower East Side's immigrant population. Its non-sectarian programmes,

funded mostly by private donations, included music lessons, dramatic performances along with poetry, dance, verse and theatre venues. George Gershwin gave his first public recital in the building's third-floor auditorium. Its life has been as varied as the neighbourhood it still towers above. Appropriately enough, it was converted to private apartments in 1987. Its occupants have included, among others, James Osterberg, aka Iggy Pop, whose latest album is entitled *Avenue B*.

Next, take a quick foray to Allen Ginsberg's first East Village home. Go south on Avenue B and then make a left on to 7th Street, heading east. In 1951, Ginsberg moved into 206 East 7th Street, a narrow but handsome tenement with a steep stoop. In 1953, a couple of years after fatally missing, with a bullet, a glass on his wife's head, William Burroughs moved in with him. Jack Kerouac would often drop in and it was here that Kerouac met the woman whom he would portray as Mardou Fox in *The Subterraneans*. It was also in 1953 that Ginsberg and Kerouac left for California. In 1955 Ginsberg read *Howl* for the first time in San Francisco and the Beats were bound for counter-cultural iconoclasm. *Howl* famously starts with the stanza:

*I saw the best minds of my generation destroyed by madness, starving, hysterical naked,*
    *dragging themselves through the negro streets at dawn looking for an angry fix,*
    *anghelheaded hipsters burning for the ancient heavenly connection to the starry dynamo in the machinery of night…*

Ginsberg's poem is saturated with images of drugs, sex, insanity and New York City, including the Lower East Side. He returned to the East Village in 1958 to take an apartment on East 2nd Street, which we'll visit later. In a 1971 interview, Ginsberg said of the relationships between the Beats and the Lower East

Side: 'This was the loam or soil out of which a lot of it grew… the apocalyptic sensibility, the interest in the mystic arts, the marginal leavings, the garbage of society… the beginning of the Department of Sanitation culture.'

Head back through Tompkins Square Park and walk west along 9th Street. Between Avenue A and Second Avenue, 9th Street is lined on either side by an eclectic variety of small restaurants and petite shops that sell everything from Bali furniture and antique watches to trendy Manhattan Portage bags, handmade pottery, and used moviemaking equipment. Perhaps portentously, a few upscale women's clothing stores have recently opened along this somewhat tattered but folksy two-block parade of shops. Because the storefronts are uniformly small, spanning only the first floors of narrow tenement buildings, it's a near *Alice in Wonderland* shopping experience, the small window displays colourful and funky by necessity, the sidewalk uneven and narrow in stretches. On the north-east corner of First Avenue and 9th Street you can't help but run into the massive PS 122. Founded in 1979 and soon thereafter established as a risk-taking theatrical, dance and performance space, this converted public school has become a major contributor to the cultural life of the city. 'PS 122,' says its mission statement, 'has achieved national and international recognition as one of [America's] most important and innovative alternative presenting organizations.' Among previous unknowns who got their start here were Spalding Gray. Look for postings of current shows in front of the First Avenue façade.

Recently coined 'Little Tokyo', 9th Street between Second and Third Avenues boasts an assortment of Japanese restaurants, some less than a year old, some nearly a decade. Decibel, a *sake* bar that falls into the latter category, occupies the basement of 240 East 9th and

offers a huge assortment of rice wine as well as interesting munchies, including salted soybeans still in their pods and cooked lotus root. Ironically, the increased popularity of Little Tokyo has also brought attention to one of my favourite restaurants, Col Legno, a hanger-on from the hairier days of the neighbourhood, whose wood-burning oven often pollutes the air of my apartment in the late afternoon, but whose pizza and grilled Tuscan fare are tops.

Continue west on East 9th Street. Before you actually reach Third Avenue and another string of Japanese restaurants, you will hit the intersection with Stuyvesant Street, the oldest street in Manhattan laid out on a true east–west axis, pre-dating the city's grid plan. Within the triangular George Hecht Viewing Gardens at 9th Street and Third Avenue, a giant compass dial has been installed, apparently to commemorate Stuyvesant Street's truth in geographic orientation. Make an acute right on to Stuyvesant Street, heading east, and observe the beautifully restored Federal-style houses on the north side. This area was originally the farm of Governor Peter Stuyvesant, who was the fourth director general (or governor) of New Amsterdam from 1646 to 1664. He was dedicated and efficient, pompous and unpopular – the prototypical New Yorker – and ended his military career by surrendering the colony to the British without a fight in 1664 after a surprise naval attack. No.21, the Stuyvesant Fish House, was built in 1804 as a gift for one of his great-great-granddaughters.

The intersection of Stuyvesant Street and Second Avenue is dominated by St Mark's-in-the-Bowery Church, built in 1799 on the former site of Stuyvesant's family chapel. Its Greek Revival steeple can be seen from the low-rise rooftops up and down Second Avenue, a view that has changed very little for nearly a century. It was restored in the late 1970s, severely damaged by a fire shortly thereafter, and

**St Mark's-in-the-Bowery** – local landmark.

restored again in the early 1980s. A full history of this Episcopal church and its surroundings is detailed on plaques lining the exterior of the wrought iron fence that surrounds the grounds. Since the 1920s, St Mark's Church has been host to a variety of avant-garde artistic performances, from William Carlos Williams to Allen Ginsberg, whose memorial service was also held there. The pews have been removed to make room for performers of all kinds. It's worth taking a stroll around the grounds – Peter Stuyvesant and Commodore Perry are buried here.

Directly across the avenue, at the corner of 10th Street, is the Second Avenue Deli, an icon that serves a wide variety of kosher Jewish-American fare. Tall pastrami sandwiches, matzoh ball soup, chopped (chicken) liver and knishes are among the most popular dishes ordered. Their chopped liver approaches the perfection of my Grandma Molly's, but can't quite match it (sorry, guys). If you can't eat a whole sandwich, ask to take half of it home and the waiter will come by with sheets of aluminium foil and a paper bag. Don't be shy – act like a regular and throw a pickle (they give you a plate of them when you sit down) and some extra bread in there to take with you, too. They'll respect you. Outside the restaurant, memorialised in Hollywood-style sidewalk inlays, are the names of stars of the Yiddish theatre, of which this area was once the centre. The owner and founder of the deli, Abe Lebewohl, was robbed and shot in 1996 while depositing the deli's receipts at his bank on East 4th Street – the tiny flower garden at the base of the flagpole outside St Mark's opposite is dedicated to his memory. A suspect has yet to be caught and an award of $100,000 is being offered for information that leads to an arrest.

Head south on Second Avenue, stopping briefly in front of No.135 (between 9th Street and St Mark's Place), the Ottendorfer Branch of the New York Public Library (under renovation at the time of this writing). This was the first building in Manhattan built as a free public library. Designed by William Schickel and erected in 1884, it was a gift from Oswald Ottendorfer, a wealthy editor, to the then heavily German population of the neighbourhood. Regarding the inscription on the façade, 'Freie Bibliothek und Lesehalle', the building's genesis was as the German-language branch of the Free Circulating Library, but it eventually became part of the city's public library system. It is also significant for its early use of moulded terracotta in its interior.

Continue south on Second Avenue. At the south-west corner of 7th Street the tinted-windowed Kiev Restaurant might beckon you with borscht (cold beet soup) or pierogi (Ukrainian dumplings stuffed with meat, sauerkraut, cheese or potatoes) or kasha varnishkes (buckwheat with bow-tie noodles) with mushroom gravy. This is the granddaddy of 24-hour Ukrainian diners, a culinary species unto themselves and one peculiar to the East Village. While its main competitor, Veselka, back at 9th Street and Second Avenue, has become very popular, I prefer the Kiev with its understated interior, its mercurial waitresses and inexpensive, hardy food that can set you up for a long day of walking or help you recover from a heavy night of drinking. To see the Kiev with full somnambulistic jitters, you'd have to come here after the bars close, at five or six in the morning, on a weekend.

Directly next door to the Kiev is Moishe's kosher bakery where I stop in regularly for their hamentachen, a triangular-shaped pastry filled with thick confections of raspberries or prunes or apricots or, my favourite, poppy seeds. Traditionally eaten on Purim, a Jewish holiday, you can thankfully buy them here all year round. Moishe's is a wonderful vestige of the days when the community was predominantly Jewish and I often wonder how much longer they can survive without serving lattes and mochaccinos.

Continue south on Second Avenue one more block and then head east on to 6th Street; 6th Street between First and Second Avenues is called Little India or Curry Row and is much more established than the nascent Little Tokyo. You'll immediately see that both sides of the block, though the south side more than the north, are lined with Indian restaurants. Starting at around seven at night, representatives from many of them will try to entice you to enter their establishment with coupons or boasts or obsequious smiles. Many of the coupons can legitimately save you money. If you're planning to eat there, it's worth walking each side of the block once before settling on a restaurant. The real draw here is not exquisite quality – and many say the food has lately taken a bit of a dive – but very low prices. To my knowledge, there's nowhere else in Manhattan where you can get a meal for so little – about $10 to $14 for a filling three-course, full-service meal, sometimes accompanied with live sitar music, and about $5 for the equivalent lunch.

**Moishe's Homemade Kosher Bakery** – still serving hamentachen, still resisting the latte.

Eddie's sculpture – just one example of local art in the **6th and B Community Garden**.

Additionally, many of the restaurants encourage you to bring your own booze. Almost everyone arrives with bags of cold beer or wine. The deli on the north-west corner of 6th Street and First Avenue has exploited this niche and offers an amazingly wide variety of chilled beers at decent prices. The strip of restaurants continues with a few more around the corner on First Avenue, heading south. The common, and now clichéd, joke is that though there may be 20-plus restaurants on this block, there's only one kitchen.

Continue east on 6th Street and head, once again, into the land of lettered avenues. On the corner with Avenue B you'll come across the 6th and B Community Garden, a 17,000-square-foot oasis. Note the unusual fence. The hand cutouts along its perimeter are meant to represent the community's contribution in creating the garden. Begun in 1983 in a vacant lot where a crumbling building had recently been razed and cleared, the garden's future was uncertain until 1996, when a prolonged grassroots campaign

culminated in an agreement between the Parks Department and the local community, providing a permanent status. The garden now boasts 15 fruiting trees, 50 flowering shrubs, along with myriad flowers, vegetables and herbs. If the gates are open, go inside, sit on a bench, smell the air, listen to the birds. East of Avenue A you will come across more community gardens, some nearly as grand as this one. Like the 6th and B Garden, they are transformations of once crime-ridden, rubble-strewn, graffiti-covered lots to oases of green. Many of their fates were uncertain until very recently. In May 1999 the Giuliani administration was preparing to auction off those other gardens, which technically were owned by the City, to the highest bidders. The mayor's view was that the gardens should be replaced by housing, which would also increase the city's tax revenue. Panic struck at the hearts of the communities who'd rehabilitated the brick-littered lots. Before the auctioning began at full swing, Bette Midler and her New York Restoration Project, along with

The mosaic marvel on the rear of **Iglesia San Isedro Y San Leandro** at 345 East 4th Street.

other advocacy groups, raised $4 million to buy up some 115 gardens, many in the poorest neighbourhoods, and a great number in Alphabet City.

Most of the earliest gardens were established around 1980, with a handful pre-dating that. After nearly two decades, many have evolved into intricate, loving manifestations of their surrounding communities. The garden at 6th and B is one of the largest and oldest ones that dots Alphabet City. In its south-east corner a sculpture composed of scrap wood, stuffed animals and other, semi-identifiable objects found on the streets of New York climbs 37 feet to a pyramidal peak. I'm not sure what the garden member, described as 'Eddie', intended, but its message has always been clear to me: make junk into beauty.

Next, go south on Avenue B to Blackout Books at 50 Avenue B, between 3rd and 4th Streets. The store, anarchistic by definition – it's a co-operative – but a hell of a lot of fun in practice, covers about every political and social issue you can imagine – women's issues, vegetarianism, race, class, sexual orientation; it also boasts an impressive selection of books on international labour practices. Additionally, you'll find an eclectic selection of free or almost-free zines, such as *Veggie Head Wilson*, a small compendium of Xeroxed and stapled typewritten personal diatribes that costs 50¢, and *The Chain Ring Ate My Pants*, a free miniature zine promoting the use of bicycles over motor vehicles. The staff are friendly and unpaid, the shoppers interesting, the stock worth perusing.

Briefly head back north on Avenue B and then make a right on to 4th Street and head east towards Avenue C. Heading this far east is not a great idea late at night if you're not sure what your destination is, but it's still much safer than it used to be. Avenue C is also called Loisaida Avenue, Spanglish for Lower East Side and the same term, dating from the 1970s, that used to be applied to the entirety of

Alphabet City when the area was overwhelmingly Hispanic. The population here is still mostly Puerto Rican and Dominican. Two churches, the Iglesia Pentecostal Camino, at 289 East 4th, and San Isedro Y San Leandro, at 345 East 4th, serve the local Catholic community. The real excitement is on the latter's rear façade. Make a left on Avenue D and another left on 5th Street and gaze across a lot to the colourful mural and folk-art embellishments that entirely cover the back of the church. To get a further sense of the cultures that have passed through this neighbourhood, note that the garden across 4th Street from the church, Orchard Alley – established in 1980 and saved by Ms Midler and co – grew out of the lot where the synagogue Cheva Bikur Cholim B'nai Israel had previously stood. In turn, this synagogue-cum-community garden is directly across the street from a Russian Orthodox Church-cum-Hispanic Orthodox Church with folk embellishments. It is in places like this that I often glimpse the blur of history in New York, and sense the speed with which one culture builds upon the artefacts of another; and it is places like this that seem to have a poetic structure of their own, uneven stanzas piled on top of each other, a kind of historical stream-of-consciousness poem.

It's now time to head to the East River Park, a rarely promoted gem of the Lower East Side. Head north on Avenue D to 6th Street, and there make a right. You'll pass the Jacob Riis Houses, on the left, and the Lillian Wald Houses, on the right, both of which are subsidised housing projects for low- and middle-income families. There's bound to be a good amount of activity, from kids riding bikes to men playing dominoes out on the sidewalk. Not that it's perfectly idyllic – poverty and crime exist, the latter at lower rates than it used to, but at night there is still the potential of danger. At the end of 6th Street walk over the pedestrian bridge that spans the FDR

Join the dots – a game of dominoes pulls the crowds by the **Jacob Riis Houses**, Avenue D.

Drive. Then walk to the East River, which will be clearly visible.

On a clear day you should be able to see most of the east side of Manhattan, north to the 59th Street Bridge and further, south to the Williamsburg Bridge. You're also bound to see runners, Rollerbladers and bicyclists. Directly across the river is Williamsburg, Brooklyn and what remains of a once-thriving industrial centre. Still resident there are Domino Sugar and Norval Cement. When I first would go on runs down here in 1990, the huge silver storage tanks had the Pfizer logo emblazoned on their sides. Walk south towards the Williamsburg Bridge. In fact, if you're up for it, walk to the Williamsburg Bridge, which rises vertiginously over the esplanade and provides a visually stunning and non-clichéd photo opportunity.

As you walk south, athletic fields and then baseball and tennis courts will be on your right. On a warm afternoon, especially a weekend afternoon, the fields should be brimming with baseball games, football games, soccer matches and

ultimate Frisbee games, the last in which you might see the author participating. Once you've explored the park and taken in the views, exit the East River Park at Houston Street. You can see the walkway intersect the large athletic field about midway. It's the pedestrian exit south of the one you entered the park through. Houston Street is the equivalent of 'zeroth' street on the grid, and in these parts it is the divider between the East Village and the Lower East Side.

After carefully crossing the busy intersection at the top of the ramp, proceed west on Houston Street on its north side. At Avenue C, make a right and then make a left on to 3rd Street. The Nuyorican (from New York and Puerto Rican) Poets' Cafe occupies the industrial-looking building at 236 East 3rd Street, between Avenues B and C. For 25 years, the Nuyorican has been the poetic core of Alphabet City. Their poetry slams have become legendary. Put simply, a slam is a competition wherein a group of poets individually perform their poems on stage and are rated by selected

**Williamsburg Bridge** spans the East River.

judges from the audience. Winners of one round will continue on to slam against winners of another round. At the end of each week a champion is crowned. For the most part, this is hard-hitting urban poetry that is not shy about subject matter, not in the least. Expect to hear at least a few rants on race relations, screwing (lots of it), the cops, not to mention love-in-the-city. This is good stuff, honestly written, beautifully performed and thankfully not concerned with political correctness in the least. Stop back in on a Friday night at ten. Pay the $5 cover and settle in for the slam and $4 beers.

Continue west on 3rd Street, past yet another little garden, this one dotted with sculptures. At 3rd Street and Avenue B you have two excellent choices for food. The first, and more expensive, would be to sit down and have a meal at Pierrot, 28 Avenue B, a newish and somewhat upscale bistro with entrées such as seared sirloin au poivre and Portobello goat

cheese panzanella. If you arrive at the right time of day there will also be virtual *tableaux vivants* of good-looking, hip, nouveau East Villagers. Or you could instead go around the corner to Mama's Food Shop, and get yourself some home-made comfort food that will make you happy to the soul. Because they don't have a licence to sell liquor, you can pick up a bottle of wine or a few bottles of beer at a bodega first. Order at the counter – one, two or three items off a blackboard menu – then grab a table and chow down your fried chicken or meatloaf or grilled salmon with any number of tasty sides. The menu changes daily, but the hefty staples mentioned above remain pretty much static and are always a delight. Note that you might have to share a table with some strangers, but what better way to get to know the local scene? Directly across the street is Step Mama, where you can get sandwiches.

Get back on to Avenue B and head south, making a right on to 2nd Street and stopping in front of 170 2nd Street. This is Allen Ginsberg's second East Village residence. He returned from visiting Burroughs in Tangier in 1958 and took up residence in apartment 16 of this red-brick building with white-stone trim. There he wrote *Kaddish* and edited Burroughs' *Naked Lunch*. A plaque gives some more details, such that 'His signal poem, *Howl*, helped launch the Beat Generation.' Continue west on 2nd Street until you hit Avenue A, then make a left until you hit 1st Street. Make a right on to 1st Street and head over to the intersection of 1st Street and First Avenue.

This intersection is usually full of activity. You can get Asian food served by transvestites at Lucky Cheng's, Brazilian food at Boca Chica, or check out any number of small cafés and restaurants that line the north side of 1st Street west of First Avenue. Lucky Cheng's is a popular destination for out-of-towners looking for a venue off the beaten path, but not too far off. Though the place can be a hoot, you should be warned that diners are often 'volunteered' to step into the cabaret spotlight and participate in a variety of games or contests. For example, if your dream is to be plucked from your table, placed on stage and encouraged, by an energetic group of pansexuals, to fellate a banana, then this joint might be for you. If you'd rather dine in relative obscurity, skip Lucky Cheng's.

You've been walking for a while by now and doubtless you need to settle down for a few pints of beer, if you haven't yet. Walk north on First Avenue to d.b.a., at No.41, which stands for 'doing business as' or 'drink better ale'. At last count, they had 19 beers on tap and over 150 in bottles, not to mention a huge assortment of single malt Scotches and a small batch

Anyone home? – **Hell's Angels HQ**.

tequilas. They're one of the best beer bars in Manhattan but you'd never know it, judging by the bar's understated façade. They serve hand-drawn, cask-conditioned ales as well as seasonal brews from around the United States. The crowd gets a bit yuppie on week nights as Wall Street types stop in for a few swift scoops, but there's generally a relaxed vibe in the place. Out back is a pleasant garden for summer drinking. If you're a fan of rich, dark stouts, try the Brooklyn Chocolate Stout, a favourite of mine that's brewed across the river in Williamsburg.

Afterwards, continue to head north on First Avenue (that's a left out of d.b.a.) and then make a left on to East 3rd Street. A few buildings in on the right side of the street you'll see the Hell's Angels Headquarters, a six-storey tenement with a one-storey false brick and column façade adorned with the Angel's death's-head trademark along with a sign that reads 'Hell's Angels Welcomes You to New York City'. If you're lucky, a half-dozen customised chromed hogs will be parked out front and maybe some Angels themselves will even be there to lour at you as you pass them. An array of security cameras mounted on the building keeps an eye on things outside HQ. The building also contains the offices of their Big Red Machine website, which sells Hell's Angels paraphernalia. While they once were perceived as toughies hanging on the tattered edge of the village, the Hell's Angels now seem like toughies who've landed some good real estate in an up-and-coming neighbourhood and have started a dot com to boot.

Continue up 3rd Street and then make a left on to Second Avenue, walking to the south-east corner of Second Avenue and 2nd Street where you'll find the Anthology Film Archives. Once a somewhat grim institution intended only for the serious film scholar, the Archives have recently revamped their programming and now offer a wide array of films that you won't find showing in mainstream theatres anywhere. At the time of this writing, a Sam Peckinpah festival was in full swing. Movies and their showtimes are posted on the side of the building; tickets are available only on the day of the show.

Cross Second Avenue and head west on 2nd Street to Bowery, then make a left and head south to No.319, the tall white building with the folksy mural of singers painted on its side. This is the Amato Opera. Now celebrating its 52nd consecutive season under the direction of husband and wife team Anthony and Sally Amato, self-proclaimed missionaries of music, the Amato has brought opera to those who can't afford, or don't want to pay, uptown prices. The company has a repertory of some 60 operas, from Verdi and Mozart to the Brazilian composer Gomes and the Italian Boito. Aspiring singers perform here, many of whom have day jobs and some of whom move on to fame. Anthony's, Sally's and their company's longevity has recently brought a great deal of attention to this tiny opera house, hopefully for the better. It's also fitting that they are located on the Bowery, which for nearly the entire 19th century was the Broadway of the working classes.

Almost next door, at 315 Bowery, is the infamous CBGBs, a music venue of a different sort. Its full designation, CBGB – OMFUG, stands for Country BlueGrass Blues and Other Music For Uplifting Gourmandizers; it was host to some of the first sounds of US punk, including the Ramones, Television, Debbie Harry, Patti Smith, Talking Heads, and the Plasmatics. A black hole of a place that befits stripped-down raucous hard-core riffs, CBGBs is also legendary for the most harrowing bathrooms in New York City. I have vivid memories of being in the club as a teenager, having tagged along with my older brother who drove us in from the suburbs of Westchester in his 1970 Plymouth Valiant. I was requisitely stoned, undoubtedly drunk as well, and I recall watching my brother vanish into

the seething floor of slamdancers while I, an enervated cross-country runner at the time, wondered what the hell this was all about. Would he emerge? (He always did, and with a wide grin plastered on his face and sweat saturating his shirt.) I don't even recall who was playing those few times I went, but it might well be that I was witnessing the ascendancy of legendary bands. I've since gone back many times, but the foreboding is gone and I'm at the age where I put cotton in my ears. A while back CBGBs opened an annexe next door, 313 Lounge and Gallery, which hosts venues that tend towards folk, jazz, soul and vocal experimentation. They have poetry slams along with performance art; 313 also has art exhibitions during the day that are open to the public free of charge.

Now walk north back up the Bowery towards East 4th Street. You'll notice on the other side of Bowery a bar-restaurant called Marion's, at No.354. This is the only bar in New York from which this writer is banned. It's a long story. They're very hip in a retro, I-wear-1960s-eyeglasses-in-an-ironic-fashion sort of way, and they're known for their well-made Martinis. Make a right on to East 4th Street. This is the heart of Off-Off-Broadway. Several inexpensive theatres employing amateur to semi-professional actors are on East 4th Street, among them the New York Theater Workshop, at 79 East 4th, where *Rent*, the now very popular Broadway show, got its start, as well as La MaMa etc, at 74A East 4th, which for over three decades has been putting on avant-garde dance pieces.

Up a steep flight of steps at 85 East 4th Street you'll find KGB Bar, a regular destination for New York's 'literary crowd, shoegazing Eurotrash debutantes, and assorted downtown dissidents' (from their website). Supposedly owned by Lucky Luciano in the 1920s, it was then used as a communist den during the cold war. The decor consists of Soviet propaganda posters, portraits of prominent communists, various permutations of the Soviet flag, and lots and lots of red. On any given night you'll find a good assortment of black-clad smokers from New York University along with editors from slick literary magazines and, yes, as always, some posers. Over the years their reputation has grown for hosting readings by prominent and not-at-all-prominent young authors. They've even put out an anthology, *The KGB Reader* (William Morrow & Co), edited by Ken Foster. Continue east on 4th Street to the corner of Second Avenue. On your left, at 87 East 4th Street, is Cucina di Pesce, an Italian restaurant that has great pasta and seafood for a good price. They also offer a three-course early-bird special that's a bargain. If you have to wait for a table, you can eat free steamed mussels at the bar while doing so, which is a real draw in itself.

Make a left on to Second Avenue and head north, then make a left on to East 5th Street. Naturally, it's time for another few pints of beer. Stop in at the Scratcher, a downstairs Irish bar at 209 East 5th, close to Bowery. They serve a good pint of Guinness and are one of the few simple, unpretentious bars around. There's lots of varnished wood and tables with benches. Sometimes there's live Irish music as well. No sign adorns the exterior of this bar, so you'll have to take a look into the windows below sidewalk level to confirm you've come to the right spot.

Fortified now by several pints, you're ready to begin the last leg of the walk. Make a left on to Bowery, cross the street, and make a right on to East 4th Street. The Merchant House Museum is located at 29 East 4th Street, midway between Bowery and Lafayette. This red-brick house, which they tell me is an excellent example of the combination of Federal and Greek Revival styles, contains three floors of the original possessions of Seabury Tredwell and his descendants who lived in it from 1835 to 1933. Everything from furniture, clothing,

family memorabilia, along with a 'secret garden', are on display. In the early 1800s row houses such as this one – and there's a dilapidated, boarded-up, urine-stained, graffiti-tagged version of one just to the east – used to lie on the outskirts of the city and lined this block of East 4th Street.

Across the street is Swift's Hibernian Lounge, another Irish bar of note that pours an excellent pint of Guinness, some say the best in town. Much larger and more popular than Scratcher's, the walls are decorated with murals depicting scenes from Jonathan Swift's *Gulliver's Travels*. You can almost always find a place to sit in the massive back room, which also hosts live music on Tuesday nights. They've got a large assortment of beers on tap as well as wines by the bottle or glass. Recently, while I was enjoying a frothy stout with a friend of mine, an entourage of security men in dark suits came through the door, cleared a corridor, and then Gerry Adams swept past us and into the back room, which was that night closed off for a private function. There's also a rumour that Harvey Keitel stops in for a sharpener now and again.

From Swift's, head west to Lafayette Street then make a right. Cross over to the west side of Lafayette. Well ahead of you will be Astor Place. You'll notice how different this long block is from the rest of the East Village. This is the border between the East and West Village, although some would say that this is NoHo (North of Houston). Either way, it's certainly not the East Village proper, with its lack of tenements and small store fronts, and its strange absence of cross-streets between East 4th Street and Astor Place. From 428 to 434 Lafayette is the distinctive-looking Colonnade Row, also called LaGrange Terrace, four of an original nine row houses built speculatively by Seth Geer far from the bustling centre of business in 1833 for the mercantile elite. Those columns were built by Sing Sing prisoners. At the time of their completion, these marble-fronted houses sold for as much as $30,000 apiece and were considered *the* place to live in Manhattan. The Delanos, Astors and Vanderbilts lived there until Fifth Avenue eclipsed Lafayette Street as the pinnacle of moneyed living, a reputation that it ardently holds on to today. Sadly, the Corinthian colonnade is slowly eroding away and the second-storey porticoes are slathered in roofing tar, but Colonnade Row makes a solid period on the final stanza of the meandering beatnik poem of the East Village.

# Eating & drinking

## Boca Chica

*13 1st Avenue, at First Street (212 473 0108).* **Open** 5.30-11pm Mon-Thur; 5.30-midnight Fri, Sat; noon-11pm Sun. Latin American trad dishes, and less typical concoctions, in a lively setting.

## Col Legno

*231 East 9th Street, between Second & Third Avenues (212 777 4650).* **Open** 6-11.30pm Tue-Sun. The restaurant every mediocre Manhattan pizza-and-pasta joint wishes it could be.

## Cucina di Pesce

*87 East 4th Street, between Second & Third Avenues (212 260 6800).* **Open** 3pm-midnight Mon-Thur, Sun; 3pm-1am Fri, Sat. The godmother of cheap East Village Italian eateries, with sidewalk seating.

## d.b.a.

*41 First Avenue, between 2nd & 3rd Streets (212 475 5097).* **Open** 1pm-4am daily. Get dizzy looking at the beer list, or simply sample the malts in the garden out back.

## Decibel Sake Bar

*240 East 9th Street, between Second & Third Avenues (212 979 2733).* **Open** 8pm-3am Mon-Sat; 8pm-1am Sun. More *sake* bar than restaurant in this hip little subterranean grotto.

## KGB

*85 East 4th Street, between Second & Third Avenues (212 505 3360).* **Open** 7pm-4am daily. A variety of vodkas, and a variety of readings.

## Kiev Restaurant

*117 Second Avenue, at 7th Street (212 674 4040).* **Open** 24hrs daily. You don't get much more old-school East Village than this Polish diner.

## Lucky Cheng's

*24 First Avenue, between 1st & 2nd Streets (212 473 0516).* **Open** 6pm-midnight (drag shows 8pm, 9.30pm, 11pm) Mon-Thur, Sun; 6pm-1am (shows 7.30pm, 11pm) Fri, Sat. Pan-Asian fare, karaoke and bawdy rapport with waiters in drag.

## Mama's Food Shop

*200 East 3rd Street, at Avenue B (212 777 4425).* **Open** 11am-10.30pm Mon-Sat. Generous portions in this nostalgia-food joint – a *TONY* 100.

## Marion's

*354 Bowery, between 3rd & 4th Streets (212 475 7621).* **Open** 6pm-2am daily. Lowbrow, upbeat and lively, American dishes in this glam '50s time warp.

## Moishe's Homemade Kosher Bakery

*115 Second Avenue, between 6th & 7th Streets (212 505 8555).* **Open** 7am-9pm Mon-Thur, Sun; 7am-7pm Fri.

## Pierrot Bistro & Bar

*28 Avenue B, between 2nd & 3rd Streets (212 673 1999).* **Open** 5pm-1am Mon-Fri; noon-midnight Sat, Sun. A solid multi-ethnic menu in this spacious bistro.

## St Mark's Pizza

*23 Third Avenue, between St Mark's Place & 9th Street (212 420 9531).* **Open** 11.30am-11pm daily.

## The Scratcher

*209 East 5th Street, between Bowery & Second Avenue (212 477 0030).* **Open** 11.30am-4am daily. Traditional dark-wood Irish joint, but fortunately they don't make a song and dance about the Irish bit.

## Second Avenue Deli

*156 Second Avenue, between 9th & 10th Streets (212 677 0606).* **Open** 7am-midnight Mon-Thur, Sun; 7am-3am Fri, Sat. The crowds testify to the quality of the food – you won't find a better pastrami sandwich in town. A *TONY* 100.

## Stepmama

*199 East 3rd Street, between Avenues A & B (212 228 2663).* **Open** 11am-10.30pm Mon-Sat.

## Swift Hibernian Lounge

*34 East 4th Street, between Bowery & Lafayette Street (212 260 3600).* **Open** noon-4am daily. One of the best pints of Guinness drawn in New York, but also a wide beer selection, bottle and tap.

## Veselka

*144 Second Avenue, at 9th Street (212 228 9682).* **Open** 24hrs daily. This cheap Eastern European venue is a 1999 *TONY* winner for best late-night eats, and as such attracts an assorted crowd of East Village insomniacs. The cold borscht here is famous.

## Churches

### Iglesia Penetecostal Camino a Damasco

*289 East 4th Street, between Avenues B & C (212 228 5544).* **Open** ring for details.

### St Mark's in-the-Bowery

*131 East 10th Street, at Second Avenue (212 674 6377).* **Open** 10am-6pm Mon-Fri.

## Shopping

### 13 St Mark's

*13 St Mark's Place, between Second & Third Avenues (212 477 4376).* **Open** noon-10pm Mon-Thur; noon-11pm Fri, Sat; noon-9pm Sun.

### Blackout Books

*50 Avenue B, between 3rd & 4th Streets (212 777 1967).* **Open** 11am-9pm Mon-Sat; noon-9pm Sun.

### Joe's Compact Discs

*11 St Mark's Place, between Second & Third Avenues (212 673 4606).* **Open** 11am-11pm Mon-Thur; 11am-midnight Fri, Sat; 11am-9pm Sun.

### Mondo Kim's

*6 St Mark's Place, between Second & Third Avenues (212 598 9985).* **Open** 9am-midnight daily.

## Parks & gardens

### Community Garden

*corner of 6th Street & Avenue B (212 420 8651).* **Open** 6-8pm Wed; 2-4pm Sun.

### Department of Parks & Recreation

*888 NY PARKS/212 360 2774.*

### East River Park

*Montgomery Street to East 12th Street, FDR Drive.*

### Tompkins Square Park

*Between East 7th & East 10th Streets and Avenues A & B.*

## Theatres

### Amato Opera Theater

*319 Bowery, at 2nd Street (212 228 8200).* **Open** *Box office* 1-5pm daily.

### CBGBs

*315 Bowery, at Bleecker Street (212 982 4052).* **Open** ring for details. **Admission** $3-$12. **No credit cards.**

### CB's 313 Gallery

*313 Bowery, at Bleecker Street (212 677 0455).* **Open** *club* noon-2am Mon-Fri; noon-4am. **Admission** $6-$10. *Gallery* noon-6pm daily. Free.

### La MaMa etc

*74A East 4th Street, between Bowery & Second Avenue (212 460 5475).* **Open** ring for details.

### New York Theater Workshop

*79 East 4th Street, between Bowery & Second Avenue (212 460 5475).* **Open** *office* 10am-6pm; *box office* 6-8pm.

### The Nuyorican

*236 East 3rd Street, between Avenues B & C (212 505 8183).* **Open** call for dates and times.

### PS 122

*150 First Avenue, at 9th Street (212 477 5288).* **Open** *box office* 2-6pm Tue-Sat.

## Literature

**Naked Lunch** William S Burroughs (1959)
**Howl and Other Poems** Allen Ginsberg (1956)
**Kaddish and Other Poems** Allen Ginsberg (1961)

## Others

### Anthology Film Archives

*32 Second Avenue, at 2nd Street (212 505 5110/5181).* **Open** *Office* 10am-6pm Mon Fri. **Admission** $8; $5 concessions.

### Merchant House Museum

*29 East 4th Street, between Lafayette Street & Bowery (212 777 1089).* **Open** 1-5pm Mon, Thur-Sun. *Guided tours* Sat, Sun. **Admission** $5; $3 concessions; free under-12s.

### New York Restoration Project

*212 258 2333.*

### Wigstock

*Pier 54, West Street, between 12th & 13th Streets (212 439 5139).* Labor Day weekend.

# On the rights track

Peter & Renata Singer

Trailing animal liberation from theory to practice.

**Start:** Washington Square Arch
**Finish:** corner of 85th Street &
Central Park West
**Time:** 3-4 hours
**Distance:** 4 miles/6km
**Getting there:** subway trains A, B,
C, E, F or Q to West 4th Street-
Washington Square station
**Getting back:** subway trains B or
C from 86th Street station
**Note:** the American Museum
of Natural History has free
admission during the last hour
of each day. There is the option
of a subway journey midway
through this walk. The restaurants
listed at the end of the piece are
noted for their vegetarian menus.
Maitland McDonagh's walk,
*You Gotta Have Park*, also
visits the American Museum
of Natural History.

A thinking man's diet – *Animal Liberation*.

We first came to New York in 1973, when Peter was offered a one-year visiting position at New York University (NYU). The essay *Animal Liberation* had appeared in the *New York Review of Books* in April of that year. It argued that we humans are 'speciesists', enslaving other animals and using them as tools to serve our ends, just as in the past racists enslaved members of other races and sexist men treated women as their chattels. Three years earlier, when we first started thinking about the ethics of how humans relate to animals, we had become vegetarians so that we would not support the abuse of animals reared, often entirely indoors in close confinement, to produce food for us. To think and act in this way about animals was then so novel as to make most people think of us as cranks. In an attempt to change this attitude, Peter had brought to New York a draft of two chapters of a book that he planned would be a careful, calm and irrefutable attack on society's attitudes to animals, and the things that those attitudes led people to do to them. One of the tasks for the year was to complete the book and, hopefully, find a publisher for it.

As for the city itself, we were not sure what we would find. We had arranged to sublet an apartment in New York University housing, and we had images of

# On the rights track

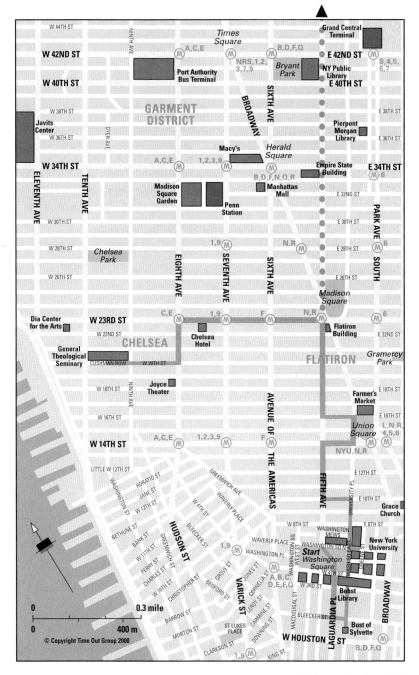

Time Out New York Walks **217**

living in an impersonal concrete jungle. Instead, we found ourselves living in Greenwich Village, near Washington Square Park, the kind of place where the woman who happens to be sitting beside you on the bench insists on showing you photos of her grand-daughter.

Our walk begins in Washington Square, and will take you to places associated with the writing of *Animal Liberation* and the subsequent development of the animal rights movement into a practical force capable of challenging giant corporations and persuading them to cease inflicting needless pain on animals. (We will also take in other points of interest en route.)

We start off under the arch in Washington Square at the bottom of Fifth Avenue, named after America's first President, George Washington (1732-99). It was finished in 1892, replacing an earlier wooden arch built to commemorate the centennial of Washington's inauguration. The architect Stanford White modelled his design on the Arc de Triomphe in Paris. Looking south, if the clouds are not hanging too low, the arch frames one icon of downtown New York, the twin towers of the World Trade Center.

On this quiet Sunday morning in April the trees are still blossoming or newly green, and yellow tulips glow in the flower beds. Greenwich Village is not a morning place: the shops struggle to open by 11 or midday. Washington Square's 9.75 acres harbour some trees, a few worn patches of grass and many ungreen features including a dog run, children's playgrounds, a skateboarding ramp, statues, a corner devoted to chess tables and a fountain in the centre to cool off in on hot summer days. On warm evenings the park is packed with people using these facilities and crowding around the buskers – magicians, fire eaters and groups of amateur musicians jamming. Before you leave the arch, take a look at the row of houses on Washington Square North, some of which date back to the

1830s and appear in works by Henry James and Edith Wharton.

Walk south and a little east to a statue of Garibaldi, a reminder that the Village was once an Italian neighbourhood. Continue directly south towards a massive square building covered in reddish stone. This is New York University's Bobst Library, designed by Philip Johnson and heavily criticised for its lack of proportion with the other buildings of Washington Square. Continue south on La Guardia Place. The area has improved since the 1970s, when the contrast of public squalor and private affluence was all too apparent. Today there's far less danger of falling in a pothole, the hedges are no longer straggly and instead of a rubbish-filled strip of dirt that separates the roadway from a little row of shops and restaurants, there are daffodils in bloom that no one has pulled up or trampled on. As you proceed to Bleecker Street, note the applauding and jovial statue of a rotund Fiorello La Guardia, Mayor of New York from 1934 to 1945. Current Mayors would probably desire a more dignified appearance, but they are unlikely to be remembered as warmly as Fiorello.

Soon we reach Bleecker Street. The stretch from La Guardia Place to Sixth Avenue (also known as the Avenue of the Americas) to the right is famous for its music venues. On hectic weekends the crowds from the suburbs compete for pavement space with the tourists outside the Bitter End and other venues. (The Bitter End has been rewarded with a 'Bitter End Day' in recognition of its contribution to the city's artistic life.) In the '70s, the large white brick building on the corner of Thompson and Bleecker was a dosshouse where homeless people congregated. Now it contains fashionable apartments. Also gone is the 'Ugliest Clothes in the World' shop where you could buy a new suit for $10, but it certainly earned its title. The locals mutter about the creeping 'mallification' of New

NYU accommodation in the **Silver Towers** allows a view on to the colossal *Bust of Sylvette*.

York, with the area now dotted with Gap, Starbucks, Banana Republic and the big drugstore chains such as Duane Reade and Rite Aid.

Cross Bleecker Street and walk half a block east from La Guardia Place to the entrance to three 30-storey buildings called 'Silver Towers', where we spent our first year in New York, and where *Animal Liberation* was begun. A large Picasso-designed statue, *Bust of Sylvette*, sits on the grassy forecourt. Though designed by IM Pei (also responsible for the glass pyramid outside the Louvre in Paris), the towers haven't weathered well. Their dreary beige façades are rain-stained and the institutional functionalism of the architecture is out of keeping with the domestic low rise of the Village and the ornate cast-iron of Soho on the other side of Houston Street. But inside, the apartments are spacious and light.

To return to Washington Square, we can go under the arch directly opposite the entrance to Silver Towers – it has the number 3 on it – that takes us through another set of NYU faculty buildings to

come out alongside the Bobst Library. Walk past the Founder's Memorial and at the corner of Washington Place and Washington Square is NYU's main building. It's here that Peter gave his first course on Animal Liberation, in the winter of 1973-4. It was offered as a continuing education course, one evening a week, and his teaching materials were the draft chapters of the book he was writing. Among the largely middle-class and female attendees, one man stood out because of his burly appearance, working-class New York accent and blunt way of putting things. His name was Henry Spira and he had worked most of his life as a merchant seaman. He brought to the course 30 years of experience fighting for the weak and oppressed, from civil rights marches in the South to standing up for his fellow seamen against the bosses who ran the National Maritime Union. Now he was starting to see that in our dealings with the animals we use for food and research, we humans are the oppressors, and the animals are the weak and powerless. No one knew it at the time, but

Henry was about to become the most effective activist of the modern American animal rights movement.

At the time NYU was a middle-ranking university in bad financial shape. It even had to sell off a campus in the Bronx to avoid bankruptcy. Its fortunes have improved along with those of the city. In the '70s New York was seen as an undesirable place in which to live – dirty, crime-ridden and in economic decline as industries fled to the suburbs. Now more and more people want to live, study and work here. When Peter was teaching at NYU he was part of the Philosophy Department, which was on the top floor of Rufus Hall, a thin nine-storey building at 25 Waverley Place. Its lop-sided architectural charms include a façade decorated with neo-classical Greek motifs. Just a little further north up University Place on the left is Washington Mews, a cobbled lane between two-storey individual houses. It is also owned by NYU, but in contrast to other university property, it retains the gracious atmosphere of the mid-19th century.

Turn west on tree-lined 10th Street, with its typical Greenwich Village mix of three- and four-storey brick dwellings, brownstones and the taller solid apartment buildings built earlier this century. These smaller streets usually have one building that stands out and on this stretch of 10th Street it's No.7. Built in 1887 by Lockwood De Forest, a painter who travelled to India and became concerned that the Indian tradition of teak carving was dying out, No.7, with its intricately carved oriel window, was conceived as a home and showroom for this work. It is now the Edgar Bronfman Center for Jewish Life. Two minutes later we turn right into Fifth Avenue, and come to an irresistible example of Italianate fancy – the balconies of No.39.

Fourteenth Street used to be the street for cheap clothes and household goods. Half-hearted salesmen's patter fails to entice the people rushing by to come into the dingy shops. The street is now in a hiatus between bargain shopping mecca and final gentrification. Detour one block east to Broadway and 14th Street where in

One-time union leader **Henry Spira**, who went from student to activist for animals' rights.

**Washington Mews**' 19th-century charm...

... and the Indian oriel at **7 10th Street**.

Union Square you'll find a statue of
Gandhi, marooned among the honking
taxis and frenetic pedestrians. If you get
here on the right days, you can also stop
to buy bread and fruit at the ever popular
Farmers' Market.

Return to Fifth Avenue and continue up
towards the Empire State Building.
Although not included in this walk, a trip
to the top is not to be missed. Don't be put
off, just because it seems a touristy thing
to do – though the queue is a problem in
busy periods. Day and night you get an
airy view over New York that allows you
to appreciate its beauty without the fumes
and the noise and to get a sense of how
the place hangs together.

At 18th Street we pass the original
Barnes & Noble, the world's largest
bookstore, built in 1873 when they
couldn't have envisaged the way the
shops have mushroomed. At 23rd Street,
where Broadway meets Fifth Avenue,
cross to the north side for the best view
of the Flatiron Building. Its prow looks

set to sail like a luxury liner up Fifth
Avenue. An insistent urban myth claims
that the Flatiron's distinctive wedge
shape derives from the days when cattle
were driven down to markets on Union
Square. If the building had been square,
they would have run slap-bang into it.
The theory doesn't give much credit to
bovine intelligence.

Head west along busy, noisy, 23rd
Street where there are many buildings
worth looking at, including No.32, an
enormous white, ornate building that was
once HL Stern's Department Store (it's
now Hasbro offices). If you're interested in
the heyday of the department store,
glance down Sixth Avenue as you cross it
and you'll see some of the most
extravagant examples built in this era of
temples to consumerism. After Sixth
Avenue the buildings become more
residential again.

Crossing Seventh Avenue you come to
the Carteret Building, as interesting to
look at as its next-door neighbour the

famous Chelsea Hotel, though its denizens are not as well known. The Chelsea, with its distinctive cast-iron balconies (best viewed from across the road), was built as one of the city's first co-operative buildings in 1884 and became a hotel in about 1905. The famous and infamous who have stayed there include O Henry, Thomas Wolfe, Brendan Behan, Arthur Miller and, of course, Dylan Thomas, about whom the plaque states, 'from here sailed out to die' – he drowned in drink.

Across the street in the architecturally unimpressive cream brick building at 255 West 23rd Street is where we lived after the year at NYU had ended, and where *Animal Liberation* was completed. Chelsea was a run-down neighbourhood in the 1970s, and this building didn't look nearly as good as it does today, with daffodils in the garden and the dogwood flowering. Our stay in New York came to an end at Christmas 1974, and the day before we left for Australia, Peter handed the typescript of the book to Bob Silvers of the *New York Review of Books*, who had agreed to publish it. Neither of us, nor Bob, of course, had any idea that *Animal Liberation* would, after a slow start, eventually sell half a million copies and, more importantly, would be credited with triggering the modern animal rights movement.

Chelsea's gentrification, which began in the late 1980s, coincided with large numbers of gays moving into the area. It is worth taking a little time to explore Chelsea further. Check out the cafés and restaurants on Eighth Avenue and the Greek-revival Cushman Row townhouses on 20th Street between Ninth and Tenth Avenues. These houses, dating from 1840, retain many original details: small wreath-encircled attic windows, deeply recessed doorways with brownstone frames, and striking iron balustrades and fences. Pineapples, a traditional symbol of welcome, perch atop the newels in front of Nos.416 and 418. Chelsea Square, covering the area stretching between Ninth and

Tenth Avenues from 20th to 21st Streets, is home to the Gothic-style General Theological Seminary of the Episcopal Church, part of the Anglican communion. A city landmark since 1826, the central garden or 'close' provides a welcome haven of secluded tranquillity from big city noise and hustle.

We are catching the subway at Eighth Avenue and 23rd, but, if you want a longer walk, return to Fifth Avenue and walk straight up to Central Park. (If you walk, after the Empire State Building and before you get to 42nd Street, you'll come to the New York Public Library. Peter was there almost every day, all day, during the summer months when he was researching *Animal Liberation*, drawing on the library's excellent selection of farming trade journals, which provided the examples used in the chapter 'Down on the Factory Farm'.)

Statue of Gandhi in **Union Square**.

We subway riders get off at 59th Street-Columbus Circle station, emerging at the south-west corner of Central Park. Make your way, either along Central Park South or via the path just inside the park itself, to the corner of Fifth Avenue and 59th Street (where the subway riders' route rejoins the hardier souls who walked straight up Fifth Avenue).

The narrow skyscraper with vertical white lines, now labelled Trump, used to be the General Motors Building, and Revlon had its headquarters there. In June 1979, Henry Spira found himself inside in a luxurious upper-floor office overlooking Central Park, explaining to Frank Johnson, Revlon's Vice-President for Public Relations, that he had obtained documents showing that Revlon was testing its cosmetics by putting them into the eyes of thousands of fully conscious rabbits, held immobile in stocks. He suggested that Revlon might like to find less painful ways of testing its products. Johnson listened politely, and made the right noises, but for nearly a year Revlon did nothing. Henry found a donor who would pay for a full-page advertisement in the *New York Times*, asking 'How Many Rabbits Does Revlon Blind for Beauty's Sake?' Then he organised a demonstration. On 13 May 1980, the forecourt of the General Motors Building was filled with people, many of them in bunny costumes, telling Revlon to stop the cruelty. Since animal rights demonstrations were still something of a novelty then, every major newspaper and television network had its reporters and cameras there. As another Revlon executive put it: 'We took a beating the likes of which no opponent of Muhammed

The **Cushman Row** townhouses retain many of their original features, pineapples and all.

Ali ever took.' Frank Johnson lost his job, and soon Henry found himself talking to someone who was prepared to do a deal with him. Revlon agreed to put $750,000 into a search for an alternative to testing its products on animals, and Henry called off the campaign. Together with matching funds Henry then obtained from other cosmetics manufacturers, that paved the way for the eventual elimination of animal testing by virtually all cosmetics corporations.

# How many rabbits does Revlon blind for beauty's sake?

### WHAT IS THE DRAIZE RABBIT EYE TEST?

### FOR RABBITS THE ONLY RELIEF IS…DEATH!

### THE TERRIBLE IRONY: THE RELIABILITY OF THE DRAIZE TEST IS QUESTIONABLE!

### IN THE NAME OF SANITY: STOP THE AGONY!

### THE ALTERNATIVE: NON-ANIMAL TESTING!

### AND HERE'S WHAT YOU CAN DO!

Our walk now takes us across Central Park to the site of another historically significant action for animals, the Natural History Museum at Central Park West and 77th Street. The park is a pleasure to walk through at all times of the year, with its heady mix of natural beauty and embellished structures, plus the human activity pulsing through it. Probably the only creatures who do not enjoy their life in the park are those crammed into the zoo that occupies the eastern side of the park around 65th Street. Central Park Zoo has made some improvements in recent years, but there is just no excuse for keeping animals if you don't have the space to meet their needs. So we will avoid it, walking north along Fifth Avenue for about 50 metres, and then going down the first set of steps to our left, just near the information booth. This leads to the Pond, and we go around the right-hand side of it.

On a warm April afternoon we enjoy the scent and sight of the blossom, huge magnolia trees in bloom and bright yellow massed forsythea. Leaving the pond at the stone moss-covered bridge (Gapstow Bridge), we stroll between the road and the Wollman ice skating rink, wending our way north-west. Coming round the northern end of the skating rink, look back at the sweeping vista of the Plaza Hotel and the other buildings of Fifth Avenue and Central Park South. A path to the right leads to the quaint slate-roofed Dairy, now a Visitors' Centre where you can pick up a map if you want to explore Central Park more thoroughly.

Keep heading north over one of the roads that takes traffic through the park, deep in a cutting to dampen its noise. Cross another road at the traffic lights and look past Sheep Meadow, a vast open lawn, towards the twin-spired Dakota Building. That's the direction in which we are heading. The Dakota Building was home to John Lennon and Yoko Ono. Lennon was shot dead outside its front door by Mark Chapman in 1980.

Keeping Sheep Meadow to your left, you are in an area that on weekends is popular with Rollerblade and rollerskate dancers. There's usually someone dressed to be noticed doing daredevil stunts. Ahead is a larger road, and beyond that, The Lake, where you can go boating. But leave that for another day, and briefly follow the road left towards the western edge of Central Park. Cross another road behind a statue of Senator Daniel Webster (1782-1852) in Napoleonic pose, and a small sign, nearly hidden by bushes, tells us that we're entering Strawberry Fields, an area restored by Yoko Ono in 1985 in memory of John Lennon. Walk up the slope on a small path between the shrubs. On a rock to the left is a plaque: 'Strawberry Fields. Imagine all the people living life in peace.' Below is a long list of nations who endorsed peace. The inclusion of countries such as Yugoslavia makes 'endorsing peace' seem just a little too easy. But avoid negative thoughts, or Strawberry Fields may dissolve before your eyes. Instead, be positive and you will come to a tiled area with 'Imagine' engraved on it, where people leave offerings of notes and flowers in memory of Lennon.

If you want to look more closely at the Dakota Building, you can leave the park at this point; otherwise continue north along the western edge of the park and leave it at 77th Street and cross Central Park West to the American Museum of Natural History.

The museum's grand steps and huge arched entrance were a fine setting for the first successful campaign against animal experimentation in the United States. This too was Henry Spira's achievement. At the conclusion of the NYU course he attended, he stood up and asked members of the class if they wanted to meet, not for more discussions about ethics and animals, but

'Curiosity kills the cats' reads one placard at the 1976 demo against animal testing at the **American Museum of Natural History**.

to take concrete steps that could make a difference to animals. In his apartment, a little group met and agreed on a strategy that was then new to the anti-vivisection movement: to target a single set of experiments that could be stopped. Henry's idea was that the abolition of all animal experimentation was an unwinnable goal, at least for the foreseeable future; if particular experiments could be stopped, however, that would not only help some animals, but would provide a stepping stone that could be used to move on to bigger targets.

Using the Freedom of Information Act, Henry discovered that in the upper floor laboratories of the Natural History Museum experimenters were taking cats, destroying their sense of smell and cutting nerves in their sex organs in order to see how the mutilations affected their sexual behaviour. The experiments had been going on for 14 years, and had cost the government $435,000. In further grant applications the experimenters proposed to blind and deafen the cats as well. In July 1976, Henry's group, supported by other animal advocacy groups, began picketing the museum and publicising the experiments. Instead of asking people to boycott the museum, they took advantage of the fact that admission was by a 'suggested donation' – then $3. They gave visitors a penny, and suggested that they use it as their donation, to show the museum what they thought of the cat experiments. Congressman Ed Koch, later to become Mayor of New York, visited the museum to check on the experiments and later queried the National Institutes of Health about why they were funding this research. All through the winter of 1976-7 and the following spring, Henry and his supporters were there, every weekend. Finally, in May, the National Institutes of Health said that the experimenters' grant would not be renewed, and the museum subsequently ceased doing invasive research on animals.

This first-ever victory in 100 years of anti-vivisection activity in America saved about 70 cats a year from distressing mutilitations. More significantly it was, as Henry had hoped, a stepping stone to the larger achievement of stopping cosmetics testing on animals. Other gains for animals have followed, although in many respects the United States still lags far behind Europe in its protection of animals.

If you continue north along Central Park West, you will see that when Henry and his friends met, in Henry's apartment, to look for some indefensible experiments against which to campaign, they didn't need to look far. Henry lived at 1 West 85th Street, on the corner of Central Park West. Between 1976 and Henry's death in 1998, Peter stayed regularly in Henry's apartment and would often go up on to the roof with Henry for a 360-degree view over the park and the city.

# Eating & drinking

### Bitter End
*147 Bleecker Street, at Thompson Street (212 673 7030).* **Open** 7.30pm-2am Mon-Thur; 8pm-4am Fri, Sat; 8pm-2am Sun.

### Eisenberg's Sandwich Shop
*174 Fifth Avenue, between 22nd & 23rd Streets (212 675 5096).* **Open** 6am-5pm Mon-Fri; 8am-4pm Sat. You won't find a better tuna salad in the city.

### Hangawi
*12 East 32nd Street, between Fifth & Madison Avenues (212 213 0077).* **Open** noon-3pm, 5-10.30pm Mon-Thur; noon-3pm, 5-11pm Fri; 1-3pm, 5-11pm Sat; 1-3pm, 5-10pm Sun. A bit out of your way, but this elegant Korean vegetarian restaurant creates a experience you won't want to miss.

### Ozu
*566 Amsterdam Avenue, between 86th & 87th Streets (212 787 3816).* **Open** 11.30am-10.30pm Mon-Sat; 11.30am-10pm Sun. Small café serving macrobiotic Japanese food – fish and vegetarian – at reasonable prices. The vegetable dumplings are particularly good.

### Popover Cafe
*551 Amsterdan Avenue, between 86th & 87th Streets (212 595 8555).* **Open** 8am-10pm Mon-Thur; 8am-11pm Fri; 9am-11pm Sat; 9am-10pm

343443444444

Sun. The speciality is the popover – a giant hollow Yorkshire-pudding-like thing you eat with strawberry or apple butter. This was a favourite haunt of Henry Spira's.

### Souen
*28 East 13th Street, between University Place & Fifth Avenue (212 627 7150).* **Open** 10am-11pm Mon-Sat; 10am-10pm Sun. A macrobiotic shrine, Souen has been serving organic Japanese vegan offerings and fish dishes for over two decades.

### The Temple in the Village
*74 West 3rd Street, between La Guardia Place & Thompson Street (212 475 5670).* **Open** 11am-9.30pm Mon-Sat. **No credit cards.** Essentially a vegetarian hot-and-cold salad bar that puts other Korean delis to shame – take-out to eat and bask in Washington Square.

### Zen Palate
*34 Union Square East, at 16th Street (212 614 9291).* **Open** 11am-11pm Mon-Thur; 11am-midnight Fri, Sat; noon-10.30pm Sun. A 1999 *TONY* winner for Best Vegetarian, this restaurant combines classy design, great service and delicious Asian-vegetarian food. No alcohol, though you can BYO beer.

## Books & learning

### Barnes & Noble
*105 Fifth Avenue, at 18th Street (212 807 0099).* **Open** 9.30am-7.45pm Mon-Fri; 9.30am-6.15pm Sat; 11am-5.45pm Sun.

### Bobst Library
*70 Washington Square South, at La Guardia Place (212 998 2500).* **Open** 8am-10pm Mon-Thur; 8am-7pm Fri; 10am-6pm Sat. *Aug* 9am-7pm Mon-Fri.

### Edgar M Bronfman Center for Jewish Life
*7 East 10th Street, between University Place & Fifth Avenue (212 998 4114).* **Open** 8am-10pm Mon-Thur; 8am-5pm Fri; noon-8pm Sun.

### General Theological Seminary
*175 Ninth Avenue, between 20th & 21st Streets (212 243 5150).* **Open** *garden* noon-3pm Mon-Fri; 11am-3pm Sat. **Admission** free. You can walk through the grounds of the seminary or take a guided tour in summer (call for details).

### New York Review of Books
*1755 Broadway, between 56th & 57th Streets (212 757 8070).* **Open** 9am-5pm Mon-Fri.

### New York Public Library
*42nd Street, at Fifth Avenue (212 930 0830/recorded information 212 869 8089).* **Open** 10am-6pm Mon, Thur-Sat; 11am-7.30pm Tue, Wed. Some sections closed Mon.

### The New York Times
*229 West 43rd Street, between Seventh & Eighth Avenues (212 597 8001).*

## Museums & sightseeing

### American Museum of Natural History/Rose Center for Earth and Space
*Central Park West, at 79th Street (212 769 5000/recorded information 212 769 5100).* **Open** 10am-5.45pm Mon-Thur, Sun; 10am-8.45pm Fri, Sat. **Admission** *suggested donation* $8; $4-$5 concessions. **No credit cards.**

### Central Park Wildlife Center
*Fifth Avenue, at 64th Street (212 861 6030).* **Open** 10am-5pm Mon-Fri; 10.30am-5.30pm Sat, Sun. **Admission** $3.50; 50¢-$1.25 concessions; free under-3s. **No credit cards.**

### The Dairy
*Mid-park, at 64th Street (212 794 6564).* **Open** *Apr-Sept* 11am-5pm Tue-Sun; *Oct-Mar* 11am-4pm Tue-Sun. **Admission** free. The dairy is now the park's information centre.

### Empire State Building
*350 Fifth Avenue, between 33rd & 34th Streets (212 736 3100).* **Open** *observatories* 9.30am-11.30pm daily. **Admission** (last tickets sold at 11.25pm) $7; $4 concessions. **No credit cards.**

## Others

### Farmers' Market (Greenmarket)
*Union Square, 17th Street, between Broadway & Park Avenue South (212 477 3220).* **Open** 8am-6pm Mon, Wed, Fri, Sat.

### The Plaza Hotel
*768 Fifth Avenue, at 59th Street (212 759 3000/800 759 3000).*

### Wollman Memorial Rink
*Central Park, enter at Fifth or Sixth Avenue at 59th Street (212 396 1010).* **Open** *mid-Oct-31 Mar* 10am-3pm Mon, Tue; 10am-9.30pm Wed, Thur; 10am-11pm Fri, Sat; 10am-9pm Sun. **Admission** $7; $3.50 concessions; skate rental $3.50; lockers $6.75.

# Urban jungle safari

Cristina Verán

Tags, pieces, writers' benches – hip hop-inspired graffiti is another language, another world.

**Start:** West 96th Street station
**Finish:** El Museo del Barrio, Fifth Avenue
**Time:** 6-7 hours
**Distance:** 10.5 miles/17km
**Getting there:** subway trains 1, 2, 3 or 9 to West 96th Street station
**Getting back:** subway train 6 from East 103rd Street station
**Note:** this is a very lengthy walk, and is probably best done with frequent rides on the subway. If you wish to dip in and out of the walk, then the numbers in the text can be traced on the map – and you can plan your route accordingly.

Spots that dot the maps of typical tourists' tours are beacons of bygone civilisations: Rome's Colosseum, the pyramids of Teotihuacan, and the temples of Angkor Wat… all are shells that remain as mere hints of the grandeur they once embodied. In the midst of New York City's megalopolis moderne, conversely, a cultural movement – also global in its impact – sprang not from society's shining monuments, but rather from its very ruins. From the seeds of poverty and urban decay planted in rows of public housing and abandoned tenements in a Bronx ghetto garden, hip hop sprang forth as a magical beanstalk for the talented inner city teens who used it to climb from the bottom rung to the top of the charts.

While a music star of today's hip hop nation might prefer partying in a plush Lexus wearing a Rolex, the humble beginnings of this culture (as opposed to the commercial industry) were testament to the creative soul of the multihued hodge-podge of Black Americans and Caribbeans, Latinos – and yes, even ethnic whites – who inhabited similar socio-economic enclaves. It wasn't about buying expensive accoutrements, but rather skilfully creating your own style without, literally, having to pay the price.

In what were often the bleakest of surroundings there bloomed the brightest graffiti murals, the boldest dance moves, the most poigniant rap-rhymes, and super-dextrous DJs. Thus announcing their arrival to the world, the world listened and heeded the call.

In a reversal of civilisation's rise-and-fall chronos, a quarter-century since hip hop's birth, many of its once-faded foundries – the original nightclubs, community centres and so on where the first wave of rap stars, DJs and breakdancing b-boys and girls honed their crafts – have since been shallacked in shiny coats of paint and enjoyed facelifts courtesy of urban-renewal revivals. To experience the environment in its essence, the touring spirit must look beyond the surface for the soul of the old school; the Nazareth of this new religion.

A dozen years after the Transit Authority finally won its long war against the hordes of graffiti conquistadors, the trains now run unadorned by the controversial artform. Books such as *Subway Art* can offer a window on to the kaleidoscopic chaos that was, and on the streets above, this hip hop-inspired

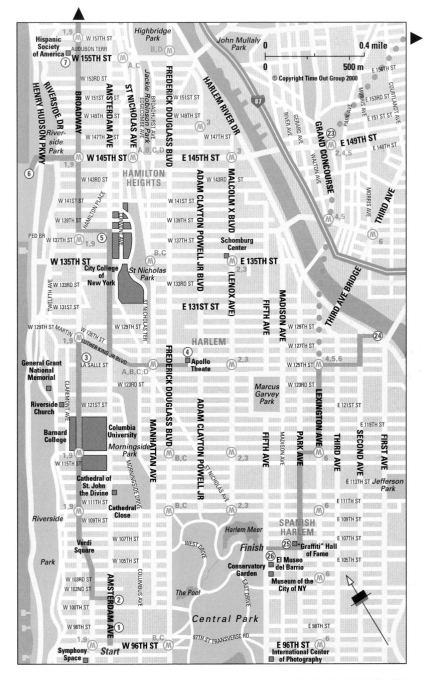

**Urban jungle safari**

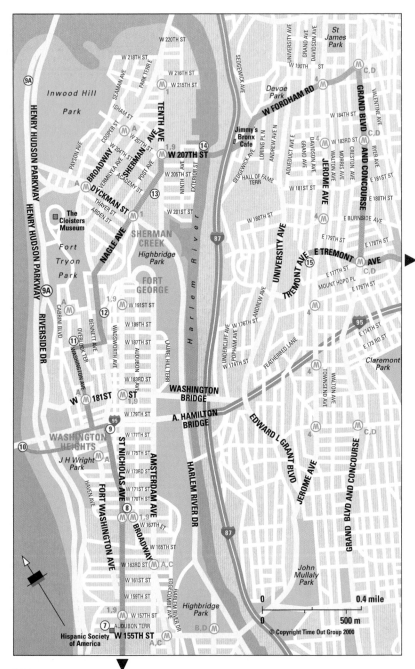

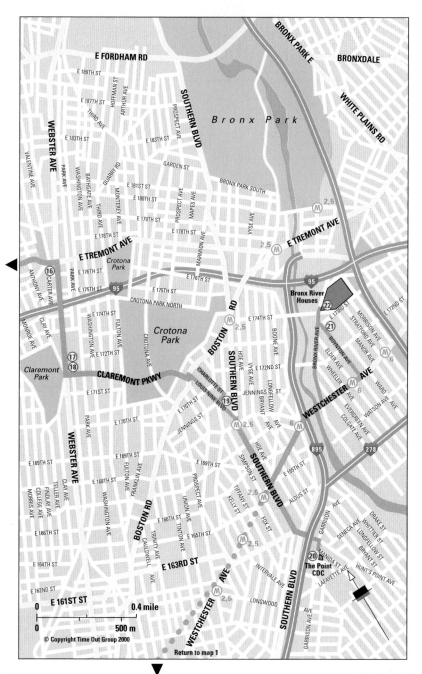

E FORDHAM RD

E 189TH ST

E 187TH ST

THIRD AVE

HOFFMAN ST

ARTHUR AVE

E 183RD ST

E 181ST ST

MONTEREY AVE

E 180TH ST

THIRD AVE

E 179TH ST

E 178TH ST

BRONX PARK E

BRONXDALE

WHITE PLAINS RD

SOUTHERN BLVD

PROSPECT AVE

*Bronx Park*

GARDEN ST

BRONX PARK SOUTH

MAPES AVE

PROSPECT AVE

E 183RD ST

QUARRY RD

WEBSTER AVE

VALENTINE AVE

PARK AVE

WASHINGTON AVE

BATHGATE AVE

E 178TH ST

MARMION AVE

VYSE AVE

E TREMONT AVE

(M) 2,5

E TREMONT AVE

(16)

ANTHONY AVE

CARTER AVE

PARK AVE

*Crotona Park*

E 176TH ST

E 175TH ST

95

E 175TH ST

CROTONA PARK NORTH

E 174TH ST

*Crotona Park*

CLAY AVE

MONROE AVE

WASHINGTON AVE

FULTON AVE

E 172ND ST

CROTONA AVE

(17)
(18)

*Claremont Park*

CLAREMONT PKWY

E 171ST ST

E 170TH ST

PARK AVE

E 169TH ST

WEBSTER AVE

CLAY AVE

TELLER AVE

FINDLAY AVE

COLLEGE AVE

MORRIS AVE

E 166TH ST

E 164TH ST

E 162ND ST

FULTON AVE

WASHINGTON AVE

FRANKLIN AVE

E 168TH ST

E 169TH ST

BOSTON RD

TRINITY AVE

CAULDWELL AVE

E 163RD ST

E 166TH ST

UNION AVE

TINTON AVE

E 165TH ST

BOSTON RD

(M) 2,5

E 174TH ST

BOONE AVE

SOUTHERN BLVD

HOE AVE

VYSE AVE

E 172ND ST

CHARLOTTE ST

LOUIS NINE BLVD

(19)

JENNINGS

BRYANT

LONGFELLOW

AVE

E 170TH ST

JENNINGS ST

(M) 2,5

6

95

Bronx River
Houses

(22)

E 173RD ST

(21)

BRONX RIVER AVE

MORRISON AVE

STRATFORD AVE

MANOR AVE

ELDER AVE

BOYNTON AVE

WHEELER AVE

WESTCHESTER AVE

(M) 6

6

EVERGREEN AVE

COLGATE AVE

WATSON AVE

WARD AVE

E 172ND ST

(M) 6

895

278

E 169TH ST

PROSPECT AVE

HOE AVE

SIMPSON ST

E 165TH ST

ALDUS ST

GARRISON AVE

DRAKE ST

WHITTIER ST

LONGFELLOW ST

BRYANT ST

SENECA AVE

HUNT'S POINT AVE

LAFAYETTE AVE

(20)

MANIDA ST

The Point
CDC

TIFFANY ST

KELLY ST

FOX ST

(M) 2,5

(M) 2,5

INTERVALE AVE

WESTCHESTER

AVE

(M) 2,5

LONGWOOD

SOUTHERN BLVD

GARRISON AVE

AVE

0        0.4 mile

E 161ST ST

0        500 m

© Copyright Time Out Group 2000

Return to map 1

Black Muslim leader and
latter-day hip hop icon
Malcolm X was shot at the
**Audobon Ballroom**.

artform lives on in the stationary exile of brick walls and schoolyard 'galleries'.

While cities from Auckland to Amsterdam to Accra now boast their own provincial hip hop scenes, NYC remains the mecca with which to be reckoned. Walk the walk, board the bus, and ride the rail, and see it all for yourself.

From whichever hostel, hotel, motel, or wherever you've ensconced yourself, begin your journey on the subway and disembark on West 96th Street and Broadway – on Manhattan's Upper West Side, a region that inspired a musical of the same name, as multi-ethnic and class-clashing as it ever was. Here, near-skyscraping condo towers cast their shadows across the rooftops of low-grade public housing blocks – 'Da Projects' in local parlance.

One block east to Amsterdam Avenue, then two north to 98th Street is the Rocksteady Park (official name: 'Happy Warrior Playground' **[1]**), the historical homebase for the legendary group of b-boys and girls who helped make breakdancing a worldwide phenomenon, the Rocksteady Crew. Back in the early '80s, both Malcolm McClaren's 'Buffalo Gals' and RSC's own 'Hey You, The Rocksteady Crew' videos were filmed here, a place where the elite hip hop dancers have converged and competed for two decades.

Three blocks to the north is Douglass Playground **[2]**, at 101st Street; it's here that local basketball legend Earl 'The Goat' Manigault coached his champion street league teams, so noteworthy that his life story became a TV movie a few years back.

One block east back to Broadway, walk or hop the 104 bus uptown, past Columbia University to 121st Street, where the No.1 line emerges from the depths to an elevated track. The aged concrete retaining walls supporting the track at La Salle Street are a living memorial to the notable pioneering graffiti artist Futura 2000, whose signature 'tag', circa 1981,

can be seen on the eastside **[3]**. Next to it is an equally significant signing of Ali, representing the seminal 'Soul Artists of Zoo York'.

Three blocks north is Harlem's famed centre of commerce and culture, the newly revitalised 125th Street. Walking east for four blocks you'll come to the renowned Apollo Theater **[4]**, whose stage has welcomed hip hop and other Black music legends for ages. Retracing your route westerly to Amsterdam Avenue, a 101 bus or a 12-block uphill hike past the Gothic-designed City University of New York's arts centre Aaron Davis Hall will bring you to the schoolyard aerosol artspace at 137th Street **[5]**. Its unofficial exhibitions change with each season, pending the approval of aerosol artform's old guard.

From there, walk west three blocks to the island's edge at the Hudson River, taking the walkway over the West Side Highway for the grand views at Riverbank State Park **[6]**; a controversial curiosity, too, because it was built covering the active sewage treatment plant below. Here's hoping the wind's in your favour!

The M5 bus on Broadway going uptown once again will take you past the landmark Hispanic Society Museum on the left side at 155th Street **[7]**, where an ornate Spanish Renaissance court hides behind the majestic façade, and El Greco, Goya and Velázquez grace the museum walls.

Continuing north to 168th Street, and here, in the midst of the vast Columbia University Medical School, is the former Audobon Ballroom **[8]**, now a bio-medical centre still proudly adorned by its Beaux Arts façade (in part thanks to community and conservationists' protests). This is the landmark where Black Muslim leader and latter-day hip hop icon El Hajj Malik El-Shabazz – better known as Malcolm X – was assassinated in 1965. A memorial mini-museum established in his honour is set for a fall 2000 opening. In the early 1980s, the Audobon was a place where

Over and under highways, through **woods**...

... and, lo, there's a **Little Red Lighthouse**.

world-renowned DJ Grandmaster Flash and his musical co-conspirators held court at hip hop jams.

From there, continue ten blocks north to 178th Street, where a large, multi-artist graffiti mural adorns the south-east corner **[9]**. Cross the street to your left, walking past the Port Authority Bus Terminal, three blocks west, then one south to Haven Avenue.

Mid-block, you'll find a path bridge that traverses the highway, and which descends zig-zaggingly to the roadway below (taking this route after dusk is not recommended, as it becomes home to homeless people after that). From here, you can take your pick of paths under the motorway, amid the colossal concrete pilings adorned with original 1970s and early '80s graffiti tags (and a splattering of new-style markings).

Pick a footpath heading westward down to the river, where you can walk about a mile in each direction along the waterfront, past tennis courts, soccer-playing Central and South Americans, and families picnicking under the sun. Directly under the overshadowing George Washington Bridge you'll see the famous Little Red Lighthouse – the only one of its kind in Manhattan **[10]**.

Continue northward or retrace your pathways back to the streets above, heading to Fort Washington Avenue, past the busy shops on 181st Street to 187th Street, where a refreshment or two at Santiago should replenish your sapping strength. On your right is a concrete stairway descending to Overlook Terrace below **[11]**. Midway down, the upper right side of the wall is emblazoned with early '70s graffiti tags from legends Stitch, Snake and Diana (all of whom feature in various international graffiti art books).

From Overlook, continue two blocks east to Broadway and stride north to Fairview Avenue, the south-east corner of which features a long multi-artist graffiti mural **[12]**, including work by

Keep an eye out for
this beauty spot on
the corner of
**Jennings Street**.

TATS Cru graffiti muralists have left their mark on the **Point Community Center**.

GARRISON AV

illustrious artist Zephyr, featured prominently in the cult hip hop documentary *Style Wars*.

Continue two blocks north to Nagle Avenue, pass El Rancho Jubilee, a Dominican watering hole, and walk five and a half blocks north-east, crossing the Dyckman Street commercial strip, and walking along under the railtracks. On your right is the Dyckman Housing Projects [13], whose basketball court and playground was the setting for the Rocksteady Crew's outdoor breakdancing segment of *Style Wars*.

Head north three blocks to 207th Street at Tenth Avenue, turning east to cross the 207th Street Bridge over the Harlem River and in to the Bronx [14]. Midway across, look back toward the 207th Street subway yards along the river's edge, where idle trains are parked and repaired, and where, once upon a time, death- and law-defying teenagers used to 'bomb' with spray paint the very same cars, evading rivals, police squads and the electrified third-rails all the while.

From the Bronx side of the bridge you can't miss the famous Jimmy's Bronx Café, a restaurant and dance club frequented by rap stars of today, from Fat Joe to Puff Daddy, as well as Yankee baseball stars and other notables. Continue eastward along Fordham Road, the main shopping district in the Bronx (and the best place in NYC to buy sneakers), across Jerome Avenue, where the No.4 elevated subway line screeches past overhead, and on again four blocks to the Grand Concourse.

Hop on a Bx1 or 2 bus heading south, past the now-closed baroque landmark Loews Paradise Theater, until you arrive at East Tremont Avenue. A five-block stroll to the right will bring you to Intermediate School 306 at Grand Avenue [15]. Enter via the alleyway on the left side of the building, passing through a mural-adorned alleyway that leads to a vast playground and handball court festooned by major graffiti art murals by

artists in prominent aerosol collectives such as Fame City and TC5.

Heading back to Tremont Avenue, then eastward three to four blocks over to Webster Avenue, the tenuously stationed south-west corner building is a shell of an important late '80s/early '90s hip hop nightclub known as the Devil's Nest, later a reborn incarnation of Disco Fever [16].

Head five blocks south on Webster to Belmont, and on the left side of the street you'll notice an advertisement mural for Tulnoy Lumber [17] painted by legendary graffitist Tracy 168, featuring cartoon characters in various fracas with timber. Just a half block further, the Diana Sands School's yard [18] comprises an outdoor art gallery for an ever-changing number of artists, including local graffiti celebs from the Hard Rocs and BT graffiti crews.

The avenue immediately past this school is Claremont, where a walk eastward brings you to Crotona Park. Cross through, emerging on Louis Nine Boulevard, and stroll eastward to Jennings Street, where a long and low wall hosts an entire block of graffiti murals by the members of COD crew and other prominent groups [19].

Just north of Jennings is the once-infamous Charlotte Street, used by presidents Reagan and Carter during televised speeches against urban decay during their 1980 campaigns. What was once, during hip hop's old school heyday, a seemingly endless sea of rubble-strewn lots is now a surrealistic American dream setting of pseudo-suburban houses, complete with barbecue grills and more than a few picket fences.

From here, venture onward one block east to Southern Boulevard, turn right and continue several blocks south, past the Westchester Avenue elevated train tracks, then two more long blocks through the shopping strip to Hunts Point Avenue. Cross beneath the Bruckner Expressway, and you'll soon come upon Garrison Avenue. One block to your right at Manida Street you'll find the Point **[20]** – a performance space and community centre with city-wide recognition, whose Live From the Edge Theater features music, art and dance performances for and by urban youth. Frequented by and featuring classes taught by hip hop luminaries, the locale is also the professional homebase for the TATS Cru graffiti muralists, whose works appear in myriad music videos and commercials.

Retrace your path back to Southern Boulevard and Westchester Avenue, and turn right.

Go seven blocks straight ahead, and cross the bridge over the Bronx River, to Bronx River Avenue. Turning left and continuing two blocks ahead to 173rd Street, you'll come to Monroe High School **[21]**, where you can have a look at the massive graffiti murals in the schoolyard within. You're now just a block away from point zero, the Bronx River Projects **[22]**. These otherwise drab, unassuming public housing cubes are where hip hop forefather and DJ Afrika Bambaata spent his adolescence. With his resignation from the once-mighty Black Spades gang, it was here that his quasi-spiritual hip hop collective known as the Zulu Nation arose nearly three decades ago. For many years, hip hop concerts with the culture's top rap artists and b-boy dancers would converge here, though sadly, conflicts with the NYC Housing Authority in recent years doomed the famous Zulu murals to being painted over.

From there, head on back along Westchester Avenue, past Southern Boulevard to the Simpson Street train station. From here, catch the No.5 train downtown to 149th Street and Grand Concourse **[23]**. Disembark, yet do not exit the station, for this is the location of the former Writers' Bench. It featured prominently in *Style Wars* as the place where the graffiti art elite, 'kings' of each subway line, would gather

*en masse* to team up, trade sketches and tales of adventure.

Hopping back on the 5 line, downtown, get off at 125th Street at Lexington Avenue. From here, trek two blocks east, then north to 128th Street at Second Avenue, and you'll come to a large handball court that doubles as an original installation by the artist Keith Haring, who began his pop-art fame quest in the subways as well **[24]**. Entitled *Crack Is Wack*, these pieces have been there since the mid-'80s and, amazingly enough, remain unblemished by the ravages of time, weather or rival graffitists.

Back to 125th Street, and you've got the option of a 19-block stroll southward, through the heart of Spanish Harlem, or a bus ride down the less festive Lexington Avenue, to East 106th Street. Turn left and walk two blocks, under the elevated Metro North commuter rail line, to the Park Avenue playground and basketball courts of the Jackie Robinson School **[25]**, otherwise known as – and with a mural announcing its world-renowned, 20-plus-year-old incarnation as – New York City's Graffiti Hall of Fame.

It is here that the elite echelons of the aerosol arts not only from NYC and other US cities, but sometimes even Europe and beyond, have come to paint their majestic, multicolour masterpieces on the grandest scale of all. Work is periodically redone and you've hit the jackpot if you're fortunate enough to visit on a weekend when the artists have gathered to paint. Bring along a sketchbook and in true graffiti art tradition, they might just oblige you with an autograph sketch.

Finally, as a fitting end to your pilgrimage through history and the 'hood, visit El Museo del Barrio **[26]** on nearby Fifth Avenue at Central Park. The museum features Latin American and local artists, many of whose lives, like your own perhaps, have been touched and influenced by hip hop and these city streets from which this now-global culture was born.

# Eating & drinking

## Bleu Evolution

*808 West 187th Street, between Pinehurst Boulevard & Fort Washington Avenue (212 928 6006).* **Open** 5pm-midnight Mon-Fri; 10am-midnight Sat, Sun. Thai, Mediterranean and Middle Eastern cuisines in bordello-like eaterie.

## Café con Leche

*726 Amsterdam Avenue, between 95th & 96th Streets (212 678 7000).* **Open** 11am-11pm daily. Good, authentic Dominican food – very busy for weekend brunch.

## Copeland's

*547 West 145th Street, between Amsterdam Avenue & Broadway (212 234 2357).* **Open** 4.30pm-midnight Mon-Sat; noon-9pm Sun. Cajun and soul food, and a Sunday Gospel Brunch with post-church crowds to boot.

## El Rancho Jubilee

*1 Nagle Avenue, at Broadway (212 304 0100).* **Open** 7pm-2am daily.

## Flor de Mayo

*2651 Broadway, between 100th & 101st Streets (212 663 5520).* **Open** noon-midnight daily. Cheap Chino-Latino food, but its Peruvian roasted chicken is the star dish.

## Jimmy's Bronx Café

*281 West Fordham Road, between Cedar Avenue & Major Deegan Expressway (718 329 2000).* **Open** 10am-2am Mon-Wed; 10am-4am Thur-Sun. A Puerto Rican entertainment mecca with home-style dishes, nightclub and sports bar.

## Obaa Koryoe

*3143 Broadway, between Tiemann Place & La Salle Street (212 316 2950).* **Open** 11am-midnight daily.

## Sal & Carmine's Pizza

*2671 Broadway, between 101st & 102nd Streets (212 663 7651).* **Open** 11.30am-11pm daily.

## Santiago

*589 Fort Washington Avenue, at 187th Street (212 543 9888).* **Open** 7am-8pm Mon-Fri; 8am-8pm Sat, Sun.

# Museums

## El Museo del Barrio

*1230 Fifth Avenue, between 104th & 105th Streets (212 831 7272).* **Open** 11am-5pm Wed-Sun. **Admission** $4; $2 concessions. **No credit cards.**

## Hispanic Society of America

*Audobon Terrace, Broadway, between 155th & 156th Streets (212 926 2234).* **Open** 10am-4.30pm Tue-Sun; 1-4pm Sun.

# Arts centres

## Aoron Davis Hall

*West 130th Street, at Convent Avenue (212 650 6900).* **Open** 9am-5pm daily.

## Audobon Ballroom

*3940 Broadway, at 168th Street (212 928 6288).*

## The Point CDC

*Garrison Avenue, at Manida Street (718 542 4139).*

# Parks

## Crotona Park

*Fulton Avenue to Crotona Park East, Crotona Park North to Crotona Park South.*

## Dyckman Houses Playground

*West 204th Street, between Tenth & Nagle Avenues.*

## Fort Washington Park

*Riverside Drive to Hudson River, West 155th to West 179th Streets.*

## Riverbank State Park

*Hudson River, between West 137th & West 145th Streets.* **Open** 6am-11pm daily.

## Frederick Douglass Playground

*Amsterdam Avenue, between 100th & 102nd Streets.*

# Others

## Apollo Theater

*253 West 125th Street, between Adam Clayton Powell Jr & Frederick Douglass Boulevards (Seventh & Eighth Avenues) (212 749 5838).*

## Columbia University

*Between Broadway & Amsterdam Avenue & 114th to 120th Streets (212 854 1754).*

## Intermediate School 306

*2580 West 149th Street on Seventh Avenue (718 283 8366).* **Open** 9am-5pm daily.

## Monroe High School

*1300 Boyton Avenue (718 893 5800).*

## Tulnoy Lumber

*1620 Webster Avenue, between East 173rd Street & Claremont Parkway (212 901 1700).* **Open** 8am-5pm Mon-Fri.

# Town and gown

Rachel Wetzsteon

Wander through college campuses, linger in airy churches, trot the Harlem globe.

**Start:** 125th Street station
**Finish:** 125th Street station
**Time:** 3-4 hours
**Distance:** 4 miles/6.5km
**Getting there:** subway trains 1 or 9 to 125th Street station
**Getting back:** subway trains 1 or 9 from 125th Street station
**Note:** the early part of this walk has some overlap with Maitland McDonagh's walk, *You Gotta Have Park*.

This is a walk about contrasts – between the cool elegance of Morningside Heights and the spirited bustle of Harlem; the hushed interior of Riverside Church and the famous façade of the Apollo Theater; the quiet refinement of Claremont Avenue and the loud vitality of 125th Street. It's also a quick lesson in what makes New York City such an amazing place. By tracing this route, you'll get a good sense of one of the things New Yorkers love most about their city: that a walk of a few hours can reveal so many faces and places, traditions and tastes along the way.

Begin at the 125th Street subway. Head west along Tiemann Avenue, which will quickly take you to Riverside Drive. For my money, this is the loveliest street in all of Manhattan; and you'd have to have a heart of stone not to stare down it – stately buildings to your left, swaying

The cherry trees give the name to the perfectly formed **Sakura Park** – and some shade.

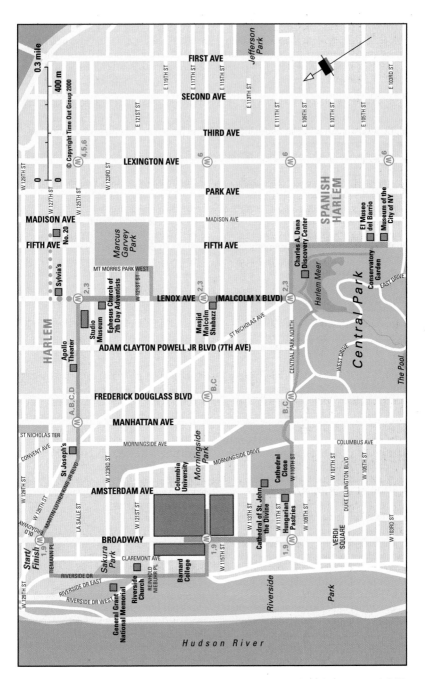

trees and Riverside Park to your right – and let out a long sigh. Walk south for a block or so, being sure to notice the plaque on the corner at 549 Riverside Drive: this is the building where the French philosopher Simone Weil lived for a few months in 1942.

You will shortly come upon Sakura Park, a tiny patch of green that happens to be my favourite park in the city. Sakura means 'cherry blossom', and the park is so named because of the 2,000 cherry trees that were delivered to New York parks from Japan in 1912. It's been renovated several times, most recently in 1981, and currently features a pavilion and a play area for children. There's also, in the south-east corner, a monument to the Civil War general Daniel Butterfield (who was, incidentally, the composer of *Taps*). I love this park because of its small scale – there's something tragic yet inspiring about the way it stands just across the road from its immense neighbour – and because of the huge variety of people who pass through it: if you linger for just a few minutes, you're likely to see families picnicking, people practising tai chi, and graduate students scurrying home with big bags of books in their hands.

Cut across the street to Grant's Tomb, whose noble marble exterior will be hard to miss. After its cornerstone was laid in 1892, seven years after Grant's death, it took six years to build and eventually reached a height of 150 feet; 90,000 American citizens contributed to its construction, including many members of the Harlem community.

Once inside, you can look up at the paintings depicting various stages of Grant's life, and down into the crypt to the tombs of both Grant and his wife Julia, who joined him in 1902.

Cross Riverside Drive again and enter Riverside Church. This 21-storey steel structure with a Gothic exterior was inspired by Chartres Cathedral, and funded by John D Rockefeller Jr, in 1930.

You'll find the interior wonderfully airy and open; and you should also make a point of seeing the small Christ Chapel on the main level, as well as the Second Gallery, with its stark and haunting sculpture of Christ by Jacob Epstein.

Once you've wandered around a bit, take the elevator up to the bell tower. You'll have to walk up several flights of stairs once the elevator drops you off; from a platform on the first level of the bell chamber, you'll see five large bells including the enormous Bourdon, or hour bell, which weighs 40,926 pounds and helps make the church's carillon the largest in the world. You'll soon reach the observation platform, where – from a height of 355 feet – you'll have fantastic views of the entire terrain covered by this walk, as well as the Hudson River, lower Manhattan, the New Jersey Shore and the George Washington Bridge. Be warned: it may be very windy up there.

Stumble breathlessly out of the church, and continue down Riverside Drive to 116th Street. As you do so, you'll pass many buildings where Columbia faculty members live. (Do the apartments come with the jobs, or is it the other way around?) Look left on 120th Street for a nice view of Union Theological Seminary and Teacher's College. At 116th Street, walk left to Broadway; halfway there you'll pass a crescent-shaped building that marks the beginning of Claremont Avenue, another gorgeous faculty block: stare covetously down it, then head onward to Broadway.

You are now at the epicentre of the Columbia and Barnard campuses, and if you're taking this walk when classes are in session, you can expect a sudden increase in the numbers of people (many of them scarily young, beautiful and hip) surrounding you. It's probably best to check out Barnard – Columbia's renowned, all-female sister school founded in 1889 – first, which you can do by taking a few steps up Broadway. The Barnard campus is extremely attractive,

Jacob Epstein's Christ looms in
**Riverside Church.**

but you may be surprised by how small it is: you can take in the whole thing in a matter of minutes. On your left after you've entered the Barnard gate, peer into the pretty Sulzberger Courtyard, around which cluster many student dorms; then walk to the other side of campus along a shrub-lined brick path, admiring the welcoming Lehman Library on your left and the equally welcoming rectangle of grass on your right: its wooden benches might be a good place to sit down for a quick rest.

Exit Barnard through the same gate you entered, and cross Broadway on 117th Street. Then walk down a block to 116th Street, where you'll see another, larger gate: this is the entrance to College Walk, which will take you into the Columbia campus. Columbia, in which 19,000 students are currently enrolled, was founded in 1754 as King's College, and was first situated near where the World Trade Center now stands, and later at Park Avenue and 49th Street. Work began on its present campus in 1897, on the site of what had been New York Hospital's Bloomingdale Insane Asylum. The McKim, Mead and White campus, with its stunning Beaux Arts marriage of bricks and marble, will make you nostalgic for every school you ever attended, and give you plenty of clues as to why Morningside Heights sometimes gets called 'the Acropolis of Manhattan'.

You could spend hours roaming around the Columbia campus, but if you want to conserve some energy for later stops on the walk, a few must-see buildings should suffice. First, of course, there are the libraries: on your left, the domed Low Library, modelled on the Roman Pantheon, and currently the home of the Columbia administration (notice the bronze statue of *Alma Mater* in the middle of Low's stairs; in 1968 she survived a bomb blast by student protesters); and on your right, the Parthenon-like Butler Library, on the pediment of which you can read the names of the classical writers – Herodotus, Plato,

Cicero, Virgil – whose works still make up a large portion of all undergraduates' required reading. A few years ago, a group of campus feminists hung a banner below the pediment that featured the names of prominent women writers; but sadly, the banner is long gone.

If you walk up the first two flights of the Low stairs, then hang a right and walk up the flight of stairs directly in front of you, you'll find yourself approaching Philosophy Hall, the home of many humanities departments in front of which stands a copy of Rodin's *Thinker*. Walk north from Philosophy, and you'll soon behold St Paul's Chapel, a lovely, intimate building in the style of the Northern Italian Renaissance, where weddings, convocations and other Columbia-related ceremonies are often held. Head back to College Walk and make a quick detour to the snazzy, controversial new Lerner Student Center, which can best be reached by following one of the paths from College Walk to Butler Library, then walking toward Broadway. This building, designed by Bernard Tschumi, Dean of Columbia's Graduate School of Architecture, and completed in 1999, is a quirky and rather in-your-face structure, with see-through glass walls and ramps connecting its many different levels. Depending on who you ask, Lerner is either a fun, interesting place to spend time, or a voyeuristic nightmare – but whatever you think of it, you're bound to be impressed that a campus can accommodate so much variety and still feel like one campus.

Walk from Lerner back to Broadway and 115th Street, and head south. This stretch of street is one of the most pleasant and interesting in the city; and though it's been massively gentrified in recent years – in went the swank restaurants, out went the smoky cafés – it's still got a mix of energy and elegance that's hard to beat. If you're feeling hungry, you'll have your pick of places to eat. For people-watching, Ollie's Noodle

**St Paul's Chapel** is just one of the gems on Columbia University campus.

Shop on the corner of Broadway and 116th is probably your best bet; there's also the West End Café, for burgers and beer; the Tamarind Seed, with its good take-out health food; Le Monde, for affordable French fare; Caffé Pertutti, with its eclectic menu and wonderful fruit juices; Tom's Diner, famous from the Suzanne Vega song and *Seinfeld*; and many more. In nicer weather, many of the restaurants and cafés set up breezy outdoor areas. Also notice the way Starbucks has invaded (surprise, surprise!) the neighbourhood. If you're on the lookout for books, duck into Papyrus books on 114th Street, the Bank Street Bookstore – which mostly stocks books for and about kids – on 112th, or simply linger at the numerous bookstalls lining the street. You'll also find elegant boutiques, well-stocked stationery stores, open-all-night Xerox shops, magazine emporia, and whatever else your heart is likely to desire.

Turn left on 112th Street, and head towards Amsterdam Avenue, watching the momentous façade of the Cathedral of St John the Divine grow nearer. At 545 West 112th, stop and view the building where the philosopher and educational reformer John Dewey lived from 1913 to 1927. Cross the street as soon as you catch sight of Labyrinth Books on the other side; although it's only a few years old, it's quickly become the unofficial Columbia bookstore, and one of the best bibliophile haunts in the city (it's especially great if you're in the market for academic releases, sale books or journals of all kinds). Continue walking down 112th, but once you reach Amsterdam, don't head for the Cathedral just yet – first you'll want to check out the legendary Hungarian Pastry Shop on the corner of Amsterdam Avenue and 111th Street. As a miserable and impecunious graduate student, I lived for several years just around the corner from this tiny café, with its flimsy wooden tables, its delicious desserts and endearingly terrible coffee, its local cat

Gateway to heaven – **St John the Divine**.

and sweetly addled waitresses, its smutty-cum-erudite graffiti ('I need God!', '"The first draft of everything is shit" – Hemingway'), and its array of Columbia types huddled over computers pretending to work, staring into space, or arguing over the latest academic fads and oldest philosophical questions.

Once you've tanked up on coffee and atmosphere, cross the street and let the majestic cathedral lure you into its sacred domain. Such grandeur didn't come about overnight; in fact, over a hundred years after building began in 1892, it still isn't finished. Its history is a long and complex one: after the sanctuary and choir had been built according to an original Romanesque design, a new architect was appointed in 1911, and constructed the nave in Gothic style. The outbreak of war in 1939 brought building to a halt, and it only began again in the late 1970s. Recently it has developed a well-earned reputation as a community church, and currently houses a soup kitchen and homeless shelter, as well as playing host to temporary art exhibits, regular concerts, an annual Blessing of the Animals, and countless other activities. It's estimated that the cathedral will finally be complete in 2050, at which time it will be the largest in the world – big enough to swallow both Notre Dame and Chartres whole, or the size, if you prefer athletic analogies, of two football fields. You can look at a scale model of the projected design in the cathedral gift shop.

As you enter the cathedral, notice the Portals of Paradise, which contain both Biblical figures and more modern scenes, including a mushroom cloud floating over Manhattan. You'll quickly sense the difference between this interior and that of its uptown cousin, Riverside Church: it's a larger, darker and altogether more mysterious space. When you've walked a few paces, turn around and marvel at the two stunning rose windows.

Strolling up the left side, notice the Poets' Corner, into which two new American poets are inducted every year; also wander through the poignant Columbarium. Approaching the apse, tiptoe reverently past seven small chapels, each of which honours a different ethnic group. As you walk back to the front of the cathedral, be sure to notice the very moving AIDS memorial.

After enjoying to the full the eclectic opulence inside, head outside for the quieter pleasures of the Cathedral Gardens next door. You'll be charmed by the big bronze fountain with its bizarre assortment of figures (a moon? a man with wings?), and by the dozens of bronze animal sculptures, all made by children, stationed on the railings at the fountain's base: *Polite Elephant*, *Mandarin Horse*, *Free as a Chimpanzee* and *Owls With Talking Eyes* are some of my favourite titles. These sculptures were winners of city-wide competitions, and 12 new works are selected each year. Scattered around the garden are many bronze, book-shaped

plaques, also designed by children, which illustrate and commemorate the lives of artistic luminaries like Twain, Chagall, O'Keeffe and Thoreau.

You have now seen most of the major sights that Morningside Heights has to offer, and you're ready for something new. Leave the Cathedral Gardens and go south along Amsterdam until you reach 110th Street, otherwise known as Cathedral Parkway. Walk a block east to Morningside Drive – another elegant Columbia block – and drift briefly into Morningside Park, the 13-block-long strip of green that runs parallel to it. This park, which was landscaped by Frederick Law Olmsted in 1887, may come as a surprise: far more gritty and run-down than anything you've encountered so far, it will jolt you back into the real world, where buildings are rarely made of marble, litter exists, and not all parks are picturesquely perfect. But would New York be New York without these quick trips from fantasy to reality, these brutal yet bracing eye-openers?

Exit Morningside Park at Manhattan Avenue, and continue walking east on 110th Street, which – no, you aren't lost – has become Central Park North. You are now poised to explore the northernmost tip of Central Park, the biggest and most varied park in Manhattan. You can enter through any of several paths that cut into it from Central Park West, but I'd suggest the first one, simply because it will give you a good sense of the width of the park, and lead you efficiently and briskly to the beautifully landscaped, placenta-shaped Harlem Meer, a lake where you can rent boats, go fishing, or just sit and watch the geese, ducks and pigeons wade and cavort. Along the path you'll also find the Charles A Dana Discovery Center, where you'll find a wealth of information about the park: children's activities, environmental facts, and whatever else you want to know. Just south of the lake is the six-acre Conservatory Garden, Central Park's only formal garden. It's divided

Pick your spot on placenta-shaped **Harlem Meer** and you could be almost anywhere.

into three smaller gardens, each of which has a distinct look: there's the mazy south garden, the rounded north garden, and the central garden with its graceful fountain.

Leave the park through the Vanderbilt Gate, which will deposit you at 105th Street and Fifth Avenue, all set to begin your tour of Harlem. But first take note of the two excellent museums across the street: El Museo del Barrio, which houses a large selection of Puerto Rican and Latin American art; and, a block farther down, the Museum of the City of New York, whose permanent exhibit offers a concise history of the city.

Walk up Fifth Avenue until you're back at Central Park North; then go a block west to Lenox (aka Malcolm X) Avenue, and start heading uptown.

Lenox Avenue was once widely known for its entertainment spots, but these days it's lined primarily by housing developments, stores and the occasional church. You'll immediately be struck by its width, which may remind you of upper Broadway even though the two streets are otherwise so different; and also by its

light, which, mostly due to Harlem's relative dearth of tall buildings, is wonderfully bright. Near the south-west corner of 116th and Lenox, you'll see the green-domed Masjid Malcolm Shabazz, the mosque where Malcolm X ministered to rapt listeners before his life was brutally cut short.

Head east on 120th, and you'll find yourself strolling down a pretty, brownstone-lined block, one of several that make up the historic Mount Morris section of Harlem, which stretches from 119th to 124th Streets and was a favourite neighbourhood of German Jews in the 19th century. Harlem's inhabitants were mostly white at the turn of the century, but there was a massive wave of black emigration from the south starting around 1910. Although the area has fallen into considerable disrepair, and many of the houses are boarded up or run-down, it's still very beautiful. At the end of the block, stare across Mount Morris Park West to Marcus Garvey Park, which runs the entire length of this little neighbourhood and was originally known, fittingly, as Mount Morris Park. But it was renamed in 1973 to honour the black activist who came to Harlem from Jamaica in 1916, founded the Universal Negro Improvement Agency, organised the back-to-Africa movement, and tirelessly promoted racial pride. The park is also the home of New York's last fire watchtower, a cast iron structure built in 1856 on the summit of the central mound. (Many of the others, being wooden, burned down.) But unfortunately, it's also quite run-down, and you may want to skip it in order to conserve your energy for 125th Street, where you'll need it.

Head back to Lenox Avenue along any of Mount Morris's graceful streets; my vote would be for 121st, because it will give you a good view of Riverside Church and allow you to reflect – as New Yorkers so often do – on how far you've come by travelling such a short distance. At Lenox and 123rd, check out the Ephesus Church of Seventh Day Adventists, where, if you're lucky, you may be treated to a fervent open-air sermon, one of which was in full swing the last time I took this walk.

As you approach 125th Street, aka Martin Luther King Jr Boulevard, you'll feel your senses being violently but pleasantly assailed: this is Harlem's most active thoroughfare, the pulsing site of stores and restaurants and churches and much more.

But first, if you're in the mood for culinary and literary detours, you might want to saunter up Lenox to 127th Street, where you'll find Sylvia's, Harlem's most famous soul-food restaurant, and, a few blocks farther east, the lovely, ivy-covered brownstone at 20 East 127th Street where Langston Hughes lived from 1947 until his death in 1967.

Standing at the intersection of 125th and Lenox, gaze around and take in the extraordinary clash (or is it a mesh?) of styles surrounding you – represented most clearly by the funky hat and shoe store at the south-west corner, looking for all the world like a backdrop for a '70s movie, and the Starbucks at the north-east corner, a more recent arrival. The two shopfronts glower at each other from their

**Marcus Garvey Park** – renamed in honour of the black activist of tireless energy.

opposite corners like two boxers preparing for a showdown. As you walk west, you'll soon stumble upon the Studio Museum, which started in 1969 as a hangout for local artists, and evolved into the most important centre for African and African-American art in the country. At the corner of 125th and Adam Clayton Powell Jr Boulevard is a massive office building, named after the influential pastor and politician who did so much to spur Harlem's development. And everywhere you look, the street is full to bursting: with zealots handing out religious leaflets; with booksellers hawking their wares; with shops blaring gospel or soul or hip hop music. The further east you go, the more you'll be struck by the street's gentrification: another Starbucks! Even, Lord help us, a Disney Store! But no amount of snazzing-up has killed 125th Street's unique electricity – at least not yet. Visit it on a weekend, and it will feel a lot like a bazaar; visit it anytime, and it will make you feel more alive.

The next block boasts the world-famous Apollo Theater, which opened in 1914 as a whites-only opera house, but after race riots in the 1930s began to feature black performers – and soon became Harlem's most renowned showcase, well known for its amateur nights on Wednesdays and for launching the careers of such megastars as Sarah Vaughan, Pearl Bailey, James Brown and Gladys Knight.

Continue west, and as the subway stop – and the end of your walk – looms closer, notice the pretty, unassuming Church of St Joseph of the Holy Family at 125th and Morningside Avenue; also check out the massive General Grant housing projects on the other side of the street. And all of a sudden you're back – can it be true? – where you started, weary from your travels but amazed at all you've seen. Only in New York City can you walk around a neighbourhood and feel like you've journeyed around the world.

# Eating & drinking

### Caffé Pertutti
*2888 Broadway, between 112th & 113th Streets (212 864 1143).* **Open** 10am-1am Mon-Fri; 10am-2am Fri, Sat; 10am-midnight Sun.

### Hungarian Pastry Shop
*1030 Amsterdam Avenue, at 111th Street (212 866 4230).* **Open** 8am-11.30pm Mon-Fri; 8.30am-10pm Sun. A Morningside Heights original with a deserved reputation beyond its plain appearance.

### Le Monde
*2885 Broadway, between 112th & 113th Streets (212 531 3939).* **Open** 11.30am-2am Mon-Fri; 10.30am-2am Sat, Sun. A classic French brasserie.

### Ollie's Noodle Shop & Grille
*2957 Broadway, at 116th Street (212 932 3300/3301/3302).* **Open** 7am-2am Mon-Sat; 7am-11.30pm Sun. Don't be scared to stray from the traditional Chinese dishes.

### Sylvia's
*328 Lenox Avenue, between 126th & 127th Streets (212 996 0660).* **Open** 8am-10.30pm Mon-Sat; 11am-8pm Sun. The Queen of Soul Food reigns in this comfort-food hall of fame.

### Tamarind Seed
*2935 Broadway, at 115th Street (212 864 3360).* **Open** 8am-10pm Mon-Fri; 9am-10pm Sat; 10am-9pm Sun.

### Tom's Restaurant
*2880 Broadway, at 112th Street (212 864 6137).* **Open** 6am-1.30am Mon-Wed, Sun; 24hrs Thur-Sat. A diner frequented by Columbia University students and *Seinfeld* fans.

### The West End
*2911 Broadway, between 113th & 114th Streets (212 662 8830).* **Open** 11am-3am (varies) daily. The wide draught selection still draws students from Columbia University.

# Bookshops

### Bank Street Bookstore
*2879 Broadway, at 112th Street (212 678 1654).* **Open** *Sept-June* 10am-8pm Mon-Thur; 10am-6pm Fri, Sat; noon-5pm Sun. *July, Aug* closed Sun.

### Labyrinth Books
*536 West 112th Street, between Amsterdam Avenue & Broadway (212 865 1588).* **Open** 9am-10pm Mon-Fri; 10am-8pm Sat; 11am-7pm Sun.

**Papyrus**
*2915 Broadway, at 114th Street (212 222 3350).*
**Open** 10am-11pm daily.

# Museums

### El Museo del Barrio
*1230 Fifth Avenue, between 104th & 105th
Streets (212 831 7272).* **Open** 11am-5pm
Wed-Sun. **Admission** $4; $2 concessions.
**No credit cards.**

### General Grant
### National Memorial
*Riverside Drive, at 122nd Street (212 666 1640).*
**Open** 9am-5pm daily.

### Museum of the
### City of New York
*1220 Fifth Avenue, at 103rd Street (212 534
1672).* **Open** 10am-5pm Wed-Sat; noon-5pm Sun.
**Admission** *suggested donation* $5; $4
concessions; $10 family ticket. **No credit cards.**

### Studio Museum
*144 West 125th Street, between Seventh Avenue
& Lenox Avenue (212 864 4500).* **Open** 10am-
5pm Wed-Fri; 1-6pm Sat, Sun. **Admission** $5;
$1-$3 concessions; free 1st Sat of every month.
**No credit cards.**

# Parks

### Charles A Dana
### Discovery Center
*Enter from Fifth Avenue, at 110th Street (212
860 1370).* **Open** 10am-5pm Tue-Sun.
**Admission** free.

### Conservatory Garden
*Enter from Fifth Avenue, between 104th &105th
Streets.* **Open** 8am-dusk daily.

### Department of
### Parks & Recreation
*888 NY PARKS/212 360 2774.*

### Morningside Park
*West 110th Street to West 123rd Street,
Manhattan Avenue to Morningside Drive.*

### Riverside Park
*Riverside Drive to Hudson River, West 72nd
Street to Clair Place.*

### Sakura Park
*Riverside Drive, Claremont Avenue to West
122nd Street.*

# Religion

### Riverside Church
*490 Riverside Drive, at 122nd Street (212 870
6700).* **Open** 9am-4pm daily. *Bell tower* 11am-
4pm Tue-Sat; 12.30-4pm Sun.

### Cathedral of St John the Divine
*1047 Amsterdam Avenue, at 112th Street (212
316 7490).* **Open** 7am-6pm Mon-Sat; 7am-
8.30pm Sun. **Services** 8am, 8.30am, 12.15pm,
5.30pm Mon-Sat; 8am, 9am, 9.30am (Spanish),
11am, 7pm Sun.

### Ephesus Church of
### Seventh Day Adventists
*101 West 123rd Street, at Lenox Avenue (212
662 5536).* **Open** services 9.15am, 11am, 5.30pm
Sat; noon, 7pm Wed.

### Church of St Joseph
### of the Holy Family
*405 West 125th Street, at Morningside Avenue
(212 662 9125).* **Open** *services* 9am, 10.30am,
noon (Spanish) Sun; *mass* 7am Mon-Fri.

### Masjid Malcolm Shabaz
*116th Street, at Lenox Avenue (212 662 2200)*

### Union Theological Seminary
*3041 Broadway, between West 120th &
122nd Streets (212 280 1317).* **Open** 9am-5pm
Mon-Fri.

# Music

**Tom's Diner** Suzanne Vega from *Solitude
Standing* (1987)

# Others

### Apollo Theater
*253 West 125th Street, between Adam Clayton
Powell Jr & Frederick Douglass Boulevards (212
749 5838).*

### Barnard College
*3009 Broadway, between 116th & 120th Streets
(212 854 5262/office 212 854 2014).* **Open**
*office* 9am-5pm Mon-Fri. Call to arrange tours.

### Columbia University
*Between Broadway & Amsterdam Avenue &
114th to 120th Streets (212 854 1754).*

### Disney Store
*300 West 125th Street, at Frederick Douglass
Boulevard (212 749 8390).* **Open** 10am-8am
Mon-Sat; 11am-6pm Sun.

# Down and out and up again

Lee Stringer

Walking freestyle through the Upper East Side and sleeping rough in Central Park

---

**Start:** corner of East 97th Street
& Third Avenue
**Finish:** corner of Central Park
South & Fifth Avenue
**Time:** 2-3 hours
**Distance:** 4 miles/6.5km
**Getting there:** subway train 6 to
96th Street station followed by
short walk
**Getting back:** subway trains N or
R from Fifth Avenue station
**Note:** if you are planning to visit
any of the galleries on Fifth
Avenue, note that most are
closed on Mondays.

---

For most of my 25 years in Manhattan I was no different from other veteran New Yorkers who, convinced of our great importance as we are, are known less for leisurely strolls than for frantic dashes from here to there. But over ten of those years, homeless, drug-dazed and wandering the pavement, I developed an intimate street-level relationship with this city of towers.

Of the many walks I took at that time, the most memorable (because I made it again and again) began around 100th Street, just above Yorkville – as the once sleepy but increasingly manic Upper East Side is known – on the periphery of Spanish Harlem, where on any given night any number of young gangstas-in-training would be huddled in the shadows of the projects ready to serve up my substance

of choice (crack cocaine at the time).

I'd hustle around the nearest corner after copping my stuff, 'slam dunk' a good chunk of my stash and, hyperenergised by the coke rush, blunder along the streets frog-eyed and crook-necked, my gaze everywhere at once, not stopping – except to lean into the odd phone booth for a surreptitious refresher blast – until I found myself 50 blocks south, at Grand Central Terminal, under the roof of which was the crawlspace I then called home.

My thought was to reconstruct a good part of this walk in the fresh light of my now cleaner, saner existence. The result is a more interior than exterior tour, one that some of you might find more suited to armchair rumination than for shoe-leather witness. All the same, it's a walk that perhaps will give new eyes to any of you contemplating a trip here, a different way of seeing the New York you will see.

I start out at 97th and Third, on the corner where a scant half-dozen years ago a sleek and modern mosque ascended on what was then a huge rubble-strewn lot. I remember considering it something of an anomaly when it first appeared, situated as it was on the brink of the projects and the dusty, low-rise tenements surrounding them, its beige, domed façade tucked into the farthest corner of the property so that what first struck your eyes was a brilliant green desert of lawn, testifying to a serenity for which Manhattan is not known.

But this day I find the place under siege, surrounded by huge mud-stained, steel-limbed, earth-altering monsters;

# Down and out and up again

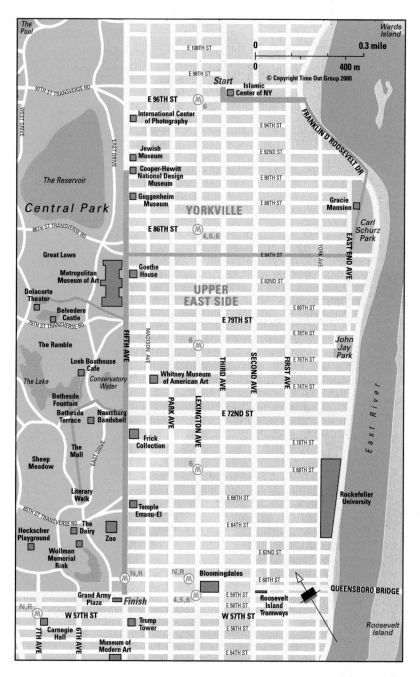

The Pool

Wards Island

E 100TH ST

0     0.3 mile

E 98TH ST

0     400 m

*Start*

© Copyright Time Out Group 2000

Islamic Center of NY

97TH ST TRANSVERSE RD

E 96TH ST

Ⓜ 6

FRANKLIN D ROOSEVELT DR

International Center of Photography

E 94TH ST

WEST DRIVE

Jewish Museum

E 92ND ST

Cooper-Hewitt National Design Museum

E 90TH ST

The Reservoir

Guggenheim Museum

E 88TH ST

Gracie Mansion

**Central Park**

YORKVILLE

EAST DRIVE

86TH ST TRANSVERSE RD

E 86TH ST

Ⓜ 4,5,6

Carl Schurz Park

E 84TH ST

YORK AVE

EAST END AVE

Great Lawn

Goethe House

E 82ND ST

Metropolitan Museum of Art

UPPER EAST SIDE

E 80TH ST

Delacorte Theater

E 79TH ST

E 78TH ST

Belvedere Castle

79TH ST TRANSVERSE RD

Ⓜ 6

E 76TH ST

John Jay Park

The Ramble

FIFTH AVE

MADISON AVE

THIRD AVE

SECOND AVE

FIRST AVE

Loeb Boathouse Cafe

Whitney Museum of American Art

E 74TH ST

The Lake

Conservatory Water

PARK AVE

LEXINGTON AVE

East River

Bethesda Fountain

Bethesda Terrace

Naumburg Bandshell

E 72ND ST

Sheep Meadow

The Mall

EAST DRIVE

Frick Collection

E 70TH ST

Ⓜ 6

E 68TH ST

Literary Walk

65TH ST TRANSVERSE RD

Temple Emanu-El

E 66TH ST

Rockefeller University

Heckscher Playground

The Dairy

E 64TH ST

Zoo

Wollman Memorial Rink

E 62ND ST

Ⓜ N,R

Ⓜ N,R

Bloomingdales

E 60TH ST

QUEENSBORO BRIDGE

Grand Army Plaza

*Finish*

E 59TH ST

Roosevelt Island Tramways

Ⓜ N,R

4,5,6

E 58TH ST

W 57TH ST

Ⓜ

W 57TH ST

Trump Tower

E 56TH ST

Roosevelt Island

7TH AVE

6TH AVE

Carnegie Hall

Museum of Modern Art

E 54TH ST

Mosque at 97th and Third, where
construction was in progress as
this book went to press.

everything is sheathed in dirty gray construction shrouds, an ugly skinless four-square cinderblock structure-in-progress now rudely intruding across the once resplendent grass. As I make the turn east at 96th Street, I spot a huge plywood sign standing sentry and announcing, to all who care, the coming of the Islamic Cultural Center School.

I stroll down to 96th, waving at the five-storey walk-up between Lexington and Third in which I once lived and that is now dwarfed by the soaring, cocoa-brown Normandy Towers directly across the street, an apartment complex that sprouted during the go-go '80s and that has no actual sister building in its namesake region. I am headed for the promenade of sorts that fronts the East River and runs, in rough parallel to the FDR Drive, right down to Manhattan's southern end. Heidelberg has its Philosopher's Mile, which snakes upward from the river into the hills and which I have seen. But for my money the ying and yang of sauntering along this promenade – quietude of the river riding one shoulder, angry snarling traffic riding the other – seldom fails to provoke the kind of internal debate upon which the best of philosophy is founded.

It's a warm day, cooled by a breeze off the river, which is never in a particular hurry, only rambles along, like a wise and weary old soul. The usual scattering of people are enjoying the sunshine: on one of the benches, a young couple, limbs entwined, their lunch things already laid bare and ravaged beside them, making a sweet dessert of each other's lips; a desk jockey flies by pumping and panting with the regularity of a pile driver, as he jogs off the consequences of a sedentary existence; sun-baked fishermen sweating into their portable coolers, rods soldiering along the guardrail. They smile back when I wish them luck and it occurs to me that one cannot be a good fisherman without embracing a bit of Zen.

A fisherman casts out into the **East River**.

North of them the Wards Island footbridge sits low above the river. Despite its ugly chalky-green hue, its profile – tall, narrow, twin towers ascending astride the apex of the arch its seemingly pencil-thin span barely makes – always strikes me as unfussy and kind of eloquent. Lonesome, too. One of New York's dozen or so movable bridges, it stands ever ready to raise its centre wing in welcome to tall ships that, alas, rarely if ever happen by.

Speaking of which, downriver a bit lies Roosevelt Island, the blur of land visible across the water that was once known as Welfare Island, back during an earlier attempt to consign the poor to oblivion in the 1920s. Even in its previous incarnation as Blackwell's Island – after the husband of Mary Manningham who had inherited it from her stepfather in 1686 – this site had for the most part served as a repository for the unwanted, having hosted a prison (in

A brace of bridges to **Wards Island** can be viewed from the East River promenade.

which Mae West was once incarcerated for obscenity), an insane asylum (about the terrace of which Charles Dickens once waxed euphoric) and a smallpox isolation hospital.

In 1973, however, under the auspices of the Urban Development Corporation, it was transformed into a city planner's wet dream, an impossible, multi-ethnic, mixed-income haven from the ruder influences of urban existence. Even those most venerable icons of city life – trash cans and garbage trucks – were factored out, replaced by an automated conveyance system that hurtles the discards of life along underground faster than a speeding subway train.

A side trip to get a gander at this city of the future might be worth your time. The tram ride over from 59th Street – eight storeys up, dangling out over the water, heaving to and fro on the wind – is an attraction in and of itself. And the view of Manhattan's skyline – ever more majestic as it falls beneath your toes – is sure to start camera shutters winking. Climb aboard a Green Line bus when you alight

(one leaves about every 15 minutes) and circle the entire 147-acre island for ten cents. You'll find five of New York's landmarks here: the 128-year-old James Renwick Jr-designed stone lighthouse still standing on its northern end (Renwick was also responsible for St Patrick's Cathedral); New York's original mental hospital, its octagonal shape considered an architectural marvel at the time; the Strecker Laboratory, built in 1892 and now home to the Russell Sage Institute of Pathology; the 200-plus-year-old wooden Blackwell House, one of New York's oldest; and the Chapel of the Good Shepherd, erected in 1888.

But back to the promenade.

Most of my former walks along here were after dark, when a more threadbare crowd was in evidence: pipe-heads scraping on their stems for that last hit of 'res'; crashed-out canners tethered to their shopping carts so no one would steal them in the night; a wino or two, perhaps, making merry with themselves. Eventually, the constant honk and growl of traffic would invariably begin to rattle my hyped-up brain and set my teeth on edge and I would end up scrambling down the promenade to 90th Street where it tapers off into Carl Schurz Park.

Like pretty much everything else in New York, ownership of this 15-acre plot can be traced back to 16th-century Dutch settlers. Under entitlement to a fellow with the unfortunate name of Sybout Classen, what we now call Carl Schurz Park remained blissfully undeveloped for over a century. A subsequent owner, Jacob Walton, built a house on the property in 1770, but it was reduced to rubble during the Revolution half a dozen years later and the Continental Army – which had built a stronghold around the house against the possible invasion of Hell Gate, the strategic shipping passage there – was routed by the Brits.

Another good 100 years passed before the city bought the land, during which time Archibald Gracie built the mansion that still bears his name and that in 1932 became, after an eight-year stint housing the Museum of New York, the official Mayor's residence.

My first time ever seeing Gracie Mansion was during the early '70s when, training as a newsreel cameraman and staying at the 34th Street Y, I got swept up in a protest march bearing down Fifth Avenue. Giddy at the prospect of being part of an actual protest, revelling in the anarchy of it all, I plunged into the human tide. Someone shouted, 'Let's take it to the Mayor's house,' which we did, chanting thunderously all the way, then stood vigil at the Mayor's doorstep demanding he give us an audience.

As I recall, Mayor John Lindsey never came out. And I remember feeling righteous indignation over this, even though, truth be told, I was only along on a lark. I don't even remember exactly what we were protesting – something to do with Vietnam, I suppose – but I do remember the march.

It was a little after the turn of the century that the property got its present name, after Carl Schurz, an émigré from Cologne, Germany, who first made his bones here turning out the German vote for Abraham Lincoln. During the war he commandeered the 26th Regiment of the

**Carl Schurz Park**, named in honour of a German immigrant, senator and newspaper editor.

Continental Army, which earned the nickname 'The Flying Dutchmen' after their controversial retreat at Mayes Hill. Inglorious as this defeat may have been, it didn't prove particularly detrimental to Schurz's upward mobility. He went on to the US Senate, later became Secretary of the Interior, and later still took to journalism – perhaps the last refuge of a statesman – as editor of the *New York Tribune*.

Besides the usual addenda of municipal parks – playgrounds, basketball courts, winding blacktop trails – Carl Schurz Park offers some pleasant grassy knolls upon which the melanin-challenged can burnish in a summer tan. Or, if the heat is too much, just inside the northernmost entrance there's a kind of a cul-de-sac ringed by trees in the shade of which are a number of benches. And the seven-block, bench-lined waterfront boardwalk is a dream for midnight strolls, particularly with a full moon silvering the ripples of the river.

During the time I was hanging out there, the park had a resident contingent of nightly squatters who, sometimes and sometimes not, clashed mightily with the regular crew of upscale sexual mavericks out for a casual tryst with whatever willing tight-jeaned young man. Some people saw it as a shame that the Mayor should permit his backyard to be so littered with down-and-outs. I saw it differently. To me it was a vivid symbol of a democracy strong enough to take a punch.

Of course, all that is now finished. Thanks to the combined efforts of the City Parks Department and Carl Schurz Park Association, the site has been by and large disencumbered of the quirks of human existence. The homeless have been cleared out, the shrubbery has been trimmed back enough to put a damper on clandestine coupling, no matter what the gender, and – as I intuit from the new signage – the most pressing problem now seems to be canines who do their business in other than the designated area.

I emerge at the park's south end, 84th Street and East End Avenue, along which pre- and post-war apartment buildings

**Gracie Mansion**, Carl Shurz Park – New York's official mayoral residence since 1942.

loom over small, one- and two-room shops, which, in the tradition of an older Yorkville, are put to bed each day at dusk. I walk west, past brownstones mostly with tidy little stoops, upon which it is no longer the vogue, sadly, to seek the cool of the night; past a club that on weekend nights never fails to draw an anxious queue of young urban scene-makers begging a nod from the surly, black-clad bouncer stationed at the door; past 84th and Third, which I'll always think of as my corner. This is where I hawked copies of *Street News* – the preferred meal ticket of many New York down-and-outers – just about every night for years. Tourists are finding their way to this spot, drawn by the bars, clubs, restaurants, cafés and specialty shops that have proliferated over the last decade or so. From 93rd Street down to the mid-70s, along First, Second and Third Avenues, every block is littered with them – too many to survive on the locals' patronage alone.

Yet the residents, refusing to cede their turf completely to commerce, are always out in force as well. You see them 'walking their dogs, chatting with their neighbours, closing the details of deals on the corner, dashing in and out of taxis, dipping in and out of the joints, zipping by on skateboards, on bicycles, on Rollerblades, laughing, singing, shouting to the sky.' (I commit the cardinal sin of quoting myself here, for which I'll doubtless burn in literary hell.) It's a great opportunity to catch real New Yorkers in the act of being themselves and, in concert with the reckless cacophony raised by restless wanderers who descend after dark, it makes for a special brand of kinetic fever you don't quite get on the Upper West Side.

Of course, whenever I was 'skeed up', I would find all this a bit too frenetic and cut up to Fifth Avenue for a more bucolic meander along the edge of Central Park and down what is known as Museum Mile. It's more than a mile, actually, encompassing some 20 blocks. Along it

you will find about ten museums or galleries. It's quite an eclectic convening of art and culture and history, but merely a bite out of the endless move-through feast Manhattan has to offer along these lines. But these are among – if not *the* – biggest in the world. Size definitely matters to us, whatever our pretenses to culture and civilisation. It ever remains New York's foremost crowing point.

North of where you join Fifth Avenue lies the Cooper-Hewitt National Design Museum. I've never been in but I am always impressed by it whenever I pass, impressed by the grounds, like a chunk of English countryside plopped down amidst New York's relentlessly vertical thrust. I have been in the Guggenheim. When I was in high school we had a class trip to see an exhibition of Italian sculpture. But for me it was the design of the museum itself, wherein you take an elevator to the top and work your way down the long, winding helix of a ramp, that floored me. Years later I had the notion of making an art video by climbing into a shopping cart and taping the art as it sailed by with greater and greater velocity as the cart shot down the spiral. The fact that I'm here to tell about it testifies to the fact that I never actually tried to do this.

About 20 years ago, I treated a visiting friend to the whole tourist thing and we made half a day out of roaming through the Metropolitan Museum's many rooms. We got separated at one point and looking for him I happened into this large sitting room filled with tables and chairs in which sat about three dozen people – at least I *think* they were people, because they were all silent and stony faced as statues. To this day I wonder what that was all about.

It was many years later, while 'living rough', that I was reintroduced to the Metropolitan. Following a particularly exhaustive nocturnal crawl, I crashed just inside the park, on the slope that tilts down from the atrium on the north side of the Metropolitan Museum. I woke up the

Let the winding helix of the **Guggenheim Museum** run you past the art.

next day to find a groundskeeper looming over me, a crisp $20 in his hands. 'Here,' he said with a kindly smile, 'I think you dropped this.'

Another night I met a man there who, coincidentally, lived just down the block from the corner on which I sold *Street News*. Recognising me, he suggested that I might use his shower every now and again if need be – an offer of which I was happy to avail myself quite regularly. With this good karma recommending it, I chose the slope by the museum whenever sleeping outdoors, and eventually grew quite fond of the atrium, its huge glass and aluminum geodesic planes slanting skyward in a narrowing grid, lending

breathtaking scale to the Egyptian artefacts visible through the lowest panes. Gaping at those crude but somehow eloquent slab stone dwellings I realised that peeking down from a 20th-floor living room is the anomaly, not stretching out for the night on the grass.

My usual walk would take me straight down Fifth Avenue to 59th Street before crossing east to Madison and on to Grand Central Terminal. Fifth Avenue may be best known as an upmarket shoppers' mecca, but, for the people who can afford to shop there, the real Fifth Avenue lies above 59th where nothing so crude and vulgar as a store or shop has ever been tolerated. Even gods of fashion such as

along here some balmy night, raise a bottle of cheap wine to the mammoth brownstones shouldered along the opposite side of the street and gloat over the grand bargain of it all.

It was the wealthy who first urged construction of Central Park upon city officials. And using the government's right of eminent domain – which is a nice way of saying seizure without due process – 1,600 poor families were put out of their homes to make way for it (it wouldn't do for the rich to have their park on development-worthy terra firma). For its first decade or so, the park's rules and regs were openly hostile to those without means, and the panoply of public attractions that one now finds there exist chiefly due to political agitation over the years from advocates for the poor and working class.

Nowadays during summer months the park is never without something going on for the masses. The most democratic of these are, for my money, the Delacorte Theater (Shakespeare) and the free concerts (opera and orchestras on the great lawn). I would either walk along outside the park or dip in one of the six entrances between 85th and 59th – the first of these being just north of the Metropolitan Museum and the last being just above the zoo. The zoo remains one of the biggest park attractions. It was renovated and upscaled during the '80s and a very pleasant café has been added with a thought for weary adults run ragged by tireless children.

The 79th Street entrance takes you past the south end of the Metropolitan Museum to the Great Lawn, where every summer a number of free concerts are staged; and the Delacorte Theater, in which one can see Shakespeare played as nowhere else, with the rocky edge of bluff leading to Belvedere Castle as a natural backdrop.

As a homeless person I had an inside edge on grabbing the best seats for these events, having more free time and being able to arrive earlier than most. Some of

Gucci, Versace and Tiffany wouldn't dare think of emblazoning their logos here.

During my days on the street I thought of this stretch as Doorman's Row. At night you see them peering out at the street, silhouetted in the blue-green fluorescence of artificial light, sentries at the gates of Babylon, perhaps. No matter how threadbare and ragged-edged I ever was, stumbling down the park side of the street, I could always squeeze a bit of bemused satisfaction out of the knowledge that the postcard-perfect views the rich and famous pay so dearly to behold from their bedroom windows are equally available to even the most penniless soul. Sit on one of the benches

Familiarity breeds affection – sleeping rough in the shadow of the **Met**'s Egyptian temple.

us had a cottage industry as professional 'waiters' for the more affluent set who couldn't be bothered idling in line for four hours to snag the first-come-first-served free tickets. Not entirely fair, I'll give you, but quite lucrative.

Enter at 72nd and you can traipse around The Mall, a long, tree-lined corridor with asphalt footpaths on either side; make your way westward, to the great band shell, the ever gurgling Bethesda Fountain and the Boat House by the lake. Summer nights I'd be lured by music and voices on the air and find my way to the Boathouse Café and the romance of cocktails and jazz served up by the shimmering moonlit lake.

More often than not, I would skim the edge of the park, go in one entrance, stop for a refresher blast on one of the benches or in one of the deserted playgrounds, then scramble down and out the next. This trip, however, I am content to stroll under the shade of the trees overhanging the sidewalk and people-watch.

By the time I reach 59th Street, that enduring hub of swank where several of

New York's priciest boulevards converge on Grand Army Plaza, the sky has taken on the red-orange glow of early dusk. It is my favourite time of day, one that seldom fails to drudge up a bit of sentimentality in me. I decide to end my walk here, where eely limos ferry a luckier breed than I to the imported marble steps of the Plaza Hotel; where horse-drawn hansom cabs-to-nowhere idle, waiting upon the pleasure of the next romantic; where Asian portrait artists line the benches just inside the park, their charcoal sticks at the ready; where peals of child laughter ascend from Central Park Zoo and break on the still air. I will leave you with the last thing I see as I am jotting this down: a balloon, silver on one side, pink and blue pastel on the other, has won its freedom, has broken loose of its string, and heads merrily skyward, to whatever its next adventure.

## Galleries & museums

### Cooper-Hewitt National Design Museum

*2 East 91st Street, at Fifth Avenue (212 849 8400).* **Open** 10am-9pm Tue; 10am-5pm Wed-

Sat; noon-5pm Sun. **Admission** $5; free 5-9pm Tue, under-12s at all times. **No credit cards.**

### El Museo del Barrio
*1230 Fifth Avenue, between 104th & 105th Streets (212 831 7272).* **Open** 11am-5pm Wed-Sun. **Admission** $4; $2 concessions. **No credit cards.**

### Frick Collection
*1 East 70th Street, at Fifth Avenue (212 288 0700).* **Open** 10am-6pm Tue-Sat; 1-6pm Sun. **Admission** $7; $5 concessions; under-10s not admitted, ages 10-16 must be accompanied by an adult. **No credit cards.**

### Jewish Museum
*1109 Fifth Avenue, at 92nd Street (212 423 3230).* **Open** 11am-5.45pm Mon, Wed, Thur, Sun; 11am-8pm Tue. **Admission** $8; free 5-8pm Tue, under-12s at all times. **No credit cards.**

### International Center of Photography
*1130 Fifth Avenue, at 94th Street (212 860 1777).* **Open** 10am-5pm Tue-Thur; 10am-8pm Fri; 10am-6pm Sat, Sun. **Admission** $6; $4 concessions; voluntary contributions 5-8pm Fri.

### Metropolitan Museum of Art
*1000 Fifth Avenue, at 82nd Street (212 535 7710).* **Open** 9.30am-5.15pm Tue-Thur, Sun; 9.30am-8.45pm Fri, Sat. **Admission** *suggested donation* $10; $5 concessions; free under-12s. **No credit cards.** No pushchairs on Sundays.

### Museum of the City of New York
*1220 Fifth Avenue, at 103rd Street (212 534 1672).* **Open** 10am-5pm Wed-Sat; noon-5pm Sun. **Admission** *suggested donation* $5; $4 concessions; $10 family ticket. **No credit cards.**

### National Academy of Design
*1083 Fifth Avenue, at 89th Street (212 369 4880).* **Open** noon-5pm Wed, Thur, Sat, Sun; 10am-6pm Fri. **Admission** $8; free 5-8pm Fri, under-5s at all times. **No credit cards.**

### Solomon R Guggenheim Museum
*1071 Fifth Avenue, at 88th Street (212 423 3500).* **Open** 9am-6pm Mon-Wed, Sun; 9am-8pm Fri, Sat. **Admission** $12; $7 concessions; free under-12s; voluntary donation 6-8pm Fri.

## Others

### Central Park Wildlife Center
*Fifth Avenue, at 64th Street (212 861 6030).* **Open** 10am-5pm Mon-Fri; 10.30am-

5.30pm Sat, Sun. **Admission** $3.50; 50¢-$1.25 concessions; free under-3s. **No credit cards.**

### Gracie Mansion
*Carl Schurz Park, 88th Street at East End Avenue (212 570 4751).* **Open** *Mar-Nov* tours by appointment only. Call for details.

### Islamic Cultural Center of New York
*96th Street & Third Avenue (212 722 5234).* **Open** *office* 9am-5pm daily.

### Loeb Boathouse
*The Lake, near Fifth Avenue & East 17th Street (212 517 4723).* **Open** *May-Oct* noon-4pm Mon-Fri; 11am-4pm Sat, Sun.

### Carl Schurz Park
*East End Avenue to East River, East 84th to East 90th Streets.*

### Department of Parks & Recreation
*888 NY PARKS/212 360 2774.*

### Roosevelt Island Operating Corporation
*591 Main Street, Roosevelt Island (212 832 4540).* **Open** 9am-5pm Mon-Fri. Call for details of events and free maps of the island.
**Getting there** Tramways (Cable cars) leave from the corner of 59th Street & Second Avenue (212 832 4543). **Open** 6am-2am Mon-Thur, Sun; 6am-3.30am Fri, Sat. **Frequency** *rush hours* (Mon-Fri) 7am-11am, 4-7pm every 5 minutes; *all other times* every 15 minutes. **Admission** $1.50 each way.

### Street News
*144-46 76th Avenue, Flushing, Queens (718 268 5165).*

## Shopping

### Gucci
*685 Fifth Avenue, at 54th Street (212 826 2600).* **Open** 10am-6.30pm Mon-Wed, Fri; 10am-7pm Thur, Sat; noon-6pm Sun.

### Tiffany & Co
*757 Fifth Avenue, at 57th Street (212 755 8000).* **Open** 10am-6pm Mon-Wed, Fri, Sat; 10am-7pm Thur.

### Gianni Versace
*647 Fifth Avenue, between 51st & 52nd Streets (212 317 0224).* **Open** 10am-6.30pm Mon-Sat.

# The Bunny hop

## Lady Bunny

Gay abandon with the Queen of New York.

**Start:** Tompkins Square Park
**Finish:** Pier 54, Hudson River
**Time:** 2-3 hours
**Distance:** 3.5 miles/6km
**Getting there:** subway train 6 to Astor Place, followed by five-minute walk
**Getting back:** short walk along West 14th St to 14th St station (subway trains A C or E)
**Note:** this walk is best done in the afternoon or early evening, although it is worth noting that the walk up the edge of the Hudson River to Pier 54 is probably best done in daylight. Also note that Greg Sanders' walk, *Men of Letters*, and Anna Sui's walk, *Rock & Roll Shopping Spree*, cover some of the same areas.

Gorgeous, stylish and talented – **Lady Bunny**.

In sharp contrast to the architectural, botanical and historical references of the other contributors to this series, my points of interest consist mainly of inexpensive eateries, bargain basements, and places to meet men. Just call me a cheap slut – with an eating disorder! So prudes, children and dieters may want to skip this walk – fellow sluts, read on!

But back to me! I'm a 'gender illusionist' who organises an outdoor festival known as Wigstock. It all began in 1984 – gosh, I'm 22 now, I must have started this shit at the tender age of – oh, you do the math! [editor's note: Bunny appears to be at least 40] – when a bunch of drunken employees were thrown out of the Pyramid nightclub and began to clown around, beers in hand,

on the (now razed) bandshell in nearby Tompkins Square Park. Together Wendy Wild, Hattie B DeMille, Kitty Duprée, members of a rock group called the Fleshtones and I hit upon the idea of spoofing the 1969 Woodstock concert, utilising the wealth of offbeat talent (mainly drag queens and alternative rockers) that headlined at the club.

The idea might have faded with the next day's hangover had I not secured the necessary permits, rented the sound system and booked the acts: thus, Wigstock was born. The first show attracted a few hundred enthusiastic (if bombed) East Village residents, that number multiplying with each successive festival until we were forced

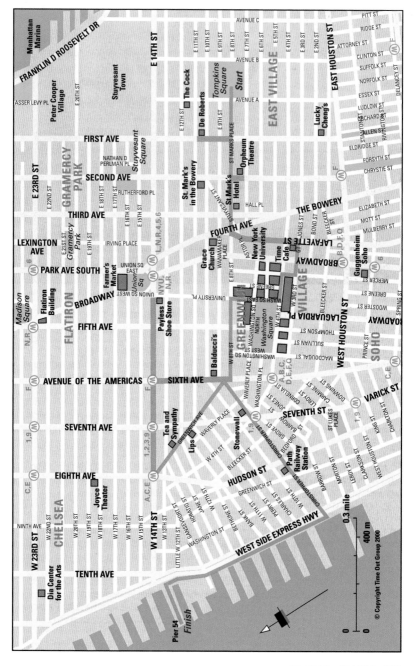

From tattoos to music to deli stores, the wacky meets the mundane along **St Mark's Place**.

to pack up our wigs and gowns and relocate to the larger West Side piers, our current (and hopefully future) home. So like Wigstock, we'll begin in Tompkins Square, and walk across town to the Hudson River, zig-zagging (you didn't expect my walk to be straight, didja?) through one of Manhattan's liveliest and most charming 'hoods.

Gentrification has transformed the East Village considerably in the past 15 years. When a Gap store opened on St Mark's Place in the early 1990s, local bohemians felt it was the nail in the coffin of their beloved turf. Indeed, the soaring rents that have accompanied the fancy shops and restaurants have forced many young, broke artist-types out to Williamsburg in Brooklyn – it's even called the 'new East Village'. But there are positive aspects to gentrification. One is the beautification of Tompkins Square Park. I certainly don't mind the police dispersing the evil skinhead gangs known for their fag-bashing – one devil pummelled his victims with a billiard ball in a sock. Plus, it's nice to have a few benches not

exclusively reserved by the homeless, whose presence (and smell) was so strong at one point that I considered printing up 'Homeless Go Home' T-shirts.

The park is still gritty. This morning I heard a homeless-looking guy shouting, 'C'mon, I haven't smoked a fucking joint all day, man!' That's my dad for ya! But basically, the litter-strewn park is what it's always been, a place for villagers, tired of their cramped apartments, to soak up some dogs or walk their rays. Many kooky characters still inhabit the nabe and make Tompkins Square a people-watching paradise.

Unlike most cities in the US where one drives to get to the house next door, few people in the Village own cars, which makes for a vital street scene. Unlike cities that shut down at night, there's a 24-hour store on almost every other corner – the Korean ones even sell health food! And *everything* can be delivered.

Cross Avenue A and walk half a block on the opposite side. Between 7th Street and St Mark's Place you'll find Ray's Candy (though the sign says 'Newsday'), a tiny, 25-year-old newsstand that serves an old-fashioned New York treat: the egg cream. It's a foamy, refreshing mixture of seltzer water, milk and syrup – but no egg. Chocolate and vanilla were the only choices for years, but now 'gentrified' flavours like licorice and sky blue raspberry (yuck!) share the bill. If you'd prefer something more substantial, there are cheap eats on every block. I also urge you to poke around the funky shops in the area, that offer everything from used CDs, books, clothing and jewellery – lots of trendy young designers, too. Take a left on St Mark's Place and you'll pass Stingy Lulu's, a cosy diner with drag hostesses. (Lucky Cheng's at First Avenue and 2nd Street has an entire drag waitstaff with nightly performances.) If you're here at night, you'll want to check out the Cock at Avenue A and 12th Street, a horny, jam-packed bar that's considered 'the new Pyramid'. The Pyramid itself has resurged in recent years and enjoys a very popular '80s night on Fridays.

On First Avenue between St Mark's Place and 10th Street, drug dealers hawk their wares – mostly marijuana and cocaine. Don't worry about recognising them, just linger a little near any corner on the east side of First Avenue looking a little lost and they'll find you – they're quite aggressive. Don't get me wrong, I'm certainly not advocating drug use. In fact I try to live by Nancy Reagan's 'Just Say No' to drugs motto, but the drugs don't always listen, do they? Be warned: aspirin is sometimes sold as Ecstasy – uh, I'm told. For a legal, natural high try the herbs at Angelica.

Walk up First Avenue a bit and you'll find PS 122, a haven for performance artists, and DeRobertis, a bustling, old-world pasticceria, established in 1904. Careful, it's addictive! Or directly across the street there's the Five Roses – I call it the Five Noses after its proprietress's grand profile – with affordable spicy Italian fare. Don't dally too long, or you'll end up with my figure!

Go back along First Avenue to St Mark's Place and turn right towards Second Avenue, passing the Holiday Cocktail Lounge – a fave among the rock set and a classic dive that inspired Madonna's smash, 'Holiday'. Go on to Second Avenue where you'll see the Orpheum Theater, home of the long running *Stomp!*, a percussive masterpiece that *can* be beat. It's highly recommended by someone who dislikes most musicals. There's also a cheap Mexican joint called San Loco that features salsa in four strengths: mild, hot, serious and stupid. With typically irreverent East Village humour, their menu once described their chilli as using an old family recipe. Some nut put a period after family – and they left it that way for years!

St Mark's between Second and Third Avenues is the main promenade for those crazy kids with wacky hair colours, tattoos, and earrings in their eyebrows for Chrissakes! On this block you can purchase trendy/fetish gear in shops like Religious Sex or the famed Trash and Vaudeville, or perhaps you'd prefer a touristy T-shirt with a slogan like, 'If I gave a shit, you'd be the 1st person I'd give it to' – a perfect gift for older relatives! There's also a super cheap Japanese restaurant called Dojo that has a healthy Japanese vibe, and the inexpensive St Mark's Hotel.

Keep west over Third Avenue and you'll hit Astor Place, in the middle of which sits a giant cubic sculpture. Rambunctious youths frequently surround, grip and rotate the cube on its axis, accompanied by the customary hoots and hollers of any rite of passage. (Ah, testosterone!) This remains one of the few surviving outlets for remotely anarchic behaviour before Mayor Giuliani sanitised the city. Hated by liberals, Giuliani has proposed idiotic ideas like mandatory school uniforms and abolishing the quintessential New York hot-dog stands. While these proposals were instantly rejected, unfortunately many of his others

West 8th Street is the home to all sorts of dressing-up opportunities, including **l'Impasse**.

went into effect. He managed to enforce archaic 'soft' laws like no dancing in bars without cabaret licences, which led to the closure of nearby Coney Island High, a popular live music venue that's now up for sale. The space was formerly the Boybar, where many of New York City's top transvestite showgirls cut their drag teeth, many of them in costumes purchased from the dozens of street vendors who once lined the streets of Cooper Square. These gypsies are now shooed away instantly by the Gestapo, I mean the coppers – and I tell ya, my wardrobe has never quite recovered. Besides, if you lived in the area and were robbed, you'd know right where to go to buy back your belongings!

Turn south down Lafayette. There are still plenty of shows to catch along here, including the Public Theater (large-scale productions, often Shakespeare) and Joe's Pub, a cabaret/performance art space. The Blue Man Group show with its paint splattering (not the kind of 'blue' material I'm fond of) has been playing for an eternity at the Astor Place

Theater. Moroccon-themed Fez, underneath Time Café, books everything from live jazz to, well, me.

Turn right and follow across Broadway (though if you're in a shopping mode, there are hip boutiques on your left all the way down to Canal Street, Chinatown's main drag) and walk up toward University Place. On your left is Washington Square Park, where you can 'take a load off'. NYU *stud*-ents, dealers, street performers and cruising men – this last one is hearsay, I assure you! – have made this their hangout.

Proceed up to 8th Street and turn west. You'll note a dazzling array of low-to-medium-priced shoe and clothing stores on both sides of the street, such as Untitled, or L'Impasse, selling clingy, sexy fashions. The first you'll come to, before Fifth Avenue, and the grandmomma of 'em all, is Patricia Field.

Open since the '70s, Pat Field has a tremendous talent for stocking the latest in flashy gear and accessories. (Do I get my discount now, Pat?) Even if you dress conservatively and can't imagine yourself sporting an oversized fun-fur backpack, you should pop in for a look at the merchandise and freaky staff. Many of the salesgirls weren't born girls, including photographer David LaChapelle's pouty muse Amanda Lepore, in the cosmetics department. Upstairs, there's a wig and hair salon with excellent (I know I get my discount now!) colourists and stylists. And trust me, these 'girls' know a few things about fake hair.

Further along the block you'll pass Electric Lady Studios, set up by Jimi Hendrix and famed for its superior acoustics. On the corner of Sixth Avenue and 8th Street take note of Gray's Papaya, a weird New York chainlet that sells only 'gourmet' hot dogs and fruit juices. Make a right and head up Sixth Avenue. For you seitan-worshippers, there's a fab health food store called LifeThyme, and also Balducci's where the rich villagers shop for gourmet provisions and the poor ones nab free samples. At least splurge on a chocolate-dipped strawberry! And I don't care how stuffed you are, try a pumpernickel bagel with maple walnut cream cheese from Murray's.

You'll find bargains galore on 14th Street between Third and Seventh Avenues: cheap audio equipment, clothing and shoes (Payless at Union Square sells women's heels in sizes up to 13!), and of course the wig boutiques. Ms Wigs and Wigs & Plus stock the cheapest *perruques* in town, along with a huge assortment of fake eyelashes, fake nails and those delightfully tacky nail decals. There is also Union Square, a pleasant park popular with the work crowd at lunch, and the site of a large farmers' market. (This was also the one-time home of Wigstock when Tompkins Square Park closed for refurbishment after the homeless riots.)

Perhaps lured by the wigs, big heels and/or the welfare headquarters, 14th Street is a prime spot to 'spook' (ie recognise as men) transsexuals, which is one of my favourite pastimes. Recently

seen: in studded leather costumes that might have been Mr T's castoffs from *The A-Team*, a couple of militant black Muslims were braying out their extremist nonsense to passers-by, taking special care to loudly denounce any gays. You can imagine the hoo-hah that ensued when a gaggle of teenage black trannies sashayed by, hips swishing, hair weaves flipping and gum smacking. With 'her' long nail wagging in one Muslim's face, one screeched, 'Unh uh, honey. God accepts everybody!' The small crowd cheered and the big-mouth 'preachers' had finally met their match. In an attempt to win back their audience they began a call and response chant of 'The Lord says man shall not wear a woman's garment! The Lord says what?' Unfortunately, their gospel-infused rhythm was so infectious that the queens outdid them once again by bursting into an impromptu voguing set, one brandishing her water balloon boobs when they flopped out of her bra at an especially titillating moment! Only in New York, kids.

Continue west until you hit Eighth Avenue and make a short left turn on to Greenwich Avenue (not to be confused with nearby Greenwich Street), a quaint thoroughfare that connects Sixth and Eighth Avenues. The numbered grid of streets and avenues mutates quite a bit in the West Village – at one especially confusing point 4th Street is on the next block down from 12th Street. At No.106 you'll encounter Tea & Sympathy, a perfect treat for homesick British for it serves English food that's actually tasty – something of a contradiction. Even the bubble and squeak! Plus the proprietress, Nicky, is a right ol' scrubber who's quick with a saucy wink and a salty joke.

Since it attracts many celebrities who reside in the area, Tea & Sympathy is a mandatory stop for 'star-gazing'. Regulars include Quentin Tarantino, Uma Thurman, Rupert Everett, Sandra Bernhard, Julianne Moore, Marisa Tomei and Paula Cole. Other celebrity residents:

Gwyneth Paltrow, RuPaul, Amber Valetta, Shalom Harlow, Christy Turlington and an extremely gorgeous, stylish and talented blonde outdoor festival-organising female impersonator whose enchanting name escapes me at the moment.

Oh, and there are local luminaries to watch for, too. Keep your eyes peeled for the toothless junkie who makes such a realistic distressed cat squawk that everyone who passes looks around thinking, 'Where is that poor kitty?'; the older, bearded gent who daily dons the garb of a medieval European courtier, complete with a walking staff; and the jovial black bum who panhandles saying, 'Trying to raise $1,000,000 for wine research'.

Right off Greenwich Avenue on Bank Street you'll find a drag restaurant by the name of Lips. With personal items donated by every local gender-bender, the setting is a crossdressing museum with drag waitresses who perform numbers while slinging hash. Items on the menu are named after drag stars, so do stop in and eat me!

Keep straight on Greenwich and, if you're sober, this should look familiar – you were just on the opposite side of Sixth Avenue half an hour ago. If you aren't, you're in luck – here the chameleon-like 8th Street changes names one last time, becoming the legendary Christopher Street, and there's no shortage of watering holes on this, the gayest of gay stradas. Between Sixth and Seventh Avenues pop into Pieces (just so you can say 'I went to Pieces in New York City!'). At Christopher Park there's the Monster, the West Village's grandest establishment (catch the 'monstrous' painting near the entrance), with a piano bar on the ground floor around which show tunes are belted, and dancing with Monday and Wednesday drag shows down under. Walk through the tiny park opposite, which features entertaining if smelly street types congregating around an odd 'gay' sculpture – a fave for tourist snapshots.

On the other side of the park you'll find – get ready, drumroll please – the birthplace of the gay liberation movement, Stonewall, where in 1969 inebriated drag

Sculpture in **Christopher Park** – handy for taking the shopping once in a while.

The gayest of gay stradas, **Christopher Street** is alive with bars and late-night shopping.

queens, sick of police raids and shattered by the death of Judy Garland, fought back at the cops throwing bricks, mugs, etc. The funny thing is we're still fighting that battle. (Maybe we should try the bricks again.) The Club at Stonewall, as the bar is now known, is a small, sleazy and fun club with porno, strippers and drag acts.

Carry on west across Seventh Avenue to a bustling smorgasbord of everything gay. The ancient Village Cigars even still sells strong brown bottles of poppers – well, I'm just giving you the info that I might like to have in an unknown city! As you work your way down Christopher you'll pass many gay bars – let me just run through all of them quickly (as I do every night) to help you make a more educated choice. Or you could pick up one of the free weekly gay rags, *HX* (Homo Extra) and *Next*, on any corner – uh, I mean after you've bought *Time Out New York*, of course!

1) Boots and Saddle – really trashy leather bar with cheap beer and an even cheaper clientele.

2) The Original Espresso Bar – popular cruising ground for the AA set, who have several meetings nearby.

3) Ty's – the leather customers here always make me feel so young – so I stop in often.

4) The Hangar – the new kid on the block, a great mix, usually packed, with a pool table, video and occasional strippers.

5) chi chiz – a new black bar, very popular.

6) Two Potato – (not to be confused with the nearby restaurant One Potato) a black bar with outrageous drag shows by queens with monikers like Princess Janae and Harmonica Sunbeam.

7) Dugout – raunchy sports bar with crowded Sunday afternoon beer busts.

This street also boasts several sex toy shops, despite a new Giuliani zoning law that restricts both their merchandise and 'activity'. But, oh, how I used to adore these small cinemas. The beauty of these fine 'art films' literally brought me to my knees on more than one occasion. And there I'd stay for hours taking it all in… The horny can still check out the Christopher Street Bookstore, the Harmony Theater, and Bad Lands Video.

As gym culture took over in the late '80s, the pumped-up 'Marys' deserted Christopher Street and flocked to Chelsea, making it the primary gay stomping ground. This left behind the 'second tier' of older and ethnic types. The ethnic gays are particularly fascinating. Most live outside of Manhattan in the outer boroughs or New Jersey, where to be openly gay is to be a target for violence. So when they arrive in the Village to hang out they 'do shows, Miss Thing'. Expect to see the latest in street style on stunning models. Many too young to enter the clubs, they head across the highway to the piers, turning it into a club of their own with no admission charge for the hip hop and house music blaring from boom-boxes or mini-audio systems in the backs of cars. Last weekend a drag queen whose boom box conked out mid-show delighted her fans by explaining, 'I knew I shouldn't have used up the batteries in my vibrator last night.' You'll still see some voguing, or an occassional legend like Madonna's dancers from 'Truth or Dare', Jose and Luis Extravaganza, or Octavia St Laurent, the would-be model from *Paris Is Burning*.

A touch of danger adds excitement although local merchants aren't too excited. They feel that the kids scare away their customers. The further you get towards the piers the more the tension in the air increases. And there are plenty of lowlifes. As I sat on a stoop outside the Path train station on Christopher Street, a very young black guy was whacking garbage cans with a metal pipe taller than he was. A friend warned him about the increased police presence, and he replied, 'What the fuck do I care? If I don't come home with some money I get my ass whooped. If I go to jail I get my ass whooped. What's the difference?' Ah, life's grand dilemmas…

Around the corner on 10th Street between the highway (called West Street) and Hudson Street, you'll notice hustlers plying their trade. They're some of the cheapest escorts around, but be careful.

The ancy, drugged-out ones are liable to rob/stab you, plus crack often prevents them from 'rising' to the occasion – I only know this because of the painstaking research I've done for the sake of this article. Honest!

Cross the highway at Christopher and you're on the piers. The Hudson Park River Conservatory (HPRC)is revamping the entire area into a spiffy promenade with jogging/cycling/Rollerblading lanes, dog-runs, cafés and flowerbeds. So far the restoration is pleasing. New chairs and tables make it a perfect picnic spot and trees are being added for shade – which has traditionally been supplied only by the shady voguers. Once outdoor sex clubs by night, many of the piers are crumbling (talk about pier pressure! Ba-dump-pum!), and therefore closed to the public. The HPRC has a long way to go and I can't imagine they'll manage to cover up the view of New Jersey, the so-called 'armpit of New York'.

Walk north to Pier 54 (at 13th Street) and you're at the home of Wigstock. It's also the site of the annual Dance on the Pier, that finishes off the Gay Pride Parade. With a rusted iron arch welcoming you, it's a desolate sight, but each year on the Sunday before Labor Day, that old Wigstock magic and a ton of paint, powder and synthetic hairpieces transform the dingy pier into a wigged-out wonderland, attracting thousands of spectators. Of course, in '99, torrential rain turned the event into 'Wetstock' starring 'Lady Runny', but even that couldn't dampen our spirits too much.

And now, back to my cramped, overpriced apartment for a nap. This is a rather lengthy walk and I'm covered in bumps and bruises – it's not easy writing and walking at the same time! Of course, you will only have to do the walking part, but I do recommend sensible shoes, which Lady Bunion needs to try next time. Right now, to quote Jesus on the cross, 'Oh Mary; get me some flats. These spikes are killing me!'

# Eating & drinking

### Angelica's
*147 First Avenue, at 9th Street (212 677 1549 ).* **Open** 1-7pm daily.

### Balducci's
*424 Sixth Avenue, at 9th Street (212 673 2600).* **Open** 7am-8.30pm daily. This gourmet shop is solidly rooted in Southern Italian traditions, and is a New York institution. Heaven couldn't be better stocked.

### Boots & Saddle
*76 Christopher Street, between Seventh Avenue South & Bleecker Street (212 929 9684).* **Open** 8am-4am Mon-Sat; noon-4am Sun. One of NYC's premier gay bars, this hard-drinkin' leather bar played a key role (the infamous sweaty scene) in the 1980 movie *Cruising.*

### chi chiz
*135 Christopher Street, between Hudson & Greenwich Streets (212 462 0027).* **Open** 2pm-4am Mon-Fri; noon-4am Sat, Sun.

### DeRobertis
*176 First Avenue, at 11th Street (212 674 7137).* **Open** 9am-11pm Tue-Thur, Sun; 9am-midnight Fri, Sat. It has remained exactly what it has been since 1904 – a cosy family-run café and pastry shop.

Rusting **Pier 54**, the current site for...

... **Wigstock**, an annual celebration of glamour and drag, for people of all eras.

## Dojo

*24-26 St Mark's Place, between Second & Third Avenues (212 674 9821).* **Open** 11am-1am daily. Enormous healthy dishes at incredibly reasonable prices. Some say that this is the best deal in town.

## Dugout

*185 Christopher Street, at Weehawken Street (212 242 9113).* **Open** 5pm-2am Mon-Thur; 4pm-2am Fri, Sat; 1pm-1am Sun.

## Five Roses Pizza

*173 First Avenue, between 10th & 11th Streets (212 228 2840).* **Open** 10am-10pm Mon-Wed, Sun; 10am-midnight Thur-Sat.

## Gray's Papaya

*402 Sixth Avenue, at 8th Street (212 260 3532).* **Open** 24hrs daily. Hot-dogs, fries and tropical fruit drinks – fast.

## The Hangar

*115 Christopher Street, between Bedford & Bleecker Streets (212 627 2044).* **Open** 3pm-4am Mon-Fri; 2pm-4am Sat; 1pm-4am Sun.

## Holiday Cocktail Lounge

*75 St Mark's Place, between First & Second Avenues (212 777 9637).* **Open** 2pm-1am daily. It started as a '20s speakeasy, and it's still one of the cheapest Manhattan bars.

## Joe's Pub

*425 Lafayette Street, between Astor Place & 4th Street (212 539 8770).* **Open** 6pm-4am daily. Sip a well-turned Martini, dip into oysters Rockefeller, and watch the cabaret.

## LifeThyme

*410 Sixth Avenue, between 8th & 9th Streets (212 420 9099).* **Open** 8am-10pm daily.

## The Monster

*80 Grove Street, at Sheridan Square (212 924 3558).* **Open** 4pm-4am Mon-Fri; 2pm-4am Sat, Sun. Crowd round the piano for show tunes, or dance in the disco downstairs in this old-school gay bar.

## Murray's Bagels

*500 Sixth Avenue, between 12th & 13th Streets (212 462-2830).* **Open** 6.30am-8pm Mon-Fri; 6.30am-7pm Sat, Sun.

## The Original Espresso Bar

*82 Christopher Street, between Sixth & Seventh Avenues (212 627 3870).* **Open** 7am-midnight daily.

## Pieces

*8 Christopher Street, between Greenwich & Gay Streets (212 929 9291).* **Open** 2pm-4am daily.

## Ray's Candy

*113 Avenue, between 7th & 8th Streets (212 505 7609).* **Open** 24hrs daily.

## San Loco

*124 Second Avenue, between 7th & 8th Streets (212 260 7948).* **Open** 11am-4am Mon-Wed, Sun; 11am-5am Thur-Sat.

## Stingy Lulu's

*129 St Mark's Place, between Avenue A & First Avenue (212 674 3545).* **Open** 11am-4am Mon-Thur; 11am-5am Fri; 10am-5am Sat; 10am-4am Sun. A stylised '50s diner, heavy on kitsch – expect to be served Martinis by the drag queen staff. The menu ranges from Thai through to the basic burger.

## The Stonewall

*53 Christopher Street, between Sixth & Seventh Avenues (212 463 0950).* **Open** 3pm-4am daily. Here, they say, is where it all began – ask the bartender to talk you through it. Or else just go to drink and you might find a dancing partner.

## Tea and Sympathy

*108 Greenwich Avenue, between 12th & 13th Streets (212 807 8329).* **Open** 11.30am-10pm Mon-Fri; 9.30am-10pm Sat, Sun. A taste of the UK, and a fine one at that.

## Two Potato Bar

*143 Christopher Street, at Greenwich Street (212 242 9304).* **Open** noon-4am daily.

## Ty's

*114 Christopher Street, between Bedford & Bleecker Streets (212 741 9641).* **Open** 3pm-4am daily.

# Clubs & theatres

## Astor Place Theater

*434 Lafayette Street, between Astor Place & 4th Street (212 254 4370/Ticketmaster 212 307 4100).*

## The Cock

*188 Avenue A, at 12th Street (212 946 1871).* **Open** 9.30pm-4am daily. **No credit cards.**

## Fez

*Inside Time Cafe, 380 Lafayette Street, between Great Jones & 4th Streets (212 533 2680).* **Open** 6pm-2am Mon-Thur, Sun; 6pm-4am Fri, Sat.

## The Bunny hop

### Lips
*2 Bank Street, at Greenwich Avenue (212 675 7710).* **Open** 5.30pm-midnight Mon-Thur; 5.30pm-2am Fri, Sat; 11.30am-4pm, 5.30pm-midnight Sun.

### Lucky Cheng's
*24 First Avenue, between 1st & 2nd Streets (212 473 0516).* **Open** 6pm-midnight (drag shows 8, 9.30, 11pm) Mon-Thur, Sun; 6pm-1am (shows 7.30, 11pm) Fri, Sat.

### Orpheum Theater
*126 Second Avenue, between 7th Street & St Mark's Place (212 477 2477).* **Open** *box office* 1-6pm Mon; 1-7pm Tue-Fri; 1-9pm Sat; noon-6pm Sun.

### PS 122
*150 First Avenue, at 9th Street (212 477 5288).* **Open** *box office* 2-6pm Tue-Sat.

### Pyramid Club
*101 Avenue A, between 6th & 7th Street (212 473 7184).* **Open** phone for details.

## Shopping

### Bad Lands Video
*388 West Street, at Christopher Street (212 255 1110).* **Open** 24hrs daily.

### Christopher Street Bookstore
*500 Hudson Street, at Christopher Street (212 463 0657).* **Open** noon-4am daily.

### Farmers' Market (Greenmarket)
*Union Square, 17th Street, between Broadway & Park Avenue South (212 477 3220).* **Open** 8am-6pm Mon, Wed, Fri, Sat.

### Harmony Video
*139 Christopher Street, at Hudson Street (212 366 9059).* **Open** 9am-1am Mon-Wed; 24hrs Thur-Sun.

### L'Impasse
*29 West 8th Street, upstairs, between Fifth & Sixth Avenues (212 533 3255).* **Open** 11am-9pm Mon-Sat; noon-8pm Sun.

### Patricia Field
*10 East 8th Street, at Fifth Avenue (212 254 1699).* **Open** noon-8pm Mon-Sat; 1-7pm Sun.

### Payless
*34 14th Street, between Fifth Avenue & Union Square (212 924 1492).* **Open** 9.30am-7pm Mon-Sat; 11am-6pm Sun.

### Religious Sex
*7 St Mark's Place, between Second & Third Avenues (212 477 9037).* **Open** noon-8pm Mon-Wed; noon-9pm Thur-Sat; 1-8pm Sun.

### Ms Wigs
*55 West 14th Street, between Fifth & Sixth Avenues (212 229 1814).* **Open** 10am-6.30pm Mon-Sat.

### Trash & Vaudeville
*4 St Mark's Place, between Second & Third Avenues (212 982 3590).* **Open** noon-8pm Mon-Thur; 11.30am-8.30pm Fri; 11.30am-9pm Sat; 1-7.30pm Sun.

### Untitled
*26 West 8th Street, between Fifth & Sixth Avenues (212 505 9725).* **Open** 11.30am-9pm Mon-Sat; noon-9pm Sun.

### Village Cigars
*110 Seventh Avenue, at Christopher Street (212 242 3877).* **Open** 8am-10pm daily.

### Wigs & Plus
*49 West 14th Street, between Fifth & Sixth Avenues (212 675 4129).* **Open** 10am-7pm Mon-Sat; noon-6.30pm Sun.

## Festivals

### Wigstock
*Pier 54, West Street, between 12th & 13th Streets (212 439 5139).* Labor Day (first Monday in September) weekend.

### Gay & Lesbian Pride March
*From Columbus Circle, along Fifth Avenue to Christopher Street (212 807 7433).* Late June.

## Other

### Electric Lady Sound Studios
*52 West 8th Street, between Fifth & Sixth Avenues (212 677 4700; www.electricladystudios.com).*

### Hudson Park River Conservatory
*North End Avenue, at Warren Street, (212 791 2530).* **Open** 9am-5.30pm Mon-Fri.

### St Mark's Hotel
*2 St Mark's Place, at Third Avenue (212 791 2530).*

### Tompkins Square Park
*Between 7th & 10th Streets and Avenues A & B (212 387 7684).* **Open** dawn-1am.

# Moody waters

Thomas Beller

River views, twin towers, movie sets – Robert Bingham and Baby Doll.

**Start:** by the Hudson River at the end of 11th Street
**Finish:** The Liquor Store, White Street
**Time:** 1-2 hours
**Distance:** 2.5 miles/4km
**Getting there:** subway trains 1 or 9 to Christopher Street station
**Getting back:** subway trains 1 or 9 from Franklin Street station
**Note:** this can be a pleasant dusk walk, and is quieter on Sundays.

New York is a moody town. For some reason I have always felt the mercurial force of these moods most acutely along the Hudson River. For some time now I've lived downtown in the West Village and often I stroll down to 11th Street and lean against the railing, staring out at the colour of the water, and taking in the strange open space with the city's crunch to my back. As with so many things, looking out, away from the city, makes your thoughts drift inward, towards it. Turning south, one is confronted by the almost comic spectacle of the Financial District, which, from that distance, seems to be at once awesome and absurd, the product of some child's overly exuberant session with Lego.

Down by the water is where you feel this city's (and probably most cities') moods and ironies most raw in your face. At times, when the weather is good, the water is so placid as to mock all the anxiety that the scampering city dwellers bring to their town, and when the weather is rough the water can be so turbulent and ominous and scary and beautiful as to

give all us New Yorkers a subtle pat on the back in acknowledging what a good place this is to have a life.

Almost immediately upon heading south from 11th Street one comes upon what may be the most appealing feature of this entire walkway down to the Battery Park – the old crumbling piers whose remains sit in the water like Roman ruins. The entire stretch of waterfront up to 11th Street has been relandscaped; there is a smooth pavement for Rollerbladers, and patches of well-ordered green and trees and flowers, and it is a delight. But for me the signs of another, crumbling archaic waterfront are extremely satisfying. The grand crumbling piers one passes are so rich in memories of other times, and you feel the sedimentary quality of life – and memory – that comes with being in such a fast-paced city. The crumbling ruins of these piers are beautiful and harrowing; they remind you how fast things change. Right now, as I walk south on a sunny afternoon, what is changing is the light on the river. It's a summertime river I'm talking about – not the ice-spiked terrifying blue of winter, when the wakes of the tug boats seem so sombre. This is a summer river, dark but somehow verdant. Fish are swimming in it, against all toxic odds. To my left are the new strict grids of lawn on which people gambol and loll, stunned, in various states of mild 'I'm-on-grass!' ecstasy (and perhaps other kinds of ecstasy, too, depending on the time of day or night).

This is not a walk that lends itself to pure leisure. For one thing, there is the ominous Financial District looming ahead,

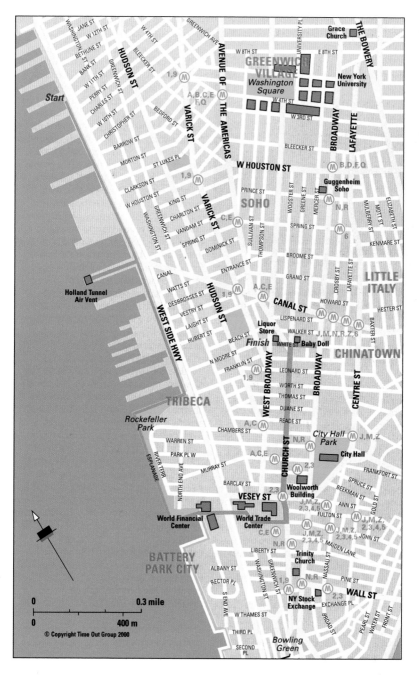

Start

JANE ST
W 12TH ST
BETHUNE ST
BANK ST
W 11TH ST
PERRY ST
CHARLES ST
W 10TH ST
CHRISTOPHER ST
BARROW ST
MORTON ST

WASHINGTON ST
GREENWICH ST
HUDSON ST
BEDFORD ST
BLEECKER ST
W 4TH ST

GREENWICH AVE
AVENUE OF THE AMERICAS

W 8TH ST
GREENWICH
VILLAGE
Washington
Square
W 4TH ST
W 3RD ST

UNIVERSITY PL
E 8TH ST
Grace
Church
THE BOWERY
New York
University
BROADWAY
LAFAYETTE

1,9 Ⓜ
A,B,C,E
F,Q

VARICK ST

ST LUKES PL
CLARKSON ST
W HOUSTON ST

1,9 Ⓜ
W HOUSTON ST

KING ST
CHARLTON ST
VANDAM ST
SPRING ST

VARICK ST
WASHINGTON ST
GREENWICH ST

BLEECKER ST

SOHO
PRINCE ST
C,E Ⓜ
SPRING ST

WOOSTER ST
GREENE ST
MERCER ST
SULLIVAN ST
THOMPSON ST

Guggenheim
Soho
N,R Ⓜ
6 Ⓜ

ELIZABETH ST
MOTT ST
MULBERRY ST
KENMARE ST

W HOUSTON ST Ⓜ B,D,F,Q

DOMINICK ST

BROOME ST

LITTLE
ITALY

CANAL
WATTS ST
DESBROSSES ST
VESTRY ST
LAIGHT ST
HUBERT ST

HUDSON ST

ENTRANCE ST
GRAND ST

CROSBY ST
LAFAYETTE ST

HOWARD ST
HESTER ST

1,9 Ⓜ
A,C,E Ⓜ
CANAL ST
LISPENARD ST
WALKER ST

Holland Tunnel
Air Vent

WEST SIDE HWY

BEACH ST
N MOORE ST
FRANKLIN ST

Liquor
Store
Finish
WHITE ST Baby Doll

J,M,N,R,Z,6 Ⓜ Ⓜ Ⓜ

CHINATOWN

1,9 Ⓜ
LEONARD ST
WORTH ST
THOMAS ST
DUANE ST
READE ST

WEST BROADWAY
BROADWAY
CENTRE ST

TRIBECA
Rockefeller
Park

A,C Ⓜ
CHAMBERS ST
WARREN ST
PARK PL W
MURRAY ST

RIVER TERR
ESPLANADE
NORTH END AVE

A,C,E Ⓜ
CHURCH ST

N,R Ⓜ
2,3 Ⓜ

City Hall
Park
City Hall
J,M,Z Ⓜ
FRANKFORT ST
SPRUCE ST
BEEKMAN ST

BARCLAY ST
VESEY ST
2,3 Ⓜ
Woolworth
Building
World Financial
Center
World Trade
Center
C,E Ⓜ
N,R Ⓜ

J,M,Z Ⓜ
2,3,4,5 Ⓜ
FULTON ST
ANN ST
GOLD ST
J,M,Z,
2,3,4,5 Ⓜ
JOHN ST
2,3,4,5 Ⓜ
MAIDEN LANE

BATTERY
PARK CITY

ALBANY ST
RECTOR PL
S END AVE
W THAMES ST
THIRD PL
SECOND
PL

GREENWICH ST
WASHINGTON ST

LIBERTY ST
Trinity
Church
1,9 Ⓜ
NY Stock
Exchange
N,R Ⓜ
PINE ST
2,3 Ⓜ
WALL ST
EXCHANGE PL
BROAD ST
NASSAU ST
PEARL ST
WATER ST
FRONT ST

Bowling
Green

0 _____ 0.3 mile
0 _____ 400 m
© Copyright Time Out Group 2000

**Relandscaped waterfront**, Rollerblade fun.

and for another, the well-paved racetrack on which New Yorkers – as they are wont to do – race. Bicyclers, Rollerbladers, roller skaters, runners, lovers, they are all on this little Indie Five Hundred stretch of smooth pavement. The Rollerbladers are especially exultant. Up ahead sits the World Trade Center. From this distance, it looks pleasingly manageable and small. The World Trade Center is not small. They tried to blow it up once, and the bombers lived across the Hudson in Jersey City. There is a particularly striking view of the World Trade Center from Jersey City, and Robert Stone, the author of *Dog Soldiers* and other classics, once pointed out that the bombers must have grown to hate it, and fear it, too, living always in its presence across the river. It would have been almost funny to see such an immovable thing crack in half like a Twix bar and fall into the river.

At Christopher Street everything changes very quickly. It is the tawdry, gay, sexual Wild West of drag queens and transvestites and junkies and very intensely fucked-up and sympathetic people (as portrayed in the documentary *Paris Is Burning*), and it is a certain kids-away-from-home lost world, a shirtless summer world of anxious glances. Just south is pier 40, a massive parking lot among other thing that juts far out on to the river. I walk out to the end, past the people sitting patiently with fishing rods, and all the way to the very end where there is a magnificent view of the Statue of Liberty, Ellis Island, the Verrazano Narrows Bridge. At sunset this is an incredibly nice and romantic place.

Just a bit further south is another pier, modern, and not as long, at the end of which is one of the stranger and more futuristically haunted structures to be found on this walk. It looks like a giant chess piece (castle) and in fact is a vent from the Holland Tunnel. Though this pier affords less spectacular views, it's worth walking out if only for the odd sensation of walking towards such a peculiar structure. South of that there are some rather unpleasant attractions notable mostly because they remind you how nice the park you have just walked through was – miniature golf, an awful stretch of Tarmac with some beverage stands, and, a bit more interestingly, a kyak centre, where kids scream and life jackets are handed out – and then one makes a sharp right and is back in the carefully conceived landscaping of the riverfront. One of the buildings you walk past is the Stuyvesant school, one of the city's three public high schools reserved for gifted children who grind it out in the usual state of numb high school perplexity, get great SAT scores, are captains of the chess club or ukelele club or whatever, and then don't get into the college of their choice because, they discover, the top schools can only take so many applicants from the same school and if everyone is so gifted… It's a great new facility from what I've heard and seen, much better than the cramped

Air vent, **Holland Tunnel**.

Peering from the end of a pier puts a river between you and the **Financial District**.

dwelling on East 19th where Frank McCourt spent so many years educating.

And then you are on the river again, with grassy patches and the odd handball court and even a very impressive pond with water lilies and bright orange goldfish swimming around. The water is as beautiful, the grass is as green, but the difference is that the wildly futuristic megalopolis is no longer off in the distance, it is upon you, beside you, engulfing you, and this is slightly unpleasant. The scale of a skyline is best seen either from a distance, or from very up close, and so I recommend taking a detour over to the World Trade Center's plaza. This is not to slight the lovely, interesting little design fillips the park has so considerately put in, and there is a nice meditative square patch of grass (which a sign explicitly says is for meditative activity and which asks people to be quiet) that has a lovely view of the Statue of Liberty; but for me, with those huge buildings packed above me, I want to force the issue, make it weird, and there is nothing like the World Trade Center to

make one feel as if the world has gone slightly mad. So I turn my back on the river, that enormous and blank thing upon which one throws one's hopes and fears and pleasures, and stride inland.

In the vast and rather forlorn promenade that sits between the two structures, they seem surreal and lonely, shooting up into the sky. On weekdays the madness of the crowds makes you lonely in a nice way, and on weekends the bareness of the people makes you feel lonely, too, and exhilarated.

They have about them – even seen from below – the quality of a lighthouse, something perched at the edge. And of course they symbolise every colonising, accumulating ethic New York is known and often disliked for. They are what they are, and among other things, they are enormous and blank.

From the World Trade Center's wide, windswept and rather alienating plaza I turn north and head up Church Street. The first few blocks are a bit seedy and overrun; the shops have that grimy overused feel of places where harried office workers scamper down for a quick lunch and cigarette, but soon a different ambience takes hold, and one enters the rough, post-industrial world of Tribeca. This is where the cheese district once was, and the coffee district, and any number of other specialised wholesale outlets providing for the city's appetites, and though these buildings have almost all been converted into residential lofts, their exteriors still exude the gritty and rather beautiful aura and architectural detail of that bygone era. Just a few blocks north of the World Trade Center, starting at Murray Street, one can dip off the main drag of Church Street and peek at the various cast-iron buildings on the side streets. Most of these buildings were built in the 1850s and '60s when cast iron provided architects with a cheap means to reproduce architectural detail, and so the façades are a riot of Doric and Corinthian and who-knows-what columns and arches. For me the aura is less 1860 than 1960 and '70s – the pioneers of Soho and Tribeca, the radicals, free spirits, artists and fuck-ups are on the run, but the architecture and sense of space is redolent of that time.

My favourite bit of architecture on this stretch isn't from another era, however; it is the massive and nearly windowless structure that sits on Church and Worth Streets, a reddish brown concrete structure that looks like a giant gun turret and is owned by AT&T. Neighbourhood lore has it that it is in fact a secret government centre where sensitive communications operations are housed in such a way as to make them resistant to nuclear attack. This sounds paranoid but to look at this bizarre thing one becomes, quite naturally, a little suspicious, and the fact that AT&T couldn't come up with any explanation for the building's use after repeated calls doesn't exactly put the matter to rest. Regardless of its use, though, it is an almost absurd and rather enjoyable bit of paranoia. In the film *Boiler Room* (which burrows into the rather ungenteel world of stock market

hustling) the building is shot at dusk as an exterior for FBI headquarters.

At White Street, I take a right for a brief stroll towards Broadway. This block is full of beautiful cast-iron buildings, as well as a very bizarre bit of modern architecture that functions as a synagoge – it's composed of white tiles that undulate, like a lava lamp frozen in time. For me, though, the significance of the block is literary, and personal. Robert Bingham, author of a collection of stories, *Pure Slaughter Value*, and a novel, *Lightning on the Sun*, lived at 38 White Street until his death, at the age of 33, in 1999. On the corner of White and Church is the Baby Doll Lounge, a topless bar. Like just about every other establishment of that nature in Manhattan, it's very much down on its heels due to the Mayor's legal manoeuvres. Most of the strip clubs in New York are now glossy places where women with fake breasts strut around for businessmen, but the Baby Doll, which has been in operation since the '50s, was always a rather neighbourly place. I mention it partly because its combination of seediness and homeliness is from an older, '70s-era New York that has more or less vanished from the cleaned-up, spruced-up and decidedly upscale Manhattan of the current decade; and partly because a variation of the Baby Doll appears, thinly disguised, in *Lightning on the Sun*, which if you haven't read it you should. The Baby Doll is to Bingham what the White Horse Tavern is to Dylan Thomas, more or less, and if this sounds like an aggrandising claim for a writer you may not have heard of, read Bingham's work and tell me I'm wrong.

From here, standing in front of the dilapidated neon sign of the Baby Doll, I cross the street heading east, across that broad swath of avenue where Church and Sixth Avenue split (Church ending its fine run from the base of the island a few blocks north at Canal Street; and Sixth just gaining momentum, swelling with pride around the curve as it heads across Canal and up through the heart of

To infinity and beyond –
the **World Trade Center.**

downtown and then midtown – a wide majestic avenue, the Avenue of the Americas, which cabbies always prefer because, as they say, 'It moves') and end up a block west at White and West Broadway. This is a quiet little street, West Broadway having just started from a dead end a few blocks north, and White concluding, a lost little intersection where one can find, happily, a bar called the Liquor Store. The Liquor Store was, for many years, a liquor store, and the old sign still hangs there. It is small and cosy and in the warmer months there are tables out on the sidewalks. Just around the corner is the old firehouse, still operational, where they shot *Ghostbusters*, and this strange little intersection is, for better and for worse, a favourite location for shooting movies. It is pleasant and, more than that, neighbourly, a local, one of my favourite bars in the city, and a place where all that vastness encountered along the river and under the huge World Trade Center becomes shrunk down. The view is more limited here, the scale more human; it is a place to collect oneself amid relatively peaceful surroundings, a place where one no longer feels small. I knock back a drink, and, refreshed, begin to fill up and expand and again think of the city in the way nearly everyone who has been here secretly regards it: as my own.

## Eating & drinking

### Arqua
*281 Church Street, at White Street (212 334 1888). Open noon-3pm, 5.30-10pm Mon-Thur; noon-3pm, 5.30-11pm Fri; 5.30-11pm Sat; 5.30-10pm Sun.* Understated, romantic elegance in the decor, hearty Tuscan-inspired food.

### Baby Doll Lounge
*34 White Street, at Church Street (212 226 4870). Open noon-4am Mon-Fri.* Find a stool and enjoy the show.

### Montrachet
*239 West Broadway, between White & Walker Streets (212 219 2777). Open 6.30-10.30pm Mon-Thur; noon-2pm, 6.30-10pm Fri; 6.30-10.30pm Sat.* A magnificent eaterie with a world-class wine list and subtly impressive French fare.

### The Liquor Store Bar
*235 West Broadway, at White Street (212 226 7121). Open noon-4am daily.* A snug bar that evokes an early New York saloon feel.

### Obeca Li
*62 Thomas Street, between Church Street & West Broadway (212 393 9887). Open 11.30am-3pm, 6-11pm Mon-Wed; 11.30am-3pm, 6pm-midnight Thur, Fri; 6pm-midnight Sat; 6-11pm Sun.* Gracefully fused Japanese and French cuisine in a cavernous space – the inventive cooking merits the expense.

### Pierino
*107 Reade Street, between Church Street & West Broadway (212 513 0610). Open noon-3pm, 5-11pm Mon-Fri; 5-11.30pm Sat.* The decor is unlikely to distract you from the fine, thoughtful and generous Neapolitan cuisine here, but the chairs are unaccountably comfortable.

### White Horse Tavern
*567 Hudson Street, at 11th Street (212 989 3956). Open 11am-2am Mon-Thur, Sun; 11am-4am Fri, Sat.* As the name suggests, reminiscent of an English pub, now popular with young tourists.

## Buildings

### World Trade Center
*Church Street to West Street, between Liberty & Vesey Streets (212 323 2340/groups 212 323 2350). Open Tower 2 Observation deck/rooftop promenade (open weather permitting) Sept-May 9.30am-9.30pm daily; Jun-Aug 9.30am-11.30pm daily. Admission $13; $6.50-$11 concessions; free under-6s.*

## Literature & film

**The Boiler Room** (Ben Younger, 2000, US)
**Paris Is Burning** (Jennie Livingston, 1990, US)
**Dog Soldiers** Robert Stone (1974)
**Pure Slaughter Value** Robert Bingham (1997)
**Lightning on the Sun** Robert Bingham (2000)

## Parks

### Battery Park
*Between State Street & Whitehall Street & Battery Place.*

### Department of Parks & Recreation
*888 NY PARKS/212 360 2774.*

# Contributors

**Thomas Beller** is a founding editor of the literary journal *Open City*, and the website mrbellersneighborhood.com. He has worked as a staff writer for the *Cambodia Daily* and the *New Yorker*, and is the author of two books of fiction, *Seduction Theory*, a collection of short stories, and *The Sleep-Over Artist*, a novel.

Inspired by Gertrude Stein – whose answer to the question 'What do writers do when they don't write?' was 'Walk' – **Victor Bockris** has been walking around NYC interviewing himself since 1972. Walking has helped him overcome every problem on his path, whether it be how to begin the next sentence, how to find the next friend, even on occasion how to find the next dollar. Graduating from the University of Manhattan in 1979, after a six-year course with professors Warhol, Burroughs and Ali, he wrote ten books between 1980 and 2000. He is about to embark on a cultural history of the '70s in New York.

**William Boyd** is the author of ten books: seven novels, two collections of short stories and the fictional biography of the American painter Nat Tate. In 1999 he wrote and directed his first feature film, *The Trench*. He has been visiting New York regularly since 1980.

**Lady Bunny**, one of New York's most colourful characters, is perhaps best known as the organiser and MC of Wigstock, the outrageous annual drag festival that she founded in 1984. Bunny has also starred in *Wigstock: The Movie* and HBO's 1998 documentary *Dragtime*, along with cameos in *Party Girl* and *To Wong Foo*. Bunny's writing credits include *Interview*, the *Advocate*, *Visionaire* and *Time Out New York*. Bunny tours the US and UK with her bawdy stage review, but is most at home on the heavenly streets of NYC.

**Edwin G Burrows** is Professor of History at Brooklyn College of the City University of New York. He is the co-author of *Gotham: A History of New York City to 1898* (Oxford University Press) and winner of the 1999 Pulitzer Prize for History.

**Kim Deitch** was born in LA but has been in and out of New York all his life. He's been drawing and writing comics for years, and also does fine art prints. His work has appeared in *Details*, the *New Yorker* and *Nickelodeon* magazine.

**Jason Epstein**, who lives in Soho, has written about New York for the *New York Review of Books*, the *New Yorker* and *Condé Nast Traveller*. He makes his living as a book publisher.

**Robert Heide** and **John Gilman** are Greenwich Village residents and authors of *Greenwich Village, O' New Jersey, New Jersey Art of the State, Disneyana, The Mickey Mouse Watch, Box Office Buckaroos* and *Popular Art Deco*. Heide, a noted Off-Broadway playwright, worked with Andy Warhol, who filmed his play *The Bed*. Heide also wrote *Lupe* for Warhol and Edie Sedgwick as well as appearing in Warhol's *Camp* and *Dracula/Batman* opposite Jack Smith. Gilman, actor, writer and photographer, bought a 1930s Sunbeam Mixmaster, photographed it for a book, and was then commissioned by the postal service, which turned the photo into a US postage stamp in the Celebrate the Century series.

**Phillip Lopate** is the author of several personal essay collections, including *Bachelorhood, Against Joie de Vivre* and *Portrait of my Body*, and the editor of *Writing New York*. He teaches at Hofstra University and lives in Brooklyn.

**Maitland McDonagh** has lived her entire life in Manhattan. A senior editor at *TV Guide Online*, she's the author of three books – *Broken Mirrors, Broken Minds: The Dark Dreams of Dario Arganto, The 50 Most Erotic Films of All Time* and *Filmmaking on the Fringe* – and numerous magazine and newspaper pieces.

**Marion Meade**'s six biographies recreate the lives of Woody Allen, Buster Keaton, Dorothy Parker (*What Fresh Hell Is This?* Penguin, 1987), Eleanor of Aquitaine, Madame Blavatksy and Victoria Woodhull. She has also written two novels about medieval France, *Stealing Heaven: The Love Story of Heloïse and Abelard*, and *Sybille*. She lives in Manhattan, in the same vicinity on the Upper West Side where Dorothy Rothschild Parker grew up.

**Barry Miles** knew Allen Ginsberg and William Burroughs for more than 30 years. He has published and edited many books on the Beats including *Allen Ginsberg: A Biography, William Burroughs: El Hombre Invisible, Jack Kerouac: King of the Beats* and *The Beat Hotel*.

# Contributors

**Minda Novek** is a writer and filmmaker on cultural history. She has worked on numerous PBS documentaries, most notably *School: Voices & Visions* and *The Ten Year Lunch: The Wit and Legend of the Algonquin Round Table*. Her project, *Times Square: Crossroads of the World*, is currently in development. She appeared on *Time Squared*, a CNN Newsstand: Entertainment Weekly story. She has been an exhibit consultant for the World of Merrill Lynch, Tenement Museum, Federation of Jewish Philanthropies and the *Daily News*. Her articles have been published widely.

**Greg Sanders'** short stories have appeared in *Mississippi Review*, *Time Out*'s neonlit.com and the anthology *Blue Cathedral* (Red Hen Press, 2000), among other places. He is currently working on a novel called *Grey's Device*. He was born in 1965 and grew up in the hilly New York suburb of Hastings-on-Hudson. In 1988 he graduated from the University of Vermont where he double-majored in mathematics and literature. He moved to Manhattan in 1990 and has held a variety of jobs, from wine salesman to actuary.

**Peter Singer** was born in Melbourne, Australia, in 1946 and studied at the University of Melbourne and the University of Oxford, where he taught for two years before going to New York University. His books include *Animal Liberation*, *Practical Ethics*, *How Are We to Live?*, *Rethinking Life and Death* and *A Darwinian Left*. He is currently DeCamp Professor of Bioethics at Princeton University and lives in New York City.

**Renata Singer** was born in Walbzych, Poland, in 1946 and now lives in Melbourne, Australia, and New York City. Most recently she was employed as publications manager for Oxfam Australia. Her books include *Goodbye and Hello* and *True Stories From the Land of Divorce. The Front of the Family*, her first novel, is due from Bruce Sims Publishing in February 2001.

**Valerie Stivers** is an associate editor for Eat Out and Check Out, and the travel editor at *Time Out New York*. Her work has appeared in *Rolling Stone, Mademoiselle, React, Paper, Details*, the *New York Observer*, the *Moscow Tribune* and the *Exile*. She first moved to NYC in 1994.

**Lee Stringer** is a New Yorker first, discovering writing as a vocation only after a decade living rough on the streets. Author of *Grand Central Winter*, a memoir of those years, and *Like Shaking Hands with God: A Conversation on Writing* (with Kurt Vonnegut), Stringer now lives in Mamaroneck, NY, and is at work on a third book, *Sleepaway School*.

**Anna Sui's** first fashion show in NYC in the spring of 1991 earned her international acclaim. She now has 250 worldwide accounts and two Anna Sui boutiques in the US (in New York and LA) and two in Japan (in Tokyo and Osaka). Anna Sui has a cosmetics range and is launching her second fragrance, Sui Dreams, in 2000. She lives in Greenwich Village.

New York journalist and historian **Cristina Verán** has documented cultural movements, locally and globally, for print, radio and online media outlets including *Vibe, NPR*, the *Source, Newsday, Islands, Latina Magazine*. Her history of the dance element in hip hop is featured in *Vibe: History of Hip Hop* (Crown/Three Rivers). Pre-dating her professional accomplishments, however, she has been a proud member of the Rocksteady Crew, the internationally acclaimed graffiti artists collective TC5, and a former rap MC with the Flygirls 3.

**John Waldman** is an aquatic biologist and writer who works for the Hudson River Foundation in Manhattan and who lives not too far from the water in Sea Cliff, New York State. He is a contributor to the *New York Times* and other newspapers and magazines, and is editor of *Stripers: An Angler's Anthology* (1998) and author of *Heartbeats in the Muck: The History, Sea Life, and Environment of New York Harbor* (1999).

**Rachel Wetzsteon** is the author of two books of poems, *The Other Stars* and *Home and Away*, both published by Penguin. A native New Yorker, she received a PhD in English from Columbia in 1999 and currently teaches literature and writing at Iona College in New Rochelle (commuting from Morningside Heights).

**Linda Yablonsky**, a New Yorker since 1966, has written on art and artists for a number of magazines and is the author of *The Story of Junk*, a novel. She was the creator and host of NightLight Readings, a series of monthly literary events, from 1991 to 1998, and last year became editorial director of the EdificeRex.com website. She is currently at work on a new novel.

Born in Maspeth, Queens, **Peter Zaremba** spent his teenage years in Flushing. He joined the 'punk rock revolution' early on when he became a founding member of the Fleshtones in 1976. In the 1980s he hosted *The Cutting Edge* on MTV, its first programme devoted to what became known as 'alternative music'. Besides performing with the Fleshtones, he is also a contributing editor for *Time Out New York*, writes for the *New York Daily News* on table topics, and is working on his autobiography, *Did I Do That?*

# Further reading

## In-depth guides

**Eleanor Berman** *Away for the Weekend: New York* Trips within a 200-mile radius of New York City.
**Eleanor Berman** *New York Neighborhoods.* Ethnic enclaves abound in this food lover's guide.
**Arthur S Brown** *Vegetarian Dining in New York City.* Includes vegan places.
**Eve Claxton** *New York's 100 Best Little Places to Shop.*
**William Corbett** *New York Literary Lights.* An encyclopedic collection of info about NYC's literary past.
**Sam Freund and Elizabeth Carpenter** *Kids Eat New York.* A guide to child-friendly restaurants.
**Alfred Gingold and Helen Rogan** *The New Ultra Cool Parents Guide to All of New York.*
**Hagstrom** *New York City 5 Borough Pocket Atlas.*
**Chuck Katz** *Manhattan on Film.* A must for movie buffs.
**Ruth Leon** *Applause: New York's Guide to the Performing Arts.* Detailed directory of performance venues.
*Sexy New York City 2000* Hot stuff.
**Lyn Skreczko and Virginia Bell** *The Manhattan Health Pages.* Everything from aerobics to Zen.
**Earl Steinbicker** *Daytrips from New York.*
*Time Out New York Eating & Drinking 2001.* A comprehensive guide to more than 2,000 places to eat and drink in the five boroughs. Written by food critics.
*Where to Wear 2000* A fix for shopoholics.
**Zagat** *New York City Restaurants.* Popular opinion guide.

## Architecture

**Margot Gayle** *Cast Iron Architecture in New York.*
**Karl Sabbagh** *Skyscraper.* How the tall ones are built.
**Robert AM Stern** *New York 1930.* A massive coffee-table slab with stunning pictures.
**Robert AM Stern** *New York 1960.* Another.
**Elliot Willensky and Norval White** *American Institute of Architects Guide to New York City.* A comprehensive directory of important buildings.
**Gerard R Wolfe** *A Guide to the Metropolis.* Historical and architectural walking tours.

## Culture & recollections

**Candace Bushnell** *Sex and the City.* Smart woman, superficial New York.
**George Chauncey** *Gay New York.* Gay life from the 1890s.
**William Cole (ed)** *Quotable New York.*
**Martha Cooper and Henry Chalfant** *Subway Art.*
**Josh Alan Friedman** *Tales of Times Square.* Sleaze, scum, filth and depredation in Times Square.
**Nelson George** *Hip-Hop America.* The history of hip-hop.
**Pat Hackett** *The Andy Warhol Diaries.*
**AJ Liebling** *Back Where I Came From.* Personal recollections from the famous *New Yorker* columnist.
**Legs McNeil** *Please Kill Me.* Oral history of the city's punk scene in the 1970s.
**Joseph Mitchell** *Up in the Old Hotel.* An anthology of the late journalist's most colorful reporting.
**Frank O'Hara** *The Collected Poems of Frank O'Hara.* The great NYC poet found inspiration in his hometown.
**Andrea Wyatt Sexton (ed)** *The Brooklyn Reader.*
**Andrés Torres** *Between Melting Pot and Mosaic.* African-American and Puerto Rican life in the city.

## Fiction

**Paul Auster** *The New York Trilogy.* A search for the madness behind the method of Manhattan's grid.
**Kevin Baker** *Dreamland* A poetic novel about Coney Island's glory days.
**James Baldwin** *Another Country.* Racism under the bohemian veneer of the 1960s.
**Caleb Carr** *The Alienist.* Hunting a serial killer in New York's turn-of-the-century demimonde.
**EL Doctorow** *The Waterworks.* A tale inspired by Edgar Allan Poe and set in late 19th-century New York.
**Bret Easton Ellis** *American Psycho.* A serial killer is loose among the young and fabulous in 1980s Manhattan.
**Ralph Ellison** *Invisible Man.* Coming of age as a black man in 1950s New York.
**F Scott Fitzgerald** *The Beautiful and Damned.* A New York couple squanders their fortune during the Jazz Age.
**Larry Kramer** *Faggots.* Hilarious gay New York.
**Jonathan Lethem** *Motherless Brooklyn.* An orphan-cum-detective discovers the intricacies of Brooklyn.
**Phillip Lopate** *Writing New York.* Excellent anthology of short stories, essays and poems set in New York.
**Toni Morrison** *Jazz.* Music and glamour of 1920s Harlem.
**Hubert Selby Jr** *Last Exit to Brooklyn.* Brooklyn dockland degradation, circa the 1960s.
**Betty Smith** *A Tree Grows in Brooklyn.* An Irish girl in 1930s Brooklyn.
**Edith Wharton** *Old New York.* Four novellas of 19th-century New York, by the author of *The Age of Innocence.*
**Tom Wolfe** *The Bonfire of the Vanities.* Rich/poor, black/white. An unmatched slice of 1980s New York.

## History

**Irving Lewis Allen** *The City in Slang.* How New York living has spawned hundreds of new words and phrases.
**Robert A Caro** *The Power Broker.* A biography of Robert Moses, the early and mid-20th century master builder in New York, and his political practices.
**Federal Writers' Project** *The WPA Guide to New York City.* A wonderful snapshot of 1930s New York by writers employed under FDR's New Deal.
**Clifton Hood** *722 Miles: The Building of the Subways and How They Transformed New York.*
**Kenneth T Jackson:** *The Encyclopedia of New York City.* The authoritative reference work.
**Rem Koolhaas** *Delirious New York.* New York as a terminal city. Urbanism and the culture of congestion.
**David Levering Lewis** *When Harlem Was in Vogue.* A study of the 1920s Harlem Renaissance.
**Shaun O'Connell** *Remarkable, Unspeakable New York.* The history of New York as literary inspiration.
**Jacob Riis** *How the Other Half Lives.* A pioneering photojournalistic record of gruesome tenement life.
**Roy Rosenzweig and Elizabeth Blackmar** *The Park and the People.* A lengthy history of Central Park.
**Luc Sante** *Low Life.* Opium dens, brothels, tenements and suicide salons in 1840–1920s New York.
**Bayrd Still** *Mirror for Gotham.* New York as seen by its inhabitants, from Dutch days to the present.
**Mike Wallace and Edwin G Burrows** *Gotham: A History of New York City to 1898.* The first volume in a planned mammoth history of NYC.

# Walks for...

## Architecture
**Thomas Beller** – the twin towers of the World Trade Center. **Edwin G Burrows** – Lower Manhattan's historic mix. **Jason Epstein** – the cast iron façades of Soho. **Phillip Lopate** – brownstone bliss in Brooklyn. **Peter Zaremba** – salt houses of Flushing's past.

## Art
**William Boyd** – Hopper at the Whitney. **Jason Epstein** – Last Supper, Warhol style, in the Guggenheim Soho. **Robert Heide & John Gilman** – private and public galleries in Chelsea and Museum Mile. **Cristina Verán** – graffiti galleries around the Bronx.

## Eating & drinking
**Lady Bunny** – go on, just a small piece. **Jason Epstein** – restaurants and delis in fashionable Soho. **Greg Sanders** – some of the best Jewish delis in town. **Valerie Stivers** – Moscow by the sea. **Linda Yablonsky** – pickles and bagels in the Lower East Side.

## Parks
**Victor Bockris** or **Peter & Renata Singer** – up and away in Central Park. **Robert Heide & John Gilman** – dip into the Conservatory Garden in Central Park. **Maitland McDonagh** – along Riverside Park. **Greg Sanders** – strolls along East River Park. **Lee Stringer** – wanders in Carl Schurz Park. **Rachel Wetzsteon** – Harlem Meer in Central Park and Marcus Garvey Park. **Peter Zaremba** – the finale in Flushing Meadows-Corona Park.

## History
**Edwin G Burrows** – Lower Manhattan's evolution from earliest colonisation. **Marion Meade** or **Minda Novek** Midtown in the '20s and '30s. **Peter & Renata Singer** – the emergence of the animal rights movement. **Peter Zaremba** – Flushing's old town.

## Literature
**William Boyd** – small independent bookshops dot the Upper East Side. **Kim Deitch** – drown in books at the Strand Book Store. **Marion Meade** – Dorothy Parker and the Algonquin Round Table. **Barry Miles** – in the footsteps of the Beats. **Minda Novek** – Broadway tales by Damon Runyon.

## Nightime
**Thomas Beller** – dusk along the Hudson. **Lady Bunny** – have a high time in Greenwich Village. **Minda Novek** – the neon lights of the Theater District and Times Square. **Lee Stringer** – a homeless view of the Upper East Side.

## Parents with children
**Thomas Beller** – river, piers and the occasional playground. **Maitland McDonagh** – Children's Museum of Manhattan, and the American Museum of Natural History. **Peter & Renata Singer** – Central Park and the American Museum of Natural History. **Valerie Stivers** – funfair frolics and seaside beaches on Coney Island.

## Shopping
**Victor Bockris** – fashion stores on Madison, bargains on Eighth Avenue. **William Boyd** – Madison Avenue for the fashion-conscious with wallets to match. **Lady Bunny** – expert guidance for buying your boas and wigs. **Kim Deitch** – take your pick from a number of flea markets. **Jason Epstein** – Soho's an extension to Madison's fashion stores. **Anna Sui** – the self-confessed shopaholic shares her fix.

## Views
**Thomas Beller** – the Hudson shimmers beneath the piers. **Edwin G Burrows** – if you take the Staten Island Ferry…. **Phillip Lopate** – spectacular vistas from on or under Brooklyn Bridge. **Maitland McDonagh** or **Rachel Wetzsteon** – Manhattan spread before you from Riverside Church tower. **Greg Sanders** – East River Park looks out over Williamsburg. **Lee Stringer** – Wards Island from the East River promenade.

## Water
**Thomas Beller** – enjoy the piers on the Hudson River. **Phillip Lopate** – over and by Brooklyn Bridge and on the esplanade. **Maitland McDonagh** – just as it says, Riverside Park. **Greg Sanders** – East River Park offers sports and strolling opportunities. **Valerie Stivers** – nothing less than the Atlantic at Brighton Beach. **Lee Stringer** – a riverside promenade along the East River. **John Waldman** – the Gowanus canal revitalised.

# Index

# Index

# Index

# Manhattan Subway Map

MTA Metropolitan Transportation Authority

January 2000

©2000 Metropolitan Transportation Authority. Unauthorized duplication prohibited.

LEGEND

Terminal
Local Stop
Express Stop
Express and Local Stop
Route Name
Free Transfer

Station Name

Brooklyn Bridge 4·5·6

Terminal

Full-time Service (6 AM – midnight)
Part-time Service